World Inflation and the Developing Countries

World Inflation and the Developing Countries

WILLIAM R. CLINE AND ASSOCIATES

SURJIT S. BHALLA

GABRIEL SIRI *and* LUIS RAÚL DOMÍNGUEZ

R. CHANDER, C. L. ROBLESS, *and* K. P. TEH

THE BROOKINGS INSTITUTION

Washington, D.C.

1775 Massachusetts Avenue, N.W., Washington, D.C. 20036

Library of Congress Cataloging in Publication data:

Cline, William R

World inflation and the developing countries.

Includes bibliographical references and index.

1. Underdeveloped areas—Inflation—Addresses, essays, lectures. I. Title.

HG1496.C56 332.4'1'091724 80-25426

ISBN 0-8157-1468-8
ISBN 0-8157-1467-X (pbk.)

9 8 7 6 5 4 3 2 1

THE BROOKINGS INSTITUTION is an independent organization devoted to nonpartisan research, education, and publication in economics, government, foreign policy, and the social sciences generally. Its principal purposes are to aid in the development of sound public policies and to promote public understanding of issues of national importance.

The Institution was founded on December 8, 1927, to merge the activities of the Institute for Government Research, founded in 1916, the Institute of Economics, founded in 1922, and the Robert Brookings Graduate School of Economics and Government, founded in 1924.

The Board of Trustees is responsible for the general administration of the Institution, while the immediate direction of the policies, program, and staff is vested in the President, assisted by an advisory committee of the officers and staff. The by-laws of the Institution state: "It is the function of the Trustees to make possible the conduct of scientific research, and publication, under the most favorable conditions, and to safeguard the independence of the research staff in the pursuit of their studies and in the publication of the results of such studies. It is not a part of their function to determine, control, or influence the conduct of particular investigations or the conclusions reached."

The President bears final responsibility for the decision to publish a manuscript as a Brookings book. In reaching his judgment on the competence, accuracy, and objectivity of each study, the President is advised by the director of the appropriate research program and weighs the views of a panel of expert outside readers who report to him in confidence on the quality of the work. Publication of a work signifies that it is deemed a competent treatment worthy of public consideration but does not imply endorsement of conclusions or recommendations.

The Institution maintains its position of neutrality on issues of public policy in order to safeguard the intellectual freedom of the staff. Hence interpretations or conclusions in Brookings publications should be understood to be solely those of the authors and should not be attributed to the Institution, to its trustees, officers, or other staff members, or to the organizations that support its research.

Foreword

IN THE 1970s inflation became a severe problem of global dimensions. Following remarkable stability in the 1960s, prices rose sharply in 1973 and 1974. High international liquidity associated with dollar outflows from the United States in the early 1970s, coordinated business-cycle booms in industrial countries in 1973, sharp increases of grain prices following poor weather in 1972, and the fourfold oil price increase in 1973–74 all contributed. Industrial countries had an average inflation rate of 10.1 percent in 1973 and 1974, compared with an average of 4.5 percent in the period from 1967 to 1972. The inflationary surge helped provoke the global recession of 1974–75, as many governments took restrictive measures despite the contractionary influence of higher oil import bills. By the turn of the decade, the industrial countries had still not found an answer to the problem of stagflation.

The developing countries did not pass through these economic disruptions unscathed. Global inflation swept them along, and even regions with traditions of price stability experienced high domestic inflation rates. Inflation in Asia and Africa, for example, averaged 18 percent in 1973–74, in contrast to a 1967–72 rate of 5 percent. Moreover, the global recession that followed the inflationary surge of 1973–74 cut back the export markets of developing countries, curbing their growth despite a substantial increase in foreign borrowing that cushioned the shock.

This volume examines how the global inflation and subsequent recession affected developing countries. By the application of quantitative methods, it demonstrates the dominant role of oil prices in worsening the terms of trade of most developing countries, measures the transmission of external inflation into their domestic economies, explores the policy responses of representative countries, and analyzes a number of other issues, including the effect of world inflation and recession on debt burdens and capital needs. The questions examined touch on issues such as commodity price stabilization, alternative responses to external shocks, appropriate levels of development assistance, and the effects of industrialized nations' macroeconomic decisions on developing countries. This study is part of a Brookings series of studies on worldwide inflation.

William R. Cline, the principal author of this volume and the coordinator of the research on which it is based, is a senior fellow in the Brookings Foreign Policy Studies program. The contributors are Surjit S. Bhalla, a Brookings research associate at the time this study was prepared, and currently at the Delhi School of Economics; Gabriel Siri and Luis Raúl Domínguez, both senior fellows of the Center for Central American Studies of Integration and Development of the Permanent Secretariat of the General Treaty of Central American Economic Integration at the time this study was prepared; R. Chander and C. L. Robless, both on leave from the Malaysian government and currently associated with the World Bank; and K. P. Teh of the World Bank.

The principal author thanks William H. Branson, Andrew Crockett, and Carlos Diaz-Alejandro for comments on the manuscript, Alice M. Carroll for editing it, Delores Burton and Julia Sternberg for typing it, and Kathryn M. Tidyman for preparing the index.

This study was financed by the Alfred P. Sloan Foundation, the U.S. Agency for International Development, and the Inter-American Development Bank. The views presented in this book are those of the authors alone and should not be ascribed to the persons or organizations whose assistance is acknowledged above, or to the trustees, officers, or other staff members of the Brookings Institution.

BRUCE K. MAC LAURY
President

January 1981
Washington, D.C.

Contents

1. Introduction 1
William R. Cline
Dimensions of the Worldwide Cycle, 1972–75 *3*
External Sources of Instability *4*
Country Studies *8*
Implications for Future Policy *8*

2. Real Economic Effects of World Inflation and Recession 10
William R. Cline
Terms of Trade *11*
Prices of Major Commodities *17*
Capital Requirements and Availability *19*
External Debt and Reserves *28*
Inflation and the Distribution of World Income *37*
Protection, Exchange Rates, and Inflation *45*
Conclusion *47*
Appendix *48*

3. The Transmission of Inflation into Developing Economies 52
Surjit S. Bhalla
The Inflation Boom *53*
Domestic Causes of Expansion of the Money Supply *63*
International Causes of Expansion of the Money Supply *69*
Econometric Models of Price Inflation *76*
Results of Econometric Tests *84*
A Cross-Country Analysis *89*
Conclusion *94*
Appendix *95*

4. Brazil's Aggressive Response to External Shocks 102
William R. Cline
The Monetary Impact of World Inflation *103*
Inflation Imported through the Trade Channel *106*
Macroeconomic Developments, 1975–77 *115*
The Impact of External Recession *117*
Response to External Fluctuations *122*
Conclusion *132*

5. India's Closed Economy and World Inflation 136
Surjit S. Bhalla
Real Activity and Inflation *137*
Food Prices *138*
The External Sector *141*
Import and Export Prices *142*
The Oil Price Increase *145*
Exchange-Rate Policy *147*
Monetary and Fiscal Policy *149*
Econometric Models of Inflation *151*
Conclusion *160*
Appendix *161*

6. Central American Accommodation to External Disruptions 166
Gabriel Siri and Luis Raúl Domínguez
External Influences on the Economies *167*
Government Response to Instability *175*
Empirical Analysis of Inflationary Sources *182*
Conclusions *204*

7. Malaysian Growth and Price Stabilization 208
R. Chander, C. L. Robless, and K. P. Teh
Inflation in the 1970s *210*
Policy Issues and Responses *217*
An Evaluation *224*

8. Policy Response to External Fluctuations 228
William R. Cline
Policy Responses in the 1970s *230*
Future Strategies *236*

Appendix: Cyclical Growth Links between Industrial and Developing Countries 240
William R. Cline

Index 257

Text Tables

1-1. Inflation Rates in Industrial and Developing Countries, 1967–77 3
1-2. Average Growth Rates of Industrial and Developing Countries, 1960–70 and 1970–75 4
2-1. Index of Terms of Trade of Twenty-five Developing Countries, 1975 15
2-2. Variability in Real Prices of Primary Commodities Measured against OECD Export Prices, 1960s and 1970s 19
2-3. Trends in Nominal and Real Official Development Assistance, 1970–76 20
2-4. Nominal and Real Official Development Assistance from the Four Largest Donors, 1970–76 21
2-5. Increase over 1972 Trade-Balance Deficit Caused by International Inflation, Fifty-two Developing Countries, 1973, 1974, and 1975 24
2-6. Impact of World Inflation in 1973 and 1974 on the Real Value of External Debt and Reserves of Fifty-five Developing Countries 32
2-7. Index of Unit Value of Twenty Major Commodities in World Trade, 1972–75 40
2-8. Impact of Price Changes in Twenty Major Traded Commodities on the Real Incomes of Sixty-eight Countries, 1972–75 41
2-9. Measures of World Income Distribution under 1972 and 1975 Commodity Prices 43
2-10. Terms-of-Trade Indexes of Fifty-two Developing Countries, 1973–77 48
3-1. Rate of Change in the Consumer Price Index, Thirty Developing Countries, 1956–76 56
3-2. Rate of Growth of the Money Supply, Thirty Developing Countries, 1956–76 58
3-3. Rates of Growth and Acceleration of the Money Supply and Consumer Prices, Twenty-six Developing Countries, 1961–76 60
3-4. Annual Growth Rates and Deviation from the Trend of Industrial Production of Developed and Developing Countries, 1956–75 61
3-5. Rates of Growth of Import and Export Prices of Developed and Developing Countries, 1956–76 62
3-6. Changes in the Index of Food Production per Capita, Twenty-eight Developing Countries, 1968–74 65
3-7. Changes in the Relative Price of Food, Thirty Developing Countries, 1972–75 66
3-8. Budget Deficits as a Percentage of GNP, Thirty Developing Countries, 1967–74 67
3-9. Rate of Growth of Wages, Twenty-three Developing Countries, Selected Years, 1965–75 68
3-10. Ratio of External Reserves to Value of Imports, Thirty Developing Countries, 1966–75 70

3-11. Percentage Changes in External Reserves, Thirty Developing Countries, 1965–75 71
3-12. Changes in External Reserves, Major Industrial Countries and Four Groups of Developing Countries, 1961–75 72
3-13. Level and Change in the Trade Balance, Thirty Developing Countries, 1966, 1970, and 1972 73
3-14. Results of Regression Analysis: Changes in Domestic Money Supply Related to Changes in Reserves, Twenty-eight Developing Countries, 1956–72 74
3-15. Ratio of the Change in Foreign Reserves to the Previous Year's Money Supply, Twenty-nine Developing Countries, 1966, 1970, 1972, 1973, and 1975 77
3-16. Relation of Import Price Inflation and Openness of the Economy, Thirty Developing Countries, 1956–75 87
3-17. Contribution of Imported Inflation to Total Inflation, Thirty Developing Countries, 1970, 1972, 1974, and 1975 88
3-18. Results of Regression Analyses of Inflation in Twenty-eight Developing Countries as a Group, 1971–75 90
3-19. Results of Regression Analysis of Best Representation of the Inflationary Process in Twenty-eight Developing Countries as a Group, 1971–75 93
3-20. Results of Basic and Hybrid Monetarist Models of Inflation, Twenty-nine Developing Countries, 1956–75 96
4-1. Growth in Brazil's International Reserves, Money Supply, and Domestic Credit, 1962–77 104
4-2. Indicators of Imported Inflation and Associated Factors in Brazil, 1961–77 110
4-3. Value of Principal Brazilian Exports, 1973–77 118
4-4. Indexes of Brazilian Export Volume and Price and World Demand, 1960–77 119
4-5. Comparison of Expected Brazilian Exports under Cyclical and Steady Growth Conditions, 1973–77 121
4-6. Index of Real Exchange Rate of Brazilian Cruzeiro, 1970–77 129
5-1. Measures of Price Inflation in India, 1956–76 137
5-2. Indicators of Real Activity in India, 1956–76 138
5-3. Production and Per Capita Supply of Food Grains in India, 1956–77 139
5-4. Domestic and International Prices of Agricultural Goods Important to India, 1970–76 141
5-5. Trade Volume and Trade Share of India's GDP, 1961–76 142
5-6. Percent Change in Indian Trade Price Indexes, 1956–76 143
5-7. Commodity Composition of India's Exports and Imports, 1970–76 144
5-8. Oil and Related Statistics for India, 1970–76 146
5-9. Sources of Variation in India's Money Supply, M_1, 1969–76 148

5-10. Position of the Central and State Governments of India, Fiscal 1970–76 150
5-11. Demand Model of Price Inflation in India, 1956–72 and 1956–76 154
5-12. Monetarist Model of Price Inflation in India, 1956–72 and 1956–76 156
5-13. Econometric Projections of Indian Inflation, 1970–76 159
5-14. Summary Statistics on Series Used for Causality Tests 162
5-15. Results of Causality Tests 164
6-1. Sources of Monetary Financing and Absorption in Guatemala and El Salvador, 1967–77 168
6-2. Increase in Trade Deficits of Guatemala and El Salvador Attributable to Changes in World Prices of Commodities, 1973–76 172
6-3. Deviation of Export and Import Volumes from 1955–71 Trend, Guatemala and El Salvador, 1972–76 173
6-4. Pattern of Government's Reaction to External and Internal Imbalance Signals, Guatemala and El Salvador, 1970–76 180
6-5. Change in Indicators of Potential Inflation, Guatemala and El Salvador, 1966–76 183
6-6 Deficit in the Central Government Account, Guatemala and El Salvador, 1967–77 184
6-7. Production and Imports of Basic Grains, Guatemala and El Salvador, 1960–76 188
6-8. Monthly Average Salaries in Guatemala, by Economic Activity, 1971 and 1976 190
6-9. Exchange Rate Indexes of Guatemala and El Salvador, 1969–76 191
6-10. Regression Analysis of Changes in Domestic Assets of the Central Banks of Guatemala and El Salvador, before and after 1972 194
6-11. Excess Liquidity of Commercial Banks in Guatemala, 1969–77 195
6-12. Regression Results of an Excess Demand Model of Inflation in Guatemala and El Salvador, 1957–75 198
6-13. Regression Results of a Cost-Push Model of Inflation in Guatemala and El Salvador, 1956–75 200
6-14. Regression Results of a Monetary Model of Inflation in Guatemala, 1956–75, and El Salvador, 1957–75 202
7-1. Consumer, Export, and Import Price Indexes, Malaysia, 1960–71 209
7-2. Federal Government Revenue, Expenditure, and Deficits, Malaysia, 1961–76 210
7-3. Consumer Price Index, Malaysia, 1970–75 211
7-4. Import Price Index, Malaysia, 1971–75 213
7-5. Unit Value and Volume of Malaysia's Major Exports of Primary Commodities, 1971–75 214

7-6. Money Supply and Its Determinants, Malaysia, 1970–75 216
7-7. Monetary Measures Affecting Malaysian Commercial Banks, 1972–75 220
7-8. Increases in Consumer Prices of Malaysia and Selected Industrial and Asian Countries, 1970–75 225
8-1. Inflationary Experience of Thirty Developing Countries, 1975–77 232

Appendix Tables

A-1. Real Rates of Growth of Gross Domestic Product, OECD and Non-Oil-Exporting Developing Countries, 1960–77 241
A-2. Rates of Inflation, Unemployment, and Growth under Various Macroeconomic Policies for the United States 248
A-3. Rates of Real Growth of Gross National Product under Various Macroeconomic Policies for Europe and Japan 251
A-4. Growth Rates and Level of Gross Domestic Product for Developing Countries after Institution of Various Macroeconomic Policies in Industrial Countries 252

Text Figures

2-1. Fluctuation in Prices of Developing Countries' Major Export Commodities and of OECD Exports, 1960–77 16
6-1. Growth Pattern of Trade Prices and Real GDP of Guatemala and El Salvador Compared with OECD Pattern, 1971–76 170
6-2. Indexes of Import and Export Prices and Their Main Components, Guatemala and El Salvador, 1971–75 174
6-3. Imports and Exports of Goods and Services and Corresponding Trade Balance, Guatemala and El Salvador, 1950–75 176

World Inflation and the Developing Countries

CHAPTER ONE

Introduction

WILLIAM R. CLINE

INTERNATIONAL economic fluctuations in the early 1970s confronted the developing countries that do not export oil with a series of economic shocks. Unprecedented global inflation in 1973 and 1974, including the quadrupling of oil prices in 1974, was followed in 1974 and 1975 by the most severe world recession since the Great Depression of the 1930s. The sharp worldwide business cycle of 1973–75 followed a long period of buoyancy in the international economy, marked by high and relatively steady growth in both industrial and developing countries and by price stability in most industrial countries (except for the brief inflation associated with the Korean War). During this long phase of international prosperity, industrial countries progressively lowered their tariff barriers to trade and moved from a patchwork of controlled national capital markets to an internationally integrated financial system with freedom of capital movement and with a growing role played by the new Eurodollar market.

In the 1960s the developing world produced a number of remarkable success stories as countries such as Korea, Taiwan, and Brazil achieved especially high growth rates. A common theme of their success was the outstanding performance of their exports. Their "economic miracles" arose in part from an unusually favorable international economic environment.

The external climate began to turn hostile as the Bretton Woods monetary system weakened, with the massive flow of dollars out of the United States in 1971, the suspension of the dollar's convertibility into gold, and the realignment of exchange rates. The international economy accelerated into a sharp business cycle in 1973 when commodity prices rose dramatically, led by food price increases brought on by crop failures in 1972, and nourished by demand pressures from the internationally synchronous boom of 1973. Commodity price inflation continued into 1974 and rose still higher with the fourfold rise of oil prices. In the ensuing down phase of the global cycle, growth of gross national product in industrial countries fell to practically zero in 1974, and GNP actually declined by nearly 1 percent in 1975—a contraction of unheard of dimensions in the years since World War II. Clearly, an encouraging, steady, and reliable international climate for growth in developing countries had first become unpredictable but perhaps lucrative and then turned into an outright hostile world economic environment.

This study examines the impact of the worldwide economic disruption on the developing countries, focusing on the effects of the Great Inflation of 1973 and 1974.[1] The shocks of this upheaval were so severe and extraordinary that they warrant investigation in their own right. By examining the various economic impacts on developing countries, including how external inflation led to domestic inflation, and the policy actions that developing countries took to deal with international inflation, it should be possible to suggest how they should respond to future outbreaks. Calculations of the effects of external inflationary forces on the developing countries can also be useful to donor governments in planning their capital assistance programs.

The world recession of 1974–75, the worst since the 1930s, may be viewed in large part as a consequence of the Great Inflation. Many industrial nations began demand-restraining measures in 1973 in response to inflation during that year's worldwide boom in domestic business cycles. The explosion of oil prices in 1974 continued the inflationary pressures but also imposed a contractionary force leading to world recession, by acting like an enormous excise tax depressing aggregate demand. The assessments in this study thus incorporate the impact of world recession on the developing countries.

Chapters 2 and 3 examine empirical analyses of the effects of world inflation and recession on a large number of developing countries. The generalized conclusions developed from analysis of international data are reinforced by the insights suggested by case studies in chapters 4–7 of the transmission of inflation into individual economies and their responses to external forces.

1. The initial Brookings study of the effects of inflation in the early 1970s examined industrial countries primarily. See Lawrence B. Krause and Walter S. Salant, eds., *Worldwide Inflation: Theory and Recent Experience* (Brookings Institution, 1977).

Table 1-1. *Inflation Rates in Industrial and Developing Countries, 1967–77*
Percent

Group	*Change in consumer price index* 1967–72 (annual average)	1973	1974	1975	1976	1977
Industrial countries	4.5	7.5	12.6	10.7	7.7	7.8
Oil-exporting countries	8.0	11.3	17.0	19.0	16.2	15.0
Non-oil-exporting developing countries	10.1	22.1	33.0	32.9	32.3	31.5
			(25.0[a])	(17.0[a])	(16.0[a])	(22.0[a])
Africa	4.8	9.3	18.6	16.4	18.8	25.0
Asia	5.4	14.9	27.8	11.5	1.5	8.8
Latin America	15.9	30.8	40.9	54.6	62.7	51.6
			(25.0[a])	(22.0[a])	(28.0[a])	(34.0[a])
Middle East	4.3	12.7	21.8	20.3	17.4	24.2

Sources: International Monetary Fund, *Annual Report 1978*, p. 11; *International Financial Statistics*, vol. 30 (May 1977), p. 53, and vol. 31 (April 1978), p. 29.
a. Excludes Argentina, Chile, and Uruguay.

Dimensions of the Worldwide Cycle, 1972–75

World inflation in 1973 and 1974 was dramatic. After holding remarkably steady through the 1950s and 1960s, prices of internationally traded goods rose by 24 percent in 1973 and by 39 percent in 1974.[2] Domestic inflation rates in the industrial countries rose from an average of 4.5 percent in 1967–72 to 7.5 percent in 1973 and 12.6 percent in 1974 (table 1-1). At the same time, inflation in the non-oil-exporting developing countries more than doubled from its 1967–72 average of 10.1 percent to 22.1 percent in 1973 and 33 percent in 1974. The simultaneous occurrence of these surges in inflation represented a new phenomenon of inflation on a worldwide basis. Whereas rapid inflation had previously occurred in selected developing countries (especially such Latin American countries as Argentina, Brazil, and Chile), it became a general pattern among developing countries in 1973 and 1974, although inflation rates dropped (especially in Asia) thereafter.

2. Based on world indexes of export and import unit values. *International Financial Statistics,* vol. 31 (May 1978), pp. 49–51.

Table 1-2. *Average Growth Rates of Industrial and Developing Countries, 1960–70 and 1970–75*

Percent

Group	*1960–70*	*1970–75*
Industrial countries	4.9	2.8
North America	4.0	2.4
Japan and Oceania	9.4	5.0
Western and Northern Europe	4.7	2.5
Developing countries	5.5	5.9
Low-income Asia	2.4	3.9
Low-income Africa	4.3	2.8
Middle income[a]	6.3	6.4
Centrally planned economies	6.8	6.4

Source: World Bank, *World Development Report, 1978* (Washington: World Bank, 1978), pp. 13, 27.
a. Includes several oil-exporting nations, whose gains from higher oil prices are not reflected because the data are for real GNP and not gross income adjusted for terms of trade.

The virulent global inflation of 1972–74 was followed by a recession that caused the growth of gross domestic product in the industrial countries to fall from a peak of 5.9 percent in 1973 to 0.2 percent in 1974 and −0.9 percent in 1975, before recovering to 5.2 percent in 1976. The non-oil-exporting developing countries managed to hold real growth at higher levels than the industrial countries; their average growth rate fell from a peak of 7.3 percent in 1973 to 5.3 percent in 1974 and 4.1 percent in 1975, recovering to 4.8 percent in 1976 (see the appendix to this study).

The developing countries seem to have been swept along by the world inflation, but they appear to have been much less affected by the following recession than the industrial countries. The average growth rate for industrial countries fell by almost half from the 1960s to the early 1970s (table 1-2). For the developing countries, by contrast, real gross domestic product actually grew faster in the first half of the 1970s than in the 1960s (except for low-income African countries).

External Sources of Instability

Much of the economic instability in developing countries in the 1970s seems to have originated from the international economy rather than from inside their own economies. The increased problems of inflation, balance-of-payments deficits, and slower growth in developing countries after 1973 have been attributed to external economic events. A joint study by the United Nations Development Program and United Nations Conference on Trade and Development isolates as new sources of instability: higher prices of commodities and manufactured goods, the counterpart deficits corresponding to the structural balance-of-trade surpluses of oil-exporting countries, slackened world demand for developing countries' exports because of recession in industrial countries, and increased protectionism in industrial countries.[3] Whereas deteriorations in trade balances were typically attributable to increases in import volume in the past, in 1973–76 they were more frequently attributable to import price surges and thus to external influences instead of domestic demand pressures.[4] The UNDP–UNCTAD study recommends that developing countries adjusting to problems caused mainly by outside forces be given more lenient "conditionality" requirements and larger loans by the International Monetary Fund. A statistical analysis by Stanley W. Black supports the view that external forces contributed to economic instability in developing countries in the early 1970s, but finds that internal policies also made a major difference in their respective economic experiences.[5]

Chapters 2 and 3 of this study provide estimates of the role of external inflation and recession in causing inflation, trade-balance problems, and slower growth in developing countries, while the detailed country studies presented in chapters 4–7 shed light on the relative weight of external factors and internal policies in determining their economic performance.

TERMS OF TRADE. One salient issue is whether the process of world inflation leads systematically to a deterioration in the terms of trade for the developing countries. An UNCTAD study argues that it does, because commodity prices fluctuate but prices of manufactured goods (which increase in response to higher prices of raw materials inputs) only rise (because of elements such as imperfect competition). As a result, according to the UNCTAD argument, even though developing countries' commodity exports may temporarily enjoy a sharp price rise, such increases

3. United Nations Development Program–United Nations Conference on Trade and Development, *The Balance of Payments Adjustment Process in Developing Countries: Report to the Group of Twenty-Four,* UNDP/UNCTAD Project INT/75/015, January 2, 1979.

4. Ibid., pp. 1–2.

5. Stanley W. Black, "The Impact of Changes in the World Economy on Stabilization Policies in Developing Countries in the 1970's," paper prepared for a conference on Economic Stabilization Policies in Developing Countries, Brookings Institution, October 25–26, 1979.

eventually lead to higher prices for their manufactured imports; when their commodity export prices subsequently fall, they will experience a deterioration in their terms of trade.[6]

Chapter 2 examines the behavior of developing countries' terms of trade (export prices relative to import prices) in the 1970s. Although changes in terms of trade represent changes in relative prices, not a rise in the general price level, an investigation of these changes is important in assessing the impact of world inflation on developing countries. A significant part of the historical economic record in this period concerns the impact of varying inflation rates on terms of trade for the developing countries. Moreover, it is important to examine empirically the UNCTAD hypothesis that world inflation causes deteriorating terms of trade for developing countries.

Special attention is given to the role of higher oil prices in affecting the terms of trade of the developing countries that do not export oil. In terms of the politics of the proposed new international economic order, it is one thing if developing countries' terms of trade deteriorated because of higher prices of manufactured goods exported by the industrial countries, and quite another if the deterioration originated primarily from higher oil prices imposed by the Organization of Petroleum Exporting Countries.

TRANSMISSION OF EXTERNAL INFLATION. Chapter 3 presents detailed statistical analysis of the transmission of external inflation into the domestic economies of thirty developing countries through the monetary channel and the import price channel. As the developing country's external reserves expand because of financial inflows (which are related to capital outflows from reserve center countries, and especially the United States in the early 1970s), the monetary base and domestic money supply also expand (in part because sterilization policies are difficult to execute). The internal expansion leads to inflation.

Sharply higher prices for imports are a structural source of inflation since they enter the country's cost structure, adding to whatever infla-

6. UNCTAD, *Inflationary Processes in the International Economy and Their Impact on Developing Countries,* UN Doc. TD/B/AC.18/2, June 12, 1975. The UNCTAD thesis appears to ignore the fact that the rate of industrial price inflation in the long run would be expected to be related to the central trend in commodity prices, yielding no long-run trend in terms of trade regardless of a period of accelerated general inflation. Similarly, the troughs to which commodity prices would fall in their downswings would be expected to be determined in real, not nominal, terms, so that heightened industrial inflation would induce higher nominal commodity prices at their troughs, again ruling out a deterioration in terms of trade as the result of more rapid general inflation.

tionary pressure already exists. In the early 1970s the inflation in the price of food imports was especially destructive because it coincided with faltering domestic food production.

WINDFALL DEBT EROSION. Worldwide inflation is widely recognized as having conferred an unexpected benefit on developing countries by eroding the real value of the debt they owed to the industrial countries. The reduction in real value realized because interest rates were negotiated in expectation of much lower inflation represents a transfer of wealth from the creditor to the borrowing nation. Chapter 2 analyzes these gains, taking into account compensating factors such as the windfall losses on reserves held in foreign monetary assets whose interest rate fails to keep up with inflation, and the present discounted value of future repayment streams, which suggests a smaller erosion of debt than does the deflated value of outstanding nominal debt.

CAPITAL NEEDS. World inflation and recession in the early 1970s are widely believed to have worsened the shortage of capital flows into developing countries. Chapter 2 calculates their impact on developing countries' import and export values, and from that the change in their trade gap. Increases in the trade gap, which call for greater capital inflows if growth is to be maintained, are compared with the increases in external capital available to determine whether the breach between the two widened because of world inflation and recession.

WORLD INCOME DISTRIBUTION. One implication of the UNCTAD study's hypothesis that world inflation causes declining terms of trade for developing countries is that inflation in the early 1970s would have caused the distribution of world income to become more unequal. Chapter 2 examines the effect of the sharp changes in relative prices on the distribution of world income. Taking into account distributional inequality within and among sixty-eight industrial and developing countries, it calculates the changes in international inequality caused by the transfers of income away from countries with relatively low export price increases and high import price increases to those in the reverse situation. The estimates indicate which countries gained and which lost in this redistributional process.

CYCLICAL LINK BETWEEN INDUSTRIAL AND DEVELOPING COUNTRIES. The macroeconomic strategies that industrial countries adopt to deal with inflation substantially affect growth prospects in developing countries. The appendix to this study calculates the effects of three possible strategies, using a model that relates growth in developing countries to growth in industrial countries.

Country Studies

International analyses capture the aggregate effects of world inflation and recession on developing countries, but they do not bring out the differential impacts that the developing countries' differing policy responses cause. Chapters 4–7 are case studies of Brazil, India, Guatemala and El Salvador, and Malaysia. They examine the relative influences of external and internal factors on domestic inflation and growth, and the strategies that governments adopted in reaction to external inflation and trade-balance problems. The case studies consider whether policies on exchange rates and trade restrictions neutralized or aggravated the transmission of external inflation and investigate the response of monetary policy to increased reserves. The social welfare aspects of government policies are also given special attention. As a means of judging the policy strategies adopted in the face of worldwide inflation and recession, the case studies are extended into the late 1970s. Thus a new form of external inflationary impulse comes into the analysis: higher export prices. In particular, the sharp increases in world coffee prices in 1976 and 1977 had substantial inflationary consequences for the economies of Brazil and Central America.

Implications for Future Policy

The lessons that can be drawn from the experience of the early 1970s cannot necessarily be generalized into broad conclusions applicable to future episodes of global inflation. The historic breakdown of the Bretton Woods system of fixed exchange rates was associated with a flow of dollars out of the United States and a rapid expansion of worldwide reserves in 1971–73 that might not recur in a future inflationary surge, especially if the world remains on a regime of flexible exchange rates. The quadrupling of oil prices represented a one-time shift from near-competitive to near-monopoly pricing in the world oil market, although the doubling of oil prices in 1979 shows that recurrent oil price increases of major proportions may still be expected. The simultaneity of booms in the business cycle of the industrial countries in 1973 is also unlikely to be repeated. And such natural disasters as the Brazilian frost in 1975 that decimated the coffee trees and caused several years of high world prices can hardly be considered characteristic of world inflation.

Nevertheless, the historical record of the 1970s does contain useful lessons for both industrial and developing countries. It provides an empirical basis for determining what happens to developing economies when worldwide inflation occurs, and some of the patterns identified are likely to hold valid under a variety of inflationary conditions. For example, large increases in foreign reserves, if not sterilized, are likely to lead to domestic monetary expansion and inflation, and surges in import prices are likely to accelerate domestic inflation, no matter what causes the reserves and the prices of imports to increase. Similarly, commodity price inflation is likely to change world patterns of income distribution only minimally (chapter 2). Lessons drawn from analysis of the effect of the 1970s inflation on the terms of trade and capital requirements of developing countries cannot be easily generalized, nor can such large windfall gains from debt erosion be expected to recur (since most commercial loans to developing countries now have floating interest rates).

The case studies reflect the very different policy reactions that countries with different trade compositions, political structures, and levels of development may take to worldwide inflationary-recessionary conditions. Because of their large populations, Brazil and India are important to study for their own sake, as a means of clarifying the historical economic record of this period. They also represent the general case of the large, relatively closed economy. The other case studies are also likely to be typical of important classes of developing countries—Malaysia representing East Asian export-oriented economies, and El Salvador and Guatemala, small, open, fiscally conservative economies.

Whether the experience of the 1970s is applicable to policymaking in the future will depend on whether the world solves its inflationary problems and the Great Inflation becomes nothing more than an historical aberration. If rapid worldwide inflation remains a significant possibility (as seems likely in light of the reemergence of double-digit inflation in the United States and other countries at the end of the decade), then the findings of this study should be valuable for the policymakers who have to deal with world inflationary outbreaks.

CHAPTER TWO

Real Economic Effects of World Inflation and Recession

WILLIAM R. CLINE

THE SHOCKS of worldwide inflation and recession in 1973–75 brought a number of real economic losses and gains to the developing countries. This chapter examines these effects in four major areas: terms of trade, capital needs and availabilities, external debt, and the distribution of income among nations. The nominal effects of world inflation transmitted into developing economies through externally induced monetary expansion and price rises are examined in chapter 3.

Commodity prices are of fundamental importance to developing countries, given their reliance on commodity exports. The ratio of their export prices to import prices, or terms of trade, has major implications for their economic well-being. Moreover, increased fluctuation in commodity prices can mean disruption of their development. This chapter examines changes in the terms of trade of fifty-two developing countries from 1971–72, the two years preceding world inflation, to 1975. To determine how oil price increases influenced these countries' terms of trade in this period, it compares the total changes to changes in terms of trade excluding oil. It also examines commodity prices to determine whether fluctuations were greater under the unsettled worldwide economic conditions of the 1970s than in the 1960s.

In the 1970s, development assistance from the Organization of Petroleum Exporting Countries rose sharply but aid to developing countries from traditional donors stagnated. With the trade gap serving as a measure of requirements, the changes in export and import values caused by rising prices of traded goods during the inflationary years and the deviation from export trends in the 1975 recession are calculated for fifty-two developing

I AM grateful to Stephen Harvey and Marion Layton for their fine research assistance.

countries. The resulting estimates of increased capital needs caused by outside shocks are then compared to increases in total capital flows.

Unanticipated world inflation, especially in 1973 and 1974, reduced the real value of the external debt of developing countries, giving them a windfall gain. The net gain to these countries is calculated by balancing against the estimated gain the loss in real value of their external reserves caused by the failure of interest earnings on foreign exchange and the dollar price of special drawing rights to keep up with inflation in dollar prices (in spite of the offsetting appreciation of gold reserves).

The chapter concludes with an investigation of the relationship between changes in commodity prices and the worldwide distribution of income. There are insistent groups in the United Nations who believe that commodity price levels should be raised or maintained by a system of international support designed to redistribute income in favor of developing countries. Calculations of a simulation model of the change in world income distribution caused by changes in trade prices from 1972 to 1975 do not support such an approach to global equity, even in the unlikely event that prices of all the commodities principally exported by developing countries were quadrupled.

Terms of Trade

The old controversy over whether the terms of trade of developing countries deteriorate over time, a notion popularized by Raúl Prebisch in the 1950s,[1] revived dramatically in the 1970s. Heightened world inflation brought a series of windfall losses and gains to developing countries. Higher world grain prices in 1973–75 inflicted some $12 billion in additional costs on those that import food.[2] From 1973 to 1974, oil prices quadrupled, raising the import bills of developing countries that must buy oil by $12.5 billion annually for 1974 and 1975.[3] But along with the

1. See Raúl Prebisch, "Commercial Policy in the Underdeveloped Countries," *American Economic Review*, vol. 49 (May 1959, *Papers and Proceedings, 1958*).

2. Alexander H. Sarris, Philip C. Abbott, and Lance Taylor, "Grain Reserves, Emergency Relief and Food Aid," in William R. Cline, ed., *Policy Alternatives for a New International Economic Order: An Economic Analysis* (Praeger for the Overseas Development Council, 1979), p. 168.

3. Organization for Economic Cooperation and Development, *Development Cooperation, Efforts and Policies of the Members of the Development Assistance Committee, 1976 Review* (Paris: OECD, 1976), p. 38.

effects of import price increases, most developing countries enjoyed exceptionally large price increases for their commodity exports in 1973 and 1974. The *Economist* price index for commodities other than fuel rose by 63 percent in 1972–73 alone.[4] However, most commodity prices peaked in mid-1974, and new fears arose of serious deterioration in the terms of trade of developing countries as commodity prices backed off while the prices of industrial products continued to rise.[5]

Whether their terms of trade had indeed seriously fallen by 1975 is an empirical question of great relevance to an assessment of the economic impact of worldwide inflation and the subsequent recession on the developing countries. Although the ratio of the prices of exports to the prices of imports—the commodity terms of trade—is not a direct indicator of economic welfare (since increases in volume of exports, for instance, can offset higher import prices), it is a useful gauge of the net impact of fluctuations in the prices of traded goods.

The aggregate terms of trade of non-oil-exporting developing countries as reported by the United Nations Conference on Trade and Development reached a relatively high level in 1968–70 (although not as high as in 1954–56).[6] They had been lower in 1960–67 (average index of 91, with 1968–70 = 100), and in 1971–72 they declined again to a level (index of 93) approximately equal to that of the mid-1960s.[7] The recession year of 1970 reduced demand for commodities and led to the reduction in terms of trade.

The years 1971 and 1972 are a good base for examining the experience of the inflationary years 1973 and 1974 and the recessionary year 1975 since they are relatively representative of the whole period 1960–72 with the exception of the brief phase of high terms of trade in 1968–70. The aggregate terms of trade of non-oil-exporting developing countries showed a small improvement in 1973, a retreat to the 1971–72 base by 1974, and a substantial drop by 1975. The index of the aggregate terms of trade for these countries (1971–72 = 100) stood at 103 in 1973, at 100 in 1974,

4. "*The Economist* Indicators," *Economist,* September 6, 1975, pp. 80–81.

5. See especially United Nations Conference on Trade and Development, *Inflationary Processes in the International Economy and their Impact on Developing Countries,* UN Doc. TD/B/AC.18/2, June 12, 1975, chap. 4.

6. UNCTAD, *Handbook of International Trade and Development Statistics, 1979,* UN Doc. TD/Stat. 8, pp. 604–25.

7. A weighted index of excess capacity for the members of the OECD showed a rise from 0.6 percent in 1969 to 2.5 percent in 1970 and 3.4 percent in 1971. It then declined to 0.7 percent in 1973. UNCTAD, *Inflationary Processes,* p. 31.

and at 94 in 1975.[8] Generally in the two years of high international inflation (1973 and 1974), terms of trade appear to have improved or held even for these countries, as the commodity price boom caused a gain in their exports in 1973 which offset the price rise for their oil imports in 1974. By 1975, however, commodity prices had dropped while oil import prices remained high, eroding their terms of trade.

Terms-of-trade estimates for fifty-two of these countries with populations exceeding two million confirm the trend shown in the aggregate estimates. In 1973 and 1974 the forty-four that do not export oil were relatively evenly divided between those with terms of trade improvement and those with deterioration from the 1971–72 base. By 1975, however, two-thirds of these countries showed terms of trade below the 1971–72 base level (see appendix table 2-10). Thus, initially world inflation left their terms of trade relatively unaltered, but by 1975 at the end of the world cycle a large majority of non-oil-exporting developing countries had suffered a decline in their terms of trade. Those with substantial declines included several populous developing countries—Bangladesh's terms of trade index fell from 100 in 1971–72 to an index of 77 by 1975, Brazil's to 85, Ethiopia's to 76, India's to 78, the Republic of Korea's to 83, Pakistan's to 88, and the Philippines' to 79.

By 1976 and 1977, terms of trade had partially recovered. The aggregate index stood at 95 in 1976 and 98 in 1977,[9] while 55 percent of the forty-four non-oil-exporting countries examined had higher terms of trade in 1976 and 1977 than in 1971–72.

The recovery is attributable in part to the recovery of industrial countries, especially the United States, from the depressed level of economic activity in 1974–75. Demand for exports from developing countries increased, buoying their prices (especially those of raw materials used in industrial production). Furthermore, the price of coffee and to some extent prices of cocoa and tea—three products extremely important in the exports of developing countries—rose precipitously in both 1976 and 1977. The terms-of-trade improvement would have been even greater if the price of oil had not risen so sharply.

It is important to separate the effects of rising prices of industrial imports on the terms of trade from 1971–72 to 1975 from those of imported oil. In the context of North-South negotiations, the Organization of Petroleum Exporting Countries has tried to maintain solidarity with

8. Calculated from UNCTAD, *Handbook, 1979,* p. 62.
9. Ibid.

the non-oil-exporting developing countries despite the damage done to developing economies by higher oil prices. Representatives of OPEC have implied that the industrial countries should accede to developing countries' demands on commodity pricing or else face even more militant oil pricing strategies in the future. Yet if it is higher oil prices rather than declining commodity prices (relative to industrial prices) that are the principal source of erosion in the terms of trade of developing countries, further increases in OPEC's prices will merely add further injury to the non-oil-exporting developing countries.

When the cost of oil imports is excluded from the trade data of twenty-five developing countries, the general pattern of their terms of trade is more favorable in 1975 than in 1971–72 (table 2-1). Total terms-of-trade data including oil show a deterioration for fifteen and improvement for ten. After adjustment to remove the influence of oil import prices, however, nineteen of these countries show improvement and only six a deterioration between 1971–72 and 1975. The unadjusted data suggest that these twenty-five countries are relatively representative of the developing countries that do not export oil, because the frequency of terms-of-trade deterioration for the twenty-five (60 percent) is close to that for the group of forty-four non-oil-exporting countries examined in appendix table 2-10 (64 percent). Several key countries—India, Brazil, Korea, Pakistan, and the Philippines—move from deteriorating to improving terms of trade when oil is excluded. Furthermore, of the countries that still show declining terms of trade after the influence of oil is eliminated, only Chile and Zambia show a reduction by more than 20 percent in prices of exports relative to prices of imports other than oil, and both are major exporters of copper, whose price was declining sharply.[10]

Using 1971–72 as the base period may seem to bias the analysis in an optimistic direction since those were years of moderately low terms of trade of developing countries. Any such bias is offset, however, by a bias in the opposite direction given by using 1975, a year of worldwide recession and consequently lower commodity prices than would be expected, as the terminal year. Moreover, processed fuels, which are important in the imports of many developing countries with limited refining capacity, were not removed from the adjusted import price indexes.

The experience of twenty-five countries suggests that although ap-

10. Copper prices fell from $64.17 per 100 pounds in 1970 to $55.85 in 1975 (London market). *International Financial Statistics,* vol. 29 (November 1976), p. 28, and vol. 26 (July 1973), p. 29.

Table 2-1. *Index of Terms of Trade of Twenty-five Developing Countries, 1975*

Index, 1971–72 = 100

Country	Terms-of-trade index[a]	Crude oil as percent of total imports[b]	Import price index[c]	Index excluding oil imports: Import price[d]	Index excluding oil imports: Terms of trade[e]
Argentina	82	4.31	189	176	88
Brazil	85	16.37	215	162	113
Chile	62	13.38	209	166	78
Dominican Republic	181	7.90	178	152	213
Egypt	114	12.36	208	169	140
Ghana	116	8.75	197	169	135
Guatemala	79	10.23	188	154	96
India	78	18.45	210	148	111
Ivory Coast	92	7.32	192	169	105
Kenya	84	18.04	224	166	113
Korea, Republic of	83	14.57	196	147	111
Malagasy Republic (Madagascar)	81	14.79	201	152	107
Malaysia	107	4.49	183	169	116
Mexico	93	1.77	179	173	96
Morocco	141	8.77	194	166	165
Pakistan	88	12.22	196	156	111
Peru	87	6.68	189	168	99
Philippines	79	17.58	211	152	109
Senegal	119	8.28	192	165	138
Sri Lanka	77	17.18	214	158	105
Syria	122	9.07	196	167	143
Tanzania	102	13.53	193	147	134
Thailand	108	14.57	204	156	141
Tunisia	159	5.18	213	198	172
Zambia	69	5.37	172	154	77

a. From appendix table 2-10, 1975 data.

b. Total 1973–74 oil imports (United Nations, Economic and Social Affairs Department, Statistical Office, *World Energy Supplies, 1950–74*, UN Doc. ST/ESA/STAT/SER. J/19) at average unit value of U.S. imports (UN, *Yearbook of International Trade Statistics, 1974*, vol. 1: *Trade by Country*, UN Doc. ST/ESA/STAT/SER. G/23) as percent of total imports (*International Financial Statistics*, vol. 29 [November 1976], p. 37).

c. UN Conference on Trade and Development, *Handbook of International Trade and Development Statistics, 1979*, UN Doc. TD/Stat. 8, pp. 604–25.

d. If the total import price index is Z, the weight in the index of oil prices ϕ, and the index of oil import prices P, the price index for imports excluding oil Z^* is $(Z - \phi P)/(1 - \phi)$. (That is, the total price index equals the weighted sum of oil and non-oil import price indexes: $\phi P + [1 - \phi]Z^* = Z$; rearranging gives the expression for Z^*.) The index of oil import prices is based on the price of U.S. crude oil imports. The unit value of U.S. imports of crude oil in 1974 was 4.37 times the average level in 1971–72 (UN, *Yearbook of International Trade Statistics, 1974*, vol. 1, p. 958). From 1974 to 1975, average U.S. costs of oil imported by refiners rose from $12.52 per barrel to $13.93 per barrel (U.S. Federal Energy Agency, *Monthly Energy Review*, October 1976, p. 67). The resulting ratio of 1975 to 1971–72 prices is 4.86 (this ratio is lower than the corresponding rise in producer prices [Saudi Arabian oil] from $1.78 per barrel in 1971–72 to $10.72 per barrel in 1975 [*International Financial Statistics*, vol. 31 (May 1978), p. 55]; the higher rise in producer price reflects the absence of transport cost).

e. If the terms-of-trade index is T and the import price indexes are Z and Z^*, the terms-of-trade index excluding oil T^* is $T(Z/Z^*)$.

Figure 2-1. *Fluctuation in Prices of Developing Countries' Major Export Commodities and of OECD Exports, 1960–77*

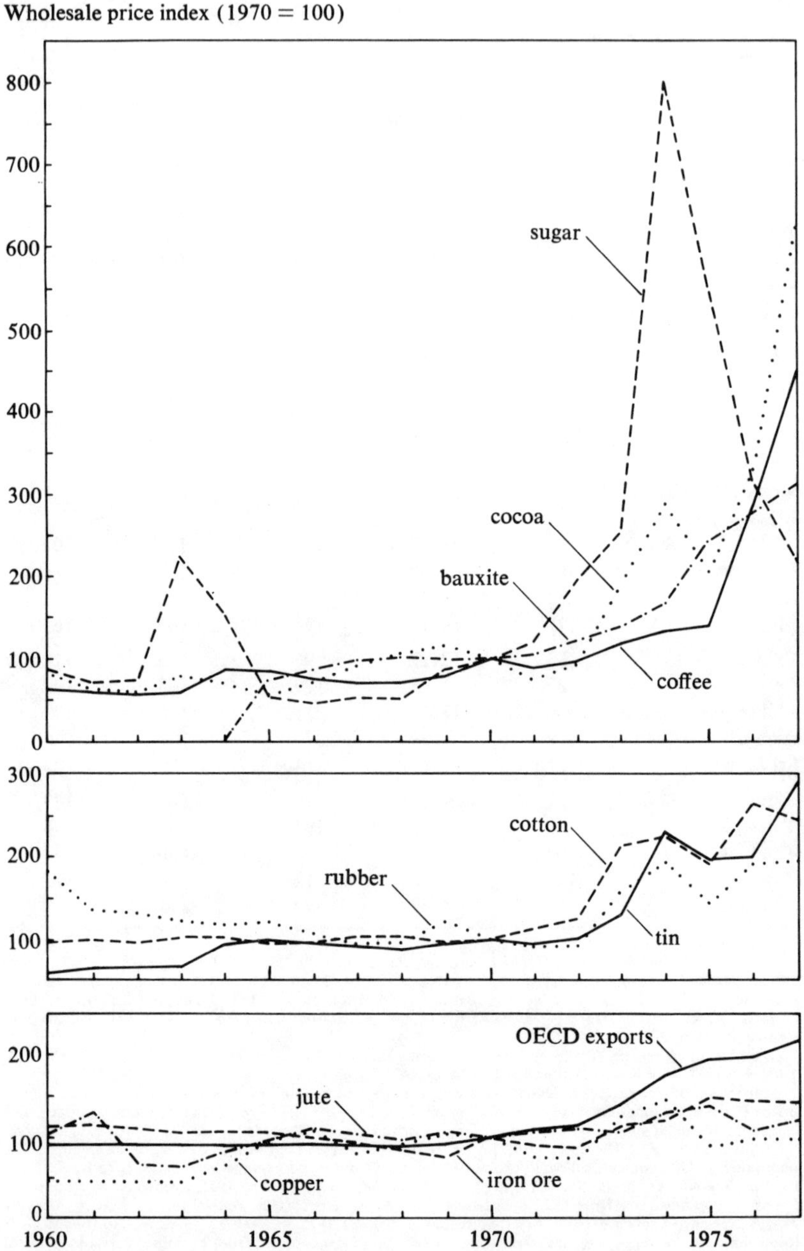

Source: *International Financial Statistics*, various issues.

proximately two-thirds of the non-oil-exporting developing countries experienced a decline in terms of trade between 1971–72 and 1975, if oil prices are eliminated the terms of trade *improved* for three-fourths of these countries. It is the price of oil, not the price of industrial goods (or food), that led to declining terms of trade for the oil-importing developing countries in the mid-1970s. Thus if worsening terms of trade should constitute a basis for petitions for special measures for developing countries (such as an integrated fund for commodity buffer stocks, and debt relief), it is oil-exporting countries, not the industrial countries, that should provide the resources required for such measures.

Prices of Major Commodities

The price indexes for the ten major commodities exported by the developing countries that are not oil exporters showed much greater variability in the period 1970–77 than in the 1960s.[11] The wholesale price index of each of the ten commodities remained relatively stable during the 1960s, as did the index of export prices of the Organization for Economic Cooperation and Development (figure 2-1). The relation to OECD export prices remained practically constant, on the average, for coffee, sugar (despite major fluctuation), bauxite, and iron ore; rose for copper, cocoa, and tin; and declined for cotton, rubber, and jute. The picture in the 1970s was radically different. The average terms of trade (commodity price relative to OECD export price) held constant only for iron ore and rubber, and even for rubber there was considerable fluctuation around the average. By contrast, the terms of trade improved dramatically for cocoa, coffee, and sugar; rose moderately for cotton and tin; declined dramatically for copper and jute; and fell moderately for bauxite.

These patterns show that commodity terms of trade were much more variable in 1970–77 than during the 1960s. Not only were fluctuations

11. Of total exports of fifteen major raw materials by developing countries in 1970–72 (but excluding petroleum, bananas, and beef), coffee accounted for 18.0 percent, copper 15.5 percent, sugar 12.6 percent, cotton 10.5 percent, bauxite 9.0 percent, iron ore 6.3 percent, rubber 6.1 percent, cocoa 4.7 percent, jute 4.1 percent, and tin 3.9 percent. Calculated from Jere R. Behrman, "International Commodity Agreements: An Evaluation of the UNCTAD Integrated Commodity Programme," in Cline, *Policy Alternatives*, pp. 126–27.

in the terms of trade of individual commodities generally greater in 1970–77 than in the 1960s, but there was a widening in the gap between the rising and declining commodities. In short, the risk to developing-country exporters of raw materials appears to have risen considerably in the 1970s.

Much of the increased variability is closely related to the boom-recession cycle of the 1970s. Thus, the price of copper (notoriously sensitive to the business cycle) first increased substantially in 1973, the year of synchronized boom in industrial countries; then it fell off dramatically in 1975 in response to world recession. The price of copper remained low as demand stayed sluggish, while pressure on the low-income countries' payments balances induced them to export more copper, whatever its price. Tin, cotton, and rubber showed much that same pattern of response in the boom and price rise of 1972–74 and the recession and price decline of 1975, although their prices began to rise again after a trough in 1975. The radical increase in the price of sugar in 1974 appears to have been caused by speculative demand fed by inflationary expectations; a reversal of expectations (as well as increased production in response to high prices) led to an equally dramatic decline in price from 1975 through 1977. A much milder speculative rise appears to have occurred for cocoa during 1972–74, followed by a relatively sharp drop in 1975. The great increase in cocoa prices during 1976 and 1977, like the rise in coffee prices starting in 1975, was unrelated to the world business cycle. Both markets were disrupted by bad harvests, and political disturbances in producing African countries also distorted cocoa prices.

The variability of the real price of each of these commodities—represented by the coefficient of variation of the price index after deflation by the index of OECD export prices—rises between 1964–70 and 1971–77 (table 2-2); the increase is dramatic for all the products except jute. Variability of the real price also rises substantially in 1971–77 over the longer period 1960–70 for all products except copper and jute.

In summary, the price indexes for the ten major export commodities suggest that the worldwide inflation of the early 1970s, and the recession that followed it, introduced considerable gyrations in the terms of trade of developing countries. They also reaffirm the finding that when oil imports are excluded, the terms of trade of developing countries tended to be higher after the world cycle of boom, recession, and recovery (especially by 1976 and 1977) than before it (1971–72).

Table 2-2. *Variability in Real Prices of Primary Commodities Measured against OECD Export Prices, 1960s and 1970s*

	Coefficient of variation of real price[a]		
Commodity	*1960–70*	*1964–70*	*1971–77*
Bauxite	0.11	0.03	0.31[b]
Cocoa	0.27	0.28	0.83
Coffee	0.16	0.15	0.68
Copper	0.34	0.16	0.27
Cotton	0.13	0.12	0.29
Iron ore	0.07	0.01	0.26[b]
Jute	0.12	0.10	0.11
Rubber	0.22	0.12	0.33
Sugar	0.57	0.48	0.70
Tin	0.19	0.07	0.41

Source: *International Financial Statistics*, various issues.
a. Nominal price index of commodity divided by index of export prices for OECD countries.
b. Based on indexes for 1971–75.

Capital Requirements and Availability

The Great Inflation of 1972–74 and the subsequent world recession adversely affected the growth in real terms of concessional development assistance. While rising prices eroded the real value of aid appropriations, the severe economic pressures of both inflation and unemployment in developed countries made the climate inhospitable for legislative increases in foreign aid. The OPEC countries in their new role as donors offset the stagnation in real aid from traditional donors, however, and the real volume of concessional assistance thus rose over the period 1970–76. Nevertheless, the real aid per capita from OECD, OPEC, and Communist countries to all countries with per capita incomes below $2,000 in 1974 (except the People's Republic of China) remained almost unchanged from 1970 to 1976 (table 2-3).

While the real value of aid from OECD countries remained nearly constant, OPEC aid rose dramatically and the already small aid given by Communist countries declined. Ironically, aid from the OECD countries remained at a nearly constant percentage of the GNP of these donors, even though their real aid fell while their real GNP was rising. The apparent divergence is explained by the fact that prices of traded goods (and therefore aid-assisted products) rose considerably more than the internal GNP deflators of the OECD countries.

Table 2-3. *Trends in Nominal and Real Official Development Assistance, 1970–76*

Item	*1970*	*1973*	*1974*	*1975*	*1976*
Nominal aid (millions of current dollars)	7,991	11,779	15,755	19,907	19,383
From OECD countries	6,811	9,351	11,304	13,585	13,656
From OPEC countries	400	1,308	3,446	5,572	5,182
From Communist countries	780	1,120	1,005	750	545
Real aid (millions of 1970 dollars)[a]	7,991	8,428	8,895	9,992	9,707
From OECD countries	6,811	6,718	6,681	7,120	7,139
From OPEC countries	400	921	1,714	2,528	2,324
From Communist countries	780	789	500	344	244
Developing country recipients[b]					
Population (millions)	1,877	1,985	2,040	2,097	2,156
Real aid per capita (1970 dollars)	4.26	4.25	4.36	4.76	4.50
Real aid as percent of GNP					
Of OECD countries	0.34	0.30	0.33	0.35	0.33
Of OPEC countries	n.a.	1.41	2.01	2.70	2.14
Of Communist countries	n.a.	0.09	0.07	0.05	0.03

Sources: Calculated from net disbursements of concessional aid in Organization for Economic Co-operation and Development, *Development Cooperation, Efforts and Policies of the Members of the Development Assistance Committee, 1977 Review* (Paris: OECD, 1977), pp. 53, 64, 84, 90, 165, 169; *International Financial Statistics*, vol. 30 (December 1977), p. 32; *World Bank Atlas: Population, Per Capita Product, and Growth Rates, 1976.*

n.a. Not available.

a. Deflators for OECD figures are those for official development assistance; for OPEC and Communist figures, the IMF index of world export prices.

b. Countries with per capita income below $2,000 in 1974, excluding the People's Republic of China.

Heightened inflation and economic difficulties during subsequent recession seriously reduced the growth of aid in real terms from the principal traditional donors, the United States, France, Germany, and Japan. The reduction in real aid from the United States is the most striking (table 2-4). American aid remained almost unchanged in nominal terms in 1970–74, reflecting a legislative climate that grudgingly produced nominal amounts of aid that repeated the previous year's level. In the meantime, prices were rising dramatically. As a result the real level of U.S. aid in 1974–76 had plunged by approximately 28 percent from its 1970–71 average.

Nominal values of aid grew more buoyantly in France, Germany, and Japan, but inflation eroded even this growth to the point that real aid grew relatively slowly in Germany and Japan and imperceptibly in France. Moreover, while real aid grew fairly rapidly in Germany and

Table 2-4. *Nominal and Real Official Development Assistance from the Four Largest Donors, 1970–76*[a]

Country and aid denomination	*1970*	*1971*	*1972*	*1973*	*1974*	*1975*	*1976*
United States							
Nominal (millions of dollars)	3,050	3,324	3,349	2,968	3,439	4,007	4,334
Real (millions of 1970 dollars)	3,050	3,262	3,121	2,303	2,200	2,203	2,375
France							
Nominal (millions of francs)	5,369	5,924	6,658	6,507	7,773	8,963	10,257
Nominal (millions of dollars)	971	1,075	1,320	1,461	1,616	2,091	2,146
Real (millions of 1970 dollars)	971	1,017	1,131	986	926	1,020	1,064
West Germany							
Nominal (millions of marks)	2,184	2,555	2,577	2,945	3,714	4,156	3,485
Nominal (millions of dollars)	599	734	808	1,102	1,433	1,689	1,384
Real (millions of 1970 dollars)	599	684	686	745	788	849	691
Japan							
Nominal (billions of yen)	164	178	185	274	328	341	328
Nominal (millions of dollars)	458	511	611	1,011	1,126	1,148	1,105
Real (millions of 1970 dollars)	458	500	520	707	658	667	623

Source: Calculated from OECD, *Development Cooperation, 1977 Review*, pp. 165, 169, and *1976 Review*, p. 207; *International Financial Statistics*, vol. 30 (December 1977), pp. 140, 148, 204.

a. Real aid is derived by using OECD deflators for official development assistance. Nominal aid in national currency is converted from dollar value at yearly average exchange rate.

Japan from 1970 to 1973, in the following three years, with the price shocks in oil and commodities and then the world recession, real aid stagnated in Germany and declined in Japan. French and U.S. aid followed a similar pattern, with the dividing point ushering in a stagnant or declining aid effort coming one year earlier, in 1972. Rapid inflation had a decidedly negative effect on the supply of real aid in 1970–76.

In developing countries, world inflation and recession also affected the demand for capital. In a sense the capital requirements for development are virtually unlimited, given the extreme disparities in living standards between rich and poor countries. But to provide a benchmark for measuring the impact of world inflation and recession, capital needs can be calculated by assuming that the limit to economic growth is set by the availability either of capital or of foreign exchange. The flow of capital required to attain any particular target growth rate then will depend on the shortfall of domestic savings from required investment—the savings gap—or the shortfall of export earnings from required import expenditures—the trade gap.[12] International inflation and recession can affect both the savings and trade gaps. For example, higher import prices for machinery will mean higher investment costs and therefore a larger gap between investment and domestic savings. Higher import prices, or a recession abroad that causes a decline in export earnings, can cause a rise in the trade gap. In either case the external capital required to meet a given growth-rate target will have risen.

In the international development strategy of the second United Nations development decade, a target of 6 percent per annum real growth was set forth for the developing countries. Estimates of their capital needs in order to attain that growth rate are altered considerably by the inflation of 1972–75. Changes in UNCTAD's and the World Bank's estimates of those needs range from approximately $2 billion to $6 billion (in 1975 prices) additional annual capital requirements as the result of world inflation.[13]

12. Hollis B. Chenery and Alan M. Strout proposed this two-gap measure in "Foreign Assistance and Development," *American Economic Review,* vol. 56 (September 1966), pp. 680–733.

13. The UNCTAD estimates of an increase of $1.8 billion in the capital requirements for oil-importing countries by 1980 represent the difference between its 1976 estimate of $90 billion in capital needs at 1975 prices and its 1972 estimate of $88.2 billion in 1975 prices (that is, $36.6 billion in 1960 prices inflated by *International Financial Statistics* index of import prices for developing countries). UNCTAD, *Trade Prospects and Capital Needs of Developing Countries during the Second United Nations Development Decade,* UN Doc. TD/118/supp. 3/Rev. 1, p. 31, and *Trade Prospects and Capital Needs of Developing Countries, 1976–1980,* UN Doc. TD/B/C.3/134, p. 4. *International Financial Statistics,* vol. 19 (January 1966), p. 31; vol. 26 (November 1963), p. 33; and vol. 30 (December 1977), p. 33. The World Bank's estimates of the increase in capital needs for 1973–76 of $3.7 billion for middle- and higher-income countries that do not export oil and $2 billion for the lower-income over the level that would have been expected based on 1967–69 prices takes account of the effects of general inflation as well as changes in the terms of trade. The Bank's estimates of the increase in concessional aid requirements of these countries over the level in 1974 is $4 billion for recipients of concessional aid in 1975 and $6 billion in 1976 (current dollars). World Bank, Development Policy Staff, *Prospects for the Developing Countries,* Report 477 (Washington: World Bank, 1974), p. 51, and *Prospects, 1976–1980,* Report 802 (1975), p. 82.

In order to obtain detailed estimates of the impact of inflation, the increases in a country's import and export expenditures caused by inflation alone are calculated by applying the increases in the import and export price indexes in 1973, 1974, and 1975 to the value of imports and exports in the base year 1972. The difference in import and export rises equals the increase in the trade deficit that may be attributed to inflationary forces. That increase represents the increase in capital requirements caused by inflation, assuming that the trade gap is an appropriate measure of those requirements.[14]

When the trade gaps of fifty-two developing countries with populations exceeding two million are examined, the results are striking. Despite its rampant pace in 1973–74, inflation apparently did not have a seriously adverse impact on the trade balances of the non-oil-exporting developing countries until 1975 (table 2-5). In fact, in 1973 both low- and middle-income non-oil-exporting countries showed a reduction in their capital requirements, as improving terms of trade relative to the 1972 base reduced the deficits in their trade balance from levels that otherwise would have occurred. This favorable effect persisted into 1974 for middle-income countries, although the low-income countries were by then experiencing a moderate rise in capital requirements. By 1975, however, inflationary developments had caused a net rise in the trade-balance deficit amounting to $3 billion for the low-income countries and $2 billion for the middle-income non-oil-exporting countries (these amounts are in the same range as the UNCTAD and World Bank estimates).

For their part, the oil-exporting countries enjoyed an enormous shift in their trade balances. The great bulk of this gain accrued to more prosperous oil countries. (It is of some note, however, that the gains of the three poor oil-exporting countries were the same size as the combined losses of the thirty low-income non-oil-exporting countries—$3 billion.) Within each group, effects vary. Thus in 1974, for example, inflation within the middle-income group caused large increases in the trade deficits of Brazil and Mexico but sizable reductions in the deficits of Malaysia, Angola, Argentina, and Peru. To the extent that financing

14. If for a given country, P_m is the price index for imports, P_x the price index for exports, M the merchandise import value, and X the merchandise export value, while superscript 0 denotes the base and 1 the terminal year, then the increase in trade balance deficit (and thus capital requirements) attributable to inflationary developments is $M^0[(P_m^1/P_m^0) - 1] - X^0[(P_x^1/P_x^0) - 1]$.

Table 2-5. *Increase over 1972 Trade-Balance Deficit Caused by International Inflation, Fifty-two Developing Countries, 1973, 1974, and 1975*[a]

Millions of current dollars

Developing country	*1973*	*1974*	*1975*
Non-oil exporters			
Low income (thirty)[b]	−166	436	3,014
Bangladesh	117	344	318
Egypt	−21	−325	−82
Ghana	−82	−284	−215
India	170	1,015	901
Kenya	26	210	267
Korea, Republic of	304	1,327	1,202
Morocco	49	−220	−406
Pakistan	96	227	240
Philippines	−246	−787	−142
Sudan	−83	−353	−192
Thailand	−319	−591	−6
Zaire	−233	−169	297
Middle income (fourteen)[c]	−2,366	−1,708	1,929
Angola	−76	−647	−609
Argentina	−512	−450	148
Brazil	−161	1,240	1,367
Chile	−324	32	646
Colombia	−99	−252	−132
Dominican Republic	−5	−109	−444
Israel	180	717	759
Malaysia	−500	−1,820	−985
Mexico	148	623	927
Peru	−635	−422	54
Tunisia	3	−200	−210
Zambia	−392	−427	249
Oil exporters			
Low income (three)[d]	−721	−4,422	−3,000
Middle and high income (five)[e]	−4,223	−52,190	−53,287

Source: Calculated from import and export price indexes in UNCTAD, *Handbook of International Trade and Development Statistics, 1976*, UN Doc. TD/STAT. 6; per capita income in *World Bank Atlas, 1976;* trade volume in *International Financial Statistics*, vol. 31 (May 1978), pp. 45, 47.

a. Countries with populations over 2 million. Negative entries indicate a reduction in deficit.

b. Per capita income below $500 in 1974. Includes Afghanistan, Bangladesh, Bolivia, Burma, Cameroon, Chad, Egypt, El Salvador, Ethiopia, Ghana, India, Ivory Coast, Kenya, Republic of Korea, Malagasy Republic (Madagascar), Malawi, Mali, Morocco, Niger, Pakistan, Philippines, Rwanda, Senegal, Sri Lanka, Sudan, Tanzania, Thailand, Uganda, Upper Volta, Zaire.

c. Per capita income of $500–$1,600 in 1974. Includes Angola, Argentina, Brazil, Chile, Colombia, Dominican Republic, Guatemala, Israel, Mexico, Malaysia, Peru, Syria, Tunisia, Zambia.

d. Per capita income below $500 in 1974; Ecuador, Indonesia, Nigeria.

e. Per capita income above $500 in 1974; Algeria, Iran, Iraq, Saudi Arabia, Venezuela.

of the increased requirements of the one group could not be met by equivalent reductions in the deficits of the more fortunate, capital requirements would have increased by more than the simple totals in the increased trade gap imply. India's receipts in concessional aid, for instance, rose by $343 million from 1973 to 1974 whereas inflation caused its trade deficit to rise by $845 million.[15] From 1973 to 1974 Korea's concessional aid receipts actually fell by $30 million and its net capital inflows by $200 million,[16] while inflation caused its trade deficit to rise $1.3 billion above the level it would otherwise have reached (table 2-5).

In order to assess how world inflation affected the global flow of aid, however, it is appropriate to aggregate across countries (by per capita income class). In principle, donors could have redirected their assistance from countries experiencing inflationary windfall gains in their trade balance to those experiencing windfall losses. Therefore the relevant figures to use for increased capital requirements are the aggregate estimates of $3 billion for low-income countries by 1975 and $2 billion for middle-income countries (table 2-5). Estimates of a joint project of the UN Conference on Trade and Development and the UN Development Programme imply similar findings. The study calculates the change in trade balance attributable to export and import price changes in 1973, 1974, and 1975, expressed as a percentage of the previous year's total exports plus imports. When those estimates are applied to trade base data for the forty-four non-oil-exporting countries in table 2-5 for 1975 relative to 1972, the results indicate that those with incomes below $300 per capita (1974 prices) would have required additional capital flows of $2.0 billion; countries with $300–$800 per capita, $0.1 billion; and countries above $800 per capita, $5.8 billion.[17] Although the losses would have been somewhat smaller for low-income countries and larger for middle-income countries than those in table 2-5, they are comparable in magnitude.

The impact of world recession on capital requirements was concentrated in 1975. The simultaneous recessions in the developed countries in 1974–75 led to a 0.73 percent reduction in the volume of exports

15. OECD, *Development Cooperation, 1977 Review,* p. 201.

16. Ibid., pp. 201–03.

17. Derived from UNCTAD, *The Balance of Payments Adjustment Process in Developing Countries: Report to the Group of Twenty-Four,* UNDP/UNCTAD Project INT/75/015, January 2, 1979, p. I-10; *International Financial Statistics,* vol. 31 (May 1978); and *World Bank Atlas, 1976.*

from the non-oil-exporting developing countries in 1975, compared with a rise of 16.9 percent in 1973 and of 5.3 percent in 1974.[18] By 1976 their export volume had rebounded again, growing by 13 percent and "more than offsetting the reduction in 1975."[19] Over the decade 1966–76 these developing countries' average real growth rate of exports was 5 percent per annum;[20] the shortfall in 1975 from that trend was thus 5.73 percent. If the export volume in 1975 had grown at the average rate for 1966–76, export earnings would have been $5.4 billion greater than they were.[21] This loss caused by the decline in export volume is additional to the losses caused by inflation ($3 billion for the low-income and $2 billion for the middle-income non-oil-exporting countries, table 2-5). The losses to each of the non-oil-exporting countries included in table 2-5 can be estimated by subtracting the percent rise in its UN export volume index in 1975 from the average growth rate of its export volume between the years 1961–62 and 1971–72 and applying the difference to its 1974 export earnings. The declines in 1975 export earnings associated with the deviation from the 1966–76 volume trend amounted to $2.6 billion for the thirty low-income countries and $1.9 billion for the fourteen middle-income countries.[22]

World inflation caused a decline in capital requirements of the thirty low-income countries in 1973, and a modest rise of $500 million by 1974. By 1975, however, the combined impact of world inflation and recession raised capital requirements for these countries by $6 billion.

During those years the total world flow of concessional assistance rose from $9.9 billion in 1972 to $11.8 billion in 1973, $15.8 billion in 1974, and $19.9 billion in 1975 in current dollar values.[23] The $10 billion increase in nominal aid flows appears to have more than kept pace with any extra aid requirements caused by world inflation and re-

18. The index of export volume for the forty-four countries is based on the dollar value of annual exports divided by the International Monetary Fund's index of export prices for these countries. *International Financial Statistics,* vol. 30 (December 1977), pp. 30, 32.

19. United Nations, *World Economic Survey, 1976: Current Trends in the World Economy,* UN Doc. ST/ESA/71, E/5995/Rev. 1 (1977), p. 6.

20. Ibid.

21. The 5.73 percent shift is applied to 1974 export earnings of $97.6 billion. *International Financial Statistics,* vol. 30 (December 1977), p. 30.

22. When countries whose 1975 export volume was higher than the 1966–76 trend are excluded from these groups, the figures are $3.4 billion and $2.7 billion. Korea alone accounts for $1.8 billion of the export shortfall for the low-income group.

23. OECD, *Development Cooperation, 1974 Review,* pp. 117, 207, and *1976 Review,* pp. 99, 297; and table 2-3.

cession through 1975.[24] Indeed, these findings imply that inflation and recession reduced developing countries' aid requirements in real terms, since the nominal increases in concessional aid necessary to hold the real value of aid constant from 1972 to 1975 would have been $7.1 billion.[25] Because inflation and recession raised concessional aid requirements very little in 1973 and 1974 and by about $6 billion in 1975, it may be said that in real terms, aid requirements were almost unaffected or even lowered slightly by world inflationary and recessionary developments in this period.

But if world inflation and recession did not cause massive increases in the developing countries' capital requirements, why were their current account deficits so large in 1974 and 1975? The aggregate current account deficits of the non-oil-exporting developing countries rose from $10.9 billion in 1973 to $29.5 billion in 1974 and $38.2 billion in 1975.[26] The explanation for this mushrooming deficit appears to lie in these countries' expansive import policies—their import volume rose by 12 percent in 1974, in response to sharply higher export earnings and foreign-exchange reserves accumulated in 1972 and 1973.[27] It appears to have been primarily the middle-income countries that chose to increase imports, whereas the increasing trade gap for the low-income countries was almost wholly related to world inflationary and recessionary forces. For the fourteen middle-income non-oil-exporting countries the current account deficit rose from $4.2 billion to $18.7 billion, and only $3.9 billion or slightly over one-fourth of the increment is explained by world inflation and recession. For the thirty low-income oil-importing countries examined in table 2-5 the current account deficit

24. Excluding countries with populations under two million from this analysis does not appear to affect this conclusion. The total population of the fifty-two countries examined was 1,377 million in 1974; the total including all other countries with per capita incomes below $500 as well was 1,501 million. Calculated from *World Bank Atlas, 1976*.

25. The OECD deflator for official development assistance rose by 68 percent (OECD, *Development Cooperation, 1977 Review*, p. 169), and general import prices for non-oil-exporting developing countries rose by 92 percent (*International Financial Statistics*, vol. 29 [September 1976], p. 31). Applying these percentage increases to 1972 OECD aid and OPEC-Communist aid, respectively, yields the $7.1 billion increase in nominal aid required to hold real aid constant by 1975.

26. International Monetary Fund, *Annual Report, 1977*, p. 21.

27. United Nations, *World Economic Survey, 1975: Fluctuations and Development in the World Economy*, UN Doc. ST/ESA/49, E/5790/Rev. 1 (1976), p. 33. In 1976 their import volume rose by 5.7 percent (calculated from their nominal dollar import totals and index of import prices, reported in *International Financial Statistics*, vol. 30 [December 1977], pp. 31, 33).

rose from $2.9 billion in 1972 to $11.7 billion in 1975, and almost three-fourths ($6 billion) of the increment of $8.8 billion is accounted for by the estimated impacts of higher prices and recession.[28] The difference in the two patterns undoubtedly reflects the greater ability of the middle-income countries to obtain financing in private markets.

In retrospect, the large increase in real imports in 1974 (primarily by the middle-income countries) represents a risky strategy, for reserves accumulated during boom years that could have been husbanded for unfavorable years were depleted. In one sense this policy may have represented a misreading of the unprecedented commodity price increases of 1972 through 1974; developing countries' planners, unprepared for their temporary nature, expanded real imports too aggressively. Thus world inflation probably complicated economic planning and led indirectly to excessive import increases, especially in 1974.

The UNCTAD-UNDP study comparing the frequency of deteriorations in the trade balance of developing countries attributable to increases in import prices and to higher import quantities concludes that the bulk of the deficits in 1973–76 was attributable to world inflation and that domestic demand pressure was a relatively minor cause.[29] But the study's estimates imply that world inflation from 1972 to 1975 caused a deterioration of $7.9 billion in 1975 in the trade balances of the forty-four non-oil-exporting countries in table 2-5, out of a total deterioration of $15.9 billion[30] (and a deterioration in the current account of $23 billion). Thus, even these estimates imply that only about one-half of the deterioration in the trade balances of the non-oil-exporting countries from 1972 to 1975 can be explained by world inflation; the other half therefore would have come from other sources, including those countries' management and growth policies.

External Debt and Reserves

Unanticipated inflation generally benefits debtors at the expense of creditors, and inflation on a worldwide scale is no exception. A major positive effect of global inflation in the early 1970s for the developing

28. Current account deficits (excluding government unrequited transfers) are calculated from International Monetary Fund, *Balance of Payments Yearbook*, vol. 29 (December 1978).

29. UNCTAD, *Balance of Payments Adjustment Process*, pp. 2, I-13.

30. *International Financial Statistics*, vol. 31 (May 1978).

countries was a reduction in the real value of the debt they owed to industrial countries. Policymakers in the developing countries appear to have become increasingly aware of the windfall gain from inflationary erosion of external debt. As President Ferdinand Marcos put it in a speech to the Philippine parliament, it is "axiomatic . . . to borrow when the prices are still down and then to repay five [or] ten years from now when everybody says the dollar will be cheaper and the prices may be higher."[31]

The great bulk of the inflationary debt relief occurred in 1973 and 1974, the years when world prices made enormous leaps. Just as inflation eroded the real value of external debt, it reduced the real value of external reserves, especially those held in the form of dollars. The windfall gains conferred on developing countries through debt erosion were equal to about two years' worth of traditional concessional aid, but almost one-half of the gain was offset by losses on the real value of external reserves.

The windfall gain from inflationary debt erosion can be measured by calculating the difference between the discounted value of the real stream of repayments and interest calculated when the debt was incurred and that when actual inflation exceeds the originally anticipated inflation (the methodology for measuring the gain is set forth in the appendix to this chapter). When actual inflation equals anticipated inflation, the two discounted values are equal and there is no debt erosion even though inflation occurs, because the interest rate negotiated in the debt contract already incorporates the inflation rate.

If the loan is on commercial terms and the time discount rate used for planning by the borrower equals the market interest rate, the discounted value of loan repayments and interest will equal the face value of the loan. In this case, when unanticipated inflation occurs, the amount of debt erosion equals the face value of the loan minus the discounted value of the real stream of repayments and interest after deflating by the revised (and unanticipated) rate of inflation. In the case of developing countries, the face value of the loan overstates the present value of repayments even in the absence of inflation, because concessional loans are made at lower than market interest rates, and the discount rate used for economic planning is often higher than the market interest rate in the international capital markets. In order to avoid overstating the amount of debt erosion, the impact of inflation must be calculated on the present discounted value of loan repayments rather than the face value of debt.

31. Mike Malloy, *Wall Street Journal,* August 28, 1979.

To calculate the originally anticipated present value of loans, it is assumed that borrowers expected zero rates of inflation on loans before 1973, in view of the remarkable stability of U.S. wholesale prices in the early 1960s.[32] The actual real value is obtained by deflating repayment streams with price deflators that incorporate inflation during 1973 and 1974, the two years of massive global inflation. For both the anticipated and actual present value of repayments, the calculations apply a discount rate of 10 percent, the rate conventionally used in analysis of the concessional element of loans to developing countries (by the OECD Development Assistance Committee, for example).[33]

The calculations apply to scheduled debt service payments for public and publicly guaranteed external debt outstanding as of the end of 1972 as well as the increment of such debt contracted in 1973. Inflation after 1974 was minor relative to the surges of 1972–74; and debt contracted in 1974 and after already had built into its interest rates an inflationary premium, or was at variable interest rates related to the London interbank overnight rate (LIBOR), which causes forecasts of interest payments to be ambiguous. Since considerable portions of outstanding debt are actually disbursed after lags of one or more years, the calculations make an allowance for the windfall gain forgone because of delayed disbursements.

The prices used to deflate debt service are simple averages of export and import price indexes for each country in question.[34] When import prices rise, then the real value of imports that must be forgone at a later date to repay a debt stated in nominal terms will be reduced; when export

32. The U.S. wholesale price index rose an average of only 0.8 percent annually in 1954–64. It rose an average of 2.7 percent in 1965–71, which may bias upward the estimate of anticipated real value of repayment streams. However, the 10 percent real discount rate may be thought of as 8 percent plus 2 percent discounting for anticipated inflation; assuming that a real time discount rate of 8 percent is plausible, there would be no bias in the calculations.

33. An alternative approach would be to obtain a discount rate based on interest rates being paid by developing countries on bonds of maturities comparable to those of the debts outstanding. However, for many developing countries there are no such bonds in the private market. Those that are able to float bond issues typically pay rates 1–2 percent above the London interbank overnight rate on dollar deposits. Even very high rates of 9–10 percent in nominal terms would generate nominal discount rates of 12 percent or less, meaning real discount rates of 7 percent or below if inflation were as low as 5 percent. Therefore the 10 percent real discount rate gives a conservative estimate of the windfall gain from debt erosion (because a lower discount rate would give a larger present discounted value of this gain).

34. UNCTAD, *Handbook of International Trade and Development Statistics, 1976,* UN Doc. TD/STAT. 6, pp. 441–59.

prices rise, the real value of exports necessary to pay the nominal debt will decline. Because there is no a priori reason to assume that adjustment will occur solely through either increased real imports or reduced exports, both price series are averaged to obtain the deflator for external debt (see the appendix to this chapter for details of the calculations).[35]

The windfall gain in 1973 and 1974 from debt erosion is shown in table 2-6 for twenty-seven developing countries that accounted for 82 percent of the external public debt of the eighty-six developing countries monitored by the World Bank.[36] Their gains amounted to $18.5 billion—19 percent of the nominal value of their outstanding external public debt at the end of 1973, and 27 percent of the nominal present discounted value of that debt. It is immediately clear that taking account of the difference between nominal debt and present discounted value of future repayments (as well as disbursement lags) reduces the estimate of inflationary debt relief below levels that might be expected at first glance. Considering that world trade prices rose by 77 percent in the two years 1973 and 1974,[37] debt erosion would have amounted to fully 44 percent of the nominal value of outstanding debt if the originally anticipated discounted value of repayments had equaled face value of loans. Even so, the magnitude of the estimated windfall gain is impressive. Moreover, the calculations in table 2-6 omit countries that account for approximately one-fifth of the total debt of developing countries. Extending the total for the twenty-seven countries examined to all developing countries produces an estimated windfall gain of $22.5 billion. As the unintended result of world inflationary developments, the creditor industrial countries transferred to the developing countries a gain substantially larger than the $17.2 billion in development assistance that they extended officially in 1973 and 1974.[38]

35. This procedure would exaggerate the windfall gain for oil-exporting countries, with their fivefold rise in export prices and the more moderate rise of import prices. The windfall gain in table 2-6 refers to the borrower's gain, which may differ in size from the loss to the lender. Gordon W. Smith also proposes an average of import and export prices as deflators and points out that the World Bank has used import prices alone for deflation of debt. "External Debt Prospects of the Non-Oil-Exporting Developing Countries," in Cline, *Policy Alternatives*, p. 324.

36. The 27 countries accounted for $81.6 billion of the 86 countries' external public debt of $99.4 billion at the end of 1972 and $96.5 billion of the $118.9 billion debt at the end of 1973 (including undisbursed funds). World Bank, *Annual Report 1974*, pp. 85–86, and *1975*, pp. 92–93.

37. *International Financial Statistics*, vol. 30 (December 1977), pp. 32–33, and vol. 28 (April 1975), pp. 34–35.

38. At 1972 prices, calculated from OECD, *Development Cooperation, 1977 Review*, pp. 165, 169.

Table 2-6. *Impact of World Inflation in 1973 and 1974 on the Real Value of External Debt and Reserves of Fifty-five Developing Countries*[a]
Millions of 1972 dollars

Country	*Windfall gain through erosion of external public debt*	*Windfall loss on reserves*	*Net (gain minus loss)*
Afghanistan	n.a.	−20	n.a.
Algeria	1,029	270	759
Argentina	844	60	784
Bangladesh	−9	81	−90
Bolivia	n.a.	2	n.a.
Brazil	1,903	1,644	259
Burma	n.a.	11	n.a.
Cameroon	n.a.	15	n.a.
Chad	n.a.	3	n.a.
China, Republic of	215	n.a.	n.a.
Chile	823	30	793
Colombia	394	95	299
Dominican Republic	n.a.	20	n.a.
Ecuador	n.a.	61	n.a.
Egypt	584	19	565
El Salvador	n.a.	9	n.a.
Ethiopia	n.a.	26	n.a.
Ghana	n.a.	44	n.a.
Greece	432	n.a.	n.a.
Guatemala	n.a.	18	n.a.
India	1,946	167	1,779
Indonesia	1,228	331	897
Iran	1,929	634	1,295
Iraq	n.a.	538	n.a.
Israel	900	325	575
Ivory Coast	128	31	97
Kenya	n.a.	88	n.a.
Korea, Republic of	701	242	459
Malagasy Republic (Madagascar)	n.a.	19	n.a.
Malawi	n.a.	10	n.a.
Malaysia	223	455	−232
Mali	n.a.	1	n.a.
Mexico	1,249	188	1,061
Morocco	282	94	188
Niger	n.a.	12	n.a.
Nigeria	413	240	173
Pakistan	880	48	832
Peru	367	172	195
Philippines	335	263	72
Rwanda	n.a.	2	n.a.

Table 2-6 (*continued*)

Country	*Windfall gain through erosion of external public debt*	*Windfall loss on reserves*	*Net (gain minus loss)*
Saudi Arabia	n.a.	1,749	n.a.
Senegal	n.a.	16	n.a.
Spain	302	n.a.	n.a.
Sri Lanka	n.a.	25	n.a.
Sudan	98	18	80
Syria	n.a.	49	n.a.
Tanzania	n.a.	52	n.a.
Thailand	n.a.	489	n.a.
Turkey	629	n.a.	n.a.
Uganda	n.a.	3	n.a.
Upper Volta	n.a.	18	n.a.
Venezuela	n.a.	1,085	n.a.
Yugoslavia	499	n.a.	n.a.
Zaire	159	33	126
Zambia	n.a.	60	n.a.
Total reserve loss, 50 countries	...	9,845	...
Total windfall gain, 27 countries	18,484	...	...
Total gain and loss, 22 countries	16,406	5,440	10,966

n.a. Not available.
a. Based on calculations described in the appendix to this chapter.

In other words, they unintentionally more than doubled their resource transfers in 1973 and 1974 as the result of inflationary erosion of external debt.[39]

39. Smith estimates reduction in the present discounted value of the debt of oil-importing developing countries caused by world inflation at $17.3 billion. "External Debt Prospects," p. 293. An UNCTAD study maintains that developing countries' cumulative current account deficit in 1973–76 was $64.3 billion above normal. Applying the increases in OECD inflation in 1973–76 over the 1965–72 rates to developing country debt, the study estimates debt erosion at $23.2 billion and concludes therefore that on balance the gains from debt erosion were more than offset by losses on terms of trade. UNCTAD Secretariat, "Some Aspects of the Impact of Inflation on the Debt Burden of Developing Countries," *World Development,* vol. 7 (February 1979), pp. 135–43. But only a portion of their increase in current account deficit can be attributed to the impact of inflation and recession on their trade deficits. In any case, terms of trade, which can easily reverse, affect trade flows and should not be compared with once-for-all changes in the real value of a stock, external debt. Even if a country has no debt or debt service, the UNCTAD formula will identify a windfall gain or loss on debt depending on terms of trade movements;

Although these estimates may contain certain biases, they tend to offset each other. The omission of further inflationary windfall gains after 1974 understates total debt erosion. Even though interest rates rose along with inflation in 1974–76, they were still too low to compensate for inflation during 1974 and 1975 and only slightly above inflation by 1976.[40] Moreover, the estimates refer only to public and publicly guaranteed debt, excluding that of private borrowers (because it is excluded from the World Bank data base). On the other hand, the analysis counts the full inflation of 1973 and 1974 as unanticipated. Some component of the inflation (say, 2–3 percent per year) was probably anticipated, but it is small relative to total inflation in the period.

The windfall losses of developing countries through the erosion of their external reserves are also strikingly large (table 2-6). The total estimated reduction in fifty countries' reserve assets is $9.8 billion. The loss is large despite favorable forces acting in opposition to the inflation: windfall gains on gold, higher interest rates on foreign-exchange reserves, and appreciation of the IMF special drawing rights relative to the dollar. To estimate the impact of world inflation, it is necessary to calculate separately the effect on foreign-exchange reserves, gold, net reserve position in the International Monetary Fund, and SDR holdings. For foreign-exchange reserves held in the form of dollars, the real loss of value from the end of 1972 to the end of 1974 corresponds to the difference between nominal holdings and real holdings as deflated by the average of the import and export price indexes from 1972 to 1974. Since most foreign-exchange reserves are held in the form of short- or medium-term official

p. 137. The comparison does not take into account erosion of reserves, which are a stock and not a flow and therefore are appropriate for comparison with erosion of debt. If increases in the trade deficit are to be mixed in with debt erosion, so should other factors, especially the rise in nominal aid flows. Furthermore, nominal erosion is not an adequate substitute for erosion of the present discounted value of repayments. In short, the UNCTAD analysis appears to overstate the damage to developing countries' terms of trade from world inflation and recession, and to mix it inappropriately with debt erosion.

40. The average interest yields on foreign and international bonds issues by developing countries were approximately 8.4 percent in 1974, 9.5 percent in 1975, and 8.7 percent in 1976, while industrial countries' consumer prices rose at rates of 12.7 percent, 10.7 percent, and 7.7 percent, and world export prices in dollars at rates of 41.5 percent, 8.5 percent, and 2.3 percent in those years. World Bank, *Annual Report 1977,* p. 121; *International Financial Statistics,* vol. 30 (December 1977), pp. 29, 32.

securities, interest earnings on these securities attributable to the rise in interest rates induced by higher inflation are subtracted from the losses.[41]

The increase in the value of gold reserves is calculated by comparing the 1972 market value ($64.90 per ounce) to the 1975 value ($140.24) because by then the market price of gold had retreated from its 1974 peak. This conservative valuation is consistent with the ambiguities raised by the uncertainty of gold prices and the thinness of the market relative to official holdings of gold.[42] The impact of inflation on SDR holdings and net reserve position in the International Monetary Fund is the net result of two opposing influences: rising dollar prices and an appreciating SDR relative to the dollar, although world dollar prices rose much more rapidly than did the dollar price of the SDR. These two categories of reserves as of the end of 1972 are converted into dollars at the end-of-1972 exchange rate, and their loss in real value is calculated by applying the average of import and export price increases from 1972 through 1974. Against the

41. The loss of real value of foreign exchange reserves, L_E, is equal to

$$R_E^{72}[1 - (\{1 + \Delta r\}/P)],$$

where R_E^{72} is the foreign-exchange reserves at end of 1972; Δr is the increase in interest rate on U.S. Treasury bills (calculated at a compounded sum of 6.87 percent over 1973 and 1974); and P is an index of the country's import and export prices (in dollars) for 1974, with 1972 as a base. *International Financial Statistics,* vol. 30 (December 1977), p. 370. Although the great bulk of foreign-exchange reserves in 1972–74 was held in dollar assets, the changes in other reserve currencies should ideally be incorporated in the analysis. In the absence of data on the currency composition of reserves, the increasing dollar value of reserves held in Deutsche marks, Swiss francs, and Japanese yen is assumed to have offset the decreasing dollar value of reserves held in pounds sterling (which devalued sharply in 1975).

42. The real windfall gain, G, from the increasing price of gold is estimated as

$$R_g^{72}[(\{1 + \dot{p}_g\}/P) - 1],$$

where R_g^{72} is the value of gold reserves at the end of 1972 at the market price of gold; $\dot{p}_g$ is the percent rise in market price of gold, 1972 to 1975; and P is the 1974 index of import and export prices for the country, with 1972 as a base. While the official price of gold rose from $38.00 an ounce in 1972 to $42.22 in 1974, the London market price rose to $112.25 in 1973 and $168.50 in 1974 and then retreated to $140.25 in 1975. The increasing irrelevance of the official price was recognized by the agreement of the IMF Interim Committee on August 31, 1975, to abolish the official price of gold. *IMF Survey,* September 15, 1975, pp. 263–65. The 1971–72 rise must be attributed primarily to the growing threat of collapse of the Bretton Woods system of fixed exchange rates. It is reasonable to attribute the 1972–74 rise to gold's function as a store of value in the face of general inflationary erosion of money.

loss there is a gain of approximately 13 percent based on the appreciation of the SDR vis-à-vis the dollar.[43]

For twenty-two countries with comparisons available, the windfall loss on reserves amounted to 33 percent of the windfall gains through debt erosion (table 2-6). The loss of real reserves caused by inflation is not a widely recognized phenomenon. Yet with an estimated $22.5 billion windfall gain for all developing countries through debt erosion, the estimated $9.8 billion windfall loss for fifty countries through erosion of reserves lowered the total gain to approximately $13 billion (1972 prices), or roughly one and a half times a year's worth of concessional assistance.

Table 2-6 indicates that the windfall gains were heavily concentrated in five countries with the largest debt erosion—Iran, India, Brazil, Mexico, and Algeria accounted for 44 percent of the total gain shown in the table. Moreover, the bulk of the gain accrued to middle-income countries since they hold the bulk of the external debt. The ten low-income countries (Bangladesh, Egypt, India, Indonesia, Morocco, Nigeria, Pakistan, Philippines, Sudan, and Zaire) accounted for only 32 percent of the total gain but represented 70 percent of the population of the twenty-seven countries examined. They hold relatively little of total debt of developing countries, and because much of their debt is on concessional terms, they have a relatively low base of discounted future repayments that can be eroded by inflation.[44] The real reserve losses also are concentrated in the middle-income countries, reflecting their relatively large share in reserve holdings. Ironically, the countries with the most favorable net results were those with large debt but low reserves—the fabled grasshoppers rather than the ants. Thus Mexico and India had large net gains. Perhaps most ironical, the net effect of inflation for Malaysia was negative, since its policy of holding high reserves led to losses in the erosion of reserves that were higher than the gains from erosion of its indebtedness. Low-income

43. The real loss on holdings of SDRs and on net reserve position in the fund, L_s, is equal to

$$R_s^{72}[1 - (\{1 + \dot{s}\}/P)],$$

where R^{72} is the nominal value of these reserves at the end of 1972 (in dollars); $\dot{s}$ is the percentage appreciation of the SDR relative to the dollar from 1972 to 1974; and P is the index of import and export prices for the country in 1974, with 1972 as a base. The value for $\dot{s}$ is 12.77 percent. *International Financial Statistics,* vol. 30 (December 1977), p. 368.

44. The present value of future repayments for Bangladesh is so low that inflationary erosion of the stream is less than the inflationary loss on debt caused by delayed disbursement, giving a negative value (table 2-6).

countries appear to have fared relatively better in the net impact of inflation than in their windfall gains on debt alone, since, holding relatively lower reserves than the middle-income countries, they had less to lose to inflationary erosion of reserves.

Inflation and the Distribution of World Income

In negotiations between industrial and developing countries in recent years, a recurrent issue has been the distribution of world income among poor and rich countries. Moreover, the recent emphasis by aid donors on programs to meet basic human needs in developing countries has caused the distribution of income within national borders to become an international political issue. (The movement has aroused considerable hostility among developing countries on the grounds that it is interventionist.)

The large changes in absolute and relative prices in the early 1970s might be expected to have had major redistributive effects. Higher oil prices alone caused a massive transfer of income to the OPEC countries from rich and poor alike. The large changes in prices of several other raw materials, as well as the high rate of inflation for industrial exports from advanced countries, could also have had significant distributional implications. Yet the impact of the commodity price explosion of 1973–75 on the world distribution of income was almost imperceptible. The minimal increases of income that commodity inflation generated, however, had an equalizing effect on the distribution of world income.

To estimate the impact of inflation on the world distribution of income, it is first necessary to estimate the world distribution in the base year, 1972 (see the methodology in the appendix). Data on real per capita income in sixty-eight developing and industrial countries, drawn from estimates by Kravis, Heston, and Summers, are already adjusted for differences in purchasing power parity among the exchange rates of various countries.[45] Broadly speaking, a poor country's currency may have three times as much purchasing power as is implied by its exchange rate, pri-

45. Irving B. Kravis, Alan W. Heston, and Robert Summers, "Real GDP Per Capita for More than One Hundred Countries," *Economic Journal,* vol. 88 (June 1978), pp. 215–42. From detailed price surveys of 16 countries they have designed a set of general functions relating the real purchasing power of a country's currency to its per capita income, at nominal, or market, exchange rates. The figures used here are for 1973 real income as estimated in the authors' preferred variant (extrapolated from 1970 with changed terms of trade).

marily because labor-intensive, nontradable service activities tend to be cheap in poor countries whereas the exchange rate is determined by tradable goods that are relatively more expensive in those countries. As a country's per capita income rises, the ratio of the currency's purchasing power to its market exchange rate approaches unity.

Changes in the world distribution of income resulting from rising commodity prices will depend not only on changes in the average per capita incomes in countries receiving windfall gains or losses but also on the extent to which incomes are equally or unequally distributed within those countries. Thus the estimates of world income distribution here incorporate data on both per capita incomes and the national income distributions for each decile in the sixty-eight countries examined.[46] The resulting estimates for the actual distribution of world income in 1972 show an extremely high degree of inequality. The income shares of the world's poorest 40 percent, next 50 percent, and richest 10 percent of families are 4.1 percent, 45.6 percent, and 50.2 percent, respectively. A considerable portion of total inequality appears to come from unusual distribution within countries as opposed to among countries. Measuring only the inequality of income among countries (implicitly assuming total equality within countries), Kravis, Heston, and Summers found, using the same basic data, respective income shares of 8.4 percent, 58.0 percent, and 33.6 percent for the sixty-eight countries.[47] The sharpest difference occurs for the world's poorest 40 percent: if inequality within countries did not exist, their share in world income would double.

To determine the change in world income distribution attributable to inflation, commodity price increases from 1972 to 1975 are applied to trade data for 1972.[48] The trade data are for twenty commodity groups,

46. Shail Jain, *Size Distribution of Income: A Compilation of Data* (Washington: World Bank, 1975); Malcolm Sawyer, "Income Distribution in OECD Countries," *OECD Economic Outlook: Occasional Studies* (July 1976), pp. 3–36. For a limited number of countries, synthetic estimates were calculated by applying the cross-country regression equations estimated by Montek S. Ahluwalia, "Inequality, Poverty and Development," *Journal of Development Economics,* vol. 3 (December 1976), pp. 307–42. Although most of these estimates are subject to error because of the typical lack of firm and consistent statistical evidence on income distribution, there is no reason to expect any systematic bias in these data toward equality or inequality, and therefore no reason to believe that the data bias the analysis here.

47. "Real GDP Per Capita," p. 239.

48. Trade data for the calculations are drawn from country-by-country issues of the United Nations' *Commodity Trade Statistics.* For prices, the analysis applied a single world export price index and a single world import price index for each commodity, across all countries. It would be possible to apply different indexes for each

including the principal raw materials exported by developing countries as well as two commodity classes important for exports of industrial countries: manufactured goods and wheat.[49] The 1975 world income distribution is estimated by computing, for each country, the addition to national income caused by rising export prices and the loss caused by rising import prices. Separate indexes of world import and export prices are estimated for each commodity, because of divergences caused by transportation costs. To account for generalized world inflation (which, if equal everywhere, would leave world income distribution unchanged), these import and export price indexes are deflated by a single global price index, a weighted average of the consumer price inflation (expressed in dollar terms) in the industrial countries in 1972–75.

The world income distribution for 1975 is calculated by applying profiles of national income distributions (assumed to remain unchanged) to the estimates of average national per capita incomes adjusted to 1973–75 commodity price changes. The 1975 estimates are designed to reflect only changes directly attributable to commodity price inflation; the difference between the 1972 and 1975 distributions measures the impact of world inflation on the world distribution of income.

The analysis assumes that commodity trade is unresponsive to price changes—that an import price rise, for example, does not reduce the quantity imported. That was true in 1972–75 of the single most important price rise, for oil, which had very little effect on the quantities imported. The price elasticities of import demand tend to be low for other raw materials as well.[50] It is also assumed that income distributions within countries were left unchanged by world inflation. Ideally the analysis would incorporate information on changes within countries, but data are not

---

country, but the variability of the corresponding unit value indexes probably would be high because of changing composition of trade within the categories. The world export and import price index for each commodity was calculated as the weighted average of the index for each country, with weights proportional to 1972 net exports (or net imports). Only net exporters were included in the index for export price and only net importers in the index for import price. Data for manufactured goods are from UN, *Monthly Bulletin of Statistics,* vol. 30 (March 1976), p. xx, and vol. 32 (March 1978), p. xxii.

49. The commodities are bauxite, cocoa, coffee, raw cotton, other cotton, copper ore, copper alloys, iron ore, jute, crude oil, refined oil, natural rubber, other rubber, raw sugar, refined sugar, tea, tin ore, tin alloys, wheat, and manufactured goods (standard international trade classification categories 5–8 excluding 68).

50. See for example, Behrman, "International Commodity Agreements," pp. 118–21.

Table 2-7. *Index of Unit Value of Twenty Major Commodities in World Trade, 1972–75*

Index, 1972 = 100

Commodity class and SITC category[a]	*1975 price index*[b]	
	Import	*Export*
Raw sugar (061.1)	369	374
Refined sugar (061.2)	335	284
Coffee (071)	138	146
Cocoa (072)	251	248
Tea (074)	137	135
Natural rubber (231.1)	173	175
Other rubber (231 less 231.1)	178	192
Raw cotton (263.1)	150	163
Other cotton (263 less 263.1)	179	152
Jute (264)	106	107
Iron ore (281)	150	161
Bauxite (283.3)	163	195
Crude oil (331)	455	498
Refined oil (332)	360	396
Copper alloys (682)	128	126
Copper ore (283.1)	133	118
Tin alloys (687)	185	169
Tin ore (283.6)	183	178
Wheat (041)	250	249
Manufactured goods (5–8 less 68)	161	161

Source: Calculated from UN, *Commodity Trade Statistics*, various issues, and *Monthly Bulletin of Statistics*, various issues.

a. Standard international trade classification category.

b. Average of the indexes, weighted by 1972 values, of countries that are net importers or exporters.

available that would permit detailed allocation of the income transfers resulting from price increases by specific commodities.[51]

For the twenty major commodities in world trade, the most dramatic increases in prices from 1972 to 1975 were those of oil, sugar, cocoa, and wheat (table 2-7). The small difference between price rises for exporters and for importers suggests that transportation costs do not act significantly to moderate price rises for importers when commodity prices rise by large amounts.

When the changes in commodity price indexes are applied to 1972

51. This procedure is preferable to omitting information on distributions within countries altogether. To ignore such distributions would be to throw away important information on the change in world distribution caused (for example) by a net transfer away from a country with a relatively equal distribution of income to another country (at the same average income level) with a highly unequal internal distribution.

Table 2-8. *Impact of Price Changes in Twenty Major Traded Commodities on the Real Incomes of Sixty-eight Countries, 1972–75*

Country	*Ratio of 1975 hypothetical to 1972 actual incomes*	*Country*	*Ratio of 1975 hypothetical to 1972 actual incomes*
Argentina	0.997	Libya	1.909
Australia	1.002	Malaysia	0.997
Austria	0.985	Mexico	0.998
Bangladesh	0.991	Morocco	0.975
Belgium-Luxembourg	0.968	Netherlands	0.966
Bolivia	1.024	New Zealand	0.967
Brazil	0.995	Nicaragua	0.995
Cameroon	0.997	Niger	0.985
Canada	1.005	Nigeria	1.123
Chile	0.980	Norway	0.951
Colombia	1.004	Pakistan	0.995
Congo	0.999	Peru	0.995
Denmark	0.957	Philippines	0.992
Ecuador	1.019	Rwanda	0.992
Egypt	1.000	Saudi Arabia	1.795
Ethiopia	0.993	Senegal	0.969
Finland	0.962	Singapore	0.956
France	0.979	Sri Lanka	1.000
Germany, Federal Republic of	0.987	Sudan	0.990
Ghana	1.013	Sweden	0.974
Honduras	0.973	Switzerland	0.969
Hong Kong	0.980	Syria	1.004
India	0.997	Tanzania	0.988
Indonesia	1.050	Thailand	0.986
Iran	1.160	Tunisia	1.014
Iraq	0.988	Turkey	0.992
Ireland	0.956	Uganda	0.999
Israel	0.969	United Kingdom	0.975
Ivory Coast	0.997	United States	0.994
Italy	0.976	Upper Volta	0.984
Japan	0.982	Venezuela	1.202
Kenya	0.973	Yugoslavia	0.987
Korea, Republic of	0.978	Zaire	0.987
Kuwait	1.944	Zambia	0.961

data on the commodities trade and real income of the sixty-eight countries (table 2-8), those that show massive increases in real income for 1975 are all major oil exporters. Kuwait, Libya, and Saudi Arabia reach a spectacular near-doubling of real income. Correspondingly, oil-importing countries (especially European countries and Japan) experience decreases in real income ranging from 2 percent to 5 percent.[52] The impact of other products is relatively limited (high cocoa prices in Ghana causing a modest increase in real income and high wheat prices in Australia and Canada a very slight increase in real income).

For the group of oil-exporting countries shown in table 2-8 (including Indonesia and Nigeria), commodity price changes from 1972 to 1975 raised real income by 23.4 percent. Among the low-income non-oil-exporting developing countries (with per capita incomes less than 10 percent of the U.S. level), these price changes reduced real income by 0.6 percent; for those with intermediate incomes (up to 40 percent of U.S. per capita income), the price changes reduced real income by 0.9 percent; and for the richer countries the price changes reduced real income by 1.4 percent.[53] Within the income groupings the distributional results are mixed; some poor countries such as Indonesia and Ecuador gained dramatically while others such as Pakistan and Kenya lost, suggesting that the inflationary rise of commodity prices had only a limited effect on the worldwide distribution of income.

Table 2-9 shows the percentage share of income for 1972 and for the 1975 simulation accruing to three world income groupings as well as two summary measures of world income distribution. The Gini coefficient, which ranges from zero for absolute equality to unity for absolute inequality, typically takes on values ranging from 0.3 for industrial countries with relatively even income distribution to 0.6 for some of the developing countries with highly unequal distributions.[54] The Atkinson measure, which also ranges from zero to unity for absolute equality and inequality, respectively, adheres to an underlying social welfare function (whereas the Gini

52. The real loss in income for the United States is understated because the calculation assumes that the physical quantities of imports remain constant at their 1972 levels, while in fact the quantity of U.S. crude oil imports rose by 48 percent from 1972 to 1974 (according to the trade data base compiled from UN, *Commodity Trade Statistics*).

53. Calculated from table 2-8. The income categories here correspond approximately to the income groups used by the World Bank: low-income ceiling, $300 (1977); middle-income, up to approximately $3,000. World Bank, *World Development Report, 1979* (Washington: Oxford University Press for the World Bank, 1979), pp. 126–27.

54. The Gini coefficient is the ratio of the area between the Lorenz curve and the diagonal to the total area under the diagonal, in a diagram of cumulative percent of income received (vertical axis) against cumulative percent of receiving units (horizontal axis). For typical estimates, see William R. Cline, *Potential Effects of Income Redistribution on Economic Growth: Latin American Cases* (Praeger, 1972), p. 111.

Table 2-9. *Measures of World Income Distribution under 1972 and 1975 Commodity Prices*

	Percent of income received by			*Distribution measure*[a]	
Year	*Lower 40 percent*	*Next 50 percent*	*Top 10 percent*	*Gini coefficient*	*Atkinson measure*
1972	4.148	45.642	50.210	0.6732	0.8335
1975[b]	4.184	45.629	50.187	0.6723	0.8328

a. Ranges from zero for absolute equality to unity for absolute inequality.
b. Simulated distribution based on 1975 commodity prices; see appendix to this chapter.

coefficient does not), but the measure itself is ambiguous in that it requires the user to specify a weight on inequality.[55] As shown in the table, the commodity price explosion of 1972 to 1975 had an extremely small effect on the world distribution of income. Equality increased by all measures but the increase was minimal. The largest proportionate change was a rise of the share of world income going to the poorest 40 percent, from 4.148 percent in 1972 to 4.184 percent after commodity price changes through 1975 are applied to the 1972 base.

The extremely limited impact of world inflation on world income distribution was due in part to the dispersion of the commodities with large price increases across exporting countries at all income levels (oil, cocoa, and sugar, for poor and middle income; wheat for rich) as well as poor and rich importing countries. And because of inequality within countries, some portion of increased export earnings was being siphoned off into a class rich by international standards even in poor or middle-income countries. Furthermore, the value of world trade in the commodities was relatively limited compared to real world income. The total value of imports of the nineteen raw materials in table 2-7 was \$48.9 billion in 1972 for the sixty-eight countries in table 2-8, and the total value of imports of manufactured goods was \$197 billion. Global real income for these same countries in 1972 was \$4,193 billion. Raw materials trade represented only 1.2 percent of world real income, and trade in manufactured goods only 4.7 percent.

55. The Atkinson measure equals $1 - (Y^e/Y)$ where Y^e is the level of per capita income which, if equally distributed, would generate the same social welfare as per capita income Y. The measure depends on the value assigned to Atkinson's epsilon, the parameter for inequality aversion; a value of 2.5 is assigned for this parameter in the calculations of table 2-9. Anthony B. Atkinson, "On the Measurement of Social Inequality," *Journal of Economic Theory,* vol. 2 (September 1970), pp. 244–63.

The equalizing effect of inflation was apparently due to price increases for oil, sugar, and cocoa (and to a lesser extent several other commodities) that more than offset increases for wheat and manufactured goods, whose benefits are concentrated on industrial countries.

An extension of this analysis, which examines distributional effects when the price of each commodity quadruples while all other prices hold constant, finds that price increases for wheat and manufactured goods concentrate income, while for each of the other raw materials (except refined sugar and other rubber) quadrupling the price equalizes world income but only by a minute degree.[56] For each commodity, the equalizing impact is a combination of the underlying proportionate distribution of exports and imports among rich and poor countries, on the one hand, and the size of the commodity in world trade, on the other. Quadrupling the price of oil (from the 1972 base) has the greatest impact on equalizing world income, but even this effect is minuscule, raising the world income share of the poorest 40 percent from 4.148 percent to only 4.211 percent. The distributional effects for oil reflect the fact that poor countries (Indonesia, Ecuador, Nigeria) as well as middle-income (Saudi Arabia, Venezuela, Iran) and rich countries (Kuwait) export oil. Quadrupling the prices of the sixteen income-equalizing commodities in table 2-7 (all except wheat, manufactured goods, refined sugar, and other rubber), while holding all other prices constant, hardly budges the world income distribution. Such a joint price explosion for exports of the poor countries represents an upper bound for any conceivable program of world income equalization through commodity pricing.

In sum, world inflation from 1972 to 1975 had an equalizing but extremely small effect on the world distribution of income. The estimates for 1972 show that the world distribution of real income is extremely unequal, and that much of this inequality comes from unequal distributions within countries. The world's poorest 40 percent would have twice as much income if incomes were equal within countries. The simulation finding that even an extreme price increase for all income-equalizing commodities would change income distribution minimally must give pause to those who attribute international inequality to low commodity export prices for developing countries.[57] The results directly challenge the argu-

56. William R. Cline, "Commodity Prices and the World Distribution of Income," *Journal of Policy Modeling,* vol. 2 (January 1980), pp. 1–17.

57. For example, Arghiri Emmanuel, *Unequal Exchange: A Study of the Imperialism of Trade,* trans. Brian Pearce (Monthly Review Press, 1972).

ment that commodity arrangements (such as the common fund negotiated in UNCTAD) should raise commodity prices to improve international equity. Such arrangements should focus on price stabilization instead.

Protection, Exchange Rates, and Inflation

The ways in which developing countries change their policies in order to deal with external shocks are examined in country case studies in chapters 4–7. Two areas of response—exchange rates and protection policy—are especially important. In Brazil, for example, authorities raised protection (instead of devaluing) to deal with a serious trade deficit in 1974 and 1975; in Malaysia the government used exchange-rate appreciation and a reduction of protection to reduce the consequences of external inflation while domestic monetary and fiscal policies were used for slowing internal inflation.

In general the choice of anti-inflationary policies will depend on the specific conditions of the external inflationary impulse. When a country's export and import prices rise by comparable amounts (the terms of trade remain unchanged), the only problem is to insulate domestic prices from external inflation, and the appropriate policy will be to neutralize the impact of higher import prices. A logical first step is to seize the unique opportunity to dismantle distorting protective barriers without worsening the balance of payments (external inflation, being higher than internal, limits imports even though protection is declining). After trade has been liberalized, appreciation of the exchange rate is the logical means of providing insulation against further external inflationary pressure. Appreciation will offset higher foreign currency prices of imports. Generally, appreciation by the percentage by which the external inflation rate exceeds the domestic rate will help insulate the economy from outside inflation without altering export incentives in real terms.

If external inflation causes a country's terms of trade to deteriorate and its trade balance to enter serious deficit, measures must be taken to reduce the trade deficit (assuming the deterioration is not considered to be strictly temporary). The choice becomes either increasing protection or devaluing in order to reduce the trade deficit (ruling out the alternative of slowing down domestic growth). Since either action will exacerbate, rather than neutralizing, external inflation, the question is which measure will do so by less.

It is relatively well established that devaluation causes some resulting domestic inflation. It has a direct, price-raising effect on imports and similar domestically produced goods, and on exports and similar products consumed at home. Indirectly, it affects the prices of services and of products with prohibitive transport costs as consumers search for substitutions when the prices of traded goods rise. The indirect price increase is higher, the lower the elasticity of supply of goods and services in the nontraded goods sector and the higher the elasticity of substitution in demand in the traded goods sector. Harberger estimates that a 50 percent devaluation in a developing country is likely to cause induced domestic inflation on the order of 30–38 percent.[58] That ratio of induced inflation to devaluation appears to be somewhat high. For the United States, every percentage point of devaluation is estimated to cause on the order of 0.15 percent domestic inflation by the end of a two-to-three-year period.[59] However, it seems indisputable that there will be some induced domestic inflation following devaluation.

Increased protection is likely to have a more inflationary impact than is devaluation. It introduces distortions in resource allocation and reduces incentives for technical change. With less efficiency in the allocation of resources there will be lower growth of output and (if growth of the money supply is unchanged) greater inflationary pressures. Higher protection is partially self-defeating because it spoils export incentives, as exporters switch to the relatively more attractive protected domestic market. This export leakage means that protection will have to rise by enough not only to reduce imports but also to compensate for an induced reduction in exports. In short, there are good reasons for expecting import protection to be even more inflationary than devaluation as the means of dealing with a serious trade deficit.[60] As a policy response, devaluation

58. Arnold C. Harberger, "Some Notes on Inflation," in Werner Baer and Issac Kerstenetzky, eds., *Inflation and Growth in Latin America* (Irwin, 1964), pp. 319–51.

59. *Economic Report of the President, January 1979*, p. 43.

60. Moreover, because devaluation applies to both importable and exportable goods and protection affects only importable goods, the proportionate price rise caused by protection will have to be higher than that caused by devaluation in order to achieve the same correction in the trade balance. (For example, an improvement in the trade balance achieved by a 10 percent devaluation might require a 20 percent tariff.) The weights of the economic sector that each affects will run in the opposite direction, so that the net impact and domestic inflation caused by devaluation and protection will be comparable (ignoring misallocation of resources and export leakage). If the export and import price elasticities are very low (that is, if Marshall-

will aggravate external inflationary impulses by less than will increased protection.

Conclusion

For most developing countries the worldwide inflation and recession of 1973–75 did reduce the terms of trade, but only because of oil price increases. Excluding oil, terms of trade improved for most developing countries from 1971–72 to 1975. The 1970s were a period of heightened fluctuation in the real terms of trade for raw materials exports.

Price inflation did not cause non-oil-exporting developing countries' capital needs to rise until 1975 (when export prices had backed off for some commodities and yet import prices of manufactured goods were continuing to rise). Even then, the magnitude of increased capital requirements was more than offset by the increased availability of capital, even of concessional aid alone for low-income countries. Indeed, the massive borrowing by developing countries to cover sharply higher trade deficits in 1974 and 1975 appears to have resulted primarily from their import and growth policies rather than from inflationary increases in the prices of traded goods per se.

World inflation conferred a major windfall gain on the developing countries by eroding the real value of their external debt (when measured by the erosion of the present discounted value of future repayments as well as by the more common measure of erosion of outstanding nominal debt). Inflation also eroded the real value of developing countries' holdings of dollars as foreign reserves, however. The net effect was still a large windfall gain, on the order of $13 billion in 1972 prices.

The Great Inflation had very little impact on the distribution of world income. From 1972 to 1975, changes in prices of traded goods had an almost imperceptible equalizing effect on income distribution. Even hypothetical radical price increases for the whole gamut of commodities exported by developing countries appear to have such an extremely small impact on income distribution that a concerted scheme to raise prices cannot be justified as a means of improving the world distribution of income.

Lerner conditions are not met), devaluation will not improve the trade balance while import quotas will. But even in this case (presumably rare), the imposition of quotas will have a domestic inflationary effect (by reducing supply).

Appendix

This appendix develops the equations for determining inflationary debt erosion and for estimating the impact of inflation on the worldwide distribution of income. Table 2-10 presents terms-of-trade indexes for the developing countries examined in this chapter.

Inflationary Debt Erosion

The windfall gain, *G*, from inflationary erosion of external debt, in 1972 prices, is equal to $(PVR^{72} - PVRD^{72}) + (PVR^{73} - PVRD^{73}) - (PVDIS^{72} - PVDISD^{72}) - (PVDIS^{73} - PVDISD^{73})$, where PRV^{72} and $PVRD^{72}$ are the present discounted value (at 10 percent discount rate) of repayment and interest stream for all public external debt outstanding (including undisbursed debt) at the end of 1972 and that value deflated for price increases over the 1972 base, and PVR^{73} and $PVRD^{73}$ the corresponding values for incremental debt contracted during 1973; and $PVDIS^{72}$ and $PVDISD^{72}$ are the present discounted value of disbursements of undisbursed debt outstanding at the end of 1972 and that value deflated for price increases, and $PVDIS^{73}$ and $PVDISD^{73}$ the corresponding values for disbursements on incremental debt contracted during 1973.

Table 2-10. *Terms-of-Trade Indexes of Fifty-two Developing Countries, 1973–77*

Index, 1971–72 average = 100

Country	*1973*	*1974*	*1975*	*1976*	*1977*
Afghanistan	100	100	111	117	123
Algeria[a]	110	265	267	279	281
Angola	96	160	157	184	192
Argentina	117	97	82	85	76
Bangladesh	87	73	77	72	68
Bolivia	102	158	142	152	145
Brazil	102	92	85	89	130
Burma	104	110	98	90	92
Cameroon	98	100	101	142	150
Chad	106	93	91	125	112
Chile	119	97	62	63	74
Colombia	107	115	108	149	177
Dominican Republic	101	122	181	131	87
Ecuador[a]	97	149	146	160	175
Egypt	99	123	114	111	94

Table 2-10 (*continued*)

Country	*1973*	*1974*	*1975*	*1976*	*1977*
El Salvador	101	88	91	120	160
Ethiopia	103	85	76	101	203
Ghana	99	112	116	145	132
Guatemala	99	84	79	111	146
India	93	75	78	77	83
Indonesia[a]	110	237	224	245	258
Iran[a]	107	332	333	351	352
Iraq[a]	106	346	349	370	364
Israel	91	82	86	83	82
Ivory Coast	95	96	92	126	138
Kenya	100	90	84	101	131
Korea, Republic of	94	78	83	82	80
Malagasy Republic (Madagascar)	99	87	81	95	105
Malawi	89	87	90	99	113
Malaysia	106	133	107	123	131
Mali	95	83	82	106	98
Mexico	98	97	93	95	123
Morocco	89	122	141	108	92
Niger	100	92	83	88	70
Nigeria[a]	113	301	293	314	318
Pakistan	90	89	88	90	77
Peru	134	117	87	99	103
Philippines	116	137	79	84	82
Rwanda	100	100	87	127	184
Saudi Arabia[a]	104	331	336	360	349
Senegal	86	110	119	103	89
Sri Lanka	91	95	77	82	126
Sudan	103	134	120	125	97
Syria	104	125	122	138	132
Tanzania	106	117	102	120	132
Thailand	125	135	108	92	84
Tunisia	111	155	159	150	134
Uganda	94	81	81	134	166
Upper Volta	95	88	83	100	91
Venezuela[a]	107	277	278	295	301
Zaire	119	109	71	81	95
Zambia	131	123	69	75	92
	Number of non-oil-exporting countries				
Terms of trade compared to 1971–72					
Improved	20	19	16	25	24
Deteriorated	20	22	28	18	20

Source: UNCTAD, *Handbook of International Trade and Development Statistics, 1979*, pp. 604–25.
a. Oil-exporting country.

The variables are

$$PVR^{72} = \sum_{t=1}^{10} S_t^{72}/(1.10)^t + D_{10}^{72}/(1.10)^{11}$$

$$PVRD^{72} = S_1^{72}/[(1.10)(P_{73})] + \sum_{t=2}^{10} S_t^{72}/(1.10)^t(P_{74}) + D_{10}^{72}/[(1.10)^{10}(P_{74})]$$

$$PVR^{73} = \left[\sum_{t=1}^{10} S_t^{73}/(1.10)^t + D_{10}^{73}/(1.10)^{11}\right] \Big/ P_{73}$$

$$PVRD^{73} = \sum_{t=1}^{10} S_t^{73}/(1.10)^t(P_{74}) + D_{10}^{73}/(1.10)^{11}(P_{74})$$

$$PVDIS^{72} = \sum_{t=1}^{10} DIS_t^{72}/(1.10)^t$$

$$PVDISD^{72} = DIS_1^{72}/[(1.10)(P_{73})] + \sum_{t=2}^{10} DIS_t^{72}/[(1.10)^t(P_{74})]$$

$$PVDIS^{73} = \sum_{t=1}^{10} DIS_t^{73}/[(1.10)^t(P_{74})],$$

where S_t^{72} and S_t^{73} are the debt service (principal and interest) on debt outstanding at the end of 1972 and on new debt contracted in 1973; D_{10}^{72} and D_{10}^{73} the unpaid principal outstanding at the end of the tenth year for debt outstanding at the end of 1972 and contracted during 1973; P_{73} and P_{74} the average of import and export price indexes for 1973 and for 1974 (with a base of 1972 prices); and DIS_t^{72} and DIS_t^{73} the disbursement in year t of undisbursed outstanding debt at the end of 1972 and debt contracted in 1973.

Inflation and World Income Distribution

Given estimates of real per capita income and national income distributions, for a particular country i the average real per capita income y of the jth decile in the base period, y_{ij}^0, is equal to $y_i^0(\phi_{ij}/0.10)$, where y_i^0 is the base period real per capita income in country i, and ϕ_{ij} is the share of decile j in total income for country i. That is, the income level of the specific decile equals national average income multiplied by the ratio of the decile's share in income to its share in population (which is 10 percent).

The number of people in decile j of country i, n_{ij}, will be equal to $0.10\ N_i$ where N_i is total population in country i.

The international distribution of income as measured by any particular distributional index (such as the Gini coefficient) for the base period, D^0, is equal to $f(y_{ij}^0, n_{ij})$, where f refers to the functional form taken by that particular measure, and all countries i to be examined are included in the overall distributional measure.

When import and export prices rise (from 1972 to 1975), real income changes in each country. The resulting changed or shocked total income, Y_i', is equal to

$$Y_i^0 - \sum_{k \epsilon M} M_k^0([PM_k/P_w] - 1) + \sum_{k \epsilon X} X_k^0([PX_k/P_w] - 1),$$

and Y_i' and Y_i^0 are total real gross domestic product in the terminal year (1975) and base year (1972); $k \epsilon M$ and $k \epsilon X$ all products in which the country is a net importer or net exporter; M_k^0 and X_k^0 the base level of net import or net export value in product k; P_w a general world index of consumer prices in dollar terms (rising from a base of 1.0 in 1972 to its 1975 level of 1.4036); and PM_k and PX_k a general index of the world import or world export price for commodity k (1972 = 1.0). Thus the hypothetical real income of the country in 1975 equals its real income in 1972 minus the increased cost of imports (in real terms, deflating by a worldwide dollar consumer price index) caused by the rise in import prices as applied to the base value of imports; plus the increased earnings from exports (again deflated) caused by the rise in export prices as applied to the base value of exports.

Once the hypothetical, commodity-price-shocked gross domestic products for 1975 are calculated, the real per capita income of country i in the terminal period, y_i', and that income for each decile j in the country, y_{ij}', can be calculated from $y_i^0\ (Y_i'/Y_i^0)$ and $y_{ij}^0\ (Y_i'/Y_i^0)$ respectively.

The distribution of world income after the impact of commodity price inflation, D, as measured by a particular criterion (such as the Gini coefficient) in the terminal period, is therefore $f(Y_{ij}', n_{ij})$. A comparison of D^0 and D', distributional measures in the base and terminal periods respectively, will then tell the impact of commodity price inflation in the period 1972–75 on the world distribution of income.

CHAPTER THREE

The Transmission of Inflation into Developing Economies

SURJIT S. BHALLA

In 1973 and 1974 inflation spread worldwide, affecting small and large countries, developed and developing. Most developing countries had gone through periods of high inflation in the past; the extraordinary feature of the 1973–74 inflation was its simultaneous spread across countries. This chapter examines the role of internal and external factors in the inflation experiences of thirty developing countries.

The simultaneous occurrence of inflation in the developing countries seems to have arisen from worldwide inflation. The principal forces in the transmission of this external inflation were the steep rise in international reserves flowing into developing countries in 1972, a sharp increase in prices of imported commodities in 1973 and 1974, and the pressure that generally poor harvests in 1972 put on food prices. The examination of the impact of the Great Inflation on twelve Latin American, eleven Asian, and seven African countries covers oil exporters, producers of primary goods, and semi-industrialized countries. Conclusions are drawn principally from the ways that individual countries are affected by outside impulses. Aggregate averages, weighted when appropriate, are used sparingly to supplement the analysis.[1]

I THANK William R. Cline for his help and guidance in the preparation of this chapter and Robert Z. Lawrence for extensive discussions on the subject matter. I also thank Babi Gupta and Linda Likar for their very able research assistance.

1. The appropriateness of weighting depends on the variable being analyzed. For inflation, when a major country avoids high inflation a weighted index will understate the phenomenon of universal inflation, whereas the inclusion of a country suffering from hyperinflation will make unweighted averages meaningless. Therefore, both weighted and unweighted averages must be taken into account. For variables such as an index of industrial production, weighting is clearly preferable.

The Inflation Boom

For very few of the thirty developing countries was the acceleration of inflation significant during 1971–72, but in 1973 it was both rapid and synchronized (table 3-1). Furthermore almost all countries showed inflation in 1973–74 that was close to their historical peaks.[2] While those earlier peaks were dispersed over fifteen years, almost all of the countries reached record levels during the single two-year period, 1973–74.

It is the universal and synchronous nature of the inflationary experience in the 1970s that makes it unique.[3] Analyses of the period have produced explanations ranging from crop failures and the oil shock to excessive monetary demand, generalized wage push, and disputes over the division of income. They have commonly identified four channels through which inflation is transmitted internationally: external demand which, operating through the trade account, can bid up the prices of domestic goods (assuming either that there is full employment or that the elasticity of supply of exportable goods is low); external prices, which tend to bring the prices of domestic goods in line with those of traded goods; excess liquidity created by increased external reserves which encourages spending on goods whose prices rise until the equilibrium level of real balances is reached; and indirect stimuli such as international trade union activity, wage boosts and social gains elsewhere, and international inflationary expectations.[4] This chapter investigates the trade, price, and reserve chan-

2. Peak years exclude those of hyperinflation for Bolivia, Indonesia, and Taiwan.

3. The inflation during the Korean War (1950–52), though comparable, was shorter and relatively damped in its acceleration.

4. See Lawrence B. Krause and Walter S. Salant, eds., *Worldwide Inflation: Theory and Recent Experience* (Brookings Institution, 1977); David I. Meiselman and Arthur B. Laffer, eds., *The Phenomenon of Worldwide Inflation* (American Enterprise Institute for Public Policy Research, 1975); Michael Parkin and George Zis, eds., *Inflation in Open Economies* (Manchester University Press, 1976); Richard J. Sweeney and Thomas D. Willett, "The International Transmission of Inflation: Mechanisms, Issues and Evidence," Proceedings of the Conference on Bank Credit, Money and Inflation in Open Economies, Leuven, Belgium, September 12–13, 1974, supplement to *Kredit und Kapital,* Heft 3 (Berlin: Dunker and Humblot, 1976), pp. 441–517; Organization for Economic Cooperation and Development, "The International Transmission of Inflation," Special Section, *Economic Outlook,* no. 13 (July 1973), pp. 81–96.

nels[5] of transmission of inflation (other channels are not examined because they are of little relevance for most developing countries). Data on international trade and reserves and on domestic money supply and production are examined in two models of inflation, one emphasizing monetary factors and the other the degree of demand pressure (as measured by real activity) in each economy during 1956–75.

A popular candidate for the high inflation of 1973–74 is the OPEC increase in oil prices. The figures in table 3-1 should remove OPEC's action from the list of initiating factors since the Organization of Petroleum Exporting Countries did not raise oil prices until November 1973, after the boom had set in (some of the effects of higher oil prices are contained in the 1973 inflation rate, of course).[6] The bad weather of 1972–73 and subsequent poor food harvests were among the causes of inflation. But most of the blame seems to rest with economic factors that can broadly be classified under the expansion of real activity and the creation of excess liquidity (especially before 1973).

In contrast to the pattern of inflation, which increased only in 1973, there was a large growth in money supply in 1972 (table 3-2).[7] Of the twenty-six countries whose past inflation rates can be regarded as normal, eight showed a higher growth in money supply in 1972 than at any time between 1956 and 1970 (only one country showed higher inflation) and most of the others showed increases close to their earlier peaks (again, not true for price inflation).

5. All three channels are incorporated in the monetary theory of the balance of payments. This revival of the Humean mechanisms of transmission has led to the creation of a new set of international monetarists who view national inflation rates as intimately linked with the world inflation rate in a world of fixed exchange rates and argue that this rate is determined by prior movements in the world money supply and world prices. See Harry G. Johnson, "The Monetary Approach to Balance-of-Payments Theory," *Further Essays in Monetary Economics* (London: Allen and Unwin, 1972; Harvard University Press, 1973), chap. 9; Michael Parkin, "A 'Monetarist' Analysis of the Generation and Transmission of World Inflation: 1958–71," *American Economic Review*, vol. 67 (February 1977, *Papers and Proceedings, 1976*), pp. 164–71.

6. Quarterly figures show that the 1973 acceleration in inflation rates occurred before November. *International Financial Statistics,* various issues.

7. For developed countries 1971 was the year of greatest acceleration. According to aggregate IMF figures, the industrial countries' money supply accelerated in 1968–69 by 7.0 percent, in 1970 by 6.0 percent, in 1971 by 11.3 percent, in 1972 by 11.5 percent, in 1973 by 10.1 percent, in 1974 by 6.6 percent, and in 1975 by 8.0 percent. The previous peak (since 1951) was 7.4 percent in 1963.

What is remarkable about 1972 is not only that for individual countries the money-supply growth rates were extreme, but also the simultaneity with which almost all of the rates accelerated. (Argentina, Brazil, Chile, and Indonesia are excluded from the normal group because they have suffered from hyperinflation.) The average growth in the money supply for the group of normal countries (which should be roughly constant, with high rates of some canceling low rates of others) ranged from 8.6 percent to 12.5 percent during 1961–69 but then increased to 14.6 percent in 1970 and 17.7 percent in 1972 (table 3-3). The average growth in consumer prices did not increase above its 1961–72 range of 2.3 percent to 5.8 percent until 1973. The acceleration or change in the growth rates of money supply and prices further dramatizes the extraordinary nature of monetary growth in 1972. In normal times, the acceleration figures should be close to zero. Indeed, for price acceleration the average ranges from −0.8 to 0.7. In 1973, however, it increases to 5.9 (it moves further up in 1974 and then falls in 1975). For the acceleration of money supply the 1968–71 range is −3.0 to 2.6. However, in 1972 the average acceleration leaps to 6.1, and in 1973 it increases to 7.4 (it then declines in 1974 and 1975).

The data in table 3-3 indicate that the acceleration in money supply preceded the acceleration in prices. This suggests that at least for 1970–72, price changes were not responsible for the money expansion—that is, increases in the money supply were not the result of an accommodating monetary policy.[8] Furthermore, the acceleration in money supply in 1972 (and in prices in 1973–74) was synchronized—a variety of developing countries experienced a boom in money supply simultaneously. If some link between money and prices is accepted, then part of the explanation for the unusual inflation of 1973–74 must lie with the prior expansion of the money supply. That expansion appears to have been caused, in part, by infusions of foreign capital (discussed below).

Another prominent determinant of inflation is excess demand. It is conventionally measured by variations in an index of resource utilization (such as capacity utilization, unemployment rate, or deviation of output from trend) and the rate of change of a demand indicator (output, unem-

8. There is no evidence to suggest that price increases, and expectations, could have had more than a partial role in generating the 1972 increase in money supply. The roles of food and import prices are examined in the econometric models in this chapter.

Table 3-1. *Rate of Change in the Consumer Price Index, Thirty Developing Countries, 1956–76*

Percent

Country	Annual average[a]			Peak, 1956–70	Annual average[a]					Acceleration in 1972 over 1966–70
	1956–60	1961–65	1966–70		1971–72	1972	1973	1973–74	1975–76	
Argentina	41.8	23.2	n.a.	111.1	46.8	58.5	60.7	42.1	313.2	n.a.
Bolivia	65.8	5.2	6.0	11.2	5.1	6.6	31.5	47.8	6.3	0.6
Brazil	25.6	63.0	n.a.	87.0	18.3	16.4	12.7	20.2	35.3	n.a.
Chile	29.4	28.6	26.8	46.0	49.2	79.1	351.9	428.7	293.2	52.3
Colombia	9.5	12.9	10.2	32.2	11.7	14.3	22.8	23.6	21.5	4.1
Dominican Republic	0.1	2.8	1.3	9.2	6.1	7.9	15.1	14.1	11.1	6.6
Ecuador	−0.1	3.9	4.7	6.5	8.2	7.9	13.0	18.1	n.a.	3.2
Egypt	1.4	3.4	4.2	14.9	2.6	2.1	4.3	7.6	10.0	−2.1
El Salvador	0.4	0.2	1.1	5.7	1.0	1.5	6.4	11.6	15.1	0.4
Ghana	1.7	11.0	4.1	25.4	8.0	13.5	10.2	17.2	46.9	9.4
Guatemala	−0.2	0.1	1.5	2.4	0.1	0.6	13.8	15.1	11.9	−0.9
India	5.2	6.0	6.9	13.8	4.4	5.8	17.4	22.4	−1.0	−1.1
Indonesia	20.1	83.8	n.a.	n.a.	9.1	12.7	31.5	36.0	19.4	n.a.
Iran	6.9	2.0	1.4	11.2	5.3	6.4	9.8	11.9	12.1	5.0
Iraq	2.1	1.1	3.5	6.5	4.4	5.2	4.9	6.6	9.9	1.7

Korea, Republic of	11.2	15.2	11.4	27.9	12.1	11.7	3.0	13.4	28.4	−0.2
Malaysia	0.4	0.5	1.4	4.6	2.4	3.2	10.6	14.0	3.6	2.8
Mexico	5.9	1.9	3.7	12.2	5.4	5.0	11.4	16.9	16.5	1.3
Morocco	3.6	4.0	0.6	6.1	3.9	3.7	4.2	10.9	8.2	3.1
Nigeria	4.1	2.8	5.9	13.9	9.4	2.8	6.0	9.2	27.6	0.1
Pakistan	4.1	2.0	4.5	11.3	7.2	5.1	23.1	24.9	14.0	0.6
Peru	8.5	9.0	9.8	19.0	7.0	7.1	9.5	13.2	28.6	−2.7
Philippines	2.2	4.7	6.1	14.4	12.4	10.2	11.0	22.7	7.1	4.1
Sri Lanka	0.6	1.7	4.2	7.4	4.5	6.3	9.6	10.9	4.0	2.1
Sudan	1.0	3.3	3.9	12.6	6.2	10.9	17.9	22.0	12.8	7.0
Syria	4.3	0.6	3.3	14.7	3.0	1.0	19.8	17.4	15.6	−2.0
Taiwan	11.2	2.4	4.4	n.a.	2.8	2.9	8.2	27.8	3.9	−1.5
Thailand	2.4	1.5	2.6	6.2	3.0	3.9	11.7	17.5	4.1	1.3
Tunisia	2.7	2.7	2.9	13.5	3.9	2.1	4.6	4.4	7.4	−0.8
Venezuela	2.4	0.4	1.6	5.0	3.1	2.9	4.1	6.2	8.9	1.0

Source: *International Financial Statistics*, various issues.
n.a. Not available.
a. Single years refer to price rises over the previous year's level, two or more years to an average over those years.

Table 3-2. *Rate of Growth of the Money Supply, Thirty Developing Countries, 1956–76*[a]

Percent

Country	Annual average			Peak, 1956–70	Annual average[b]				Acceleration in 1972 over 1966–70
	1956–60	1961–65	1966–70		1971–72	1972	1973–74	1975–76	
Argentina	53.8	18.6	10.2	23.0	17.2	22.4	39.2	20.6	12.2
Bolivia	53.8	18.6	10.2	23.0	17.2	22.4	39.2	20.6	12.2
Brazil	29.1	65.8	n.a.	87.4	32.8	34.6	39.9	37.4	n.a.
Chile	23.3	37.8	n.a.	104.5	103.8	105.7	296.7	265.2	n.a.
Colombia	n.a.	18.4	19.8	24.0	15.4	20.6	27.1	21.9	0.8
Dominican Republic	n.a.	4.9	6.8	15.7	11.9	12.6	23.6	9.0	9.8
Ecuador	6.3	9.9	15.5	25.1	18.0	17.6	38.8	22.2	2.1
Egypt	n.a.	10.4	4.0	20.2	9.4	13.0	24.0	23.4	9.0
El Salvador	1.5	3.8	3.9	12.4	9.3	11.3	25.1	22.4	7.4
Ghana	6.2	16.8	4.7	26.1	19.0	38.8	22.8	42.5	34.1
Guatemala	5.6	6.3	4.5	14.3	10.3	14.6	23.7	23.1	10.1
India	6.5	9.0	9.5	11.9	12.7	12.5	15.3	11.4	3.0
Indonesia	29.9	n.a.	n.a.	n.a.	30.0	33.8	41.0	30.5	n.a.
Iran	17.5	12.1	10.5	26.6	23.7	32.6	26.6	41.5	22.1
Iraq	17.5	6.1	9.3	44.8	7.0	11.8	27.0	31.1	2.5

Korea, Republic of	18.3	22.9	35.9	45.7	26.6	32.6	38.8	27.0	−3.3
Malaysia	6.8	4.9	6.2	15.9	10.7	14.5	27.2	11.8	8.3
Mexico	10.6	11.5	11.2	11.1	10.9	14.2	21.6	22.1	3.0
Morocco	n.a.	7.3	8.2	23.8	12.5	16.6	20.1	19.3	8.4
Nigeria	n.a.	9.6	16.1	51.9	10.7	7.8	30.6	69.8	−8.3
Pakistan	7.4	7.4	9.2	16.9	18.7	20.2	8.9	17.4	11.0
Peru	n.a.	17.3	19.4	43.7	23.4	22.2	30.1	24.3	2.8
Philippines	n.a.	8.7	11.0	27.5	16.6	18.7	23.0	15.3	7.7
Sri Lanka	3.7	6.9	3.7	10.9	6.8	6.9	15.2	12.9	3.2
Sudan	11.5	11.8	13.0	20.5	6.6	7.0	27.9	18.0	−6.0
Syria	9.6	9.4	13.9	19.3	13.1	17.3	35.5	24.1	3.4
Taiwan	15.2	21.7	17.7	36.4	24.1	20.4	29.8	19.9	2.7
Thailand	6.9	6.2	7.1	12.2	11.5	12.7	17.7	10.5	5.6
Tunisia	n.a.	9.5	2.9	21.2	19.5	21.0	17.5	15.1	18.1
Venezuela	8.7	7.2	6.6	27.9	16.1	20.7	27.5	37.7	14.1

Source: *International Financial Statistics*, various issues.
n.a. Not available.
a. Money supply refers to cash and demand deposits.
b. Single year refers to price rises over previous year's level, two or more years to an average over those years.

Table 3-3. *Rates of Growth and Acceleration of the Money Supply and Consumer Prices, Twenty-six Developing Countries, 1961–76*[a]

Percent

	Money supply[b]		*Consumer prices*	
Year	*Growth*	*Acceleration*[c]	*Growth*	*Acceleration*[c]
1961	8.86	2.58	2.93	−0.75
1962	8.65	−0.21	2.34	−0.59
1963	11.42	2.77	4.52	2.18
1964	13.82	2.40	5.40	0.98
1965	9.19	−4.63	4.29	−1.11
1966	9.04	−0.15	4.65	0.36
1967	8.80	−0.24	4.20	−0.45
1968	9.98	1.19	3.36	−0.84
1969	12.55	2.57	4.22	0.85
1970	14.63	2.08	4.90	0.68
1971	11.63	−3.00	5.20	0.30
1972	17.72	6.09	5.80	0.60
1973	25.16	7.44	11.69	5.89
1974	25.94	0.78	21.19	9.50
1975	23.64	−2.30	15.13	3.61
1976	23.60	−0.04	11.60	−3.52

a. Includes all countries listed in table 3-1 except Argentina, Brazil, Chile, and Indonesia.
b. Money supply refers to cash and demand deposits.
c. Increase over previous year's growth rate.

ployment, etc.). The level measure emphasizes the extent of resource utilization while the rate-of-change measure captures the speed at which demand changes. Both can contribute to short-run inflation.

One index of real activity that is available for an aggregate of countries is industrial production. Table 3-4 underlines the fact that, for developed countries, 1971 was a recession year (only 2 percent growth).[9] The acceleration to 6.9 percent in 1972 and 9.2 percent in 1973 brought these countries to their highest growth rate since the recovery of 1959. In short, the industrialized world moved from recession in 1971 to boom in 1973.

The developing countries, in contrast, do not show a radical break from trend in the early 1970s. During 1971 they experienced a mild deceleration, with a growth rate of 7.0 percent. Their growth then accelerated to 8.4 percent in 1972 and reached 10.3 percent in 1973, the highest since

9. Though it is a more appropriate indicator of real activity for developed countries, the industrial production index is a reasonable proxy for total output for an aggregate of developing countries.

Table 3-4. *Annual Growth Rates and Deviation from the Trend of Industrial Production of Developed and Developing Countries, 1956–75*
Percent

	Growth rate		Deviation from trend[a]	
Year	Developed countries	Developing countries	Developed countries	Developing countries
1956	6.09	5.47	3.95	−0.66
1957	1.98	6.82	0.75	−1.42
1958	−2.91	6.38	−7.36	−2.58
1959	10.00	7.00	−2.98	−3.17
1960	7.27	11.22	−1.11	0.11
1961	2.54	9.24	−3.75	1.59
1962	7.44	7.69	−1.73	1.65
1963	4.62	6.43	−2.37	0.53
1964	8.00	10.00	0.17	2.71
1965	6.48	7.27	1.30	2.37
1966	7.82	5.93	3.68	0.78
1967	3.23	5.60	1.70	−1.12
1968	7.03	7.58	3.34	−1.17
1969	7.30	9.15	5.23	0.23
1970	2.72	7.74	2.76	0.34
1971	2.00	7.00	−0.41	−0.25
1972	6.86	8.41	1.08	0.47
1973	9.17	10.34	4.70	2.97
1974	0.00	5.47	−0.45	0.94
1975	−5.88	0.74	−11.67	−5.68

Source: United Nations, *Monthly Bulletin of Statistics*, various issues. Country classifications as reported in the *Bulletin;* developed countries are industrialized countries.
a. The trend regression is based on 1955–75 data.

1960. Thus both developed and developing countries suffered a slowdown in 1971, followed by expansion in 1972 and 1973, and both reached a peak growth in 1973, at least since 1960. This synchronization of peaks in 1973 indicates that the expansion of real activity had at least some role in the inflation; whether this expansion matched the unusual nature of price changes in 1973 (and 1974) cannot be determined from growth rates alone. Since an accelerating growth rate may only indicate a recovery to normalcy, the rate of growth needs to be examined with reference to a trend growth path.

The data on deviation of industrial production from its trend suggest that the unusual activity brought developed countries a return to normalcy rather than expansion; the 4.7 percent deviation in 1973 did not

Table 3-5. *Rates of Growth of Import and Export Prices of Developed and Developing Countries, 1956–76*[a]

Percent

	Import prices		*Export prices*	
Year	*Developed countries*	*Developing countries*	*Developed countries*	*Developing countries*
1956	2.2	3.3	2.4	−1.1
1957	3.2	6.5	3.6	−1.1
1958	−7.2	−6.1	−2.3	−7.7
1959	−2.2	−4.3	−1.2	−1.2
1960	1.1	5.6	1.2	2.4
1961	−1.1	0.0	1.2	−1.2
1962	0.0	−3.2	−1.2	−3.6
1963	0.0	4.4	1.2	2.5
1964	2.3	2.1	2.3	6.0
1965	1.1	2.1	1.1	2.3
1966	2.2	−1.0	2.2	3.3
1967	0.0	−2.0	1.1	−4.3
1968	−1.1	0.0	−1.1	2.2
1969	2.2	1.0	3.3	5.5
1970	6.4	3.1	6.4	4.2
1971	5.0	3.0	5.0	−3.0
1972	7.6	6.8	8.6	5.2
1973	23.0	25.5	19.3	36.3
1974	41.7	50.7	25.7	37.4
1975	8.6	6.7	11.7	−3.1
1976	−1.4	−1.8	1.1	7.6

Source: *International Financial Statistics*, various issues.

a. Country classifications refer to "industrial" (developed) and "other less developed areas" (developing) as reported in *International Financial Statistics*, various issues.

reach the high of 1969 (table 3-4). The developing countries did have a peak deviation from trend in 1973, but the 2.97 percent deviation was not much different from the 2.7 percent expansion of 1964.

Neither growth rates nor their deviation from trend explain the extraordinary increase in money supply of 1972. Their relation to the price increase of 1973–74 is ambiguous. The expansion of real demand was prominent in 1973, and like the previous peaks (in growth rates in 1959 and 1960 and in deviation from trend in 1969 and 1964 for developed and developing countries, respectively), the figures for the 1970s do show a synchronization in real activity. The simultaneous expansion of prices in

1973 cannot be denied. But real activity was not particularly unusual in 1973. Similar periods of expansion had occurred before without a corresponding acceleration in consumer prices.

Apart from its direct effect, the excess demand arising from the synchronous international expansion in real activity caused the prices of traded goods to rise (pushed by domestic price rises in a world of fixed exchange rates).[10] In this important respect the expansion of 1973 differed from previous expansions. As table 3-5 makes clear, traded goods prices increased at record rates during the 1970s. The simultaneity of the expansion in real activity and the inflation in prices of traded goods perhaps did proportionately more to stimulate the 1973–74 inflation than either phenomenon could have done in isolation. However, the implicit link between the expansion in real activity and worldwide inflation leaves unanswered some questions about the 1970–72 experience. If the world was in a recession, then why the record increase in the prices of traded goods for the developed countries in 1970–71?[11]

Domestic Causes of Expansion of the Money Supply

Little evidence has been found that domestic causes were responsible for the acceleration of money supply in the developing countries in 1970–72. Crop failures and lagging food supply, which have often been assigned a prominent position in the list of causes of inflation, actually had a limited role in 1972. The structuralists' argument that lagging agricultural supply causes inflation is based on the assumption that food prices are flexible and other prices relatively fixed, and that imports are not used extensively to maintain a stable price level. If foreign-exchange shortages are assumed to dictate a policy that only essential imports are allowed, a food shortage can cause inflation by inducing an increase in the relative price of food. To avoid a severe decline in output when prices in the nonfarm sector are sticky, an increase in the relative price of food must be financed by an increase in nominal income and inflation.

10. If prices (and demand) expand simultaneously in a competitive world, there is no danger of much loss in market share. This is true at a worldwide level; for individual countries (except perhaps for large countries like the United States) traded goods prices are not affected by domestic price movements.

11. For the developing countries, the price rise of imports and exports is not particularly unusual during 1970–72.

In 1972, a disastrously bad crop year, world food production per capita declined by 2.8 percent (table 3-6).[12] At an aggregate level, this decline is extremely large. Indeed, the previous peak decline, in 1964–65, was 2.0 percent. Among developing countries, production shortfalls in 1972 were fairly widespread. Moreover, it was difficult to reduce the pressure of food shortages on domestic prices through imports. Prices of wheat and rice, which had been relatively stable during the 1960s, began to rise in 1972 and reached their peaks in 1973 and 1974.

By 1973–74 the relative price of food had accelerated from a fairly stable base in 1970–71 (table 3-7). Quarterly figures show that food prices began to rise in the fourth quarter of 1972.[13] But the acceleration in the rate of growth of money supply, though also rapid in the fourth quarter, had been proceeding all year. Thus food shortages may have had a limited role in causing the money supply growth of 1972, assuming an extremely short lag in an accommodating growth of money supply in response to price increases. At most, the food decline exacerbated the acceleration of the money supply. Nevertheless, the role of food declines in generating the inflation of 1973 and 1974 may be significant.

One of the important domestic causes of expansion of the money supply is government budget deficits. Although in developed countries noninflationary financing of budget deficits is the rule, in developing countries the presence of undeveloped financial markets and institutions makes difficult the financing of budget deficits through government bonds.[14] Thus budget deficits are usually financed by creating money. Though it is difficult to separate monetary and fiscal causes for budget deficits, it is of interest to note whether the deficits were expansionary in 1972–74.

The budget deficits of the thirty developing countries, as a percentage of their gross national product in 1971, 1972, and 1974, show no pro-

12. Per capita food production is a good indicator of availability if the role of food stocks is limited. The use of imports to maintain stable prices is ignored in examining production data alone. For many developing countries, imports on private account are prohibited, and the quantity of imports and domestic prices are determined by domestic production. If foreign exchange is scarce, then even if a country imports food regularly, a domestic food shortage can still have price repercussions in the economy.

13. Quarterly figures from *International Financial Statistics,* various issues.

14. In this discussion deficits are assumed to arise through a deficiency in taxation or an excess of expenditure. If there was a large imported component of government expenditures, then deficits could have been caused in 1972–74 by imported inflation. If the deficit was nonexpansionary, then there is a good case for asserting that it was not responsible either for the money supply expansion or for the extraordinary increase in prices.

Table 3-6. *Changes in the Index of Food Production per Capita, Twenty-eight Developing Countries, 1968–74*

Index, 1961–65 = 100

	Index			*Percent change*		*Index*	
Country	*1968–69*	*1970–71*	*1971*	*1972*	*1973*	*1973*	*1974*
Argentina	104.0	101.0	98	−4.1	4.3	98	102
Bolivia	106.5	110.5	110	4.5	3.5	119	118
Brazil	109.0	113.0	112	3.6	−1.7	114	118
Chile	105.0	105.5	105	−7.6	−11.3	86	100
Colombia	97.5	101.0	102	−2.0	−3.0	97	100
Dominican Republic	92.0	103.0	104	1.0	−2.9	102	103
Ecuador	105.0	101.5	100	−5.0	−1.0	94	101
Egypt	106.5	105.5	106	−0.9	−0.9	104	103
El Salvador	99.0	104.0	105	−6.7	12.2	110	105
Ghana	93.5	98.0	101	−7.9	−6.5	87	93
Guatemala	109.5	111.5	112	2.7	−1.7	113	110
India	99.5	103.0	102	−6.9	5.9	101	93
Indonesia	105.0	109.0	109	−3.7	6.7	112	116
Iran	110.5	110.5	104	6.7	0.9	112	113
Iraq	108.5	95.5	92	n.a.	n.a.	n.a.	n.a.
Korea, Republic of	108.5	111.0	110	−1.8	−0.9	107	111
Malaysia	114.0	126.0	130	3.9	5.2	142	151
Mexico	104.0	108.0	110	−3.6	−1.9	104	102
Morocco	n.a.	112.5	114	−1.8	−20.4	93	108
Nigeria	95.5	95.0	93	−4.9	−11.2	79	85
Pakistan	118.0	117.5	115	0.9	1.6	118	117
Peru	94.0	102.5	102	−2.0	1.0	101	99
Philippines	99.5	101.0	100	−4.0	8.3	104	103
Sri Lanka	104.0	101.5	103	−5.8	−1.0	96	110
Sudan	100.0	107.5	108	0.0	−1.9	106	118
Thailand	105.0	106.5	107	−7.5	13.1	112	105
Tunisia	90.5	114.0	125	−0.8	0.8	125	129
Venezuela	116.0	121.0	120	−1.7	1.7	120	123
World	105.0	106.5	107	−2.8	3.9	108	107

Source: UN, Food and Agriculture Organization, *FAO Production Yearbook*, various years.
n.a. Not available.

nounced trend away from the 1967–70 averages (table 3-8).[15] Although there appears to have been some increase in 1972, it is doubtful whether

15. A full employment budget deficit would be preferable to the actual deficit as an indicator of excess demand pressure, but no estimates of such deficits are available. In any event, for most developing countries, resource limitations rather than Keynesian unemployment restrain growth.

Table 3-7. *Changes in the Relative Price of Food, Thirty Developing Countries, 1972–75*
Base, 1970 = 1.00

Country	*1972*	*1973*	*1974*	*1975*
Argentina	1.23	1.11	0.93	0.97
Bolivia	1.00	1.06	1.07	1.31
Brazil	0.84	0.94	0.94	0.95
Chile	1.56	1.73	1.79	1.66
Colombia	1.06	1.22	1.28	1.41
Dominican Republic	0.91	0.95	1.01	1.05
Ecuador	1.02	1.14	1.30	1.38
Egypt	1.06	1.12	1.27	1.34
El Salvador	0.99	1.01	1.02	1.04
Ghana	1.04	1.22	1.34	1.25
Guatemala	0.96	1.07	1.05	1.15
India	0.98	1.06	1.14	1.09
Indonesia	0.88	1.11	1.13	1.18
Iran	1.08	1.03	1.06	1.05
Iraq	1.01	1.03	1.09	1.19
Korea, Republic of	1.14	1.13	1.21	1.32
Malaysia	1.01	1.15	1.53	1.46
Mexico	0.93	1.09	1.47	1.21
Morocco	1.08	1.11	1.15	1.15
Nigeria	1.14	0.98	1.10	1.25
Pakistan	0.89	0.94	1.00	1.02
Peru	1.01	1.02	1.05	1.23
Philippines	1.74	1.49	1.84	1.78
Sri Lanka	0.97	1.05	1.09	1.12
Sudan	0.92	0.89	0.88	0.97
Syria	0.96	1.00	1.00	1.04
Taiwan	1.10	1.17	1.45	1.55
Thailand	1.02	1.07	1.16	1.16
Tunisia	1.10	1.15	1.07	1.07
Venezuela	1.03	1.08	1.14	1.21
Normal countries[a]	1.05	1.09	1.18	1.22

Source: UN, *Monthly Bulletin of Statistics*, various issues.
a. Excludes Argentina, Brazil, Chile, and Indonesia.

it was comparable to the acceleration in money supply. Furthermore, the expansion was by no means universal (almost half the countries were below normal levels) nor was it particularly excessive. (Also, the rise in prices of imported food may have been partly responsible for the deficits.) Although the fiscal deficits may have been partially responsible for the expansion of the money supply in some of the countries, they do not

Table 3-8. *Budget Deficits as a Percentage of GNP, Thirty Developing Countries, 1967–74*[a]

Country	*Average, 1967–70*	*1971*	*1972*	*1974*
Argentina	1.3	2.6	2.7	6.2
Bolivia	3.9	4.0	3.9	n.a.
Brazil	0.9	0.2	0.1	−0.6
Chile	1.0	7.8	10.2	5.9
Colombia	0.6	0.8	2.0	0.8
Dominican Republic	1.4	1.2	0.4	0.9
Ecuador	3.4	4.3	1.9	0.6
Egypt	11.8	11.1	12.9	n.a.
El Salvador	0.6	1.1	0.8	1.4
Ghana	4.4	3.5	6.9	6.3
Guatemala	0.9	1.5	2.1	1.4
India	3.5	3.7	4.6	3.6
Indonesia	0.9	1.9	2.1	0.9
Iran	5.6	3.1	4.5	−4.5
Iraq	1.4	−1.9	5.2	n.a.
Korea, Republic of	2.4	1.8	5.4	3.5
Malaysia	4.3	7.9	9.3	6.3
Mexico	1.8	0.9	3.3	3.8
Morocco	4.5	3.0	4.5	5.3
Nigeria	5.1	−0.5	0.3	−10.9
Pakistan	8.4	6.1	n.a.	n.a.
Peru	2.4	2.8	0.9	n.a.
Philippines	1.1	0.4	1.8	−2.4
Sri Lanka	6.8	8.7	7.9	4.9
Sudan	2.5	1.3	2.1	n.a.
Syria	7.4	7.3	6.5	n.a.
Taiwan	−0.4	−0.6	−0.7	n.a.
Thailand	2.5	5.0	4.4	−0.7
Tunisia	5.5	1.1	−0.1	n.a.
Venezuela	1.2	−0.5	0.6	−2.7
Normal countries[b]	4.0	3.0	3.66	1.28

Source: *International Financial Statistics*, vol. 30 (May 1977).
n.a. Not available.
a. Negative sign indicates a surplus.
b. Excludes Argentina, Brazil, Chile, and Indonesia.

appear to have been generally responsible for the acceleration of monetary growth in 1972.

Wage inflation, which is one of the major instigators of growth in the money supply in developed economies, is generally not a source of pressure in developing countries (with exceptions such as Argentina and

Table 3-9. *Rate of Growth of Wages, Twenty-three Developing Countries, Selected Years, 1965–75*

Country	*1965*	*1968*	*1970*	*1972*	*1974*	*1975*
Argentina	32.7	3.9	18.1	45.8	28.7	171.4
Bolivia	n.a.	n.a.	n.a.	3.1	38.9	n.a.
Brazil	55.5	30.6	19.1	n.a.	n.a.	n.a.
Chile	39.4	34.1	44.2	62.6	530.0	348.9
Colombia	10.9	13.7	10.3	17.1	18.9	26.6
Dominican Republic	−6.3	11.5	−3.1	6.8	14.6	n.a.
Ecuador	1.3	9.5	8.9	19.1	21.3	n.a.
Egypt	15.8	10.6	−0.2	n.a.	n.a.	n.a.
El Salvador	5.2	3.5	2.2	3.1	9.7	n.a.
Ghana	4.7	14.4	10.6	4.8	n.a.	n.a.
Guatemala	4.5	3.2	n.a.	0.2	1.4	n.a.
India	12.0	7.0	5.2	6.6	n.a.	n.a.
Korea, Republic of	18.6	26.5	49.6	10.3	31.9	29.5
Mexico	6.9	5.2	5.1	5.7	27.8	21.6
Morocco	n.a.	n.a.	n.a.	n.a.	92.2	n.a.
Pakistan	−6.0	9.9	−1.9	6.4	n.a.	n.a.
Peru	18.1	23.3	7.3	25.0	15.0	30.0
Philippines	6.1	0.4	7.7	10.7	13.0	6.3
Sri Lanka	n.a.	16.5	2.8	2.9	18.0	16.9
Syria	0.6	1.7	1.1	1.1	n.a.	n.a.
Taiwan	8.5	11.5	n.a.	n.a.	n.a.	n.a.
Thailand	n.a.	−10.9	14.1	−116.8	n.a.	n.a.
Venezuela	5.0	8.2	9.4	4.9	22.9	4.8

Source: International Labor Office, *Labor Force Statistics*, various issues.
n.a. Not available.

Chile).[16] Labor unions typically are weak, and the bulk of the labor force is not unionized and works in agriculture rather than manufacturing. Moreover, developing economies frequently have surplus labor in the form of family farm workers or workers in the unorganized urban services sector who could be removed with little loss in output. As table 3-9 indicates, the acceleration in the developing countries' wages was unexceptional (if not absent) and certainly did not precede the money supply change of 1972.

16. See Arnold C. Harberger, "The Dynamics of Inflation in Chile," in Carl F. Christ and others, *Measurement in Economics: Studies in Mathematical Economics and Econometrics* (Stanford University Press, 1963), pp. 219–50; Carlos F. Diaz-Alejandro, *Essays on the Economic History of the Argentine Republic* (Yale University Press, 1970), and *Exchange Rate Changes in a Semi-Industrialized Country* (MIT Press, 1965).

International Causes of Expansion of the Money Supply

External factors seem to have been to a larger extent responsible for the monetary acceleration than were domestic factors. External reserves increased (for most countries) at an unusual rate in 1972 and these increases were systematically related to money supply changes.[17]

Nineteen of the thirty developing countries show a reserve availability that was excessive in 1972, compared with their 1966–70 averages. For sixteen of the twenty-six normal countries the 1972 ratio of their reserves to imports exceeded their 1966–70 average by more than 25 percent (table 3-10). Governments usually attempt to maintain reserves in a relatively fixed relation to imports, so that annual deviations from a long-run average are indicative of the excessiveness of reserves.[18]

Another indicator of unusual reserve accumulation is the percentage increase in reserves in a given year compared with the long-run degree of fluctuation (both positive and negative) in the country's reserves. For the base period 1965–69, typical reserve fluctuation is calculated as the average absolute value of annual percentage reserve change. For nineteen of the twenty-six normal inflation countries, reserve increases in 1972 were more than 25 percentage points higher than their typical fluctuations during the 1965–69 base period (table 3-11). By contrast, only ten countries showed such an excess in 1970, and seven in 1975. Many of the 1972 increases were twice the long-run average fluctuation.

Aggregate data on the movement in reserves in the developed and developing countries are striking.[19] Compared to a previous high of 7 percent in 1960, the industrialized countries show an expansion in reserves of 19.6 percent and 34.9 percent in 1970 and 1971, respectively (table 3-12). The developing countries show an expansion of 37 percent in 1972

17. If there is a link between money supply changes and inflation, then reserve changes can be a cause of the 1973–74 inflation. H. Robert Heller explicitly considers this link in "International Reserves and World-Wide Inflation," *International Monetary Fund Staff Papers*, vol. 23 (March 1976), pp. 61–87.

18. The ratio of reserves to imports is downwardly biased as an indicator because imports can be a positive function of the perceived availability of reserves. Assuming that foreign exchange is a constraint on government policy, a windfall gain in reserves will be short-lived if it allows governments to relax import controls.

19. While aggregate indexes should dampen out random fluctuations for different countries, changes for one country can dominate the aggregate movements. Brazil accounts for 77 percent of the increase in table 3-12 for developing countries in the western hemisphere in 1971–72.

Table 3-10. *Ratio of External Reserves to Value of Imports, Thirty Developing Countries, 1966–75*

	Ratio of reserves to imports					
Country	*1966–70 average*	*1971*	*1972*	*1973*	*1974*	*1975*
Argentina	0.45	0.16	0.24	0.59	0.36	0.11
Bolivia	0.27	0.32	0.32	0.31	0.50	0.28
Brazil	0.25	0.47	0.87	0.92	0.37	0.30
Chile	0.30	0.23	0.16	0.16	0.53	0.60
Colombia	0.22	0.22	0.38	0.50	0.28	0.41
Dominican Republic	0.16	0.16	0.15	0.18	0.12	0.13
Ecuador	0.29	0.19	0.45	0.61	0.31	0.30
Egypt	0.22	0.16	0.16	0.40	0.15	0.78
El Salvador	0.28	0.26	0.30	0.17	0.18	0.21
Ghana	0.26	0.11	0.37	0.42	0.11	0.19
Guatemala	0.28	0.31	0.42	0.50	0.29	0.38
India	0.31	0.50	0.58	0.36	0.26	0.22
Indonesia	0.12	0.17	0.37	0.30	0.39	0.12
Iran	0.22	0.33	0.40	0.36	1.54	0.84
Iraq	0.93	0.86	1.11	1.71	1.38	0.96
Korea, Republic of	0.32	0.24	0.29	0.26	0.15	0.21
Malaysia	0.46	0.57	0.60	0.54	0.39	0.42
Mexico	0.32	0.40	0.41	0.33	0.21	0.15
Morocco	0.18	0.25	0.30	0.23	0.22	0.15
Nigeria	0.21	0.28	0.25	0.31	2.03	0.96
Pakistan	0.22	0.21	0.42	0.49	0.27	0.19
Peru	0.27	0.57	0.61	0.53	0.63	0.18
Philippines	0.16	0.29	0.40	0.59	0.43	0.35
Sri Lanka	0.12	0.15	0.16	0.20	0.11	0.07
Sudan	0.18	0.06	0.11	0.14	0.19	0.41
Syria	0.20	0.20	0.25	0.67	0.41	0.44
Taiwan	0.45	0.38	0.41	0.30	0.17	0.20
Thailand	0.88	0.68	0.71	0.64	0.69	0.54
Tunisia	0.15	0.43	0.48	0.45	0.37	0.27
Venezuela	0.26	0.25	0.26	0.27	0.30	0.21

Source: *International Financial Statistics*, vol. 30 (May 1977).

—the previous peak of 17 percent was observed in 1965. The expansion in developing countries' reserves is also observed to be universal and extreme at regional levels. Western hemisphere countries (especially Brazil) show peak increases in 1971 and 1972 (as do the oil-exporting countries). The Asian countries' expansion—24.2 percent—is close to the prior peak of 24.4 percent in 1963. Only the African countries fail to show unusual behavior; nevertheless, their reserves expanded by 15.6 percent.

Table 3-11. *Percentage Changes in External Reserves, Thirty Developing Countries, 1965–75*

Country	*Average of absolute values of annual percentage changes, 1965–69*	*Annual percentage change* 1970	1972	1974	1975
Argentina	66.6	25.1	60.3	−0.2	−65.6
Bolivia	18.7	8.3	10.4	168.3	−19.4
Brazil	69.5	80.9	139.6	−17.8	−23.5
Chile	47.3	13.1	−33.0	−43.4	7.1
Colombia	34.3	06.8	60.1	−16.0	16.0
Dominican Republic	16.8	−19.3	4.5	3.3	27.9
Ecuador	17.5	28.0	121.6	45.1	−18.3
Egypt	17.0	15.2	−6.7	−1.9	−17.4
El Salvador	5.2	−1.7	27.0	59.2	29.1
Ghana	−14.2	−23.9	125.2	50.4	59.8
Guatemala	9.1	5.7	44.3	−4.5	50.1
India	13.9	8.6	−2.2	16.0	3.6
Indonesia	294.9	31.1	207.0	84.9	−60.7
Iran	15.2	−32.9	54.6	578.2	3.7
Iraq	17.3	−3.0	30.2	110.8	−16.7
Korea, Republic of	34.3	10.3	29.5	−3.5	46.8
Malaysia	11.3	7.1	19.9	20.6	−5.8
Mexico	0.0	12.4	22.3	3.0	9.9
Morocco	31.5	22.8	36.2	56.8	−9.6
Nigeria	16.0	68.2	−12.4	865.0	3.1
Pakistan	25.1	−42.8	48.7	−4.0	−11.9
Peru	20.2	101.2	14.2	44.9	−9.6
Philippines	20.0	107.4	44.2	44.9	−0.6
Sri Lanka	27.6	7.5	20.0	−10.3	−25.6
Sudan	12.2	−40.4	27.6	102.8	−80.7
Syria	47.6	−6.8	53.4	21.4	47.0
Taiwan	12.1	40.4	47.6	6.1	−1.8
Thailand	10.2	−8.0	20.0	42.3	−4.5
Tunisia	18.9	61.5	50.7	36.2	−7.8
Venezuela	294.9	31.1	207.0	84.9	−60.7

Source: *International Financial Statistics*, vol. 30 (May 1977).

These three measures strongly support the conclusion that there was an unusual increase in international liquidity in 1971 and 1972—and, furthermore, that a large number of the developing countries shared in this increase. In order to identify the channels of transmission of external inflation, it is important to determine whether the increase was due to

Table 3-12. *Changes in External Reserves, Major Industrial Countries and Four Groups of Developing Countries, 1961–75*
Percent

		Developing countries				
			Non-oil exporting			
Year	*Industrial countries*	*All*	*Asia*	*Western hemisphere*	*Africa*	*Oil exporting*
1961	4.1	−5.1	−2.6	−4.5	−21.8	−7.9
1962	0.4	1.0	−0.5	−21.6	33.1	−6.1
1963	3.2	15.3	24.4	19.5	−10.4	24.7
1964	3.3	−0.7	1.0	2.1	−19.0	2.2
1965	2.3	17.0	9.2	19.6	38.8	10.8
1966	1.0	6.1	10.5	−0.3	13.2	9.4
1967	1.9	7.5	8.4	4.7	−4.1	10.4
1968	1.2	11.1	7.6	19.8	15.5	8.1
1969	−1.8	10.9	14.0	14.8	25.3	9.6
1970	19.6	16.3	8.4	27.8	25.5	22.1
1971	34.9	4.6	7.8	2.1	−15.5	55.1
1972	9.8	37.0	24.2	64.9	15.6	29.1
1973	−1.8	23.3	12.7	32.8	14.7	19.9
1974	2.3	8.0	18.9	−2.4	11.5	219.0
1975	6.3	0.2	7.0	−11.9	−2.2	25.7

Source: *International Financial Statistics*, vol. 30 (May 1977).

changes in the trade balance, which primarily reflect commodity prices and movements in real activity, or to capital flows, which are the result of monetary factors.[20]

Both the level and the change of the trade balance are relevant for analysis of changes in reserves. Because developing countries in general are liable to have negative trade balances, and thus to use aid and borrowing to cover trade deficits, an unanticipated improvement in the trade balance may lead to an increase in reserves if capital flows (including aid) are kept at planned levels. Since the developed countries were emerging from a recession in 1971–72, the volume and prices of developing countries' exports were buoyed. Both the size of the trade deficit and the change over the previous year suggest a partial role for trade in explaining reserve changes in 1972 (table 3-13). Twelve of the normal countries showed a surplus in 1972, compared to seven in 1970. The changes in the trade bal-

20. Lack of developed capital markets limits developing countries' use of restrictive monetary policy to attract capital through higher domestic interest rates. Foreign capital usually comes from borrowing on public or private account.

Table 3-13. *Level and Change in the Trade Balance, Thirty Developing Countries, 1966, 1970, and 1972*

Millions of U.S. dollars

	Trade balance[a]					
	1966		1970		1972	
Country	Total	Change	Total	Change	Total	Change
Argentina	469	175	79	43	36	164
Bolivia	−11	13	−31	24	16	4
Brazil	245	−255	−110	−156	−792	5
Chile	66	33	303	135	−86	−68
Colombia	−166	−251	−100	−23	15	236
Dominican Republic	−48	−74	−93	−27	−42	73
Ecuador	−10	98	−53	−4	24	142
Egypt	−465	−191	−25	−132	−52	63
El Salvador	−31	−19	23	31	23	27
Ghana	−84	46	47	67	139	216
Guatemala	−21	63	15	7	14	28
India	−1,486	−335	−99	278	210	596
Indonesia	152	139	106	34	216	85
Iran	378	−67	961	387	1,664	−287
Iraq	423	18	514	−40	650	−25
Korea, Republic of	−466	−178	−1,149	52	−898	428
Malaysia	153	13	269	−204	80	−123
Mexico	−406	34	−1,059	−411	−1,074	−168
Morocco	−49	−26	−198	−121	−137	62
Nigeria	78	97	181	−14	641	340
Pakistan	−299	220	−428	−76	13	264
Peru	−42	11	441	170	152	−0
Philippines	−129	3	−149	251	−260	−52
Sri Lanka	−69	−168	4	109	−29	−22
Sudan	−19	−6	10	19	37	40
Syria	−116	−72	−157	6	−258	−19
Taiwan	−88	19	−100	67	396	247
Thailand	−206	−93	−583	−49	−403	52
Tunisia	−110	16	−124	−24	−151	−23
Venezuela	872	−38	639	−34	715	−97
Normal countries excluding OPEC[b]	−190		−125		−99	

Source: *International Financial Statistics*, vol. 30 (May 1977).

a. Negative sign in the total column indicates a deficit and in the change column a deterioration in the trade balance. Amount of change on previous year.

b. Does not include Argentina, Brazil, Chile, Indonesia, Iran, Iraq, Nigeria, and Venezuela.

Table 3-14. *Results of Regression Analysis: Changes in Domestic Money Supply Related to Changes in Reserves, Twenty-eight Developing Countries, 1956–72*[a]

Country	*Coefficient of determination,* $\bar{R}^2$	*Money multiplier, b*	*t-statistic*
Argentina	0.28	1.7	2.7
Bolivia	0.44	1.1	3.7
Chile	−0.06	−0.6	−0.2
Colombia	0.62	1.6	5.2
Dominican Republic	0.10	0.5	1.7
Ecuador	0.56	0.7	4.6
Egypt	−0.40	0.4	0.6
El Salvador	0.61	0.9	5.1
Ghana	0.15	0.4	2.0
Guatemala	0.58	0.6	4.8
India	0.32	1.5	2.9
Iran	0.47	1.0	3.9
Iraq	0.21	0.2	2.3
Korea, Republic of	0.87	1.6	9.8
Malaysia	0.19	0.5	2.2
Mexico	0.42	1.6	3.6
Morocco	0.00	0.8	1.0
Nigeria	0.10	0.3	1.6
Pakistan	0.25	1.1	2.5
Peru	0.88	1.8	5.9
Philippines	3.90	0.5	3.3
Sri Lanka	0.29	0.5	2.7
Sudan	−0.60	0.1	0.4
Syria	0.34	1.2	3.0
Taiwan	0.82	0.9	8.5
Thailand	0.60	0.2	1.4
Tunisia	0.70	0.8	5.6
Venezuela	0.13	0.2	1.8

Source: *International Financial Statistics*, vol. 30 (May 1977). End-of-year data, where available.

a. Derived from the equation $dM = a + bdR$, where dM is the change in the money supply and b is the multiplier associated with the change in reserves, dR.

ance are slightly more supportive of a trade explanation for increases in reserves. Nineteen countries showed an improvement in the trade balance in 1972, against sixteen in 1970. Aggregate figures are also mildly supportive of an improvement in trade balance in 1972. For normal countries excluding OPEC the trade deficit was only $99 million in 1972 as opposed to $125 million in 1970 and $190 million in 1966.

Capital movements appear to have been a more important factor than trade changes. While trade accounts were improving in the 1970s there was unusual growth in developing countries' borrowing from the private capital markets.[21] Medium- and long-term Eurocurrency credits to these countries are estimated to have gone up from \$1.8 billion in 1971 and \$4.5 billion in 1972 to \$10 billion in 1973.[22] If the developing countries' increase of \$2.7 billion in borrowing from the Eurodollar market in 1972 is compared with the \$3.1 billion increase in their reserves that year, capital flows seem a plausible explanation for reserve changes. Not only were large Eurodollar loans undertaken, but they were widely dispersed among developing countries.[23]

It appears that a greater part of the explanation of reserve changes in the early 1970s lies with the behavior of the capital market than with the trade balance. Moreover, it is likely that the reserve growth caused the money supply growth. Because developing countries lack developed financial institutions and, consequently, extensive open-market operations, reserve changes usually have a direct and immediate effect on their domestic liquidity. Capital inflows and reserve increases generally are not sterilized, and they cause expansion of the domestic money supply.

Changes in twenty-eight developing countries' money supply and reserves during the era of fixed exchange rates, 1956–72, indicate that the money multiplier associated with the change in reserves for most of them was in the range 0.75 to 1.5 (table 3-14).[24] In striking contrast to the poor

21. The improvement in the creditworthiness of developing countries during this period was directly linked with the growth of their exports. See Ishan Kapur, "An Analysis of the Supply of Euro-Currency Finance to Developing Countries," *Oxford Bulletin of Economics and Statistics,* vol. 39 (August 1977), pp. 171–88.

22. Bank for International Settlements, *Annual Report, 1974,* p. 159.

23. Of 60 countries examined, 16 borrowed in 1971, 29 in 1972, and 44 in 1973. Until the 1970s, borrowings from the private capital market by developing countries were almost nonexistent. P. A. Wellons, *Borrowing for Developing Countries on the Euro-currency Market* (Paris: Organization for Economic Cooperation and Development, 1977).

24. The monetary base, MB, equals domestic assets, DA, plus foreign assets or reserves, R. Money supply, M, is therefore $m_1DA + m_2R$, where m_1 and m_2 are the individual money multipliers. The first difference of money supply equals m_1 (dR) + m_2 (dDA). The estimating equation used here is: $dM = a + bdR$, where b may be interpreted as the money multiplier for reserves. Although the equation is misspecified because it excludes the variable dDA, the nature of the correlation between dR and dDA sets bounds on the magnitude of b. If sterilization policies are followed, then dR will be negatively correlated with dDA; thus the estimate of b is downwardly biased. However, if b is found to be positive and significantly different from zero, then this evidence suggests that reserve changes have an impact on domestic money supply, and that the government is unwilling, or fails, to sterilize the reserve inflows.

results of such tests for the OECD countries,[25] the correlation between domestic money supply and reserves for the developing countries is relatively high. For a third of them, the coefficient of determination, $\bar{R}^2$, is over 0.5 (although for some, there is no significant relationship between reserves and money supply).[26] These results suggest that reserve changes did have an impact on domestic money supply and that the governments were unwilling, or failed, to sterilize the reserve inflows.

This evidence, combined with the information on reserve growth, suggests that the domestic monetary policies of developing countries when exchange rates were fixed were influenced by external events and, in particular, by changes in their reserve levels. The role of sterilization policies cannot be determined from table 3-14, and money expansion might have occurred in the absence of reserve changes. But the table indicates that changes in domestic money supply were strongly correlated with changes in reserves. Considering the unusual expansion in the reserves of developing countries in the 1970s, that connection implies that the acceleration of money supply in 1970–72 was strongly influenced by international as opposed to domestic factors.

One index of the external, or imported, contribution to money supply growth is the ratio of reserve change to the previous year's money stock (table 3-15). Knowledge of the money multiplier is necessary in order to assess the share of reserve changes in the expansion of the money supply. However, trends in the relation of the two factors should be indicative of the relative importance of external and internal factors responsible for money expansion. Almost all the countries in table 3-15 showed an improvement in reserves and hence a positive contribution to the growth in money supply in 1972. Furthermore, the index of that contribution is historically large in 1972.

Econometric Models of Price Inflation

One means of obtaining more rigorous estimates of the relative importance of money supply, real activity, inflation in import prices, and food shortages in explaining developing countries' inflation is econometric tests.

25. Henry N. Goldstein, "Monetary Policy under Fixed and Floating Exchange Rates," National Westminster Bank, *Quarterly Review,* November 1974, pp. 15–27.

26. The higher $\bar{R}^2$ may be partly due to the damping effect of annual data. For Germany, and annual data, 1956–72, the money multiplier was estimated to be 1.05, and $\bar{R}^2$ was equal to 0.39.

Table 3-15. *Ratio of the Change in Foreign Reserves to the Previous Year's Money Supply, Twenty-nine Developing Countries, 1966, 1970, 1972, 1973, and 1975*

	Ratio of change in reserves to previous year's money supply				
Country	*1966*	*1970*	*1972*	*1973*	*1975*
Argentina	1.0	4.4	10.4	25.4	0.6
Bolivia	5.9	3.1	8.3	29.6	−17.6
Brazil	0.8	9.8	34.3	22.7	−2.4
Chile	14.8	19.5	2.1	18.3	60.4
Colombia	0.5	−0.1	12.3	17.5	7.7
Dominican Republic	−5.3	−5.0	1.2	12.5	6.1
Ecuador	10.2	12.0	29.3	29.2	−9.4
Egypt	−2.5	1.3	−0.5	8.4	−1.5
El Salvador	0.6	−0.9	12.7	−12.5	11.9
Ghana	−1.4	−6.4	28.6	16.9	9.2
Guatemala	−5.0	2.5	22.2	34.6	31.6
India	2.3	0.9	−0.1	−0.1	0.7
Indonesia	n.a.	10.4	51.6	20.4	−30.7
Iran	1.7	−6.9	16.6	5.8	5.6
Iraq	22.4	−2.5	19.4	79.5	−35.0
Korea, Republic of	41.7	11.8	25.6	27.9	34.0
Malaysia	4.8	7.0	12.4	18.9	−5.8
Mexico	1.1	2.1	4.6	3.5	1.7
Morocco	−1.6	2.5	3.4	0.4	−2.7
Pakistan	−1.2	2.5	5.2	5.8	−16.3
Peru	−3.6	2.5	5.2	5.8	−16.3
Philippines	0.2	25.8	24.7	51.5	−11.8
Sri Lanka	−8.4	1.0	3.0	8.0	−3.8
Sudan	−1.4	−5.3	2.3	6.5	−14.0
Syria	−4.6	−0.7	7.2	33.6	15.5
Taiwan	10.1	25.1	32.8	2.5	−1.0
Thailand	30.0	−9.2	17.1	20.4	−5.1
Tunisia	−3.3	6.6	12.1	8.2	−6.8
Venezuela	6.3	6.1	11.4	30.1	63.0

Source: *International Financial Statistics*, vol. 30 (May 1977).
n.a. Not available.

While detailed econometric models for each country are beyond the scope of this study, it is possible to apply a reduced-form, single-equation approach, both for individual countries over time and for a pooled cross section of countries. Two basic estimating models are used in the analysis: monetarist and Phillips curve alternatives. In each case, the analysis here applies a hybrid version to take account of the special influences of import price inflation and food shortages.

The monetarist model is adapted from Harberger's model of inflation in Chile, which he calls "a simple transformation of the liquidity preference function."[27] Specifically, demand for real money balances (M/P) is assumed to be a function of real income, Y; the cost of holding such balances, A (which as a proxy for the interest rate is the lagged acceleration or change in inflation rates); and time, t (to incorporate any changes in monetization, financial institutions, and so forth). Thus the basic monetarist model is:

$$(1) \qquad P' = -a - bY' + cA' + M'$$

where P' is the percent change in price, Y' the percent change in real income, M' the percent change in money supply, and A' the percent change in the cost of holding money. Changes in velocity are captured by the constant term, a, and changes in money supply are assumed to be exogenous.[28]

Because the relatively rigid financial structure of developing countries makes interest rates a poor measure, changes in past inflation rates are used to measure changes in the cost of holding cash, A.[29] When lagged effects of money supply on prices are introduced,[30]

$$(2) \qquad P' = a_0 + a_1Y' + a_2A' + a_3M' + a_4M'_{-1},$$

where M'_{-1} is the growth of money supply in the previous period.

27. Harberger, "Dynamics of Inflation in Chile," p. 226.

28. Tests for the exogeneity of changes in money supply have led to conflicting results for the United States (see Edgar L. Feige and Douglas K. Pearce, "Economically Rational Expectations: Are Innovations in the Rate of Inflation Independent of Innovations in Measures of Monetary and Fiscal Policy?" *Journal of Political Economy,* vol. 84 [June 1976], pp. 499–522; Arturo Brillembourg and Mohsin S. Khan, "The Relationship between Money, Income, and Prices: Has Money Mattered Historically?" *Journal of Money, Credit, and Banking,* vol. 11 [August 1979], pp. 358–65). Evidence in chapter 5, below, supports the assumption that such changes are exogenous for India. Estimation of this equation implicitly assumes that the economy is always at full employment output, or alternatively that real income and changes in it are exogenous to changes in money supply and prices. If the exogeneity does not hold, then the results of the monetarist model will be biased. However, the exogeneity of changes in real income may be a viable assumption for most developing countries since they are heavily dependent on agriculture, a sector whose output is dependent on exogenous factors like weather and technological change.

29. Harberger's choice of changes in past inflation rates is followed by Robert C. Vogel, "The Dynamics of Inflation in Latin America, 1950–1969," *American Economic Review,* vol. 64 (March 1974), pp. 102–14; and Susan M. Wachter, *Latin American Inflation* (Lexington Books, 1976).

30. In addition, lagged income variables can be used to reflect permanent income. This approach was experimented with and rejected. Generally, the coefficients for the lagged income variables were not significant.

The theoretical restrictions on the coefficients are as follows: trends in velocity are reflected in a_0 being different from zero; the coefficient on changes in real income, a_1, is expected to be negative and equal to -1 assuming there is a unitary elasticity between real income and real cash balances; a_2 is expected to be positive; and since in the long run, money supply and prices are closely associated, the sum of a_3 and a_4 (assuming there is a two-year lag in the impact of money supply) should not be significantly different from 1.

The major alternative to a monetarist model is a model of real activity based on the Phillips curve. This model relates changes in wages to the tightness of the labor market, and wage changes (usually, but not necessarily, in markup fashion) to inflation. Thus,

$$P' = f(L; X), \tag{3}$$

where L is a measure of excess demand for labor and X represents other variables. Allowing for price expectations, P^*, this equation becomes

$$P' = f(L, P^*; X). \tag{4}$$

Because the conventional unemployment rate has little meaning in most developing countries (in view of ample underemployment in agriculture), the excess demand for labor is replaced by a measure of excess aggregate demand—the percentage deviation of actual output from potential output, *GAP*.[31] The equation then becomes a conventional excess demand model, augmented by price expectations:

$$P' = b_0 + b_1\, GAP + b_3 P^*. \tag{5}$$

Allowing for lagged effects, the equation becomes

$$P' = b_0 + b_1\, GAP + b_2\, GAP_{-1} + b_3 P^*, \tag{6}$$

where GAP_{-1} is the GAP variable for the previous year.[32]

31. This is a common representation of excess aggregate demand. Admittedly, it has drawbacks. The definition of potential output is bound to be arbitrary; moreover, such a formulation ignores bottlenecks.

32. Variants of this model are used to examine OECD data in David Laidler, "Inflation—Alternative Explanations and Policies: Tests on Data Drawn from Six Countries," in Karl Brunner and Allan K. Meltzer, eds., *Institutions, Policies and Economic Performance,* Carnegie-Rochester Conference Series on Public Policy, vol. 4 (Amsterdam: North-Holland, 1976), pp. 251–306; and Robert J. Gordon, "Alternative Responses of Policy to External Supply Shocks," *Brookings Papers on Economic Activity, 1:1975,* pp. 183–204 (hereafter *BPEA*), and to examine the Philippines in K. Otani, "Inflation in an Open Economy: A Case Study of the Philippines," *IMF Staff Papers,* vol. 22 (November 1975), pp. 750–74. The use of GAP and GAP_{-1} in equation 6 is essentially equivalent to the use of growth in real income, Y', and lagged Y'.

In estimating *GAP,* potential output is measured by the logarithmic trend for gross domestic product. The signs of the coefficients b_1 and b_2 are expected to be positive, assuming excess demand results in upward pressure on the price level. Alternatively, a "business cycle" or capacity utilization approach can be taken toward the process of price formation.[33] If changes in *GAP* are represented by *GAPD,* i.e. $GAPD = GAP - GAP_{-1}$, then equation 6 can be written as

$$(7) \qquad P' = b_0' + b_1' \, GAP + b_2' \, GAPD + b_3 P^*.$$

Note that $b_1 = b_1' + b_2'$ and $b_2 = -b_2'$. The variable *GAPD* is meant to capture the effect of an upturn or downturn in the economy. An upturn could indicate an upward pressure on the price level; therefore b_2' should be positive. Alternatively, an increase in capacity utilization signified by a positive *GAPD* may lead to a decline in unit costs, and prices. Thus b_2' should be negative. A different version of essentially the same argument is the assumption that employment and prices lag behind output changes; hence, b_2' is negative.

This argument applies essentially to developed economies. For developing countries, stagflation might be the norm. If the food sector is important, the exogenous element of weather would dominate (or at least strongly influence) movements in gross output. If agricultural prices are relatively flexible, total output and the price level would be negatively related.[34] The coefficient on expected inflation, b_3, is expected to be positive and to lie between 0 and 1. It is assumed that expectations are adaptive, so that P^* is represented by the lagged inflation rate, P'_{-1}.

This real activity model and the monetarist model are both essentially demand-related models of inflation, differing in their emphasis on the nature of demand. Neither model considers either structural or cost-push causes of inflation. If monetary authorities respond to cost increases by increasing money growth to prevent real output from falling, then such effects are transmitted by changes in the money supply. Analogously, the real activity model implies that structural or cost factors are reflected through output changes. To capture the independent effect of such non-demand structural factors, two variables—food bottlenecks and import prices—are introduced into each of the basic models.

33. Neither interpretation adequately captures the inflation process in developing countries, however.

34. Strictly speaking, agricultural prices need not be completely flexible downward; all that is needed is that increases in agricultural output slow down the rise in food prices and hence the price level.

Food bottlenecks are assumed to generate inflation because developing countries' nonfarm prices are relatively fixed, whereas their agricultural prices are flexible. In Gordon's model relating inflation to supply shocks originating in agriculture, a decline in food production leads to an increase in the relative price of food, P_r.[35] Thus (if velocity is relatively constant) nonfarm output would be expected to decline, assuming nonfarm prices are fixed in the short run. In their desire to prevent such a decline, authorities may increase the money supply, and therefore nominal income. This expansion would allow the absolute and relative price of food to increase while nonfarm output and prices remain constant.

Changes in import price can also have important direct and indirect effects on domestic prices. Indeed, in a world of fixed exchange rates, external inflation may have a primary role in causing domestic inflation.[36] Inflation abroad leads to an improvement in the competitiveness of domestically produced goods, raising external and internal demand and eventually leading to equal prices for domestic and external goods. In terms of either the law of one price or excess demand leading to higher prices, internal and external inflation will be equalized. This equivalence holds strictly for the traded-goods sector and can in principle be extended to tradable goods. A large sector of any economy, however, may be composed of nontradable goods whose presence causes inflation rates to diverge.

At a micro level the influence of imported prices on domestic prices is straightforward. A rise in import prices of intermediate goods implies that costs increase and therefore prices also go up. If substitutes are available for either intermediate or final imported goods, domestic prices are likely to follow external prices.

The direct role of import price inflation argues for the addition of a term representing the change in import prices, P'_m,[37] to basic inflationary

35. Gordon, "Alternative Responses of Policy." This closed economy model abstracts from the possibility of raising imports to maintain a stable price level. Demand factors can also cause an increase in the relative price of food, if agricultural prices rise faster than industrial prices. In this chapter the relative price of food is used to represent food scarcity.

36. Gösta Edgren, Karl-Olof Faxen, and Clas-Erik Odhner, "Wages, Growth and the Distribution of Income," *Swedish Journal of Economics*, vol. 71 (September 1969), pp. 133–60; Parkin, "A 'Monetarist' Analysis."

37. It can be argued that external effects on domestic inflation are best captured by the average prices of all traded goods—exports and imports. Though appropriate for the developed countries, an average traded-goods index is not considered appropriate for the developing countries because their export goods are composed mainly

models. A major indirect effect of higher import prices—the demand deflected toward domestically produced goods—may also lead to higher prices for domestic goods.[38] However, this influence should have no additional role in explaining inflation since both models of inflation include demand changes.

If an eclectic approach is taken and both excess demand and structural factors are presumed to cause inflation, then the basic models of inflation should be extended. Thus equations 2 and 6 are modified to become:

$$(8) \qquad P' = a_0 + a_1Y' + a_2A' + a_3M' + a_4M_{-1} + a_5P'_r + a_6P'_m$$

and

$$(9) \qquad P' = b_0 + b_1GAP + b_2GAP_{-1} + b_3P_{-1} + b_4P'_r + b_5P'_m,$$

where P'_r is the percent change in the relative price of food and P'_m is the percent change of import prices.

Equations 8 and 9 are best viewed as hybrid, reduced-form models that allow for explicit tests of various presumed determinants of the inflation process. Monetarists, who hold that relative price changes are irrelevant to the determination of the overall price level, would deny any significance for the terms P'_r and P'_m.[39] This position does not deny that import prices affect inflation; rather, it asserts that their influences are captured by the money supply variables.[40]

Relative food prices have been used to explain inflation in Argentina, Brazil, and Mexico.[41] And import price inflation has increasingly appeared in inflation equations since the occurrence of import price surges in the

---

of primary commodities of which there is relatively little consumption domestically, and because their governments often create a wedge between domestic and international prices (as Brazil does for coffee and the OPEC countries for oil).

38. For open economies like England, import prices of consumer goods are also likely to affect wage demands and therefore domestic prices.

39. International monetarists (see Parkin, "A 'Monetarist' Analysis"), however, would argue for a strong relationship between P' and P'_m. But they view domestic prices as related to the world money stock and world prices.

40. Such induced changes could occur if the government accommodates price increases—of oil, for example—by expansion of the money supply.

41. Wachter, in *Latin American Inflation*, defines P_r as FPI/CPI, where FPI and CPI are the food and consumer price indexes, respectively. In this chapter the formulation is slightly different:

$$P_r + (1 - W_1)FPI/(CPI - W_1FPI),$$

where W_1 is the weight of food prices in the consumer price index. The FPI and CPI figures are as reported in UN, *Monthly Bulletin of Statistics*, various issues.

1970s (table 3-5 indicates that import prices were relatively constant in the 1960s). Generally significant results have been found in studies examining the effect of import price inflation on domestic inflation in the United States and in OECD countries.[42]

Some researchers, hesitant to assign more than an associative role to import price inflation in explaining domestic inflation, have argued that the two phenomena are determined by the same forces in an economy. Excessive growth rates in the money supply can lead to a depreciation in the exchange rate and a rise in import prices. In a fixed-exchange-rate world, a major economy like the United States can affect the world price level with repercussions in both import and domestic prices. Developing economies are too small to affect world prices. The problem of induced depreciation is partly solved by measuring P'_m in exogenous dollar prices, although because producers and consumers react to domestic prices, such an equation is difficult to interpret. When the two extended inflation models in this chapter were estimated with import price inflation in dollar terms, the estimated coefficients were significant and roughly of the same order of magnitude as those for equations 8 and 9.

A further problem is that it can be argued that the introduction of import price inflation in equations 8 and 9 will result in a spurious correlation because the import price is a component of the consumer price index used as the dependent variable. When equations were estimated with the GDP deflator (which does not suffer from this drawback) as dependent variable, almost identical results were obtained as with the consumer price index.

42. Franco Modigliani and Lucas Papademos, "Targets for Monetary Policy in the Coming Year," *BPEA, 1:1975,* pp. 141–65; Sung Y. Kwack, "The Effect of Foreign Inflation on Domestic Prices and the Relative Price Advantage of Exchange-Rate Changes," in Peter B. Clark, Dennis E. Logue, and Richard James Sweeney, eds., *The Effects of Exchange Rate Adjustments,* Proceedings of a Conference Sponsored by OASIA Research, U.S. Treasury Department, April 4–5, 1974 (U.S. Government Printing Office, 1977), pp. 387–98; William D. Nordhaus, "The Worldwide Wage Explosion," *BPEA, 2:1972,* pp. 431–64; Morris Goldstein, "Downward Price Inflexibility, Ratchet Effects, and the Inflationary Impact of Import Price Changes: Some Empirical Evidence," *IMF Staff Papers,* vol. 24 (November 1977), pp. 569–612; and Robert J. Gordon, "World Inflation and Monetary Accommodation in Eight Countries," *BPEA, 2:1977,* pp. 409–68. As a historical matter, it should be mentioned that A. W. Phillips, "The Relation Between Unemployment and the Rate of Change of Money Wage Rates in the United Kingdom, 1861–1957," *Economica,* vol. 25 (November 1958), pp. 283–99, explicitly considers the role of import price inflation. It is therefore fitting that the unemployment-inflation or output-inflation tradeoff be estimated in ceteris paribus terms, that is, holding import prices constant.

Results of Econometric Tests

The basic monetarist model of inflation (equation 2) performs remarkably well, given the diversity of the countries studied (results for the model, as estimated for twenty-nine developing countries, are reported in appendix table 3-20). Except for Korea, the adjusted coefficients of determination, $\bar{R}^2$, are high and the coefficients of the variables conform to predictions. Coefficient a_2 is usually greater than a_3, suggesting that current changes in money supply have a greater effect than lagged changes. The sum of the money variables, a_2 and a_3, is significant for twenty-five of the twenty-nine countries. For eleven of these countries the sum is not significantly different from one. The income coefficient, a_1, is negative and significant for only eleven countries, and is not significantly different from -1 for nine. The cost-of-liquidity variable, A', has the correct sign in most cases, though it is significant for only ten countries.[43] Insignificance of this coefficient can be interpreted as reflecting the fact that interest rates in most developing countries do not affect the holdings of real cash balances, or that the lagged rate of change of inflation is not a good proxy for expected costs of holding cash. The constant term is generally not significant, suggesting no trend in velocity.

The performance of the alternative model of real activity (equation 6) is disappointing. For most countries the variables representing excess demand, *GAP* and GAP_{-1}, are not significant. The price-expectations variable is significant for fourteen countries. Overall, the explanatory power of this model is poor, with only sixteen countries showing an explanatory power, $\bar{R}^2$, over 0.20. Equations similar to this have been somewhat more successful in explaining inflation in developed countries. The large agricultural sector in most developing countries causes *GAP* to represent upward pressure on prices caused by industrial demand and downward pressure caused by large agricultural output. Over time, their conflicting effects might cancel each other, leading to no systematic relation between inflation and the variable *GAP*. Whatever the reason, the results clearly emphasize that the basic real activity model is not an adequate representation of the inflation process in developing countries.

The hybrid models (equations 8 and 9) are much more satisfactory

43. Both Vogel, "Dynamics of Inflation," and Wachter, *Latin American Inflation*, reached similar results for the variable measuring the opportunity cost of money for Latin American countries.

explanators of inflation (the full results of the monetarist hybrid model appear in appendix table 3-20). The results of the demand variables are similar to those for the basic models. For virtually all of the countries the real-activity variables, GAP and GAP_{-1}, are not significant. In striking contrast, for most countries, the money-supply variables of the hybrid model retain their significance. Seventeen countries show significance for the sum of M' and M'_{-1} (coefficients a_3 and a_4); for the basic monetarist model there were twenty-five such countries. Monetary variables appear to represent the inflationary process better for developing countries than changes in real activity. Furthermore, the lagged money term, M'_{-1}, is often significant, and sizable, for most countries in which the joint influence on M' and M'_{-1} is significant. This suggests that the acceleration in the growth of the money supply that was observed in 1972 (which was caused principally by external events) had an important role to play in the subsequent inflation boom of 1973.

The structural variables, relative food price and import price inflation, turn out to be important contributors to inflation. The presence of the other variables in equations 8 and 9 is a relatively stringent test of the role of the structural variables in the generation of inflation since part of their effect may already be captured by the money-supply and excess-demand variables. The fact that their direct effect is significant strongly supports the argument that the composition of demand (as well as its magnitude) is relevant for inflation.

The results of appendix table 3-20 clearly indicate that the structural variables are important. For all of the countries the explanatory power of the monetarist model is considerably increased with the introduction of food supply bottlenecks and import price changes. Taken individually, relative food price, P'_r, is significant for ten countries and import price inflation, P'_m, is significant for sixteen.[44] Further, these coefficients are found to be of similar magnitude (and significance) for both the monetarist and real activity models. Given the divergent ways in which the two

44. During the 1970s, P'_r may partially be capturing the effect of imported prices. During 1970–75, international prices for wheat and rice (and other commodities) reached historical peaks after having remained relatively constant during the 1960s. Even though the distribution of food is controlled in most countries (see Jeffrey M. Davis, "The Fiscal Role of Food Subsidy Programs," *IMF Staff Papers,* vol. 24 [March 1977], pp. 100–27), it is likely that part of the explosive increase in prices was passed on to the consumers. Thus, the rise in P'_r during these years could have been caused to a larger extent by P'_m. Hence the emphasis on the role of P'_m.

models measure the nature of demand, this robustness in the coefficients of P'_r and P'_m attests to their relevance in the generation of inflation.

It can be argued that the susceptibility of a country to imported inflation is proportional to its degree of openness, or the share of traded goods in its production and consumption. That susceptibility can be approximated, ceteris paribus, by the coefficient a_6 in equation 8 (or b_6 in equation 9). These estimates, along with the associated *t*-statistics, are shown in table 3-16, as is a proxy for openness of the economy—the ratio of imports to gross domestic product, *Op,* in 1970–72 (ideally it would be the ratio of tradable goods to GNP). If *Op* adequately measures the role of imports, then a_6 and *Op* should be approximately equal. Instead, coefficient a_6 is generally greater than *Op*.[45] (It may be that the potential trade is usually greater than goods actually traded.) A regression between the two alternative measures of susceptibility, a_6 and *Op*, yields no suggestion of a relationship between them:

$$a_6 = \underset{(3.61)}{0.35} - \underset{(0.65)}{0.35}\,Op.$$

$$\bar{R}^2 = 0.21$$

Taken at face value, this suggests that the share of imports, a commonly used measure of openness, is an irrelevant indicator of a country's susceptibility to imported inflation.[46] Alternatively, the countries may differ much less in the ratio of their traded goods to gross national product than is indicated by their trade.

If the coefficient a_6 is accepted as a rough indicator of the impact of imported inflation on domestic inflation, then the term $a_6P'_m$ can be calculated to reflect the contribution of import price inflation to total domestic inflation. For most countries the contribution of import price inflation in the 1970s, as indicated in table 3-17, is equal to if not greater than the average of domestic inflation in the 1960s. Furthermore, the contribution

45. The impact coefficient, a_6, is greater than the share of imports in GDP in the models for the United States tested by Kwack, "Effects of Foreign Inflation," Modigliani and Papademos, "Targets for Monetary Policy," and Rudiger Dornbusch and Paul Krugman, "Flexible Exchange Rates in the Short Run," *BPEA, 3:1976,* pp. 537–75.

46. Michael Bruno reaches a similar conclusion in his analysis of inflation in the developing countries; "Exchange Rates, Import Costs, and Wage-Price Dynamics," *Journal of Political Economy,* vol. 86 (June 1978), pp. 379–403.

Table 3-16. *Relation of Import Price Inflation and Openness of the Economy, Thirty Developing Countries, 1956–75*

Country	Coefficient of: Import price inflation	Coefficient of: t-statistic	Coefficient of: Openness of economy
Non-oil exporters			
Bolivia	0.13	1.63	0.16
Colombia	0.19	3.03	0.11
Dominican Republic	0.27	1.62	0.21
Ecuador	0.22	4.50	0.18
Egypt	0.00	0.71	0.12
El Salvador	0.34[a]	2.83	0.23
Ghana	0.21	1.33	0.17
Guatemala	0.27	3.70	0.15
India	0.24	3.49	0.04
Korea, Republic of	0.28	0.90	0.25
Malaysia	0.00	0.84	0.34
Mexico	0.21	1.23	0.07
Morocco	0.26	4.94	0.19
Pakistan	0.52	1.88	0.10
Peru	0.18	1.52	0.10
Philippines	0.19[a]	4.02	0.17
Sri Lanka	0.21	3.15	0.15
Sudan	0.71	4.82	0.14
Syria	0.52	5.07	0.23
Taiwan	0.39	3.13	0.30
Thailand	0.34	5.92	0.19
Tunisia	0.12	2.00	0.21
Oil exporters			
Indonesia	n.a.	n.a.	n.a.
Iran	0.73	3.20	0.12
Iraq	0.57	3.28	0.14
Nigeria	0.30	1.30	0.16
Venezuela	0.14	0.93	0.15
Hyperinflation sufferers			
Argentina	0.55	3.77	0.07
Brazil	0.35[a]	2.89	0.07
Chile	0.38	2.47	0.09

Source: Appendix, table 3-20.
n.a. Not available.
a. Estimated from the real activity model regression because the estimate from the monetarist model is not significant.

Table 3-17. *Contribution of Imported Inflation to Total Inflation, Thirty Developing Countries, 1970, 1972, 1974, and 1975*

Percent

Country	Average inflation, 1961–70	Imported inflation			
		1970	1972	1974	1975
Argentina	21.50	7.13	51.30	21.73	131.06
Bolivia	5.56	0.54	2.96	3.98	0.48
Brazil	45.30	6.12	7.58	8.31	9.25
Chile	27.50	16.40	53.67	189.30	486.83
Colombia	11.52	2.08	3.76	8.04	4.87
Dominican Republic	2.03	1.13	1.98	7.42	2.09
Ecuador	4.31	4.36	2.44	7.18	1.76
Egypt	3.78	0.00	0.00	0.00	0.00
El Salvador	0.66	1.78	2.52	11.20	2.38
Ghana	7.54	1.11	8.03	8.12	1.16
Guatemala	0.82	1.04	1.85	6.25	2.29
India	6.46	1.00	1.86	14.20	1.72
Indonesia	90.44	n.a.	n.a.	n.a.	n.a.
Iran	1.73	3.04	6.08	16.20	7.19
Iraq	2.30	2.38	0.28	14.36	4.48
Korea, Republic of	13.28	0.97	1.66	3.89	1.85
Malaysia	0.94	0.58	−0.09	3.35	0.49
Mexico	2.78	0.88	1.94	6.90	1.58
Morocco	2.31	1.08	−0.36	13.47	−0.71
Nigeria	4.30	1.58	−0.23	8.07	1.44
Pakistan	3.21	2.17	52.8	26.00	1.69
Peru	9.39	0.75	1.50	6.72	4.11
Philippines	5.41	11.83	2.52	10.23	2.43
Sri Lanka	2.96	1.11	1.79	11.55	1.77
Sudan	3.58	3.74	5.26	24.33	4.07
Syria	1.94	1.79	3.34	18.94	1.72
Taiwan	3.40	1.37	4.78	17.66	−1.45
Thailand	2.03	1.79	2.49	15.44	2.15
Tunisia	2.28	0.50	−0.10	7.57	−0.60
Venezuela	0.98	0.63	1.02	3.55	1.38

Source: Appendix table 3-20; *International Financial Statistics*, vol. 30 (May 1977).
n.a. Not available.

shows a steep, and almost universal, drop in 1975. This close parallel with the pattern of overall inflation (table 3-1) suggests that the behavior of import prices is crucial to an understanding of both the boom and the subsequent decline in worldwide inflation.[47]

A Cross-Country Analysis

When the analysis of the inflation models is applied to pooled data on twenty-eight of the developing countries in 1971–75, the results support the conclusion that excess liquidity and import prices had an important role in causing inflation.[48] In the regressions, to correct for the great disparities in national food budgets, each country's relative food price is weighted by the share of food in the consumer price index (in India the share is 60.9 percent, in Venezuela 27.1 percent). Import price inflation, on the other hand, is not weighted to reflect the share of imports in gross domestic product because that is not a significant factor in explaining susceptibility to inflation. But the variable P'_m, changes in import prices, is adjusted to accommodate changes in exchange rates, tariffs, and the dollar price of imports (exchange-rate changes possibly have the greatest impact on the local economy).[49] If the three changes affect domestic prices in an identical manner, the effective import price is:

$$P_{em} = P_{m\$}E(1 + t_r),$$

where $P_{m\$}$ is the dollar price of imports, E the exchange rate, and t_r the tariff rate. Percentage changes in the effective import price are represented by P'_{em}. The presence of differential effects for the three components can be tested by inserting each one separately in percentage change form.

When the relationships between inflation and lagged prices, relative price of food, and import prices are compared (regressions 1, 4, and 10 of table 3-18), the best single explanatory variable is not lagged prices but

47. The share of imported inflation is another indicator of the same phenomenon. This share is greater than a third of actual inflation for twenty-three of the thirty countries in 1973, but for only five of the countries in 1975. Thus the simultaneous decline in $a_6P'_m$ and P' in 1975 suggests a reversal to the norm of the 1960s.

48. Both Chile and Argentina are excluded from the analysis because their hyperinflation would be so dominant as to skew the results of the entire group of countries.

49. Assuming that developing countries cannot affect the prices of imports, there is no bias in a regression involving P' as dependent and P'_m as independent variable.

Table 3-18. *Results of Regression Analyses of Inflation in Twenty-eight Developing Countries as a Group, 1971–75*[a]

Regression number	Constant	Lagged prices	Relative price of food[b]	Import prices	Real activity or money: Current	Real activity or money: Lagged	Change in income	Cost of liquidity	Exchange rate	Dollar price of imports	Protection[c]	Coefficient of determination, $\bar{R}^2$	Durbin-Watson
1	7.76 (6.72)	0.45 (5.60)	...	...	...	...	...	...	...	...	...	0.179	1.81
Structural model													
2	3.04 (2.52)	0.41 (5.95)	0.39 (3.05)	0.24 (6.06)	...	...	...	...	...	...	...	0.396	2.13
Monetarist model													
3	1.72 (1.11)	...	...	...	0.23 (3.69)	0.31 (4.49)	−0.21 (3.64)	0.32 (3.60)	...	...	...	0.416	1.79
4	−0.32 (0.22)	...	0.24 (2.04)	0.19 (5.45)	0.21 (3.60)	0.25 (3.87)	−0.20 (3.77)	0.31	...	...	...	0.534	2.02
5	−1.02 (0.72)	...	0.15 (1.32)	...	0.19 (3.34)	0.25 (4.08)	−0.24 (4.70)	0.31 (3.97)	0.14 (2.55)	0.29 (5.98)	0.07 (0.35)	0.561	2.04

Real activity model													
6	7.86	0.39	...	...	0.05	0.37	...	...	...	...	...	0.212	1.79
	(6.78)	(4.71)			(0.32)	(1.76)							
7	3.21	0.35	0.40	0.24	0.02	0.39	...	...	...	...	...	0.432	2.10
	(2.71)	(4.98)	(3.23)	(6.15)	(0.15)	(2.19)							
8	1.48	0.39	0.30	...	−0.03	0.39	...	...	0.16	0.35	0.19	0.463	2.18
	(1.16)	(5.66)	(2.37)		(0.23)	(2.26)			(2.62)	(6.65)	(0.91)		
9	11.24	...	0.58	...	...	...	...	...	...	...	...	0.084	1.48
	(12.50)		(3.72)										
10	7.83	...	...	0.26	...	...	...	...	...	...	...	0.188	1.77
	(6.96)			(5.76)									

a. Includes all countries listed in table 3-1 except Argentina and Chile. Absolute values of t-statistics are in parentheses.
b. Weighted for each country, by the shares of food in the consumer price index.
c. Unity plus tariff rate (percentage change).

the price of imports. The coefficient for lagged prices, 0.45, in regression 1 is almost identical to the 0.49 coefficient determined for the OECD countries for 1972–76.[50] The import price coefficient in the OECD analysis was 0.17, compared to 0.26 in regression 10. This suggests that developing countries were more susceptible to international influences in the 1970s than were developed countries, an observation that is supported by the larger acceleration of their consumer prices.

Comparison of the basic regressions (3 for the monetarist model, 6 for the real activity, and 2 for a structural model) suggests that, as with the individual country analysis, the monetarist model performs best. The real activity model does not show significance for either of the demand variables, GAP and GAP_{-1}. By contrast, all the variables in the monetarist model are significant, though neither the income nor the money variables approach their theoretical limits of -1 and $+1$, respectively.[51] The sum of the money terms is 0.54; given the large acceleration of money supply in 1972 and 1973, this suggests a strong role for money in the acceleration of inflation in 1973–74. The A' variable, changes in the cost of holding money, is significant in the cross-country analysis in contrast to its general insignificance for the individual countries over the 1956–75 period. During most of those years, inflation rates were low and relatively constant. This suggests that the demand for money is generally inelastic with respect to interest rates; however, with relatively extreme changes, such as those observed in 1972–74, a threshold is crossed and the response is elastic.

The hybrid models again indicate that both demand and structural cost variables are important. The robustness in the demand coefficients is indicated by the fact that they stay relatively constant with the addition of relative-food-price and import-price variables. As regressions 1, 9, and 10 show, import prices, P'_{em}, were the best single predictor of inflation. In regressions 4 and 7, in the presence of demand variables, import price inflation is again the most significant variable, at least in terms of its t-statistic. Furthermore, this result occurs in the presence of the relative food price variable, P'_{rw}, which was strongly affected by import prices, P'_{em}, in the 1970s. These and the results in table 3-16 and appendix table 3-20 support an international rather than domestic interpretation of developing countries' inflation in the 1970s.

50. Bruno, "Exchange Rates."

51. The income coefficient may not reach its theoretical value of –1 in part because the variable measured is current income rather than permanent income.

Table 3-19. *Results of Regression Analysis of Best Representation of the Inflationary Process in Twenty-eight Developing Countries as a Group, 1971–75*[a]

Factor	*1971*	*1972*	*1973*	*1974*	*1975*
Actual inflation	5.74	6.42	11.43	22.11	15.77
Predicted inflation	7.24	8.22	12.53	18.74	15.74
Contribution to inflation					
Money supply, M'	2.66	3.88	5.44	5.54	5.06
Lagged money supply, M'_{-1}	3.94	3.18	4.64	6.50	6.61
Import prices, P'_{em}	2.09	2.85	3.86	6.93	1.43
Food prices, P'	0.25	0.08	0.75	1.09	0.42
Income, Y'	−1.28	−1.46	−2.06	−2.83	−0.93
Cost of liquidity, A'	−0.09	0.02	0.21	1.85	2.97
Actual acceleration in inflation, P''	0.06	0.68	6.01	9.68	−6.34
Contribution to acceleration					
Money supply, M''	−0.64	1.22	1.56	0.10	−0.47
Lagged money supply, M''_{-1}	0.23	−0.76	1.46	1.86	0.11
Import prices, P''_{em}	0.51	0.43	1.60	3.57	−6.15
Food prices, P''	0.21	−0.17	0.67	0.33	−0.67
Income, Y''	0.40	−0.18	−0.60	−0.78	2.40
Cost of liquidity, A''	0.30	0.11	0.19	1.64	1.12

a. Based on regression 4, table 3-18.

When structural variables representing the openness of the economy (as measured by the share of imports in national product, 1970–72) and dependency on oil imports (measured both as the 1970–72 share of oil imports in total imports, and as share in national income) were added to the hybrid models containing the food and import price variables, neither was significant in any of the regressions. Again, openness seems to be irrelevant. Oil dependency is also unimportant, reflecting the fact that OPEC prices were increased well after the inflation boom began. Furthermore, oil dependence seems to have no role in explaining inflation beyond its contribution to the inflation of import prices.

Since regression 4 in table 3-18 appears to be the best representation of the inflationary process in developing countries, the relative importance of its variables is examined in table 3-19. Each variable's contributions to inflation and to the acceleration in inflation are evaluated. Changes in income, cost of liquidity, and the relative price of food played a relatively small role in the inflation of the 1970s. The monetary variables, M' and

M'_{-1}, and import prices are of major importance for all the years, 1972–75. And they are important in both the generation and the acceleration of inflation. In 1973, actual average inflation was 11.4 percent; the money and money-lagged variables together account for 10.1 percent and import prices contribute 3.9 percent of the inflation. In 1974, import prices increase their importance and account for 6.9 percent; the money terms contribute 12 percent, with total inflation being 22 percent. The same factors explain the acceleration of inflation. In 1973 the total acceleration of 6 percent included a 1.6 percent acceleration from import price inflation and 3 percent acceleration from the money variable. The 1974 figures suggest an increase in the contribution of import price inflation and a decline in importance of the money terms. The deceleration in inflation in 1975—a decline of 6.3 percent in consumer prices—seems to be strongly associated with the deceleration in import prices which contributed 6.2 percentage points to the total deceleration.

The cross-country analyses confirm the impression that the excess liquidity generated by foreign capital in the early 1970s can be held partly responsible for the inflation of 1973 and 1974 and that import price changes also played an important role in the generation of this inflation.

Conclusion

The monetary channel was one of the major mechanisms for the transmission of inflation in 1972–75. Large increases in foreign reserves in 1972 led to unusually high increases in the domestic money supply, setting up inflationary monetary conditions. Increased reserves reflected inflows of capital into the developing countries more than gains in their trade balances. And the capital flows appear to have been related to the expansion of both U.S. dollar outflows in 1971 and Eurodollar lending. Regression analysis indicates that the foreign reserves generally were not sterilized, so that they led to increases in the developing countries' money supply. Regression analysis also shows that import prices played an important role in these countries' domestic inflation—they accounted for well over half of domestic inflation in the thirty countries in 1973–74 and were largely responsible for the drop in inflation in 1975. Thus goods arbitrage was a channel through which inflation was imported. One of its components—the world price of grains—constituted a special vehicle for imported inflation. Widespread crop failures in 1972 and the high costs of importing food to offset shortages in 1972–73 explain the relatively strong role that food shortages register in statistical tests of inflation in 1972–74. One factor that had no role in initiating the inflation boom was the OPEC oil price increase, though oil was of course one of the influences in the rise of import prices during 1971–75.

Both the developed and the developing countries were emerging from a recession in 1971. This recession was especially severe for the industrialized world. The synchronous expansion in real output, which was of relatively high magnitude in 1973, probably caused some pressure on prices. In the developed world, changes in output have a strong role in explaining inflation. Surprisingly, both individual and cross-country analyses indicate their role is insignificant in the inflation of developing countries. One reason may be the predominantly agricultural basis of most of these economies. Thus, excess demand may have less impact on prices than do weather, technology, and the like.

Expansion of the money supply seems to have preceded the inflation boom. In 1972, when consumer prices were relatively stable, money supply expanded at an unusual rate. Neither wage inflation, budget deficits, nor food bottlenecks were major causes of the liquidity problem, though changes in external reserves were. Some role can be ascribed to trade in causing the reserve increase, but financial borrowing from the capital market (Eurodollars), which was virtually nonexistent in the late 1960s, almost equaled the reserve changes in the early 1970s. And those changes were strongly correlated with money expansion.

The monetarist model of inflation in the thirty developing countries examined in this chapter indicates that the money changes had a strong and systematic effect on the price level. Structural factors—food bottlenecks and particularly changes in import prices—were also significant. The inflation boom seems indeed to have been imported.

Appendix

Table 3-20 reports the results of the monetarist models of inflation (equations 2 and 8) for twenty-nine of the thirty countries investigated in this chapter; Indonesia is not included because complete data are not available. The results of the real activity models are not presented because in most cases they are not significant for either the basic or the hybrid model.

Table 3-20. *Results of Basic and Hybrid Monetarist Models of Inflation, Twenty-nine Developing Countries, 1956–75*[a]

Country	Model	Constant	Income, Y'	Cost of liquidity, A'	Money supply, M'	Money supply lagged, M'_{-1}	Money supply, actual plus lagged, $M' + M'_{-1}$	Relative price of food, P'_r	Import price, P'_m	Coefficient of determination, $\bar{R}^2$	Durbin-Watson
Argentina	Basic	19.35	−3.63	0.25	1.17	0.38	0.79	...	...	0.644	1.71
		(1.68)	(3.12)	(3.58)	(3.58)	(0.95)	(3.07)				
	Hybrid	6.5	−0.45	−0.03	0.31	−0.03	0.28	−0.05	0.55	0.913	2.59
		(1.04)	(0.51)	(0.37)	(1.39)	(0.13)	(1.06)	(0.08)	(3.77)		
Bolivia[b]	Basic	4.34	−1.59	0.70	0.95	−0.24	0.71	...	...	0.864	1.12
		(0.89)	(4.64)	(3.20)	(4.70)	(0.81)	(2.81)				
	Hybrid	8.71	−2.0	0.61	0.75	−0.24	0.51	0.44	0.13	0.931	1.62
		(2.35)	(7.28)	(3.85)	(3.08)	(0.97)	(2.55)	(1.92)	(1.63)		
Brazil	Basic	1.89	−0.68	0.27	0.64	0.26	0.90	...	...	0.756	1.91
		(0.25)	(1.92)	(1.03)	(2.54)	(1.22)	(5.72)				
	Hybrid	2.17	−0.61	0.27	0.52	0.24	0.76	0.12	0.12	0.740	1.84
		(0.28)	(1.64)	(0.98)	(1.69)	(1.11)	(3.21)	(0.74)	(0.50)		
Chile	Basic	−9.3	−1.27	0.81	1.14	−0.10	1.04	...	...	0.972	1.96
		(0.72)	(1.52)	(3.65)	(7.53)	(0.48)	(5.61)				
	Hybrid	4.13	−1.72	−0.23	1.14	−0.65	0.49	−0.23	0.38	0.980	2.36
		(0.33)	(2.31)	(0.46)	(8.41)	(2.23)	(1.68)	(0.46)	(2.47)		
Colombia[c]	Basic	4.62	−1.82	−0.01	0.43	0.59	1.02	...	...	0.655	1.17
		(0.76)	(5.63)	(0.05)	(1.66)	(2.93)	(3.09)				
	Hybrid	7.48	−1.17	0.08	0.12	0.35	0.47	0.41	0.19	0.937	2.02
		(2.80)	(6.41)	(1.31)	(1.07)	(2.91)	(2.69)	(4.24)	(3.03)		

Dominican Republic	Basic	−1.15	0.04	0.55	0.09	0.43	0.52	...	...	0.576	1.62
		(0.75)	(0.26)	(2.30)	(0.69)	(3.22)	(4.23)				
	Hybrid	−1.04	0.13	0.33	−0.01	0.32	0.31	0.17	0.27	0.617	1.79
		(0.71)	(0.73)	(1.29)	(0.04)	(2.23)	(1.92)	(0.81)	(1.62)		
Ecuador	Basic	−2.71	0.16	0.13	0.23	0.28	0.51	...	...	0.818	2.31
		(2.29)	(0.65)	(0.55)	(1.71)	(3.50)	(4.77)				
	Hybrid	0.44	−0.32	−0.05	0.16	0.13	0.29	0.60	0.22	0.957	2.36
		(0.60)	(2.31)	(0.41)	(2.50)	(2.94)	(4.94)	(6.85)	(4.50)		
Egypt[d]	Basic	2.93	−0.57	0.18	0.15	0.22	0.37	...	...	0.698	1.80
		(2.16)	(3.28)	(1.06)	(1.15)	(1.66)	(3.46)				
	Hybrid	2.65	−0.55	0.04	0.15	0.16	0.31	0.28	−0.05	0.719	1.86
		(1.96)	(3.27)	(0.24)	(1.16)	(1.16)	(2.32)	(1.64)	(0.71)		
El Salvador	Basic	1.79	−0.66	0.07	0.31	0.24	0.55	...	...	0.755	1.71
		(1.67)	(3.55)	(0.41)	(2.57)	(1.91)	(6.03)				
	Hybrid	1.91	−0.69	0.06	0.24	0.20	0.44	0.08	0.11	0.736	1.79
		(1.70)	(3.36)	(0.31)	(1.32)	(1.53)	(2.57)	(0.79)	(0.69)		
Ghana[e]	Basic	2.66	−0.65	0.13	0.46	0.20	0.66	...	...	0.649	1.21
		(0.79)	(2.60)	(0.64)	(3.25)	(1.15)	(3.23)				
	Hybrid	3.26	−0.76	0.30	0.36	0.10	0.46	0.18	0.21	0.659	1.10
		(0.91)	(2.92)	(1.29)	(2.37)	(0.49)	(1.89)	(0.73)	(1.33)		
Guatemala	Basic	2.94	−0.54	1.07	0.14	0.03	0.17	...	...	0.531	1.89
		(1.40)	(1.41)	(4.09)	(2.01)	(0.57)	(1.90)				
	Hybrid	2.54	−0.41	0.78	0.01	0.00	0.00	0.62	0.27	0.941	2.18
		(3.32)	(3.02)	(5.94)	(0.32)	(0.62)	(0.11)	(7.35)	(3.70)		

Table 3-20 (*continued*)

Country	Model	Constant	Income, Y'	Cost of liquidity, A'	Money supply, M'	Money supply lagged, M'_{-1}	Money supply, actual plus lagged, $M' + M'_{-1}$	Relative price of food, P'_r	Import price, P'_m	Coefficient of determination, $\bar{R}^2$	Durbin-Watson
India	Basic	−2.48	−0.88	−0.31	0.72	0.63	1.35	...	...	0.463	1.73
		(0.58)	(1.77)	(0.96)	(1.54)	(1.20)	(3.39)				
	Hybrid	0.18	−0.11	0.01	−0.13	0.60	0.47	0.48	0.24	0.762	1.91
		(0.06)	(0.31)	(0.04)	(0.35)	(1.50)	(1.36)	(2.32)	(3.49)		
Iran[b]	Basic	−0.33	0.10	0.48	0.13	0.07	0.20	...	...	0.555	1.57
		(0.18)	(1.12)	(2.07)	(1.92)	(0.69)	(1.47)				
	Hybrid	1.80	−0.15	0.36	0.04	0.04	0.08	−0.14	0.73	0.766	1.90
		(1.04)	(1.52)	(1.97)	(0.68)	(0.47)	(0.67)	(0.53)	(3.20)		
Iraq	Basic	0.60	0.006	0.40	0.13	0.06	0.19	...	...	0.438	1.45
		(0.65)	(0.21)	(2.31)	(2.74)	(1.37)	(2.88)				
	Hybrid	1.44	−0.12	0.20	0.07	0.00	0.07	0.04	0.57	0.675	2.05
		(1.94)	(2.68)	(1.4)	(1.71)	(0.13)	(1.04)	(0.27)	(3.28)		
Korea[e]	Basic	15.66	0.13	0.34	−0.27	0.13	−0.14	...	...	0.283	1.79
		(3.17)	(0.42)	(2.13)	(1.93)	(0.90)	(0.73)				
	Hybrid	11.66	0.07	0.29	−0.27	0.23	−0.04	−0.01	0.08	0.209	1.41
		(1.72)	(0.17)	(1.46)	(1.06)	(1.06)	(0.16)	(0.03)	(0.90)		
Malaysia[e]	Basic	−1.35	−0.14	0.29	0.26	0.25	0.51	...	...	0.756	2.02
		(1.02)	(0.80)	(0.99)	(2.77)	(2.46)	(5.05)				
	Hybrid	0.57	−0.13	0.20	0.18	0.04	0.22	0.23	0.11	0.858	1.72
		(0.55)	(1.04)	(0.96)	(2.69)	(0.93)	(2.07)	(2.72)	(0.84)		

Mexico	Basic	−0.89	−1.27	−0.21	0.65	0.58	1.23	...	...	0.640	1.80
		(0.32)	(3.77)	(1.17)	(3.35)	(3.13)	(5.36)				
	Hybrid	3.31	−1.26	−0.11	0.45	0.33	0.78	0.11	0.21	0.781	1.80
		(1.32)	(3.67)	(0.76)	(2.25)	(2.04)	(2.96)	(1.38)	(1.23)		
Morocco[d]	Basic	−3.07	−0.06	−0.27	0.50	0.20	0.70	...	...	0.442	1.71
		(1.19)	(0.21)	(0.79)	(2.74)	(0.91)	(3.13)				
	Hybrid	2.26	0.03	0.64	0.08	−0.16	−0.08	0.54	0.26	0.854	1.14
		(1.37)	(0.20)	(2.65)	(0.65)	(1.24)	(0.46)	(2.28)	(4.94)		
Nigeria[f]	Basic	−0.09	−0.04	−0.06	0.28	0.18	0.46	...	...	0.750	2.91
		(0.04)	(0.46)	(0.26)	(4.06)	(1.89)	(4.66)				
	Hybrid	0.64	−0.24	−0.26	0.20	0.09	−0.29	0.55	0.30	0.888	1.97
		(0.41)	(2.14)	(1.48)	(3.54)	(1.12)	(2.82)	(3.17)	(1.30)		
Pakistan[e]	Basic	8.73	−0.86	0.32	−0.12	0.43	0.31	...	...	0.206	0.84
		(1.36)	(1.50)	(0.91)	(0.32)	(1.15)	(0.73)				
	Hybrid	0.03	0.25	0.13	0.30	0.05	0.35	−0.44	0.52	0.454	1.33
		(0.00)	(0.25)	(0.41)	(0.75)	(0.14)	(0.86)	(0.66)	(1.88)		
Peru	Basic	9.57	−0.77	0.39	0.23	0.01	0.24	...	...	0.398	1.40
		(3.98)	(2.68)	(1.95)	(2.37)	(0.01)	(2.35)				
	Hybrid	9.54	−0.81	0.37	0.20	−0.04	0.16	−0.02	0.18	0.416	1.72
		(3.40)	(2.22)	(1.49)	(1.71)	(0.37)	(1.34)	(0.32)	(1.52)		
Philippines[e,g]	Basic	0.37	−0.52	−0.11	0.42	0.56	0.98	...	...	0.467	2.55
		(0.10)	(1.03)	(0.51)	(1.24)	(2.10)	(3.96)				
	Hybrid	−3.42	0.37	−0.14	0.07	0.54	0.61	0.22	0.08	0.674	1.91
		(0.92)	(0.54)	(0.70)	(0.19)	(2.20)	(1.84)	(2.15)	(1.12)		

Table 3-20 (*continued*)

Country	Model	Constant	Income, Y'	Cost of liquidity, A'	Money supply, M'	Money supply lagged, M'_{-1}	Money supply, actual plus lagged, $M' + M'_{-1}$	Relative price of food, P'_r	Import price, P'_m	Coefficient of determination, $\bar{R}^2$	Durbin-Watson
Sri Lanka	Basic	−0.22	0.24	0.71	0.19	0.18	0.37	...	...	0.428	1.20
		(0.16)	(1.32)	(2.22)	(1.32)	(1.29)	(2.14)				
	Hybrid	2:15	0.05	0.46	−0.16	0.03	−0.13	−0.04	0.21	0.631	1.54
		(1.41)	(0.30)	(1.68)	(0.97)	(0.20)	(0.60)	(0.22)	(3.15)		
Sudan[h]	Basic	−4.14	−0.10	−0.21	0.65	0.17	0.82	...	...	0.330	1.63
		(0.81)	(0.42)	(1.0)	(2.74)	(0.76)	(2.37)				
	Hybrid	3.40	−0.29	−0.12	0.11	−0.09	0.02	0.14	0.71	0.789	2.27
		(1.0)	(1.59)	(0.96)	(0.63)	(0.60)	(0.05)	(0.97)	(4.82)		
Syria	Basic	−2.43	−0.30	0.25	0.29	0.37	0.66	...	...	0.575	1.65
		(0.97)	(2.38)	(1.0)	(1.70)	(2.36)	(4.55)				
	Hybrid	−0.66	−0.26	0.18	−0.15	0.46	0.31	0.19	0.52	0.889	2.34
		(0.50)	(3.57)	(1.37)	(1.2)	(4.81)	(3.17)	(1.27)	(5.07)		
Taiwan[e]	Basic	9.44	−1.81	−0.26	0.42	0.26	0.68	...	...	0.736	2.01
		(1.70)	(5.22)	(1.57)	(2.12)	(1.50)	(2.84)				
	Hybrid	15.92	−1.26	−0.23	0.14	−0.18	0.04	0.38	0.39	0.918	1.89
		(4.52)	(5.29)	(2.01)	(1.11)	(1.3)	(−0.20)	(2.00)	(3.13)		

Thailand	Basic	−5.34	−0.10	−0.05	0.42	0.71	1.13	...	...	0.620	1.78
		(2.10)	(0.48)	(0.20)	(1.92)	(2.70)	(4.81)				
	Hybrid	−0.78	−0.08	−0.23	0.00	0.37	0.37	−0.23	0.34	0.895	1.86
		(0.51)	(0.79)	(1.64)	(0.01)	(2.50)	(2.15)	(2.79)	(5.92)		
Tunisia[d]	Basic	2.02	−0.17	−0.14	0.19	0.06	0.25	...	...	−0.013	1.35
		(1.06)	(1.10)	(0.57)	(1.30)	(0.44)	(1.57)				
	Hybrid	2.07	−0.36	−0.10	0.27	0.02	0.29	0.22	0.12	0.169	1.82
		(1.18)	(1.96)	(0.43)	(1.85)	(0.17)	(1.90)	(0.94)	(2.00)		
Venezuela	Basic	−0.02	0.03	0.34	−0.01	0.22	0.21	...	...	0.683	1.53
		(0.03)	(0.90)	(2.04)	(0.23)	(4.67)	(5.37)				
	Hybrid	0.24	−0.02	0.33	−0.05	0.21	0.16	0.16	0.14	0.704	2.04
		(0.35)	(0.36)	(1.67)	(0.75)	(3.00)	(3.54)	(0.51)	(0.93)		

Source: Data on import prices from UN Conference on Trade and Development, *Handbook of International Trade and Development Statistics, 1976*, UN Doc. TD/STAT. 6; income data from OECD, *National Accounts of Less Developed Countries, 1950–1966* (Paris: OECD, 1968), *International Financial Statistics*, various issues, and UN, *Monthly Bulletin of Statistics*, various issues.

a. Absolute values of *t*-statistics are in parentheses.
b. Based on 1960–75 data.
c. Equation estimated with a dummy variable for the year in which an extreme change in exchange rate occurred.
d. Based on 1961–75 data.
e. Based on 1959–75 data.
f. Based on 1964–75 data.
g. Based on 1958–75 data.
h. Based on 1959–74 data.

CHAPTER FOUR

Brazil's Aggressive Response to External Shocks

WILLIAM R. CLINE

BRAZIL was one of the developing countries most favorably situated to escape the international economic shocks of the early 1970s. Its economy is larger than any other developing country's and the weight of the external sector is relatively small.[1] Brazil's history of high rates of domestic inflation had prepared households, firms, and public institutions for reacting to inflation (in contrast to countries with traditions of price stability and fiscal conservatism). Furthermore, since the late 1960s Brazil had followed a policy of frequent, small devaluations of the exchange rate designed to neutralize high domestic inflation. In principle this series of minidevaluations could have been adjusted to offset accelerating external inflation. Yet the Brazilian economy did not escape the shocks of external inflation and recession.

Both inflation and real economic growth have been high in Brazil since World War II. In the 1950s real economic growth averaged 6–7 percent annually. Inflation averaged 16 percent in the mid-1950s, but the ambitious development programs of the Kubitschek regime and the political instability of the early 1960s pushed the average to 52 percent in 1959–

I AM INDEBTED to Bela Balassa, Edmar Bacha, Claudio Contador, Antonio Lemgruber, Pedro Malan, and Affonso Pastore for their helpful suggestions during the preparation of this chapter.

1. Its gross national product in 1976 was $126 billion; *World Bank Atlas, 1977.* In 1977, imports and exports represented 8.1 percent of GNP; "Parâmetros da economia brasileira," *Conjuntura econômica,* vol. 32 (February 1978), p. 19. The economy was even more closed in the mid-1960s; see William R. Cline, "Brazil's Emerging International Economic Role," in Riordan Roett, ed., *Brazil in the Seventies* (Washington: American Enterprise Institute for Public Policy Research, 1976), p. 64.

64.[2] When the military took power in 1964, growth was stagnant and inflation had reached the rate of 90.5 percent a year; the new regime applied a shock treatment that brought inflation down to 38 percent annually by 1966, but only at the cost of further slow growth. Subsequently, the government switched to a policy of gradualism in fighting inflation, while instituting reforms such as price indexing, tariff liberalization, minidevaluations (which helped exporters), and export incentives. Exports began to grow rapidly after a long period of stagnation. After 1966 the rate of inflation steadily declined, reaching a low of 15 percent in 1973. Real economic growth was even more impressive, reaching a remarkable average of 11 percent in 1968–73. In 1974 and 1975, however, inflation began to accelerate again, averaging approximately 28 percent, and in 1976 and 1977 it reached an average rate of 42 percent. At the same time, real economic growth fell to only 5.6 percent in 1975, rebounded to 9.2 percent in 1976, but fell to 4.7 percent in 1977.[3] Something had gone wrong with the Brazilian economic "miracle."[4] This chapter examines, with statistical tests, the transmission of external inflation into Brazil through the growth in international reserves in 1970–73, through the direct impact of higher prices for imported products in 1973 and 1974, and through Brazil's own protective response in 1975. It also examines the retarding effect of world recession on Brazilian exports and economic growth in 1974, 1975, and to some extent 1976. The discussion ends with an evaluation of the policy response to these external shocks.

The Monetary Impact of World Inflation

The initial phase of external inflationary pressure on the Brazilian economy began in 1972, well before the oil price increase, through the monetary channel. In that year Brazil's foreign reserves rose by 140 percent

2. See Werner Baer and Isaac Kerstenetzky, *Inflation and Growth in Latin America* (Irwin, 1964), p. 369; Antonio C. Lemgruber, "Inflation in Brazil," in Lawrence B. Krause and Walter S. Salant, eds., *Worldwide Inflation: Theory and Recent Experience* (Brookings Institution, 1977), pp. 397–401.

3. "Parâmetros da economia brasileira," p. 19.

4. Some analysts maintain that there had been no miracle; instead, the economy was merely following its natural long-term cycle, aided by an abnormally buoyant international economy. Edmar L. Bacha, "Issues and Evidence on Recent Brazilian Economic Growth," and Pedro S. Malan and Regis Bonelli, "The Brazilian Economy in the Seventies: Old and New Developments," *World Development*, vol. 5 (January–February 1977), pp. 19–45, 47–67.

Table 4-1. *Growth in Brazil's International Reserves, Money Supply, and Domestic Credit, 1962–77*

	International reserves			*Percentage growth*	
Year	*Millions of dollars*[a]	*Billions of 1970 cruzeiros*[a]	*Money supply (billions of 1970 cruzeiros)*[a]	*Dollar value of reserves*	*Domestic credit*
1962	285	2.06	25.84	−39.4	61.8
1963	219	1.18	24.07	−23.2	60.8
1964	245	2.17	24.53	11.9	76.6
1965	484	3.35	28.23	97.6	49.4
1966	425	2.09	23.21	−12.2	27.0
1967	199	0.95	26.16	−53.2	58.2
1968	257	1.40	30.28	29.1	55.6
1969	656	3.41	32.73	155.3	34.7
1970	1,187	5.88	34.74	80.9	29.3
1971	1,746	8.11	37.59	47.1	41.4
1972	4,183	18.20	44.36	139.6	31.9
1973	6,415	24.22	56.94	53.4	46.6
1974	5,272	18.42	59.43	−17.8	58.5
1975	4,034	13.46	67.43	−23.5	51.5
1976	6,541	21.16	64.22	62.1	53.7
1977	5,994[b]	17.89	60.08	−9.1	42.7

Source: *International Financial Statistics*, vol. 30 (May 1977), and vol. 31 (April 1978).
a. End of year.
b. End of November.

(table 4-1), from $1.7 billion to $4.2 billion. Monetary authorities were able to sterilize most of this enormous surge in reserves. In 1973, however, foreign reserves once again rose dramatically (by 53 percent), but this time the authorities did not make compensating reductions in other elements of the monetary base. On the contrary, the Bank of Brazil rapidly expanded lending, and very little government borrowing in the open market took place. As a result, the money supply grew at the highly inflationary rate of 48 percent over the year.[5] The inflationary pressure from increasing reserves resulted in part no doubt from the global outpouring of dollars as the Bretton Woods regime of fixed exchange rates broke down. The dollars that flowed out of the United States in anticipation of a devaluation went not only to Europe and Japan but also to developing

5. Francisco Lafaiete Lopes, "Problemas do controle da inflação," in Dionísio Dias Carneiro, ed., *Brasil: dilemas da política econômica* (Rio de Janeiro: Editôra Campus, 1977), pp. 61–79. Lopes cites the 1973 growth in money supply as the main reason for the resurgence of inflation in 1974. Import price increases in 1974, however, seem to have been more important in explaining the reacceleration.

countries—especially to credit-worthy middle-income countries like Brazil.[6]

In Brazil a strategy of debt-led growth was also at work. Relying heavily on foreign capital to supplement domestic savings in the push for rapid growth, Brazil borrowed large sums externally in the 1970s. This aggressive borrowing strategy required a large base of external reserves to serve as equity for much larger, leveraged, amounts of debt being contracted—a good credit rating depended on a fairly constant ratio of external debt to reserves.[7] The indirect, perhaps unanticipated, result of this substantial accumulation of reserves was constant pressure on the domestic money supply, which would increase by a multiple of any reserve increases that were not sterilized.

Table 4-1 shows that over the sixteen-year period 1962–77 there is a relatively close correlation in the growth of reserves and domestic money supply. There is not a close relationship in their year-to-year variation, however.[8] The data do suggest a dominant role of reserve changes in the

6. See "Comments by Edward S. Shaw," on Lemgruber, "Inflation in Brazil," pp. 442–45.

7. If creditworthiness, C, is a function, f, of the ratio of debt servicing to exports, S/X, and reserves relative to imports, R/M, then $C = f\,(S/X, R/M)$ with a negative derivative with respect to S/X and a positive derivative with respect to R/M. See Charles R. Frank, Jr., and William R. Cline, "Measurement of Debt Servicing Capacity: An Application of Discriminant Analysis," *Journal of International Economics,* vol. 1 (August 1971), pp. 327–44. Extra borrowing, ΔD will lead to extra debt service of $(i + a)\Delta D$, where i is the interest rate and a the amortization rate. If the borrowed funds are fully spent abroad, the creditworthiness indicator falls by

$$f_d'(i + a)\Delta D/X,$$

where f_d' indicates partial derivative with respect to S/X and X is the level of exports. (The indicator falls still further as imports rise when the funds are spent, because R/M falls. This fall may be offset eventually by a rise in exports generated by the investment project.) If instead some portion of the borrowings, $\phi\Delta D$, is used to build up reserves, the net decline in creditworthiness will be only

$$f_d'(i + a)\Delta D/X + f_R'\phi\Delta D/M,$$

where f_R' is the partial derivative of C with respect to R/M. Thus creditworthiness can be kept from falling as far as it otherwise would by retaining some of the borrowings as extra reserves. However, a side effect of this strategy is to raise the domestic money supply by $m\phi\Delta D$, where m is the money multiplier, unless authorities succeed in sterilizing the increase in reserves. If sterilization is difficult or impossible, there is a conflict between the objectives of establishing a good credit rating and controlling the money supply.

8. A simple regression of money supply on reserves (both in 1970 cruzeiros) shows a correlation of 0.90 which is significant at the 95 percent level. Regressions of the percentage changes of the two variables, or of their first differences, show no significant relationship, nor is there significant correlation when reserves are lagged one year in these formulations.

behavior of Brazilian money supply in the early 1970s. From 1970 through 1973, larger and larger increments in reserves were associated with increments of almost equal magnitudes in the money supply. Reserves quadrupled, growing by about 18 billion cruzeiros, while the money supply rose by 22 billion cruzeiros (both in 1970 cruzeiros). Given a money multiplier of approximately 2,[9] it is clear that Brazilian authorities were sterilizing a good portion of the increase in foreign reserves; otherwise the increase in the money supply from reserve changes alone would have been almost twice as large as it was (each extra cruzeiro in foreign reserves would have called forth two extra cruzeiros in the money supply). When the sterilization efforts largely broke down in 1973, the money supply grew by 48 percent, or by more than in any year since 1965.

Table 4-1 also illustrates the inverse relationship between the growth of foreign reserves and the growth of domestic credit in Brazil—in years when the growth of international reserves is high, the growth of domestic credit tends to be low. The inverse relationship appears to be partially the effect of sterilization efforts—the authorities reduce domestic credit (or slow its growth) when reserves are growing rapidly. But the cause of the negative relationship may be more ominous: the availability of foreign credit may provide domestic and especially multinational firms a means of circumventing monetary stringency being imposed by domestic authorities.[10] Thus, when authorities try to tighten money and slow down the growth of domestic credit, firms can borrow more abroad and the result will be an expansion of foreign reserves and a larger growth of money supply than the monetary authorities desire. In such circumstances, domestic authorities essentially lose control of the money supply.[11]

Inflation Imported through the Trade Channel

The external stimulus to inflation through the monetary channel receded in 1974 and 1975, but it was replaced by the inflation in the prices

9. "Comments by Edward S. Shaw," p. 444.

10. I am indebted to Affonso Celso Pastore for this point.

11. The stronger negative correlation between reserve growth and domestic credit growth for 1968–77 (−0.72) than for 1962–77 (−0.53) suggests that when Brazil became more credit worthy in the late 1960s by strengthening export performance, and when it introduced special instruments whereby foreign exchange could be brought in with an automatic right to reconversion, the problem of harmonizing financial inflows and domestic credit policy became more severe.

of imported goods. In 1974 Brazil's balance of payments entered a period of crisis. Imports rose from $7 billion in 1973 to $14.2 billion. Brazil's import bill for petroleum rose from $1 billion to $3.2 billion, but that was only about one-third of the total increase.[12] The price of other raw materials—wheat, copper, fruits, chemicals, coal—rose by 97 percent, although the impact was diluted by the low price rises for capital goods (8.5 percent) and consumer goods (−3.8 percent).[13] More surprising than the rise in import costs was the 40.8 percent rise in volume of imports. The total rise in import value was thus about evenly divided between the rises in prices and in quantity imported.[14] One of the causes of the rapid growth in imports appears to have been speculative stockpiling, as importers responded to rising prices of raw materials and to the prospect that the oil crisis would force the government to limit imports (as indeed it did).[15] The excessive expansion of private credit,[16] the failure of the exchange rate to depreciate in real terms,[17] and the new military government's willingness to continue its ambitious development plans all added to the burden on Brazil's imports.[18] The result was a disequilibrium in the balance of payments that was to act as the key factor limiting economic policy choices over the next three years. Clearly, world inflation, acting directly through increases in import prices, contributed to this crisis. Just as clearly, many of the pressures came from the domestic economy.

Whether imported inflation exacerbated internal Brazilian inflation is a controversial issue (with implications for whether the reacceleration of inflation in 1974 was due to domestic mismanagement or external shocks). The influential Brazilian periodical *Conjuntura econômica* in an early assessment noted that the beginning of acceleration of Brazilian inflation coincided with the increase in petroleum prices. However, it also noted that the increase followed, with a six-to-nine-month lag, the high rate of growth of money supply in 1973.[19] For its part, the United Nations Economic Commission for Latin America classified Brazil in a group of

12. *International Financial Statistics,* vol. 30 (May 1977), pp. 61, 101.

13. Computed from *Conjuntura econômica,* vol. 32 (February 1978), p. 318.

14. "Balança comercial brasileira—o impacto da crise mundial," *Conjuntura econômica,* vol. 29 (December 1975), p. 75.

15. See Malan and Bonelli, "Brazilian Economy in the Seventies," p. 30.

16. "Balança comercial brasileira," p. 79.

17. See Cline, "Brazil's Emerging International Economic Role," pp 67–70, and the subsequent discussion in this chapter.

18. Malan and Bonelli, "Brazilian Economy in the Seventies," p. 30.

19. "O Brasil e a crise mundial—impacto e ajustamento," *Conjuntura econômica,* vol. 29 (December 1975), p. 73.

five Latin American countries showing "a fairly equal combination of imported inflation and domestic factors" in 1973–74, in contrast with fourteen countries with a "predominance of imported inflation" and three with a "predominance of domestic inflationary factors."[20]

Antonio C. Lemgruber, in an econometric analysis of the role of imported inflation in Brazil for the period 1952–73, concluded that the main determinants were domestic but that "external factors—mainly exchange rate variations—certainly cannot be neglected" in explaining domestic inflation.[21] However, the time period of his tests did not cover the years 1974–76 when imported inflation was most severe; the variable for world inflation was based on consumer prices in five industrial countries instead of Brazil's own import prices; and the model's inclusion of the exchange rate as an explanatory variable for domestic inflation biased the results, as discussed below. Perhaps for these reasons Lemgruber found no significant influence of world inflation on Brazilian inflation, although he did find a significant relationship between domestic prices and the exchange rate.

The analysis here uses an index of import prices in dollars, rather than cruzeiros, to capture the influence of imported inflation. In Brazil, domestic inflation is so persistent and rapid that as a matter of course the exchange rate is devalued systematically to keep pace with domestic inflation. To use a variable in the investigation of inflation that incorporates the exchange rate (either by itself or combined with the dollar price in the domestic, cruzeiro price of imports) would cause a bias in favor of the hypothesis of imported inflation. The exchange rate and domestic inflation would inevitably be found to be moving together, leading to the conclusion of imported inflation even if world dollar prices were absolutely stable.[22]

20. United Nations, Economic and Social Council, Economic Commission for Latin America, *Economic Survey of Latin America 1975,* vol. 1, UN Doc. E/CEPAL/1014, July 1, 1976, pp. 72–73. The other countries with combined imported and domestic factors were Bolivia, Barbados, Colombia, and Costa Rica. Countries with predominantly imported inflation were Paraguay, Ecuador, Mexico, Jamaica, El Salvador, Haiti, Trinidad and Tobago, Peru, Panama, Guatemala, Guyana, Honduras, Venezuela, and the Dominican Republic. The countries with predominantly domestic inflationary sources were Argentina, Chile, and Uruguay; ibid., p. 72.

21. Lemgruber, "Inflation in Brazil," p. 431.

22. It may be shown formally that a statistical bias occurs if the exchange rate is used to represent import prices when exchange-rate policy is of the type followed by Brazilian authorities. The problem is one of simultaneity. Consider a single equation model of the form $\dot{P} = f(\dot{P}^d_m, Z)$, where $\dot{P}$ is the rate of domestic inflation, $\dot{P}^d_m$ is the rate of inflation of import prices stated in terms of domestic currency (or the rate of change of the product of the exchange rate and the import price in foreign currency), and Z represents

For Brazil, an index of dollar prices of imports seems an appropriate variable for import price inflation. In a structure in which domestic prices rise as the result of cost-push factors (including indexing of price increases), monetary expansion, and other forces, an increase of dollar prices of imports will add to cost-push inflation. If domestic inflation is running at 20 percent annually and dollar import prices suddenly rise by 40 percent, then unless the exchange rate appreciates, import prices expressed in domestic currency will rise by more than the 20 percent rise for all other good and services. The relative rise of import prices in domestic currency will cause a general acceleration of prices above the 20 percent rate.

In Brazil in 1973 and especially in 1974 the dollar price of imports inflated more rapidly than domestic prices (table 4-2); nevertheless, Brazil depreciated in both years.[23] The pressure from rising dollar prices of imports was passed on through domestic prices of imports and import substitutes into the domestic economy.

The information in table 4-2 is used in the models of imported inflation estimated here. The dependent variable is domestic inflation (based on weighted averages of the wholesale price index and the indexes of consumer prices and construction costs for Rio de Janeiro). The independent variables are the inflation rate for dollar prices of imports (based on the index of import unit values), the rate of growth of money supply (speci-

---

all other influences. Suppose that exchange-rate determination is such that $\dot{E} = \dot{P} - \dot{P}_w$, where $\dot{E}$ is the rate of depreciation of the exchange rate and $\dot{P}_w$ the rate of world inflation in foreign currency (say, dollar) prices. The second equation in fact describes the behavior of Brazilian authorities: they have devalued the cruzeiro over time at a rate equal approximately to the difference between domestic inflation and foreign inflation (as represented, for example, by wholesale price increases in the United States, Germany, and Japan). Now, by definition, $\dot{P}^d_m = \dot{P}^\$_m + \dot{E} + \dot{P}^\$_m\dot{E}$, where $\dot{P}^\$_m$ is the rate of inflation of dollar prices of imports. Therefore the first equation may be written $\dot{P} = f(\dot{P}^\$_m + \dot{E} + \dot{P}^\$_m E, Z)$. And because $\dot{E} = \dot{P} - \dot{P}_w$, this last equation may be written as $\dot{P} = f(\{\dot{P}^\$_m + [\dot{P} - \dot{P}_w] + \dot{P}^\$_m[\dot{P} - \dot{P}^\$_w]\}, Z)$. In this final equation the dependent variable $\dot{P}$ appears on both sides. Thus, the simultaneity of the first two equations causes the dependent variable to appear on both sides of the single estimating equation and there will therefore be an upward bias in the coefficient on import price when that equation is used.

23. The authorities probably were basing Brazil's depreciation on the rate of domestic inflation relative to inflation in the United States and other industrial countries, which was much lower than the dollar price inflation of Brazil's imports. In 1973 and 1974, world trade prices inflated much more rapidly than domestic prices in the industrial countries, reversing the usual relationship between the two rates. Brazil needed to depreciate the exchange rate in order to achieve external balance; the devaluation was not sufficient to do that.

Table 4-2. *Indicators of Imported Inflation and Associated Factors in Brazil, 1961–77*

Year	*Inflation rate (percent)* Domestic prices[a]	Dollar import prices[b]	Exchange-rate depreciation (percent)	Money supply growth (percent)	Index of protection[c]
1961	37.0	0.0	48.9	50.6	218
1962	51.6	0.0	68.1	63.3	254
1963	75.4	2.2	51.9	64.0	275
1964	90.5	1.1	86.2	85.9	223
1965	56.8	2.2	80.5	75.4	199
1966	38.0	0.0	24.1	16.3	163
1967	28.3	3.2	17.8	43.1	136
1968	24.2	−1.0	24.4	42.3	134
1969	20.8	−1.1	26.4	32.8	145
1970	19.8	5.3	11.6	26.7	145
1971	20.4	9.0	18.0	31.3	160
1972	17.0	8.3	12.4	38.9	151
1973	15.1	20.3	1.0	48.0	152
1974	28.7	54.9	11.7	34.8	182
1975	27.7	5.5	19.9	44.9	215
1976	41.3	1.0	31.3	33.8	224
1977	42.7	5.9	31.3	43.9	224

Sources: *Conjuntura econômica*, various issues; United Nations Conference on Trade and Development, *Handbook of International Trade and Development Statistics, 1976*, UN Doc. TD/STAT. 6, p. 442; *International Financial Statistics*, vol. 30 (May 1977), pp. 48–49, 98–99, and vol. 31 (April 1978), pp. 72, 74–75; Affonso Celso Pastore, José Roberto Mendonça de Barros, and Décio Kadota, "A teoria da paridade do poder de compra, minidesvalorizações e o equilibrio da balança comercial brasileira," *Pesquisa e planejamento econômico*, vol. 6 (August 1976), p. 299.

a. Year-over-year index of prices of goods and services for internal use. Equals weighted average of wholesale price index, consumer price index for Rio de Janeiro, and construction cost index for Rio de Janeiro.

b. Import prices are from unit value indexes.

c. The index equals 100 plus the percentage tariff equivalent of tariffs and other protective barriers. Estimates for 1975–77 are extrapolated from 1974 estimates by adding the 100 percent increase in tariffs on superfluous goods (8 percent of imports according to "Balança comercial—comportamento recente e perspectiva," *Conjuntura econômica*, vol. 29 [December 1975], p. 84) and by adding 30 percent on all others; for 1975 the cost effect of a 180-day prior deposit is added and for 1976 the effect of a 360-day prior deposit (calculated as the annual inflation rate times 0.3, the portion of imports covered by prior deposits).

fied with a six-month lag),[24] and an index of import protection (based on the annual change in the level of tariffs and other barriers to imports). Because the government responded to foreign sector crisis by raising protection, it is important to include protection as an explanatory variable for

24. Money supply was the most important variable in Lemgruber's model of inflation.

domestic inflation. It is likely that the cost-push effects of higher protection beginning in 1975 contributed substantially to accelerating inflation.[25]

The first model, which relates domestic inflation to the rate of growth of the money supply, (dollar) import price inflation, and the rate of change in the level of protection, yields the following results:

$$(1) \qquad \dot{P} = \underset{(0.07)}{0.770} + \underset{(3.85)}{0.850\dot{M}} - \underset{(0.38)}{0.115\dot{P}^m} - \underset{(0.83)}{0.253\dot{P}^m_{t-1}} + \underset{(0.72)}{0.162\dot{T}_{t-1}}$$

$$\bar{R}^2 = 0.52$$

where $\dot{P}$ is the rate of domestic inflation (percent per year), $\dot{M}$ the rate of growth of money supply with six months lag, $\dot{P}^m$ and $\dot{P}^m_{t-1}$ the rate of inflation in dollar import prices in the current and previous years, respectively, and $\dot{T}_{t-1}$ the percent change in the protection index for the previous year (*t*-statistics are in parentheses). The equation reveals the strong influence of money supply in explaining inflation, as expected. The protection variable has the correct sign, but it is not statistically significant, and the terms for import price inflation are not significant and have the wrong sign. This is not surprising since import prices were almost unchanged over the 1960s, and their large increases were concentrated in 1973 and 1974. After 1964 there was a long period of declining inflation in Brazil, followed by an abrupt increase in 1974 at just the same time as the import price explosion.

The second model of imported inflation uses as a key independent variable the previous year's rate of inflation, adding the variables for imported inflation to detect their influence in accelerating the underlying rate of inflation. It yields the following results:

$$(2) \qquad \dot{P} = \underset{(0.11)}{-0.79} + \underset{(6.37)}{0.925\dot{P}_{t-1}} + \underset{(1.04)}{0.234\dot{P}^m} + \underset{(3.25)}{0.513\dot{T}_{t-1}},$$

$$\bar{R}^2 = 0.75$$

where $\dot{P}_{t-1}$ is the domestic inflation in the previous year and the other variables are those used in equation 1.

25. Bacha suggests that import restrictions probably had a larger cost-push impact than devaluation would have had. He cites unpublished research by D. Munhoz which concludes that import restrictions have doubled the cost pressures originally caused by the oil price increase of 1973–74. Edmar L. Bacha, "Brazil's Balance of Payments Before and After the Oil Crisis," draft paper, April 1978, p. 15.

This accelerationist formulation performs much better than the initial formulation. The adjusted $\bar{R}^2$ (or fraction of variation explained) rises; the significance of the lagged inflation variable (as measured by the t-statistic) is higher than that of money supply in equation 1; the import-price variable takes on the correct sign; and the variable for protection becomes highly significant.

The results of this model show that there is almost a full repetition of the previous year's inflation (a coefficient on past inflation of 0.925) when other factors remain constant. This is what would be expected under a regime of price indexing. The system of indexing, which Brazil adopted in the 1960s, represents both a bane and a blessing for the economy.[26] It is beneficial in that it removes many of the distortions and redistributive effects that otherwise would accompany inflation at Brazilian rates. However, it aggravates the problems of the kind of cost-push inflation set off by the rise in international prices in 1973–74. The presence of indexing tends to ensure that higher costs caused by such shocks are passed on into higher prices; the induced inflation causes further rises in wages leading to a continuing spiral of inflation.[27]

Equation 2 shows that increased protection contributes substantially to inflation. On theoretical grounds, it should do so directly through its effect on prices of importable goods and indirectly by causing inefficient allocation of factors in the economy. Applying the regression coefficient of approximately 0.5 to the 1975 rise in protection (18 percent), the model would predict an increase of 9 percentage points of inflation from 1975 to 1976. In fact there was an acceleration of inflation of approximately 14 percentage points from 1975 to 1976. Therefore the model

26. For a description of the system see Lemgruber, "Inflation in Brazil"; Albert Fishlow, "Indexing Brazilian Style: Inflation without Tears?" *Brookings Papers on Economic Activity, 1:1974*, pp. 261–80; and Angelo Jorge de Souza and Janes Angelo de Souza, "A Case Study on Inflation in Latin America: Brazil," paper prepared for the 15th General Conference of the International Association for Research in Income and Wealth, University of York, August 19–25, 1977.

27. That was not always so. From 1964 through 1967, wages were indexed by a formula that calculated prospective as well as past inflation; the estimate of future inflation systematically turned out to be too low, and the result was a reduction in real wages. Since 1967, however, the indexing of wages has kept them approximately in line with inflation, largely eliminating the possibility of avoiding cost-push transmission of inflation. The flexibility probably has become even more limited as the political liberalization efforts of the mid-1970s reduced the government's leeway to deal harshly with labor. In May 1978 the government permitted the first major industrial strike (in the São Paulo automotive industry) in fourteen years of military regime.

suggests that higher protection played a key role in the acceleration of inflation by 1976.

An alternative formulation of the accelerationist model that deals directly with changes in the rates of inflation and in the independent variables relates the change in the rate of domestic inflation to changes in the rate of monetary growth, the rate of dollar import price inflation, and a protection index. Its results are:

$$(3) \qquad \Delta\dot{P} = \underset{(0.74)}{-1.97} + \underset{(1.10)}{0.155}\Delta\dot{M} + \underset{(1.64)}{0.279}\Delta\dot{P}^m + \underset{(3.45)}{0.530}\dot{T}_{t-1},$$

$$\bar{R}^2 = 0.46$$

where $\Delta\dot{P}$ is the change in rate of inflation, $\Delta\dot{M}$ the change in rate of money supply growth, and $\Delta\dot{P}^m$ the change in rate of (dollar) import price inflation. The sizes of the coefficients on import prices and on protection are approximately the same as in equation 2. Their levels of significance, however, are higher; the import price variable becomes statistically significant at approximately the 90 percent level. Equation 3 strengthens the argument that inflation is imported through the channels of dollar import prices and protection. In fact, monetary growth is weaker than the other two variables, with a coefficient on its change that is not significant. The degree of explanation, $\bar{R}^2$, is lower in equation 3 than that in equation 2, but this is expected in a model that is based on first differences of variables (general trends are easier to capture than changes from trends).

A final test of the model incorporates the rate of capacity utilization in manufacturing.[28] Because this index is an indicator of the extent of demand tightness in the economy, when it is higher the rate of inflation should be higher. Once again the accelerationist formulation was the most successful, yielding the following results:

$$(4) \quad \Delta\dot{P} = \underset{(0.62)}{-1.62} + \underset{(1.55)}{0.222}\Delta\dot{M} + \underset{(1.73)}{0.282}\Delta\dot{P}^m + \underset{(3.45)}{0.511}\dot{T}_{t-1} + \underset{(1.42)}{0.976}\Delta C,$$

$$\bar{R}^2 = 0.51$$

where ΔC is the change in the capacity utilization index and the other variables are those used in equations 1–3. Although the capacity utilization variable is not significant itself, it has the correct sign, and its inclusion

28. From data in *Conjuntura econômica* reported by Bela Balassa, "Incentive Policies in Brazil," working paper, Washington, D.C., March 17, 1979, p. 13, and for 1961–67, data interpolated from Malan and Bonelli, "Brazilian Economy in the Seventies," p. 29.

raises total explanation ($\bar{R}^2$) as well as the t-statistics of money acceleration and the acceleration of import price inflation.

In sum, the accelerationist model of inflation (especially as formulated in equations 3 and 4) provides strong evidence that imported inflation accelerated Brazilian inflation. It had a direct impact in higher dollar import prices, and a policy-induced impact through higher protection. Both factors appear to have had a cost-push effect on Brazilian inflation beginning in 1974. The calculations (based on data for 1961–77) indicate, as expected, that the full force of imported inflation was concentrated in the period 1974 to 1976. The bulk of the impact of higher protection appears to have occurred in 1976 in response to the large increase in protection in 1975. Similarly, the inflation of import prices had its greatest impact in 1974. In that year dollar import prices rose by approximately 55 percent (table 4-2), representing a rise of 35 percentage points over the rate in 1973. Applying the coefficient on the change in import price inflation in equation 4, the result should have been an estimated increase of inflation by 10 percent in 1974. And indeed inflation did accelerate in 1974, by 13.6 percentage points.[29]

When these results are combined with the findings on inflationary pressure through the monetary channel, they form a sequence of imported inflationary pressures acting through the period 1971–76. The first step was monetary expansion associated with growing international reserves, in 1971–73, the second the pressure of higher import prices on domestic inflation in 1973 but most severe in 1974, and finally the higher protection in response to the balance-of-payments crisis that led to still more inflationary pressure in 1976. Before 1971 the high rates of Brazilian inflation were almost exclusively attributable to internal factors, but from 1971 to 1976 imported inflation was operating to aggravate the underlying rate of inflation.

Another transmission channel for external inflation is the influence of the foreign sector on aggregate demand. As international inflation increases demand for the country's exports and reduces its demand for imports, aggregate demand rises and aggregate supply declines, causing inflationary pressure. However, in the years of high world inflation, 1973 and especially 1974, the foreign sector increased the net availability of

29. If the government understated inflation in 1973 and the actual rate was closer to 20 percent than the reported 15 percent, as many observers believe, then the acceleration in 1974 was even closer to the 10 percent predicted by the change in import price inflation according to equation 4.

supply to Brazil, as import volume grew by 64 percent from 1972 to 1974 while export volume rose by only 17 percent.[30] Nevertheless, by 1975–76 the channel of aggregate demand was transmitting external inflation, as radically increased prices and values of coffee exports exerted inflationary pressure on the economy.

Macroeconomic Developments, 1975–77

The Brazilian government did not react to the extreme disequilibrium in the balance of payments that arose in 1974 by attempting to deflate the economy. On the contrary, in March 1975 the monetary authorities loosened money in the fear of recession, and monetary growth reached a high 44.9 percent over the year (compared with only 34.8 percent in 1974), contributing to rapid industrial growth and high inflation in 1976.[31] Nevertheless, real GDP growth for 1975 was a slow 5.7 percent, and real income growth was even lower because lower terms of trade (due mainly to oil prices) cost Brazil approximately 1.5 percent of GDP.[32]

In the face of this slowdown, the government responded to the crisis in the foreign sector not by pursuing still more deflationary policies, but by stimulating import substitution. It established new incentives (through the Council of Industrial Development) for the development of new capital goods industries and provided new, subsidized credit for them (through the National Bank of Economic Development). The government mandated a general 15 percent reduction in public sector imports and raised tariffs on "superfluous" items by 100 percent and on raw materials and intermediate goods by 30 percent. For imports with tariffs above 37 percent, it imposed a cruzeiro deposit 180 days before the goods were received, which constitutes a severe tax in a time of rapid inflation.[33] These protective measures reversed the trend of trade liberalization begun in the mid-1960s. They did succeed in compressing imports; the nominal dollar value of imports held constant from 1974 through 1977, representing a

30. Calculated from *Conjuntura econômica,* vol. 32 (February 1978), pp. 313, 317.

31. Alberto S. Furuguem, "Aspectos da politica monetaria no Brasil," in Carneiro, *Brasil,* pp. 84–85.

32. *International Financial Statistics Yearbook,* vol. 32 (1979), p. 119; Bacha, "Brazil's Balance of Payments," p. 1.

33. "Balança comercial—comportamento recente e perspectiva," *Conjuntura econômica,* vol. 29 (December 1975), p. 84.

reduction in real imports to approximately their 1973 level (after the 40 percent surge of 1974).

While Brazil's trade balance deficit was being reduced, its current account deficit was worsening. Mounting debt service and profits remissions and a growing deficit on other services held the deficit at a staggering $7 billion in 1975 for the second year in a row.[34] By the end of 1975, external debt had risen to $22 billion from $12.6 billion at the end of 1973.[35]

The expansive monetary and fiscal policies of 1975 and a dramatic rise in world coffee prices (after the Brazilian frost in 1975)[36] brought rapid growth in 1976 (approximately 9 percent in real terms). But inflation also jumped once again, reaching 41.3 percent (or 46.4 percent for December over December).[37] Coffee, which represented approximately 3 percent of the basic price index for "total supply,"[38] added considerably to the inflation since the increase in the international price was passed on to the Brazilian consumer (from 1975 to 1977 the price quadrupled, so that its direct impact on the price index represented more than a tenth of the overall price rise of approximately 100 percent in those years). Higher coffee prices also brought extra foreign-exchange earnings and thus higher foreign reserves (which rose by 62 percent in 1976). Increased reserves meant increased pressure once again for expansion of the monetary base. And the greater income from export earnings led presumably to an even greater expansion in aggregate demand (as the Keynesian demand multiplier suggests).

Recognizing that external borrowing could not continue at the high rates of 1974 and 1975, the government began to cut back some of its ambitious capital development projects (although the full force of cuts was not felt until 1977).[39] Real growth in 1977 fell to 4.7 percent, but inflation fell (to 38.8 percent from December to December) and in the foreign sector, exports rose enough to achieve a slight surplus in the trade balance—a remarkable accomplishment considering that merchandise exports were only half the level of imports in 1974.

34. *International Financial Statistics,* vol. 30 (May 1977), p. 101.

35. Cline, "Brazil's Emerging International Economic Role," p. 71.

36. The average price for coffee exports rose from $0.50 per pound in 1975 to $1.22 in 1976 and $2.04 per pound in 1977. Coffee accounted for approximately 10 percent of export value in 1975 and 20 percent in 1976. *International Financial Statistics,* vol. 31 (April 1978), pp. 34, 74.

37. *Conjuntura econômica,* vol. 32 (February 1978), p. 303.

38. "Indices de preços por atacado—ponderações revistas," *Conjuntura econômica,* vol. 30 (July 1976), pp. 154–61.

39. João Paulo dos Reis Velloso, *Brasil: a solução positiva* (São Paulo: Abril-Tec Editôra, 1978), pp. 124–25.

The Impact of External Recession

The world recession that followed so quickly after the inflationary shocks of 1973–74 caused a slackening in export demand that had adverse consequences for Brazil's trade balance and growth. From 1974 to 1977 Brazil's exports grew by 53 percent in dollar value but only 8 percent in volume, a distinct deceleration from the growth in the three-year period 1971–74 (174 percent and 49 percent, respectively).[40] Favorable price developments for raw materials exports (especially coffee) compensated for slow growth in volume, enabling Brazil to double the dollar value of exports from 1973 to 1977 (and thereby practically close the gulf between exports and imports that opened in 1974).

Government incentives to exports were not greatly increased in response to the balance-of-payments crisis of 1974. In 1975 the government increased credit for exports and expanded the tax incentives for exporters; and firms registering plans for export expansion received exemption from taxes and prior deposits on imports.[41] However, these measures for export expansion were minor compared with the extreme measures taken to compress imports. Devaluation of the exchange rate in real terms was the policy conspicuously absent in dealing with the balance-of-payments crisis.

The wide diversification of Brazil's exports (table 4-3) provided the basis for a strong performance in at least one or two products in each year. In 1974 when the industrial countries entered recession, sugar prices were extremely high, providing a windfall gain for Brazilian exports. In 1975, while sugar export earnings remained high, export earnings from soybeans rose substantially, as the volume of Brazilian soybean production and exports responded vigorously to the dramatic increase in soybean prices of 1973 (and their persistence at relatively high levels thereafter). At the same time, export earnings from iron ore increased considerably as the result of both high prices and higher volume exported. By 1976, sugar export earnings had tumbled along with world sugar prices, but coffee export earnings soared as the world price of coffee more than doubled. By 1977, increased export earnings from cocoa (due to much higher world prices) supplemented still further increases in earnings from coffee and soybeans.

The value of Brazil's principal exports of manufactured goods also

40. Calculated from *International Financial Statistics,* vol. 30 (May 1977), p. 101; vol. 31 (April 1978), p. 74; and table 4-4 below.

41. "Balança comercial—comportamento recente e perspectiva," p. 83.

Table 4-3. *Value of Principal Brazilian Exports, 1973–77*
Millions of dollars (f.o.b.)

Export	*1973*	*1974*	*1975*	*1976*	*1977*
All exports	6,199	7,951	8,670	10,128	12,139
Principal raw materials	3,480	3,987	4,557	5,684	6,622
Coffee[a]	1,324	957	934	2,399	2,642
Soybeans[b]	917	888	1,303	1,759	2,132
Sugar[c]	553	1,259	1,100	306	463
Iron ore	363	571	902	994	908
Cocoa	89	210	220	219	436
Cotton	234	102	98	7	41
Principal manufactured goods	397	766	902	1,003	1,375
Transportation material	91	191	317	373	492
Mechanical machinery	212	455	260	266	427
Electrical machinery	d	d	160	189	281
Shoes	94	120	165	175	175

Source: *Conjuntura econômica,* various issues.
a. Includes industrialized coffee.
b. Beans, meal, and oil.
c. Crystal, natural, and refined.
d. Values of mechanical and electrical machinery reported jointly.

grew rapidly in this period (reflecting export incentives and slack domestic demand, especially in transportation equipment). There was a sharp slowdown in their real growth rates, however, from an annual rate of 26 percent in 1966–73 to 10.6 percent annually for 1973–77.[42]

Brazil's export growth in the face of weak demand from a world economy in recession was impressive but it depended on price increases rather than volume. The data in table 4-4 indicate that the external recession in 1974 and especially in 1975 had a retarding effect on Brazilian exports. The index of Brazil's export volume shows relatively strong growth in 1975 but a decline in 1976 and a 1977 level still below the 1975 peak. The negative effect of the severe world recession of 1975 on Brazil's real export volume seems to have shown up a year later, which corresponds to

42. Balassa reports the latter figure. He also reports value growth of manufactured exports as 38.5 percent annually in 1966–73. "Incentive Policies in Brazil," pp. 8 and 28. Based on export unit values for industrial countries, export prices of manufactured goods probably rose by only 8 percent in 1966–70. Based on Brazil's own price index for manufactured exports, they rose by another 75 percent in 1970–73. The 38.5 percent annual nominal growth rate represented a real growth rate of 26 percent annually for 1966–73. *International Financial Statistics,* vol. 31 (May 1978), p. 49; *Conjuntura econômica,* vol. 32 (February 1978), p. 316.

Table 4-4. *Indexes of Brazilian Export Volume and Price and World Demand, 1960–77*

Year	Brazil's export volume (1970 = 100)	Industrial production: OECD (1970 = 100)	Industrial production: World (1970 = 100)	Brazil's real export prices[a]
1960	62	57	57	2.434
1961	70	59	59	3.015
1962	63	63	63	2.408
1963	72	67	67	2.104
1964	61	72	72	2.544
1965	71	77	77	2.434
1966	78	83	83	2.200
1967	76	85	84	2.188
1968	84	92	91	2.142
1969	97	98	98	2.225
1970	100	100	100	2.189
1971	106	102	102	2.176
1972	135	108	108	2.469
1973	155	119	115	3.279
1974	158	118	119	3.978
1975	174	109	112	3.749
1976	168	119	114	4.216
1977	171	124	116	4.553

Sources: UNCTAD, *Handbook of International Trade and Development Statistics, 1976*, p. 442; *Conjuntura econômica*, vol. 32 (February 1978), p. 313; Organization for Economic Cooperation and Development, *Industrial Production*, various issues; UN, *Monthly Bulletin of Statistics*, vol. 21 (May 1967), vol. 27 (May 1973), and vol. 32 (May 1978); Pastore, Barros, and Kadota, "A teoria da paridade do poder de compra," p. 301.

a. This index, computed by Pastore, Barros, and Kadota, ibid., is based on cruzeiros per dollar at 1965–67 prices; it incorporates the exchange rate, dollar prices of exports, and the value of export incentives. Figures for 1975–77 are my extrapolations based on changing values of the exchange rate, the domestic price index, and the unit value index for exports, assuming unchanged incentives to exports. The 1976 and 1977 increases are heavily influenced by the high world price of coffee.

the normal lags of trade in response to shifts in income. The table also shows the index of real export prices, which represents the combined influences of international prices, the exchange rate, a domestic deflator, and export incentives. The information in table 4-4 is used here in models of world demand for Brazilian exports. The dependent variable is the volume of exports. The independent variables are the indexes of world industrial production (assuming that world activity affects demand for Brazil's exports with a one-year lag), the index of real export prices (assuming that the real prices paid to exporters affect supply), and a dummy representing the practice of minidevaluation of the exchange rate in 1968–77 (which encouraged exporters by giving them some assurance of the real value of their earnings). Other things being held constant, Brazilian exports should have been higher after 1968 than before.

The results of the models using natural logarithms, ln, of the data for 1961 to 1977 are:

$$(5) \quad \ln X = \underset{(0.12)}{-0.014} + \underset{(3.19)}{0.907} \ln Y^{O}_{t-1} + \underset{(3.68)}{0.492} \ln P_x + \underset{(1.23)}{0.134}D$$

$$\bar{R}^2 = 0.935$$

$$(6) \quad \ln X = \underset{(0.29)}{-0.317} + \underset{(3.64)}{0.980} \ln Y^{W}_{t-1} + \underset{(3.93)}{0.484} \ln P_x + \underset{(1.07)}{0.110}D,$$

$$\bar{R}^2 = 0.943$$

where X is the index of export volume, Y^{O}_{t-1} the OECD index and Y^{W}_{t-1} the world index of industrial activity for the previous year, P_x the index of real export prices, and D the dummy for minidevaluation, which is 1 for 1968 to 1977 and 0 for other years.

The coefficient of exports on international industrial activity in each of the equations is close to unity, meaning that in 1961–77 each percentage point of growth in external economic activity called forth approximately 1 percent growth in Brazilian exports. In each equation the coefficient on world activity is highly significant (the results closely resemble those in a model relating Brazil's trade balance to the difference between income growth in the world and in Brazil as well as other variables).[43] The coefficient of real export price is also highly significant, and in both equations it shows an elasticity of approximately 0.5 for the responsiveness of exports to real export price. The dummy variable for 1968 and after shows the correct sign but is not statistically significant in either equation. Thus there is only weak evidence that the system of minidevaluations stimulated Brazilian exports.[44]

The results imply that rising real export prices had a crucial role in ex-

43. Affonso Celso Pastore, José Roberto Mendonça de Barros, and Décio Kadota, "A teoria da paridade do poder de compra, minidesvalorizações e o equilíbrio da balança comercial brasileira," *Pesquisa e planejamento econômico,* vol. 6 (August 1976), find the elasticity of exports with respect to world income to be almost exactly unity.

44. The Pastore model also found the variable for minidevaluations (standard deviation of the real exchange rate, which became lower under the regime of minidevaluations) to have a positive influence on exports but not a statistically significant one; it did show statistical significance on the import side, however; ibid., p. 306.

Table 4-5. *Comparison of Expected Brazilian Exports under Cyclical and Steady Growth Conditions, 1973–77*[a]

	Export level					
	OECD-based model			*World-based model*		
Year	*Cyclical growth (1970 = 100)*	*Steady growth (1970 = 100)*	*Ratio of steady to cyclical level*	*Cyclical growth (1970 = 100)*	*Steady growth (1970 = 100)*	*Ratio of steady to cyclical level*
1973	141	141	1.00	143	143	1.00
1974	170	163	0.96	166	165	0.99
1975	164	167	1.02	167	170	1.02
1976	161	185	1.15	167	188	1.13
1977	181	202	1.11	176	206	1.17

a. The expected levels of exports are calculated from equations 5 and 6 in the text. The cyclical growth estimates are based on the industrial production indexes in table 4-4. The steady growth estimates are based on hypothetical continuation of the world growth rate in 1961–72 of 5.6 percent per annum.

plaining the dynamism of Brazil's exports.[45] Considering that the exchange rate barely kept up with domestic inflation, the driving force behind this variable was the rising world price index for Brazilian exports (especially coffee in 1976 and 1977). This suggests that if Brazilian authorities wish to stimulate exports without relying on world prices to rise, they have a powerful instrument in the exchange rate. By devaluing they can raise the real export price to producers.[46]

To calculate the impact of world boom and recession on Brazil's exports in 1973–77, table 4-5 compares the expected levels of exports with the actual (cyclical) level of world industrial activity in each year (based on equations 5 and 6) and the level that would have resulted from steady continuation of the 1961–72 world growth rate. The difference between the two sets of estimates indicates the net impact of the world business cycle on Brazil's exports.[47] The table probably understates the effect of the cycle on Brazilian export earnings because it captures only the quantity effect on exports. There is probably some additional price effect (higher export prices during world boom, lower during slump), although

45. If the real export price index had remained at its 1970 level instead of doubling by 1977 (table 4-4), the predicted index level for exports in the OECD-based model would have stood at only 127 instead of 181 (cyclical growth case).

46. Pastore, Barros, and Kadota reach a similar conclusion about the powerful role of exchange rates. Ibid.

47. It is not reasonable to compare the steady-growth levels directly with actual export levels because of variations in exports that are not explained by the model.

the price effect should be lower for Brazil's exports (mainly agricultural and manufactured products) than for those of countries that rely heavily on exports of products such as copper whose prices respond more sharply to the level of world industrial activity. Both the OECD and the world models indicate that Brazilian exports would have been slightly lower in 1974, higher in 1975, and much higher in 1976 and 1977 if world growth had proceeded smoothly. The lower hypothetical level for 1974 reflects the fact that under steady growth, world activity would have been lower in 1973 and Brazilian exports would have been resultingly lower after a year's lag. By contrast, steady growth would have meant higher world activity during 1974–76, and Brazilian exports during 1975–77 would thus have been higher by an average of approximately 10 percent.

Response to External Fluctuations

The conflicting goals of maintaining rapid growth and reducing imbalance in the foreign sector and inflationary pressure caused Brazilian economic policy to fluctuate between periods of monetary and fiscal stimulus (from 1972 to early 1974, and from the latter half of 1975 through 1976) and periods of deflationary policy (second quarter of 1974 to first quarter of 1975, and 1977).[48]

Brazil's external sector entered a crisis when imports doubled in value in 1974, partly because of increased prices for oil and other products but also because of speculative purchasing in anticipation of new import restrictions. A policy of mild monetary restriction in 1974 ushered in industrial stagnation, causing the government to overreact in an expansionary splurge of monetary and fiscal policies in 1975 that, in conjunction with higher coffee prices, boosted the economy to high growth in 1976. To address the balance-of-payments problem, which would have been aggravated by this expansionary policy, the government instituted highly protective measures and ambitious programs of import substitution in raw materials, basic industrial inputs, and capital goods. Nevertheless, the price of forcing a higher growth rate was a high trade deficit and the accumulation of excessive debt. By 1976 and 1977 the government had reduced its growth aspirations in order to come to grips with external imbalance, despite political pressure to deliver high growth rates during a phase of political liberalization.

48. Bacha, "Brazil's Balance of Payments," p. 12.

Growth Policy

In 1973, when world prices and activity were on the crest of boom, Brazilian policymakers held to a real growth target of 10 percent, even though the economy had virtually exhausted its excess capacity at the end of a long cycle beginning in 1965. There was enormous growth in money supply in 1973. Some analysts maintain that the economy was on a collision course between excessive stimulus and excessive capacity utilization, and that it would have entered a growth slump in 1974 even without the oil price crisis.[49] In 1974, despite the increasingly evident overheating of the economy, and the compounded problem of imported inflation with the oil price increase, the government remained committed to high growth. The new government that took control in March 1974 forecast growth rates of 10 percent per year in its planning documents.[50] It did, however, pursue a more cautious policy, allowing ambitious investment programs inherited from the previous government to continue, but reducing monetary growth and adopting a moderate fiscal policy.

Reduced stimulus plus cost-push inflation from oil prices and corrective increases for prices that had been frozen in the previous administration caused a rapid decline in industrial activity, which slumped from an annual growth rate of nearly 17 percent in the first quarter of 1974 to a rate of less than 4 percent in the first quarter of 1975. At this point "policymakers reacted in panic"; they went onto a course of intense stimulus to the economy, raising government spending by 31 percent in 1975 (while revenue rose by 24 percent), and even raising real wages 5–7 percent.[51] The government returned to a policy of rapid money growth; the money supply grew by 44.9 percent in 1975, 10 percentage points higher than in 1974, despite the fact that reserve losses were working to reduce monetary growth.

The Brazilian response in 1975 was not typical of developing countries. The majority of Latin American countries (excluding oil exporters), faced with both higher inflation and serious balance-of-payments problems, adopted restrictive economic policies.[52] The Brazilian response of

49. Edmar Bacha, "Issues and Evidence"; Malan and Bonelli, "Brazilian Economy in the Seventies."

50. Bacha, "Brazil's Balance of Payments," p. 11.

51. Bacha, "Issues and Evidence," p. 61.

52. See, for example, UN Economic Commission for Latin America, "Evolución de la economía regional en 1977," *Notas sobre la economía y el desarrollo de América Latina,* no. 274/275 (July 1978), p. 2.

expansion may have been drawn from the country's experience in dealing with internal inflation; the shock treatment of 1964–66 had had serious growth costs, but the gradualist approach of 1967–72 had been dramatically successful. It was only natural to extend the lesson to dealing with economic shocks caused by international inflation. Another factor in the Brazilian response was the considerable political pressure on the military regime to deliver high growth in order to retain its legitimacy, and beginning in 1974 it was all the more under pressure given its policy of political "decompression."[53] The decision to reapply massive stimulus to the economy in 1975 was essentially political, having emerged only after conflicting advice from alternative economic ministries, with the Planning Ministry emerging victorious at least temporarily.[54] One consequence of the decision was a critical need to take offsetting measures to deal with the balance-of-payments problem, and the result was the barrage of restrictive import controls erected in 1975.

Planning Minister Velloso has written that the government rejected the option to follow the road of the developed countries as both "ineffective" and (politically) "inconvenient."[55] "To attempt to resolve the trade balance problem through a recession, which would bring a sharp reduction of imports," would have merely postponed the balance-of-payments problem while raising unemployment and lowering living standards. The alternative Brazilian option involved only a moderate degree of deceleration in growth, combined with aggressive efforts, including increased oil exploration (and deals with foreign companies) and massive investment, to find substitutes for imports of raw materials, basic industrial inputs, and capital goods.[56] Velloso acknowledged that a necessary result of the oil price increase would be "a more moderate growth . . . on the part of the developing countries, for a certain period."[57] By the second half of 1975, according to Velloso, the government recognized that growth was becoming too rapid once again. The sizzling growth rate of 1976 appears to have been an unintended result of expansionary measures in 1975 as well as higher coffee prices. Beginning in 1976 but especially in 1977 the

53. See Thomas E. Skidmore, "Brazil's Changing Role in the International System: Implications for U.S. Policy," in Roett, *Brazil in the Seventies,* pp. 9–40.

54. Bacha, "Brazil's Balance of Payments," p. 12.

55. Velloso, *Brasil,* p. 115. My translation.

56. Velloso notes that the two previous occasions of major surges in Brazilian industrialization also occurred when the country faced balance-of-payments crisis: the Great Depression of the 1930s and the early postwar period. Ibid., p. 118.

57. Ibid., p. 65.

government decelerated its investments, seeking the target of a more intermediate growth rate "at least through 1978."[58]

Critics have dealt sharply with the inflationary growth policies of 1973, 1975, and 1976. Some emphasize the exhaustion of excess capacity by 1973 and the need for more moderate growth in order to avoid an overheating of the economy followed by recession. Perhaps the most severe criticism of the high short-run growth strategy is that Brazil had to resort to massive external borrowing in order to cover large trade deficits (which would have been lower with slower growth). Brazil's external debt catapulted from $12.5 billion at the end of 1973 to $17 billion at the end of 1974, $21 billion at the end of 1975, and $29 billion at the end of 1976.[59] Critics maintain that this debt will place serious constraints on Brazilian growth for a number of years, requiring slower growth to hold down imports just at a time when the politics of decompression require rapid growth.[60]

The fluctuation in Brazil's growth policies between highly inflationary and expansive phases (1973 and 1975–76) and relatively restrictive phases (1974 and 1977) has been associated by Planning Minister Velloso with the international economic fluctuations, which forced yearly reviews and adjustments in economic planning.[61] Nevertheless, a considerable portion of the blame would appear to lie squarely with domestic policymakers. Part of the problem may have been failure to anticipate the policy lags—the excessive monetary expansion after March 1975, for example, occurred at a time of economic slack but had its inflationary impact primarily in 1976, when the economy was overheated.

On balance, Brazilian authorities appear to have erred on the side of too much stimulus for short-term growth. They not only failed to accept slower growth rates as the economy reached full capacity (an internal factor) but attempted to grow more rapidly than the radically changed international conditions (an external factor) warranted. Even the external shock need not have implied slower growth if the deterioration in

58. Ibid., p. 124.

59. *Conjuntura econômica,* vol. 31 (March 1977), p. 114.

60. See Bacha, "Issues and Evidence," pp. 62–64; Albert Fishlow, "Debt, Growth and Hemispheric Relations: Latin American Prospects in the 1980s," draft paper, University of California—Berkeley, n.d.

61. The complications included how foreign banks would recycle OPEC earnings, how much protectionism would rise in industrial countries, how long the world recession would last, whether high prices for raw materials would last, and the future course of OPEC prices. Velloso, *Brasil,* p. 121.

Brazil's terms of trade had not been so great. The terms of trade, however, reversed sharply from a 20 percent improvement in 1966–73 to a decline of 13 percent from 1973 to 1975; the purchasing power of exports also declined by 16 percent from 1973 to 1975.[62] If world inflation had involved only an increase in nominal prices, then skillfully employed monetary and exchange-rate policies might have been able to insulate the Brazilian economy. But because the real terms of trade were deteriorating, the attempt to keep high growth rates for domestic demand inevitably meant a failure to deal with the new external constraint. Eventually the Brazilian authorities recognized that their policies were bringing high levels of external debt and accelerating domestic inflation and they accepted more moderate growth rate targets in view of balance-of-payments constraints.[63]

By 1976 the terms of trade had improved again (mainly because of high coffee prices) and stood only 1 percent below their high 1973 level; for the first three quarters of 1977 they averaged 15 percent above the 1973 level.[64] Ironically, this real recuperation did not mean that Brazil could resort to stimulus for high growth. The change was almost certainly temporary, as coffee prices began to decline from their highs of 1977. And the damage had already been done by earlier policies: high debt meant continued high debt servicing; and the dramatic escalation of Brazil's inflation rate from 1973 to 1977 left little scope for internal stimulation even though the consequences of stimulus for the external balance might have been tolerable.

The longer-term development policies that Brazil followed in 1973–77 were sound: relaxation of trade-balance constraints through the development of import substitutes in raw materials, industrial inputs, and capital goods. The government applied heavy protection of capital goods and subsidized credit for investment in these areas to achieve its goals. As a result, by 1977 approximately a hundred large projects were in progress, with investment for 1975–80 totaling $24 billion. Moreover, the projects were already yielding results and saving foreign exchange, especially in the capital goods sector.[65]

62. UN Conference on Trade and Development, *Handbook of International Trade and Development Statistics, 1976,* UN Doc. TD/STAT. 6, p. 442.

63. Velloso, *Brasil,* p. 124.

64. *Conjuntura econômica,* vol. 32 (February 1978), p. 303. Purchasing power of exports stood 5.7 percent and 25.4 percent above the 1973 level by 1976 and 1977, respectively; ibid.

65. Velloso, *Brasil,* p. 124.

Brazil's strong action to deal with the oil crisis by positive development programs is a refreshing contrast to the inaction of some countries, including the United States. In January of 1974 the government raised the real price of gasoline by 80 percent. In addition, it required that alcohol (made chiefly from sugar cane) be mixed into gasoline in proportions of up to 20 percent; it established incentives for production of oil from shale; and it granted permission for Petrobras, the state oil company, to enter into service contracts with foreign firms for exploration for new wells. By 1977 the use of gasoline had actually declined, despite rapid growth of the automotive fleet. Moreover, petroleum fell from 44 percent of all energy consumption in 1973 to 38 percent in 1977.[66]

Exchange-Rate Policy

Brazil erred in its exchange-rate policy by keeping minidevaluations along a path that represented a relatively rigid, constant "real" rate of exchange while a major devaluation in real terms (a "maxidevaluation") was called for to deal with the markedly worsened situation of the foreign sector beginning in 1974. Edward S. Shaw argues to the contrary that Brazil should have insulated itself from world inflation by devaluing even less than it did (or even appreciating) from 1970 to 1973.[67] His critique fails to recognize that in the period 1970–74 Brazil experienced a large loss in real terms of trade, and some real devaluation was necessary to deal with the resulting trade-balance decline. Moreover, an inadequate devaluation (or an appreciation) would have placed Brazil at a competitive disadvantage internationally. Though Brazil's dollar import prices rose by 20 percent and 55 percent in 1973 and 1974, respectively, and domestic inflation was only 15.1 percent and 28.7 percent in those years, wholesale prices in competitor countries were rising at rates far below the dollar import price index for Brazil (in large part because Brazil's oil import prices rose much more than wholesale prices in those countries).

Generally analyses of Brazil's real exchange rate agree that the rate held constant in the early 1970s as the frequent minidevaluations offset the difference between inflation at home and abroad. Typically these anal-

66. Major efforts were made to expand hydroelectric energy. Angelo Calmon de Sa, minister of industry and commerce of Brazil, "Brazilian Industrial Development: Strategies for the Energy Crisis," speech delivered at Johns Hopkins University School of Advanced International Studies, Center of Brazilian Studies, Washington, February 22, 1978.

67. "Comments by Edward S. Shaw," p. 444.

yses are based on differences between the rates of inflation in Brazil and the United States.[68] The dollar's depreciation in the 1970s, however, means that the cruzeiro would not necessarily need to depreciate by as much as the difference between Brazilian and U.S. inflation in order to hold a constant real purchasing power, which depends on its relation to the currencies of all of Brazil's trading partners. Table 4-6 shows that the cruzeiro was devalued almost exactly at the correct pace to keep the real exchange rate constant against the currencies of Brazil's major trading partners. The cruzeiro-dollar rate increased sufficiently to neutralize the difference between Brazilian inflation and inflation in the United States, Germany, Japan, the United Kingdom, France, Italy, and the Netherlands. Brazil's problem was that the real world did not remain constant: it imposed serious adverse shifts on Brazil's foreign sector. These shifts should have been compensated for by a devaluation in the real exchange rate. Instead, in 1974 and 1975 the cruzeiro was devalued in real terms by only 6 percent and even this small cumulative devaluation was reversed in 1976 and 1977.[69] The real shifts indicated by deteriorating terms of trade and a decline in foreign growth rate relative to domestic meant that Brazil should have devalued by a much greater amount in

68. There is some ambiguity as to whether the rate actually depreciated or appreciated. Bacha estimated that the real exchange rate appreciated by 4 percent from 1972 to 1976, deflating the cruzeiro by the GDP deflator and the dollar by the U.S. wholesale price index. Pastore, Barros, and Kadota calculate that the rate appreciated 38 percent from 1968 through 1974, but they do not take into account the decline in the real value of the dollar. *Conjuntura econômica* indicates a real devaluation from 1973 through 1975. My calculations in "Brazil's Emerging International Economic Role," pp. 68–70, indicate an appreciating real cruzeiro rate from 1969 through 1973. However, if those calculations are adjusted for dollar depreciation relative to all major currencies, and year-average exchange rates are used, no pattern of real appreciation is found for the cruzeiro. Bacha, "Brazil's Balance of Payments," p. 14; Pastore, Barros, and Kadota, "A teoria da paridade do poder de compra," p. 229; "O Brasil e a crise mundial," p. 72.

69. Balassa, "Incentive Policies in Brazil," p. 20, points out that if instead of the overall price index, the wholesale price index for industrial goods is used to deflate the cruzeiro, then the real exchange-rate index would stand at 116 for 1978, showing a larger devaluation. Although it is true that high coffee prices in 1976 and 1977 may have biased upward the overall price index as the basis for evaluating the exchange rate, it would probably be to err in the opposite extreme to use only industrial prices, thereby excluding key agricultural exports such as soybeans and excluding services (which affect the real value in terms of consumption of the dollars earned by exporters). Even accepting the industrial price index for analysis, a 16 percent devaluation would have been too small as a policy response to the massive shift in the external sector in 1974 and after.

Table 4-6. *Index of Real Exchange Rate of Brazilian Cruzeiro, 1970–77*
Index, 1973 = 100

Year	*Nominal exchange rate* — *Cruzeiros per dollar*[a]	*Nominal exchange rate* — *Index*	*Index of purchasing power parity exchange rate weighted by trade*[b]	*Index of real exchange rate*[c]
1970	4.494	73.3	79.7	91.9
1971	5.304	86.5	91.9	94.2
1972	5.960	97.2	100.6	96.6
1973	6.128	100.0	100.0	100.0
1974	6.843	111.7	106.6	104.7
1975	8.204	133.9	126.3	106.0
1976	10.770	175.7	173.1	101.5
1977	14.144	230.7	229.6	100.5

Sources: *International Financial Statistics*, various issues; International Monetary Fund, *Direction of Trade*, April 1974, p. 50.

a. Annual average.

b. Based on the dollar exchange rates and wholesale price indexes for the United States, Germany, Japan, the United Kingdom, France, Italy, and the Netherlands, weighted by each country's share of Brazil's foreign trade in 1972 (the U.S. figures include trade with countries other than the seven listed). Calculated as

$$P_t^B \sum_i \phi_i \frac{R_t^i}{R_0^i} \frac{1}{P_t^i}$$

where P_t^B is the index of Brazilian prices (*Conjuntura econômica* index number 2) in year t, ϕ_i the share of country i in Brazil's exports and imports, R_t^i and R_0^i the exchange rate of country i (currency/dollar) in year t and 1970, respectively, and P_t^i the index of wholesale prices for country i in year t. Trade weights of ϕ_i, for 1972, are: Germany, 0.113; Japan, 0.042; United Kingdom, 0.046; France, 0.037; Netherlands, 0.048; Italy, 0.053; United States and all others (considered as dollar area), 0.661.

c. Ratio of index of nominal exchange rate to index of purchasing power parity exchange rate weighted by trade.

1974.[70] But policymakers were unwilling to impose contractionary monetary and fiscal policies necessary to make devaluation work. They thought that in the short run, devaluation would be more inflationary than import restrictions. They wished to protect firms that had heavy dollar debts abroad. And they believed that a rigid formula of minidevaluation limited to adjusting for the differences between domestic and foreign inflation was best for avoiding speculation against the cruzeiro. They also feared that real devaluation would discourage borrowing abroad, cutting the flow of foreign capital at a time when it was essential.[71]

Although the government's reasons are understandable, its decision

70. Pastore, Barros, and Kadota, "A teoria da paridade do poder de compra," pp. 306–11.

71. These reasons are summarized in Bacha, "Brazil's Balance of Payments," p. 15; Malan and Bonelli, "Brazilian Economy in the Seventies," p. 36.

against devaluation was probably misguided. Fiscal and monetary restraint eventually had to be imposed. Protection rather than devaluation proved to be seriously inflationary. The possible losses of firms with external debt should hardly determine exchange-rate policy, which affects real income of the whole country. If necessary, the losses could be redressed through such measures as tax credits. Confidence in the cruzeiro could hardly be bolstered in the long run by a policy that failed to adjust the real rate to real changes in economic conditions. Finally, for a country seriously in debt the rate of external borrowing in the private sector could hardly be a major problem; if new borrowing declined too much, government borrowing could replace private. In any event, it is questionable whether a large devaluation would discourage borrowing abroad—it is the anticipation of the devaluation that would do so.

The absence of a large devaluation in real terms in 1974–77 was a serious failure of government policy to give the proper signals that the economy needed to adjust to the severe deterioration in the position of the external account.

Protection and Export Incentives

The protective measures that the Brazilian government instituted in 1975 and 1976 appear to have played a strong role in the acceleration of inflation in 1974–77. The tariff equivalent of tariffs and other protective barriers rose from an average of approximately 48 percent in 1968–73 to 82 percent in 1974, 115 percent in 1975, and 124 percent by 1976 (table 4-2). The lackluster performance of real exports in the period 1975–77, including deceleration in real growth for manufactured goods, probably was due partly to a higher incentive for producers to sell at home than abroad as protection rose. High protection in the Brazilian economy has traditionally led to severe distortions and eventual stagnation of growth, a lesson the government seemed to have learned when it liberalized imports in the mid-1960s. The new phase of protectionism in 1974–77 thus represented a major policy error.

One of the side effects of the strategy of protection, instead of devaluation, was the need to subsidize exports. As the government increased its export incentives through rebates of indirect taxes for exports and subsidized credit for manufactured exports, Brazilian goods were increasingly in jeopardy of facing extra tariffs in the United States imposed as countervailing duties. (In late 1978 the United States and Brazil reached an agreement whereby Brazil would phase down its export subsidies, thereby avoiding a potential trade war between the two countries.)

The combined effects of an overvalued exchange rate, high import protection with variation across products, and export subsidies available mainly for manufactured goods were a considerable degree of policy-induced inefficiency. Often the least efficient sectors received the greatest stimulus from this network of measures.[72] In the capital-goods sector, even though Brazil has the economies of scale, resources, and skilled labor force that can in the long run give it a comparative advantage, import incentives had caused the share of imports to rise from 14.5 percent in 1965 to 29.5 percent in 1975.[73] Nevertheless, the crash course of high protection was a far less efficient way to reduce imports of capital goods than changes in the earlier policies of import incentives would have been. The resort to much higher protection in 1975 and after introduced distortions in the Brazilian economy that aggravated inflation, discouraged exports, and probably worked against long-run efficiency.

External Debt

The large buildup in external debt represented another questionable response. From the standpoint of the rest of the world, this policy response was temporarily helpful. It meant that Brazil contributed to the maintenance of world demand just when most economies faced their most serious recession since the 1930s. For Brazil, however, the strategy was risky and probably shortsighted. While it enabled growth to continue at the relatively high rate of 5.7 percent in 1975 and the very high rate of 9.0 percent in 1976, it imposed a continuing burden for future growth in the form of debt servicing.[74]

Despite the rapid growth in debt, Brazil's credit rating has remained strong. Moreover, relative to export earnings, outstanding debt has not necessarily grown disproportionately. In 1972, year-end debt stood at a ratio of 2.38 times export earnings for the year; by 1976, the ratio had

72. Savasini and Kume found that fiscal and credit subsidies ranged from an average 3 percent of export value for products whose ratio of domestic resource costs (the ratio of domestic resources required to produce the good at home compared to those required to purchase from abroad) was below 1.25 to an average of 34 percent for those products whose ratio was above 1.35. Cited in Balassa, "Incentive Policies in Brazil," pp. 36–37.

73. Malan and Bonelli, "Brazilian Economy in the Seventies," p. 32.

74. *International Financial Statistics*, vol. 33 (August 1980), p. 92.

risen moderately to 2.86.[75] One statistical model of debt servicing indicated that as of 1976 there was no indication of serious debt servicing difficulty for Brazil, given its ratio of debt service, level of reserves relative to imports, and amortization rate.[76]

The future is more cloudy. Projections by the Wharton econometric forecasting model for Brazil indicate that with growth rates rising gradually from 6 percent to 8 percent through 1982, Brazil will experience a debt service ratio (interest and amortization relative to exports) rising from 51 percent in 1977 to approximately 65 percent in 1980–82.[77] Projections by Fishlow similarly give reason for concern that rapid growth may be incompatible with manageable external debt.[78] Moreover, the sharp deterioration of the trade balance caused by oil price increases in 1979 makes prospects even less favorable.

In broad terms Brazilian policy probably erred on the side of too much accumulation of debt in 1974–77, just as Brazilian growth policies were, on balance, excessively expansionary over this period.

Conclusion

Despite its large size and relatively closed nature, the Brazilian economy was not immune to the external shock of the 1970s. In a three-punch sequence, the international economy first induced reserve and monetary expansion (1971–73), then administered a shock of high price increases for traded commodities, especially oil (1973–74), and then delivered a final blow in the form of decreased real demand for exports as industrial countries entered serious recession (1975). Statistical tests show that a large part of the acceleration of Brazil's inflation (from a low of 15 percent in 1973 to 43 percent by 1977) was caused by the sharp rise in prices of imported goods in 1974 and by Brazil's own imposition of higher import protection in 1975.

These shocks helped interrupt the Brazilian economic miracle of 10 percent yearly growth (although internal factors such as the exhaustion

75. *Conjuntura econômica*, vol. 31 (March 1977), p. 114; *International Financial Statistics*, various issues.

76. Cline, "Brazil's Emerging International Economic Role," p. 73. However, the high level of Brazil's private debt makes the model applied a somewhat optimistic one since it applies only public debt figures.

77. As cited in Bacha, "Brazil's Balance of Payments," pp. 17–19.

78. Fishlow, "Debt, Growth, and Hemispheric Relations."

of excess capacity by 1973 also played a role). They caused a substantial decline in Brazil's terms of trade. World recession in 1975 reduced export volume by 10 percent from levels it might otherwise have reached. Policymakers explicitly rejected the contractionary measures adopted by some industrial countries in response to the oil price increase and trade-balance crisis. Despite a massive trade deficit beginning in 1974, the government adopted overexpansionary monetary and fiscal policies in 1975–76, while dealing with the balance-of-payments problem through highly protective measures and ambitious programs of import substitution in raw materials, basic industrial inputs, and capital goods (instead of choosing the more efficient option, devaluation).

Brazilian policymakers erred on the side of excessive growth stimulus in their response to the external shocks. While this result was probably preferable to the alternative of erring on the side of stagnation, the strategy left a burdensome external debt that will inhibit future efforts at high growth by preempting a large share of export earnings for debt servicing. By 1977 the government had reduced its growth aspirations in order to come to grips with external imbalance, despite political pressures to deliver high growth rates during a phase of political liberalization.

Policies on exchange rates, protection, and export subsidies erred in the direction of adjustment by control rather than by the price mechanism. A massive increase in protection staunched the growth of imports but only at the price of a serious acceleration of cost-push inflation. Authorities held the real exchange rate constant, while the serious deterioration in the trade balance called for a large devaluation. Only after three years of these control-oriented policies did Brazil (in January 1979) adopt a reform package liberalizing trade, phasing out export subsidies, and gradually devaluing the cruzeiro in real terms. In December 1979 Brazil pushed these reforms much further.[79]

Despite its flaws, the policy response of Brazil to worldwide inflation

79. A policy package of measures adopted in January 1979 provided for a gradual program over five years of eliminating fiscal export subsidies and the 100 percent prior deposit on imports, while devaluing the exchange rate in real terms by approximately 5 percent annually. In December, in the face of severe pressure caused by the doubling of oil prices in 1979, the new economic team headed by Delfim Netto went much further, devaluing the cruzeiro by 30 percent, and the prior deposit on imports, the highly protective law of similars, and export subsidies were abolished. These reforms should eliminate many of the distortions caused by the policy of overvaluation, protection, and export subsidization followed in the second half of the 1970s. "Nova estratégia de política comercial," *Conjuntura econômica,* vol. 33 (March 1979), pp. 109–12; "Um pacote de Natal," *Veja,* December 12, 1979, pp. 120–26.

and recession was still dynamic and generally coherent. In many ways its response to the oil price crisis was more adequate than that in the United States. The ambitious investment programs for import substitution began to bear fruit and to save foreign exchange; and the measures in the energy field in particular were strong and effective. If equally decisive policy actions could have been applied in different directions, accepting moderate growth earlier, and relying less on protection and more on real devaluation, the prospects for Brazil's longer-term growth and efficiency probably would have been better.

The Brazilian experience contains a number of guides for other developing countries trying to deal with external inflationary and recessionary shocks. To begin with, it shows that even large and relatively closed economies cannot fully or even largely escape the influence of these shocks. Therefore their economic planning must take into account policies designed to deal realistically with international disturbances.

A provocative lesson from the Brazilian experience is that on balance an ambitious set of growth policies designed to offset external shocks through new import substitution may be preferable to a passive response that accepts sluggish growth rates. However, the high-growth response is risky, particularly because rapid accumulation of external debt may limit future growth. Whether it is the correct response is an international variant of the old structuralist-monetarist debate in Latin American development strategy. The evidence from Brazil suggests that the growth-oriented structuralist approach to external crisis is preferable to the contractionary monetarist approach but only if applied in moderation. This conclusion has direct relevance for policies of developing countries and international lending agencies (especially the International Monetary Fund) in the context of the oil price shock of 1979.

The Brazilian resort to a large increase in protection proved to be an ill-advised response to external shock. Ironically, the strong inflationary impact of protection on the domestic economy may be an indication that it is possible to isolate the economy from external inflation by reducing protection. A decline in protection rates would offset the rise in international prices of goods. However, such a policy would be appropriate only when the basic problem is inflationary transmission of all prices, both export and import. By contrast, when the problem is primarily import price inflation and a deterioration in the terms of trade, the economy would not be in a position to undergo the deterioration in the trade balance that unilateral reductions in protection would cause. Appreciation of the exchange rate would also be a reasonable policy for insulating the economy from world inflation of both export and import prices. Indeed, in this case the ideal sequence would be unilateral liberalization of imports followed by appreciation (by amounts equal to the difference between high inflation abroad and low inflation domestically). When external shocks cause a real deterioration in the terms of trade, the response should be a real devaluation in order to adjust the trade balance.

Brazil proved during the worldwide recession that it pays to have diversified exports. Despite stagnant demand, its export earnings grew rapidly from 1974 to 1977. If a particular year was mediocre for one product, it was excellent for another (because of either world price developments or increased export supply). The benefits of diversification arose from having not only a varied list of raw materials to export, but also a wide range of exportable manufactured goods.

CHAPTER FIVE

India's Closed Economy and World Inflation

SURJIT S. BHALLA

INFLATION in India during the 1970s was unprecedented, in both its absolute magnitude and its acceleration. As measured by the consumer price index, inflation accelerated from 3 percent and 5 percent in 1971 and 1972 to 18 percent and 28 percent in 1973 and 1974 (table 5-1). By contrast, the previous high rate had been 14 percent in 1964. Despite sudden jumps, India's inflation had been fairly moderate since World War II. The 1964 jump appears to have been caused by excessive demands on industrial production and a decline in food supplies. The 11 percent and 13 percent rises in the consumer price index in 1966 and 1967 are widely regarded as having been the result of two years of drought capped by a devaluation in 1966. The drought caused food and other domestic prices to rise while the devaluation increased the price of imports.[1]

The inflation that troubled India during the 1970s was in part related to domestic factors, especially the price of food. But international factors also had a strong role in the generation of this record inflation. This chapter analyzes, with formal regression models, inflation in India between 1956 and 1976 and seeks to define the role of international fluctuations in the early 1970s.

I THANK Suman K. Bery and Robert Z. Lawrence for helpful discussions during the preparation of this chapter.

1. For an analysis of inflation in the 1960s see *Foreign Trade Regimes and Economic Development,* vol. 6: Jagdish N. Bhagwati and T. N. Srinavasan, *India* (Columbia University Press for National Bureau of Economic Research, 1975). For a structural model of price developments in the Indian economy, see Isher J. Ahluwalia, "An Analysis of Price and Output Behavior in the Indian Economy: 1951–1973," *Journal of Development Economics,* vol. 6 (September 1979), pp. 363–90.

Table 5-1. *Measures of Price Inflation in India, 1956–76*
Percent

Year	*Consumer price index*	*Wholesale price index*	*Gross domestic product deflator*	*Food price index*
1956–60	5.2	6.1	3.3	6.5
1961–65	6.0	5.2	7.0	6.6
1966–70	6.9	7.0	6.0	8.0
1969	1.7	2.2	5.3	3.9
1970	5.1	6.2	4.6	5.3
1971	3.3	3.9	5.0	1.5
1972	5.2	7.8	10.5	6.4
1973	17.8	16.3	16.4	21.3
1974	27.8	28.6	18.7	30.5
1975	5.6	3.9	−3.0	4.4
1976	−7.8	−2.0	n.a.	−12.6

Sources: *International Financial Statistics*, various issues; United Nations, *Monthly Bulletin of Statistics*, various issues.
n.a. Not available.

Real Activity and Inflation

Real aggregate activity seems neither to have caused nor contributed to the inflation of the 1970s. Industrial production and gross domestic output, the principal indicators of real activity, reflect none of the increased demand that is conventionally used to explain inflation. The years 1970–72 point to a recession—national output grew by 1.0 percent in 1971 and declined in 1972 by 1.0 percent (table 5-2). Though there was some expansion in 1973, it stopped abruptly in 1974. Excluding the drought years of 1966 and 1967, industrial production grew at a slower rate during 1970–72 than in the 1960s and in the inflation period reached its lowest rates ever—1.6 percent in 1973 and 2.1 percent in 1974.

An alternative indicator of excess demand—deviations from trend in output—reveals the same picture. National output was above trend in 1970 and 1971 and below trend from 1972 through 1976. Industrial production declined during 1973–76, with activity slightly above trend during 1971–72 and in a deep recession during 1974–75.

Table 5-2. *Indicators of Real Activity in India, 1956–76*
Percent

	Gross domestic product		*Industrial production*		
Year	*Growth rate*	*Deviation from trend*[a]	*Growth rate*	*Deviation from trend*[a]	*Growth of money supply, M_1*
1956	4.9	−0.4	9.0	−4.3	9.6
1960	7.5	0.95	11.3	−6.6	7.7
1961	5.8	3.1	9.0	2.3	4.1
1962	4.1	3.7	9.8	6.0	8.1
1963	1.8	2.0	8.3	8.3	11.2
1964	7.6	5.9	8.6	10.9	11.9
1965	−4.7	−2.4	9.1	14.0	9.6
1966	1.9	−4.0	−0.8	7.5	9.8
1967	9.1	1.3	−0.7	1.1	8.7
1968	3.3	1.1	6.5	1.7	8.0
1969	5.4	2.9	7.1	2.8	10.1
1970	4.2	3.8	4.8	1.8	10.9
1971	1.0	2.6	4.3	0.4	12.9
1972	−1.0	−1.6	5.7	0.2	12.5
1973	5.3	−1.3	1.6	−3.8	16.8
1974	0.0	−4.9	2.1	−7.5	13.7
1975	8.5	−0.14	4.4	−8.9	7.9
1976	1.3	−2.3	10.4	−4.7	14.8

Source: *International Financial Statistics,* various issues.
a. The residual from the estimated equation, $\log Z = a + bt$, where Z is the variable and t is time.

Food Prices

Problems of agricultural supply are more relevant than aggregate demand in explaining India's inflation in the 1970s. The agricultural sector accounts for 50 percent of the gross national product and employs about 70 percent of the labor force. Food accounts for 60.9 percent of the weight in the consumer price index and 41.3 percent in the wholesale price index. Furthermore, industrial prices are directly linked to the agricultural sector through the cost of industrial raw materials and the use of food as a wage good.

In 1973 and 1974, inflation in food prices was much higher than in 1966 and 1967. The drought in crop years 1965–66 and 1966–67 caused a shortfall of 17 percent in the production of food grains (table 5-3). Production in the early 1970s was above trend, though it did decline to 5.3

Table 5-3. *Production and Per Capita Supply of Food Grains in India, 1956–77*

	Gross production		Net availability[a]		
Year[b]	Millions of metric tons	Deviation from trend (percent)[c]	Per capita grams per day	Deviation from mean (percent)	Imports (millions of metric tons)
1956	69.2	0.8	430.9	−3.0	1.4
1960	76.7	1.7	447.2	0.6	5.1
1961	82.0	6.2	468.7	5.5	3.5
1962	82.7	4.6	461.0	3.7	3.6
1963	80.2	−0.9	443.8	−0.1	4.6
1964	80.6	−2.8	452.0	1.7	6.3
1965	89.4	5.4	480.2	8.0	7.5
1966	72.3	−16.8	408.2	−8.2	10.3
1967	74.2	−16.6	401.4	−9.7	8.7
1968	95.1	4.4	460.1	3.5	5.7
1969	94.0	0.8	445.2	0.2	3.9
1970	99.5	4.2	455.0	2.4	3.6
1971	108.4	10.9	468.8	5.5	2.0
1972	105.2	5.1	466.5	5.0	−0.5
1973	97.0	−5.3	422.4	−5.0	3.6
1974	104.7	−0.2	450.8	1.4	4.8
1975	99.8	−7.1	406.6	−8.5	7.4
1976	121.0	10.0	452.8	1.9	6.4
1977	111.6	−0.9	434.7	−2.2	0.4

Source: India, Ministry of Finance, *Economic Survey*, various issues.
a. The sum of net production (87.5 percent of gross), net imports, and change in government stocks.
b. Crop year, ending in June of the year indicated.
c. The residual of a regression $z = a + bt$, where z is the natural logarithm of production and t is time.

percent below trend in 1973. This shortfall, by itself, was minor compared to that in the drought years.

An alternative indicator of food supply is food availability per capita. This index has the advantage that it incorporates all factors (production, stocks, and imports) affecting food supply. For the time period 1956–77, this index shows no trend. If deviations from average represent food scarcity, then it appears that even record imports of food grains did not prevent food supply from being at a twenty-year low during 1966–67. In contrast, the food supply was near its highest per capita point in 1971–72, and though it declined in 1973, the decline was much smaller than in the 1966–67 shortage. Thus it seems unreasonable to hold the production deficit entirely responsible for the historically high inflation in India's food prices in 1973 and 1974.[2]

International inflation in food prices did make the 1970s situation unique. Prices of rice and wheat rose rapidly in late 1972 and continued to rise through 1974. The U.S. government's Public Law 480 program of subsidized food exports was no longer in operation, and India had to import food grains at record prices. Significant pressure on domestic food prices was exerted by both the domestic shortfall in production and the record import prices of rice and wheat (table 5-4).

The production decline in 1973 was singular in that it occurred during a period of record prices and a worldwide shortage. World production of food declined by 2.8 percent in 1972, at a time when world stocks of wheat were relatively low. Hence the record prices of food grains internationally and in India in 1973 and 1974.[3]

The prices of wheat, rice, sugar, and cotton on the Indian market did not move as sharply as international prices in the 1970s, suggesting that the domestic economy was insulated from the international fluctuations (table 5-4). Wheat prices varied least of all because the domestic price is usually above the world price (in 1972 it was almost double the international price, but in June 1974 the two prices were approximately equal).

In India, food imports on private account are prohibited. Furthermore, the government is intimately involved in the procurement of food grains for distribution in urban areas. Internal developments (such as weather) and government responses to a large extent determine the price of food.[4] Nevertheless, international developments in commodities appear to have had a direct effect on domestic prices. The decrease in domestic supplies (table 5-3) did not warrant the explosion of food prices (table 5-1), a

2. Nor does availability of stocks explain the paradoxical rise in food prices since the years preceding the drought were a period of relative surplus.

3. Both supply and demand factors caused abnormal price increases in food grains and other commodities during the 1970s. See Dale E. Hathaway, "Food Prices and Inflation," and Richard N. Cooper and Robert Z. Lawrence, "The 1972–75 Commodity Boom," *Brookings Papers on Economic Activity, 1:1974*, pp. 63–109, and *3:1975*, pp. 671–715.

4. The government sets the price of food grains before harvest time each year. Government purchases vary positively with the price and weather conditions. The government draws down its stocks or imports to make up any deficit in its needs for grain to be distributed to the poor on a ration basis. By changing the price of grain in its ration shops, the government can affect the price of food grains and perhaps other prices in the economy.

Table 5-4. *Domestic and International Prices of Agricultural Goods Important to India, 1970–76*
Dollars per kilogram

	Price						
Product	*1970*	*1971*	*1972*	*1973*	*1974*	*1975*	*1976*
Wheat[a]							
India	0.125	0.124	0.127	0.108	0.144	0.135	0.125
International	0.057	0.062	0.069	0.137	0.178	0.138	0.123
Rice, milled[b]							
India	0.145	0.145	0.151	0.158	0.270	0.160	0.148
International	0.144	0.129	0.147	0.350	0.542	0.363	0.255
Sugar[c]							
India	n.a.	n.a.	0.202	0.187	0.168	0.200	n.a.
International	0.081	0.099	0.160	0.208	0.653	0.448	0.253
Cotton[d]							
India	n.a.	n.a.	0.404	0.532	0.853	0.633	0.775
International	n.a.	n.a.	0.757	1.241	1.298	1.153	1.617

Sources: UN, Food and Agriculture Organization, *FAO Production Yearbook*, various years; World Bank, *Commodity Trade and Price Trends*, various years.
n.a. Not available.
a. U.S. soft red winter wheat.
b. Wholesale price, 5 percent broken, milled, f.o.b. Bangkok.
c. International Sugar Council, f.o.b.
d. Middling 1-inch American cotton, f.o.b. Liverpool.

large part of which must be credited to the international commodity price boom.

The External Sector

Traded goods represent a direct channel for the international transmission of inflation that is particularly important for small, open economies. By almost any definition, however, India is a relatively closed economy. Since 1960 its dependence on international trade has remained relatively constant. The share of imports and exports in national income fluctuated around an average of 5 percent in 1961–76 (table 5-5). The structure of Indian trade has changed, however. Well before the oil price rise of 1973, the volume of imports began a steady decline from the high point of the mid-1960s (table 5-5) despite steady dollar prices for India's imports (table 5-6). By contrast, the volume of exports steadily increased, doubling in the fifteen-year period 1960–75.

Table 5-5. *Trade Volume and Trade Share of India's GDP, 1961–76*

	Imports		*Exports*		*Gross domestic product*	
Year	*Billions of rupees*	*Volume index (1975 = 100)*	*Billions of rupees*	*Volume index (1975 = 100)*	*Billions of rupees*	*Traded goods portion (percent)*[a]
1961	11.00	80	8.02	52	159.77	5.94
1962	12.09	86	8.35	56	170.99	5.96
1963	13.63	84	9.85	63	196.56	5.97
1964	15.26	90	10.15	67	230.44	5.51
1965	14.64	108	9.32	62	241.12	4.96
1966	21.15	108	13.25	64	276.62	6.22
1967	22.01	109	15.08	62	322.94	5.75
1968	18.97	106	15.97	70	332.79	5.10
1969	17.47	88	16.25	69	368.51	4.56
1970	19.02	87	16.39	76	403.75	4.38
1971	21.75	102	17.85	76	429.83	4.61
1972	23.28	94	21.49	83	470.37	4.76
1973	29.49	103	26.58	83	576.78	4.86
1974	44.50	97	34.74	98	684.57	5.79
1975	n.a.	100	n.a.	100	720.61	n.a.
1976	n.a.	82	n.a.	118	n.a.	n.a.

Source: *International Financial Statistics*, vol. 31 (May 1978), pp. 198–99.
n.a. Not available.
a. Average of import and export shares in GDP.

The most important imports in the 1970s were food and petroleum (table 5-7). Prices of traditional Indian exports, such as tea and jute, were relatively stable during the commodity boom. Sugar is one commodity whose price boom affected India. From a base of 100 in 1969 the index of sugar prices reached a high of 394 in 1975 and the index of export volume increased to 819. Sugar exports rose from a negligible share of total exports in 1970 to 10.2 percent in 1975 and 12 percent in 1976. A nontraditional item that assumed an increasingly important role in Indian exports is engineering goods, which grew in value from $163.1 million and 7.6 percent of total exports in 1972 (and a negligible amount in the mid-1960s) to 10.4 percent of exports in 1976.

Import and Export Prices

Despite a changing structure of trade, the dependence of the Indian economy on international trade remained low. Nevertheless, inflation in

Table 5-6. *Percent Change in Indian Trade Price Indexes, 1956–76*[a]

Year	Wholesale price index (percent)	Consumer price index (percent)	Import price index: Rupee	Import price index: Dollar	Export price index: Rupee	Export price index: Dollar
1956	12.1	9.1	1.6	2.1	0.0	n.a.
1960	6.6	1.3	6.5	1.0	8.6	n.a.
1961	2.3	1.9	0.0	0.0	1.6	n.a.
1962	1.2	2.8	−4.5	0.0	−4.7	0.0
1963	4.0	2.8	3.2	2.2	0.0	−1.2
1964	10.5	14.0	1.5	1.1	0.0	3.6
1965	8.1	8.9	4.5	1.1	6.6	4.6
1966	12.0	11.3	26.1	0.0	30.8	6.7
1967	15.0	13.4	18.4	2.1	15.3	0.0
1968	−0.4	3.0	−5.8	−1.0	−4.1	−1.0
1969	2.2	1.7	4.1	0.0	7.4	0.0
1970	6.2	5.1	−1.0	4.2	−1.0	5.3
1971	3.9	3.3	−1.0	9.0	2.0	1.0
1972	7.8	5.2	2.0	6.4	9.8	8.9
1973	16.3	17.8	30.7	24.1	21.4	15.5
1974	28.6	27.8	56.1	52.1	27.2	12.3
1975	3.9	5.6	22.8	3.7	11.0	7.8
1976	−2.0	−7.8	5.1	n.a.	5.2	n.a.

Sources: UN, *Monthly Bulletin of Statistics*, various issues; *International Financial Statistics*, various issues.
n.a. Not available.
a. Unit values.

the prices of imported goods became a problem in the 1970s. Changes in the unit value indexes of imports and exports, which had been negligible compared to the changes in the indexes of wholesale and consumer prices until the mid-1960s, began to move more closely with the domestic series in 1965–70 (table 5-6). In the 1970s, however, the inflation in international prices began reaching record magnitudes. In export prices the inflation was of roughly the same magnitude as that in domestic prices, but import prices were rising at roughly twice the domestic rate during the three-year period 1972–75. (The dollar price of imports and exports showed essentially no movement until 1971–72, though import prices in domestic currency shot up in the drought years 1966–67; the devaluation of the Indian rupee from 4.745 per dollar to 7.5 in June 1966 exacerbated the drought-induced inflation.) The inflation in traded items seems to have preceded the domestic inflation of the 1970s and thus to have placed cost-push pressure on domestic prices.

Table 5-7. *Commodity Composition of India's Exports and Imports, 1970–76*[a]

Millions of dollars and, in parentheses, percent of total exports or imports

Commodity	*1969–70*	*1970–71*	*1971–72*	*1972–73*	*1973–74*	*1974–75*	*1975–76*
Exports	1,884.3	2,046.9	2,160.4	2,557.5	3,238.9	4,173.6	4,555.2
Tea	166.0	197.7	210.0	191.1	187.4	285.9	273.7
	(8.81)	(9.7)	(9.7)	(7.5)	(5.8)	(6.9)	(6.0)
Sugar	11.4	36.8	40.6	17.2	55.0	425.9	545.9
	(0.6)	(1.8)	(1.9)	(0.7)	(1.7)	(10.2)	(12.0)
Jute goods	275.5	253.9	356.4	324.4	292.0	372.1	287.0
	(14.6)	(12.4)	(16.5)	(12.7)	(9.0)	(8.9)	(6.3)
Leather and leather goods	108.7	96.2	135.3	242.0	239.5	207.4	263.4
	(5.8)	(4.7)	(6.3)	(9.5)	(7.4)	(5.0)	(5.8)
Engineering goods	n.a.	n.a.	163.1	184.9	258.9	447.1	472.3
			(7.6)	(7.2)	(8.0)	(10.7)	(10.4)
Cotton goods	162.2	168.2	177.3	235.2	392.2	396.4	422.9
	(8.6)	(8.2)	(8.2)	(9.2)	(12.1)	(9.5)	(9.3)
Imports	2,109.5	2,178.9	2,451.0	2,473.4	3,793.2	5,665.5	6,084.3
Food grains	343.1	271.8	142.5	90.9	597.0	951.3	1,537.3
	(16.3)	(12.5)	(5.8)	(3.8)	(15.7)	(16.8)	(25.3)
Fertilizers	130.5	100.9	119.5	159.2	242.8	617.6	609.5
	(6.2)	(4.6)	(4.9)	(6.6)	(6.4)	(10.9)	(10.0)
Machinery and transport equipment	527.9	526.2	632.2	690.6	836.3	872.2	1,080.0
	(25.0)	(24.1)	(25.8)	(28.5)	(22.0)	(15.4)	(17.8)
Fuels, lubricants, and related materials	183.4	181.2	260.9	264.7	719.1	1,450.5	1,416.9
	(8.7)	(8.3)	(10.6)	(10.9)	(18.9)	(25.6)	(23.3)

Source: India, Department of Commercial Intelligence and Statistics, *Monthly Statistics of Foreign Trade of India*, various issues.
n.a. Not available.
a. Financial years, beginning April 1 each year.

The Oil Price Increase

The OPEC oil price rise was not one of the originating factors in the 1970s inflation. The annual rate of inflation was already running at 22 percent when the Organization of Petroleum Exporting Countries raised oil prices in November 1973, and over the preceding twelve months inflation had averaged 17 percent. The price rise did cause later rises in the price of fuel, domestic industrial goods, and agricultural goods (through its impact on international fertilizer prices). But its effect was not catastrophic for the Indian economy. Oil imports form a relatively small proportion of India's total energy supply; traditional and noncommercial forms of energy (firewood and charcoal, dried cow dung, and vegetable wastes) account for almost 50 percent of total energy consumption.[5] The importance of petroleum is in industry—50 percent of commercial energy comes from oil and 25 percent from coal. In 1973 about 30 percent of the oil consumed was from domestic sources. Oil imports thus accounted for 70 percent of total consumption of petroleum products but only 16 percent of total energy consumption. They accounted for a large portion of scarce foreign exchange, however, amounting to 11 percent of total imports in 1973 and 26 percent in 1975 (table 5-8).

Reduction of consumption of petroleum products became an explicit part of government policy in the early 1970s. The excise duty on gasoline doubled and that on kerosene oil, an important component of household fuel consumption, increased by 30 percent. Retail prices increased 112 percent for gasoline and 58 percent for kerosene in the year ending in August 1974.[6] These and other conservation policies succeeded in reducing consumption of petroleum products by 3 percent in 1974, a significant turnaround in a rate that had increased at more than 8 percent annually since 1961.

Crude petroleum imports, which had increased 26 percent in volume in the first four years of the decade, increased only slightly in 1975 and declined the next year. Even more striking, imports of all oil-related items declined by 33 percent in 1975 after doubling over the previous four years.

5. World Bank, *India, 1973*, Country Economic Report (Washington: World Bank, 1973).

6. See Katrine Saito, "An Examination of Changes in the Retail Price and Taxation of Petroleum Products, July 1973–July 1974," Domestic Finance Studies no. 9 (World Bank, September 1975).

Table 5-8. *Oil and Related Statistics for India, 1970–76*[a]

Item	*1969–70*	*1970–71*	*1971–72*	*1972–73*	*1973–74*	*1974–75*	*1975–76*
Oil and oil-related imports							
Value (millions of dollars)	183.4	181.2	260.9	264.7	719.1	1,450.5	1,416.9
Share in total imports (percent)	8.7	8.3	10.6	10.9	18.9	25.6	23.3
Volume index	100.0	94.8	142.7	183.6	200.5	136.6	140.4
Crude petroleum							
Value (millions of dollars)	128.4	141.2	198.1	187.9	535.3	1,197.2	1,215.9
Volume index	100.0	105.5	116.9	108.2	125.7	130.6	127.9
Unit value index	100.0	104.1	130.9	139.2	344.3	758.9	854.6
Petrol price index[b]	100.0	109.7	127.8	133.2	196.2	298.3	309.9
Kerosene price index[c]	100.0	102.6	108.1	117.9	136.7	192.7	215.2
Coal production (millions of tons)	79.6	75.8	76.3	80.2	81.9	91.6	102.7

Sources: Reserve Bank of India, *Bulletin*, various issues; *Monthly Statistics of Foreign Trade of India.*
a. Financial years, beginning April 1 each year.
b. Component of the wholesale price index, weighted 9.2 percent.
c. Component of the wholesale price index, weighted 8.5 percent.

One reason was a successful government policy of expanding coal production, which rose by 25 percent in two years.

The government's pricing policy before the OPEC price rise was to allow the price of domestic oil to follow import prices. After the price rise, the petroleum component of India's wholesale price index rose, but by only a fraction of the increase in the unit value of imported petroleum (table 5-8). The politically more sensitive price of kerosene oil increased even more slowly, and at a rate very close to the change in the overall wholesale price index (kerosene oil is a major item in household expenditures, while petroleum-related goods are luxury items).

Exchange-Rate Policy

The impact of inflation in imported items on the domestic price level can be partially contained by exchange-rate changes. A revaluation can diminish the import price rise and thereby the cost effects on the rest of the economy. However, India's exchange-rate policy was one of devaluation; thus imported inflation was encouraged rather than suppressed (the rupee was devalued 1.2 percent, 1.95 percent, 4.65 percent, and 3.38 percent over the period 1972–75).

With the breakdown of the fixed-exchange-rate system, the Indian rupee, like other currencies, was allowed to float within limits. Until June 1975 it was tied to the British pound and thus declined by 10.75 percent against the dollar. This policy might have been beneficial for exports; by raising the prices of imports, however, it had an inflationary bias.

After the rupee was taken off the pound, it was tied to a secret basket of currencies. The timing of this major policy change (September 1975) indicates that, at least partly, it was an anti-inflationary measure. After a steep upward climb, domestic prices had begun to decline, and there was confidence in the government that the battle against inflation was being won (the wholesale price index had declined by 5.25 percent over the previous year). It was expected that the rupee would depreciate less if not tied to the pound, and therefore that there would be less pressure from imported inflation. During the year beginning September 1975 the rupee declined by 0.5 percent with respect to the dollar and increased in value with respect to the pound by 20 percent. The wholesale price index increased by only 1.2 percent. And from June 1975 to June 1976 the wholesale price index declined by 3 percent compared to an increase in the previous year of 22 percent. The change in exchange-rate policy and the

Table 5-9. *Sources of Variation in India's Money Supply, M_1, 1969–76*[a]

Billions of rupees and, in parentheses, percent change over previous year

Item	*1969*[b]	*1969–70*	*1970–71*	*1971–72*	*1972–73*	*1973–74*	*1974–75*	*1975–76*
Money supply	57.79	63.9	71.4	81.4	94.1	108.5	115.6	126.8
		(10.5)	(13.6)	(12.9)	(16.9)	(15.2)	(6.5)	(9.7)
Currency	36.82	40.1	43.8	48.2	54.4	63.4	63.8	67.3
Factors affecting money supply[c]								
Bank credit to government	47.0	47.3	52.4	64.2	77.4	87.0	95.0	100.3
		(0.6)	(10.8)	(22.6)	(20.6)	(12.3)	(9.3)	(5.6)
Bank credit to commercial sector	47.0	47.9	56.8	65.2	76.4	94.2	112.2	133.3
		(17.5)	(18.6)	(14.9)	(17.1)	(23.3)	(19.1)	(18.5)
Net foreign exchange assets	3.26	5.8	5.5	6.1	5.7	6.7	3.9	10.8
		(75.8)	(−5.2)	(10.9)	(−6.9)	(18.9)	(−41.6)	(174.3)
Government net currency liabilities	3.41	3.61	3.85	4.12	4.57	5.02	5.31	5.52

Source: Reserve Bank of India, *Bulletin*, various issues.
a. Financial years, beginning April 1 each year.
b. Outstanding as of March 28.
c. Nonmonetary liabilities of the banking sector are not shown.

implicit revaluation with a major trading partner, the United Kingdom, was thus supportive of anti-inflationary goals.

Monetary and Fiscal Policy

Although the inflationary forces from fiscal and monetary policy are primarily domestic, both types of policy are vulnerable to international activity. Changes in reserves, unless sterilized, interfere with monetary policy; and changes in international prices can alter reserve levels and the fiscal plans of the government. Well before the worldwide economic disruptions of 1972–75, India's fiscal deficits and money supply were increasing at record rates. The Bangladesh War of 1971 and the severe drought in 1973 had increased the rate of inflation (in the wholesale price index) to 9.9 percent.

Part of the pressure for price increases in 1974 might have been due to the unprecedented rate of growth of the money supply in the preceding three years (table 5-9).[7] It was the highest three-year growth in money supply in the 1956–76 period and it took place at a time when changes in real income were historically low (see table 5-2).

External events played a relatively small role in the change in M_1 during 1970–74. India's net foreign-exchange assets changed relatively little until 1975, when private remittances began to flow into the country (India was an exception to the pattern of growth in the reserves of developing countries leading to monetary expansion in the early 1970s). In 1975 the rate of growth of M_1 was brought down to 6.5 percent. Though money supply growth rose again the next year, to a rate of 9.7 percent, the increase was accompanied by an 8.5 percent increase in real national income (in the previous year, national income was stagnant).

The restraint in monetary growth was achieved by tightening the allocation of credit to the commercial sector—banks' cash and liquidity requirements were increased as were lending and deposit rates, and more stringent limits were put on advances against commodity purchases and on the financing of inventories. The success of these policies and the decline in the net foreign-exchange assets contributed to the moderation in the growth of money supply.

7. In the long run, if velocity is relatively constant, money changes are reflected in changes in prices and output. Though short-run changes in velocity can neutralize the effect of money on prices, net money growth must have an impact on prices—the only uncertainty is with regard to the timing.

Table 5-10. *Position of the Central and State Governments of India, Fiscal 1970–76*[a]

Item	*1970*	*1971*	*1972*	*1973*	*1974*	*1975*	*1976*
				Billions of rupees and, in parentheses, percent of total			
Revenue receipts	53.31	58.63	69.01	77.97	87.89	110.48	133.34
Tax revenue	42.00	47.75	55.75	64.36	73.89	92.23	109.13
Direct taxes	9.63	10.09	11.71	13.46	15.52	18.34	23.97
Expenditures	68.68	78.45	93.63	104.35	114.73	140.56	173.04
Nondevelopmental	33.00	36.92	44.52	47.59	53.51	59.13	71.05
	(48.1)	(47.1)	(47.6)	(45.6)	(46.6)	(42.1)	(41.1)
Developmental	31.26	35.38	43.27	48.47	53.06	66.79	81.43
	(45.5)	(45.1)	(46.2)	(46.4)	(46.2)	(47.5)	(47.1)
Capital receipts	14.80	16.23	17.52	17.90	19.10	23.54	41.76
Market borrowings	2.46	2.60	4.08	6.23	6.29	7.00	7.24
Deficit	−0.58	−3.59	−7.10	−8.48	−7.75	−6.54	+2.06
				Ratio of deficit to national income			
Indian definition of deficit[b]	−0.15	−0.89	−1.65	−1.80	−1.34	−0.96	0.29
IMF definition of deficit[c]	−2.80	−3.30	−3.70	−4.50	−2.90	−3.60	−4.90

Source: World Bank, *India, 1978*, Country Economic Report (Washington: World Bank, 1978).

a. Subentries do not represent all factors in each category.

b. The Planning Commission of India defines the deficit as the change in short-term and long-term advances by the Reserve Bank of India to the government, and the change in cash balances.

c. The International Monetary Fund defines the deficit as revenue less expenditures, minus lendings net of repayments.

The fact that inflation did decline when monetary brakes were applied (and indeed reached a negative level in 1976) suggests that the steady increase of money supply until 1974 might have been partially responsible for the inflationary experience of 1973–75.

India's fiscal policy is closely linked to its monetary policy because budget deficits are mainly financed by increases in money supply. Expansionary fiscal policy in India predates international inflation. The record budget deficit of 7.1 billion rupees in 1972 (table 5-10), which was more than the combined deficits of the preceding three years, was caused mainly by increases in military requirements, refugee assistance, and relief related to the Bangladesh War. Unexpected expenditures on drought relief measures and crash schemes to finance the winter crop caused the even larger deficit in 1973.

The government planned an austere budget for 1974, holding defense expenditures steady and imposing new taxes (including taxes based on partial integration of agricultural and nonagricultural income) and reducing outlays considered nonessential for growth. Nevertheless, the budget deficit was high once again, this time because of increases in government salaries, high food subsidies caused by record prices of food imports, and high expenditures for drought relief.

The turning point in the fight against inflation was July 1974. The next two years were marked by fiscal and monetary restraint. Increased charges for postal and telephone services, railway fares, and other government services netted some 10 billion rupees in 1975. In 1976 an incomes policy was enacted that required that all increases in wages be deposited in savings accounts, as were all cost-of-living increases; also a ceiling was imposed on the distribution of company profits. In addition, a grace period for voluntary disclosure of undeclared income netted some 2.5 billion rupees in taxes in 1976—almost 10 percent of direct tax revenue and 2 percent of total revenue. The result was a surplus in the budget. Monetary restraint and a bumper crop aided in the reduction of inflation (in the consumer price index) to minus 8 percent, certainly one of the more successful of the anti-inflationary policies in the 1970s internationally.

Econometric Models of Inflation

India's deviation in the 1970s from generally less than 5 percent inflation annually was brought on by its expansionary fiscal and monetary policies of 1970–72, caused in part by the Bangladesh War. Inflation was aggravated by sharp rises in import prices, especially for wheat and oil. It was halted by contractionary monetary and fiscal policies starting in mid-1974. A mixture of demand and cost factors seems to have contributed to the high rates of inflation during the 1970s. The results of econometric tests indicate that the impact of excess demand was limited while changes in cost-push factors were extremely disruptive. The extreme and simultaneous movements in prices generally and in the prices of food and imported goods in 1972–76, when tested using data for 1956–76 and for the more stable 1956–72 period, indicate that international inflation had a significant and disproportionate effect on the price level.

In regression models for the Indian economy (based on the monetarist and real activity models developed in chapter 3) the independent variables tested are the relative price of food, the availability of food (a factor unaffected by monetary developments), and the prices of imported goods (tables 5-11 and 5-12). Harberger's monetarist model, based on the theory of demand for real money balances, relates the inflation rate to the rates of growth of real income and money supply, and the cost of holding money.[8] It assumes that changes in money supply are exogenous rather than themselves being determined jointly with price changes (tests of this assumption are conducted in the appendix to this chapter). The model also assumes that changes in real income are exogenous, not jointly determined with money supply changes. In the Indian context this assumption is plausible, since almost half of output originates in agriculture where output depends on exogenous factors such as weather and technology.

The real activity model relates the inflation rate to the percentage deviation of output from its trend and to price expectations. For Western economies, inflation is expected to be positively related to the deviation of output from trend, following a general Phillips-curve relationship. For the predominantly agricultural economy of India, however, the expected relationship may be the reverse; that is, a stagflation relationship may be the natural one. A rise in agricultural output caused by good weather should lead to a decline or deceleration in agricultural prices and an increase in output of the industrial sector as raw material costs decline and urban wage demands are dampened.

Both models are demand-oriented, although one emphasizes monetary

8. Arnold C. Harberger, "The Dynamics of Inflation in Chile," in Carl F. Christ and others, *Measurement in Economics: Studies in Mathematical Economics and Econometrics* (Stanford University Press, 1963), pp. 219–50.

elements and the other real activity. Neither captures structural or cost-push aspects of inflation. Because these factors were important in Indian inflation, the tests here incorporate in both models variables to capture cost-push pressures from food scarcity and imported inflation. Cost-push from food scarcity is represented by the relative price of food, or alternatively the deviation of food availability per capita from its historical average (which has shown no trend over time). The rate of inflation in the price of imported goods is the other cost-push variable. If the food and import price variables are statistically significant, then inflation is affected not only by the level of aggregate demand but also by its composition.

The models are estimated both for the entire period 1956–76 and for 1956–72 in order to examine the stability of the relationships during the period of extremely high domestic and foreign inflation.[9] Surprisingly, none of the terms of the real activity model is significant in any of the equations tested (table 5-11). Aggregate changes in output apparently have no effect on the inflation rate. Admittedly, deviations from trends may not be a good measure of the nature of demand; but to find that there is no correlation with inflation is somewhat surprising.[10] Both the structural variables—food and import price changes—are significant explanators of inflation, which along with the lack of significance in the demand variables lends support to a structural explanation of inflation.

The nonsignificance of the price-expectations term—the lagged inflation rate—is also somewhat unexpected. However, if supply is taken to be the prime element in inflation, the role of expectations is irrelevant. Food output affects prices, and labor supply and union demands are irrelevant. If attempts at maintaining a real wage were successful, then there would be some autocorrelation in the price series—wages would follow prices and in turn raise prices. But the large agricultural, and unorganized, sector in India makes a wage-price spiral unlikely.

The monetarist model performs much better than the real activity model. Indeed, equation 2 in table 5-12 yields coefficients close to the

9. The years 1973–76 contain extreme and simultaneous movement in domestic, import, and relative food prices. A correlation between these variables is thus imposed by the data. This creates a dilemma; a model tested for the entire period would yield efficient estimates for the coefficients, but if most of the variation between the key variables is during 1972–76, a spurious correlation could impose a structure for the entire test period.

10. When the real activity model was estimated with a variable representing the deviation of industrial output from trend, this variable also showed no relationship with inflation, nor did the nonfood component of the consumer price index show any statistical relationship with this variable.

Table 5-11. *Demand Model of Price Inflation in India, 1956–72 and 1956–76*[a]

Percent[b]

			Change in							
			Real output							
Equation number	Time period	Constant	Trend	Change in trend	Lagged prices	Import prices	Food prices	Food availability	Coefficient of determination, $\bar{R}^2$	Durbin-Watson
1	1956–72	4.96	−0.28	0.37	0.20	...	...	...	−0.100	1.20
		(2.83)	(0.69)	(0.95)	(0.81)					
2	1956–76	5.30	−0.60	0.27	0.22	...	...	...	−0.033	1.29
		(2.16)	(0.82)	(0.44)	(0.82)					
3	1956–72	4.65	−0.01	0.21	0.10	0.22	...	...	0.046	1.66
		(2.83)	(0.03)	(0.55)	(0.42)	(1.73)				
4	1956–76	4.35	0.33	−0.07	−0.12	0.41	...	...	0.460	1.36
		(2.43)	(0.57)	(0.16)	(0.59)	(4.06)				
5	1956–72	4.13	−0.19	0.34	0.24	...	0.32	...	−0.082	1.29
		(2.18)	(0.42)	(0.89)	(0.96)		(1.10)			

6	1956–76	3.09	−0.36	0.21	0.35	...	0.91	...	0.426	1.91
		(1.60)	(0.64)	(0.48)	(1.75)		(3.82)			
7	1956–72	5.60	0.34	−0.18	0.06	...	...	−0.61	0.239	2.10
		(3.80)	(0.76)	(0.48)	(0.28)			(2.60)		
8	1956–76	5.70	−0.19	−0.16	0.16	...	...	−0.45	−0.025	1.51
		(2.30)	(0.23)	(0.22)	(0.59)			(1.10)		
9	1956–72	3.92	3.92	0.19	0.14	0.21	0.28	...	0.055	1.73
		(2.21)	(0.11)	(0.51)	(0.58)	(1.66)	(1.06)			
10	1956–76	3.00	0.27	−0.02	0.06	0.30	0.65	...	0.673	2.06
		(2.06)	(0.60)	(0.07)	(0.35)	(3.60)	(3.38)			
11	1956–72	5.30	0.36	−0.16	0.40	0.10	...	−0.51	0.207	2.13
		(3.50)	(0.78)	(0.42)	(0.18)	(0.71)		(1.85)		
12	1956–76	4.60	0.57	−0.34	−0.15	0.40	...	−0.30	0.457	1.59
		(2.50)	(0.90)	(0.65)	(0.71)	(3.90)		(0.94)		

a. Based on the equation $P' = b_0 + b_1 \text{ GAP} + b_2 \text{ GAPD} + b_3P^e$, where P' is the change in prices, GAP is the percentage deviation of output from its trend value and GAPD the difference between the current and lagged deviations, and P^e is a variable reflecting price expectations.
b. Figures in parentheses are the absolute values of the t-statistic.

Table 5-12. *Monetarist Model of Price Inflation in India, 1956–72 and 1956–76*[a]

Percent[b]

			Change in									
								Money supply				
Equation number	*Time period*	*Constant*	*Real income*	*Cost of holding money*	*Import prices*	*Food prices*	*Food availability*	*Current*	*Lagged*	*Current plus lagged*	*Coefficient of determination,* $\bar{R}^2$	*Durbin-Watson*
1	1956–72	1.20	−0.50	−0.200	...	...	...	0.12	0.63	0.75	0.075	1.52
		(0.32)	(1.1)	(0.8)				(0.25)	(0.25)	(1.80)		
2	1956–76	−1.10	−0.80	−0.020	...	...	...	0.53	0.57	1.10	0.474	2.00
		(0.14)	(1.6)	(0.0)				(1.05)	(0.98)	(2.70)		
3	1956–72	2.50	−0.50	−0.200	0.18	...	...	0.11	0.42	0.53	0.173	1.93
		(0.67)	(1.1)	(0.8)	(1.6)			(0.23)	(0.84)	(1.28)		
4	1956–76	3.20	−0.50	0.060	0.22	...	...	0.27	0.09	0.36	0.578	1.91
		(0.72)	(1.1)	(0.21)	(2.2)			(0.60)	(0.10)	(0.73)		
5	1956–72	0.14	−0.39	−0.190	...	0.34	...	−0.07	0.83	0.76	0.119	1.51
		(0.04)	(0.8)	(0.7)		(1.3)		(0.14)	(1.60)	(1.90)		

6	1956–76	−3.10 (0.87)	−0.56 (1.3)	−0.180 (0.7)	...	0.68 (3.3)	...	0.09 (0.20)	1.06 (2.20)	1.15 (3.52)	0.671	1.88
7	1956–72	1.60 (0.57)	−0.50 (1.5)	−0.110 (0.05)	...	...	−0.55 (3.4)	0.55 (1.40)	0.16 (0.40)	0.71 (2.4)	0.514	2.40
8	1956–76	0.18 (0.04)	−0.96 (1.95)	−0.025 (0.09)	...	...	−0.48 (2.0)	0.88 (1.80)	0.13 (0.22)	1.01 (2.60)	0.558	2.00
9	1956–72	1.40 (0.38)	−0.38 (0.9)	−0.170 (0.6)	0.16 (1.4)	0.29 (1.1)	...	−0.05 (0.11)	0.61 (1.20)	0.56 (1.3)	0.193	1.92
10	1956–76	0.55 (0.15)	−0.35 (0.91)	−0.090 (0.4)	0.18 (2.3)	0.61 (3.3)	...	−0.07 (0.19)	0.62 (1.30)	0.55 (1.40)	0.740	2.07
11	1956–72	1.40 (0.46)	−0.50 (1.5)	−0.110 (0.5)	−0.03 (0.2)	...	−0.58 (2.7)	0.58 (1.40)	0.16 (0.40)	0.74 (2.20)	0.470	2.41
12	1956–76	2.90 (0.65)	−0.070 (1.4)	0.040 (0.13)	0.16 (1.5)	...	−0.30 (1.19)	0.57 (1.10)	−0.06 (0.11)	0.51 (1.00)	0.599	1.94

a. Based on the equation $P' = a_0 + a_1 Y' + a_2 M' + aM'_{-1} + a_4 A'$, where P', Y', M', and A' represent percentage changes in prices, real income, money supply, M_1, and the cost of holding money, respectively.

b. Figures in parentheses are the absolute values of the t-statistic.

predicted values: the coefficient of real income is −0.8 compared to the theoretical long-run value of −1.0. The variable representing the cost of holding money is never significant in any of the equations tested. Taken at face value, this suggests that the demand for money is extremely inelastic with respect to interest rates. It might be, however, that the variable used is a crude and inappropriate proxy for changes in the cost of holding money.[11]

The sum of the coefficients on the two money-supply variables, though always of the right sign and reasonable magnitude, is not statistically significant in some of the equations in table 5-12. When both food and import prices are included in the regression, the sum is significant only in equation 10. The pattern of changes in these coefficients of money is suggestive of multicollinearity as well as a weak role for money in its influence on prices.

The food bottleneck, whether measured in terms of relative price or food availability, does affect the inflation rate. This directly contradicts the assumption of the monetarist model that relative price changes do not matter. Furthermore, the food price variable is significant even in the presence of variables reflecting demand, which suggests that supply bottlenecks have an effect independent of their role in affecting monetary demand. It is possible that changes in food prices induce changes in monetary growth. For instance, expectation of a drought can induce hoarding and increase speculation and thereby lead to an increase in the demand for credit. Statistical significance of the food-price variable in the presence of the monetary-expansion variable indicates a strong role for supply variables in the generation of inflation.

The import-price variable is significant for the 1956–76 time period and relatively significant for the 1956–72 time period as well. Thus import prices seem to have had an important role in domestic inflation. The range of the coefficient on import price inflation (0.18–0.22) is much larger than the share of imports in GNP (0.05), supporting the contention that the external inflation had a disproportionate effect on domestic prices in 1973–76. The 1956–72 coefficient in equation 9, table 5-12, implies that in the consumer price increases of 17 percent, 27 percent, and 6 percent

11. Susan M. Wachter, *Latin American Inflation* (Lexington Books, 1976), finds that the variable representing the cost of holding money is insignificant. See also Robert C. Vogel, "The Dynamics of Inflation in Latin America, 1950–1969," *American Economic Review*, vol. 64 (March 1974), pp. 102–14.

Table 5-13. *Econometric Projections of Indian Inflation, 1970–76*
Percent

	Changes in consumer price index		
		Projected	
Year	*Actual*	*Based on 1956–72 data*[a]	*Based on 1956–76 data*[b]
1970	5.3	4.2	3.1
1971	3.0	3.3	0.9
1972	5.8	4.3	5.5
1973	17.4	13.8	15.6
1974	27.3	19.3	22.1
1975	6.1	12.2	10.0
1976	−8.1	1.8	−2.5

a. Calculated from equation 9, table 5-12.
b. Calculated from equation 10, table 5-12.

during 1973, 1974, and 1975, respectively, the portions contributed by imported inflation were 4.9 percent, 9.0 percent, and 3.6 percent. This interpretation makes the high domestic inflation rates less difficult to explain.

Given the rise in international food prices during 1972–75, the import-price and food-price variables are structurally related and reflect part of the same phenomenon. However, to a considerable degree they reflect different cost-push influences. The inclusion of both variables (in equations 9 and 10) does generally increase the explanatory power of the models.

When the model estimated for 1956–72 is used to predict the inflation rates of 1970–76, it captures double-digit inflation in 1973–74, but its performance is not strong (table 5-13). But when the model estimated with 1956–76 data is used, predicted inflation rates correspond much more closely with the actual data and even anticipate the steep decline in domestic inflation in 1976.

Structural, cost-push elements seem to have played a more important role than monetary elements in India's inflation in the 1970s. Furthermore, the reduced role of money when these variables are included in the regression models suggests that both demand (i.e., money) and supply factors play important roles in explaining inflation.

Conclusion

Both domestic and external causes accounted for the leap in Indian inflation from its range of 3–5 percent yearly in the 1960s to 17 percent in 1973 and 27 percent in 1974. Agricultural supply appears to have been one important factor. Food grain production declined in 1973 when there were no more P.L. 480 imports to bridge the supply gap and when world prices of imported food were at all-time highs. The result was severe upward pressure on food prices.

For import prices more generally, with external trade only 5 percent of Indian GNP, external price movements might be expected to have a limited impact. In the specific instance of petroleum, although Indian inflation had already reached an annual rate of 22 percent before the November 1973 OPEC oil price rise, the rise did worsen inflation and the import bill (with oil rising from 10 percent to 26 percent of import value).

For its part, money supply grew excessively in the period 1970–73, reaching a peak annual growth rate of 17 percent in 1972–73. External reserves did not account for this expansion, as they did in many developing countries. Fiscal policy was also expansive in the period 1970–73, as the result of the Bangladesh War in 1971–72 and poor food crops in 1973–74 (requiring purchases of food abroad and increased government wages). By mid-1974, however, fiscal as well as monetary policy turned to restraint.

The statistical monetarist model of Indian inflation augmented by variables for import and food price inflation finds that these two variables, in addition to monetary variables, are significant in explaining inflation. The estimated coefficient of import prices in explaining domestic inflation is approximately 0.2, far in excess of the share of imports in the economy. This result indicates a major role for imported inflation. Even though India's economy is relatively closed, with traded goods constituting only 5 percent of the GNP, rising prices in the foreign sector accounted for approximately one-third of the country's inflation in 1973 and 1974. The other part of India's exceptional inflation in those years was attributable to domestic monetary and fiscal influences rather than imported inflation. After mid-1974, monetary and fiscal restraint, combined with a sharp drop in the inflationary pressure from import and food prices, enabled India to regain its earlier price stability.

Appendix

The monetarist model tested in this chapter assumes that money supply changes are exogenous to price changes. The assumption is formally tested in this section. Apart from its implications regarding simultaneous-equations bias in reduced-form models, the exogeneity of money and prices has a bearing on the controversy over causes of inflation. For instance, if changes in the money supply cause price changes as defined by Granger[12] and no reverse or contemporaneous relationship exists, then support would be received for the monetarist position that inflation is induced by changes in monetary expansion. A strictly reverse finding of price change causing money change would support a cost-push structuralist position.

Granger and Sims have developed statistical tests for causality.[13] In addition, Pierce and Haugh offer a test for the presence (rather than the direction) of a relationship between two variables.[14] The application of the causality tests is dependent on an appropriate transformation of the respective series. In particular, the series Z_t (referring to the logarithmic values of both M_1 and CPI) needs to be transformed into a random, serially uncorrelated (white noise) series, Z_t^*. This transformation, achieved through Box-Jenkins[15] or ARIMA methods, involves two steps. First, the series Z is transformed into a stationary series (stationarity is achieved for most economic time-series by an appropriate degree of differencing—for example, $Z_t' = Z_t - Z_{t-1}$, where Z_t' is the stationary series). Second, the autoregressive and autocorrelative nature of the series is identified and a residual series, Z_t^*, is obtained. The term Z_t^* represents the innovations present in the series—that is, the part of Z_t (or Z_t') that cannot be predicted

12. C. W. J. Granger, "Investigating Causal Relations by Econometric Models and Cross-Spectral Methods," *Econometrica,* vol. 37 (July 1979), pp. 424–38; the formal definition of causality states that X causes Y if present and past values of X are significant in explaining variations in Y *after* adjusting for the effect of the past values of Y on its present value.

13. Granger, ibid.; Christopher A. Sims, "Money, Income and Causality," *American Economic Review,* vol. 62 (September 1972), pp. 540–52.

14. David A. Pierce and Larry D. Haugh, "Causality in Temporal Systems: Characterizations and a Survey," *Journal of Econometrics,* vol. 5 (May 1977), pp. 265–93.

15. George E. P. Box and Gwilym M. Jenkins, *Times Series Analysis Forecasting and Control* (Holden-Day, 1970).

Table 5-14. *Summary Statistics on Series Used for Causality Tests*[a]

Equation	*Q-statistic*	*Degrees of freedom*	*Variance of residuals*
1. Prices: $(1 - L) \log P_t = U1_t$	83.7	21	0.023
2. Money: $(1 - L) \log M_t = U2_t$	93.1	21	0.019
3. Prices: $(1 - \underset{(6.14)}{0.521L})((1 - L) \log P_t - \underset{(3.14)}{0.013}) = U3_t$	32.3	18	0.004
4. Money: $(1 - \underset{(3.93)}{0.382L} - \underset{(2.46)}{0.237L^2})((1 - L) \log M_t - \underset{(4.8)}{0.020}) = U4_t$	34.3	17	0.003

a. Analysis of quarterly data, 1951–76; P_t is CPI and M_t is M_1; absolute values of the *t*-statistic are in parentheses. The *U* terms refer to residuals.

from its own past. These residuals, or innovations, are then used for formal causality tests.

Stationarity was achieved for both M_1 and CPI by taking first differences in the logarithms of the respective series. (Since percentage changes are approximately equal to first differences in the logs, the same notation is used for the latter, that is, $Z'_t = \log Z_t - \log Z_{t-1}$). ARIMA models for the two series were then identified; the CPI series was identified as ARIMA (1, 1, 1) and the M_1 series as ARIMA (1, 1, 2).[16] The stationary and ARIMA series are presented in table 5-14 with the corresponding statistics. The *Q*-statistic tests for the serial independence or white-noise nature of each series.[17]

The residuals from the ARIMA models allow the formal tests of causality to be conducted. Strictly speaking, the (somewhat) arbitrary ARIMA transformation is only necessary for the Sims and Pierce-Haugh

16. ARIMA (*l, m, n*) refers to a series with a degree of differencing equal to *l*, an autoregressive parameter of order *m*, and a moving average parameter of order *n*. See Charles R. Nelson, *Applied Time Series Analysis for Managerial Forecasting* (Holden–Day, 1973), for a good introduction to the subject of ARIMA models.

17. Formally,

$$Q = N \sum_{i=1}^{m} r_i^2,$$

where *N* is the number of observations, and r_i^2 is the square of the *i*th autocorrelation coefficient. The term *Q* is distributed asymptotically as χ^2 with $(m - n)$ degrees of freedom, where *m* is the number of autoregressive parameters and *n* the number of moving average parameters estimated.

tests, and not for the Granger test. The Sims and Pierce-Haugh tests are sensitive to the presence of autocorrelation and can yield biased results if the series have not been appropriately transformed into white noise. The Granger test involves, on the righthand side, lagged values of the dependent variable. If a sufficiently long-lagged distribution is chosen, the effects of serial correlation can be purged and F-tests appropriately applied. Thus an ARIMA transformation of the series Z'_t is not necessary. This property of the Granger test, the arbitrariness of the ARIMA method, and the relatively white-noise nature of M' and P' dictate that the causality tests be conducted for two sets of series—M' and P', and M^* and P^*. Comparison of the results should be indicative of their robustness.

The Pierce-Haugh test is used to test for independence of two series, x and y. This test states that on the null hypothesis of independence, the S-statistic,

$$S = N \sum_{k=m}^{m} r_{xy}^2(k),$$

is distributed asymptotically as χ^2 $(2m+1)$, chi-squared with $(2m+1)$ degrees of freedom. For small samples, the modified S-statistic, S^*, is suggested:

$$S^* = N^2 \sum_{k=m}^{m} (N - k)^{-1} r_{xy}^2(k),$$

where N is the number of observations, k the extent of the lag, and r_{xy}^2 the squared correlation coefficient. In either case, if S or S^* exceeds the chi-squared value at the chosen significance level, the hypothesis of independence is rejected.

The Pierce-Haugh test is unable to detect the direction of causality. For testing the nature of causality, the Granger and Sims tests can be used. The tests are equivalent, theoretically. The Granger test is simply a test of the effect of lagged x values on y, in the presence of lagged y values. If these lagged x values are jointly significant, then it can be concluded that x causes y. The Sims test involves lagged and leading values: for instance, x causes y if in a regression involving x as the dependent variable and past, present, and future y values as the independent variables, the future y values are jointly significant. The x and y variables are reversed in both tests for the test of the relationship between x and y. A contemporaneous relationship between x and y is given by the result x causes y and y causes x. More informally, the coefficient on the current value of x (or y) in a

Table 5-15. *Results of Causality Tests*[a]

Tests for independence of money and prices	
Pierce-Haugh cross-correlation test	*S-statistic*
Prices and money (*U*1 and *U*2)	68.4
Prices and money (*U*3 and *U*4)	19.1
The χ^2-statistic for *U*1 and *U*2 is significant at 1 percent level of confidence; for *U*3 and *U*4, χ^2 is not significant at the 10 percent level.	
Causality tests between money and prices	
Sims test	*F-statistic* (10, 58)
Case A. Money causes prices (*U*1 and *U*2)	2.40
Case B. Prices cause money (*U*1 and *U*2)	1.44
Case C. Money causes prices (*U*3 and *U*4)	1.80
Case D. Prices cause money (*U*3 and *U*4)	0.73
The *F*-statistic for case A is significant at 1 percent level of significance, for case C at the 10 percent level.	
Granger test	*F-statistic* (9, 67)
Case A. Money causes prices (*U*1 and *U*2)	2.98
Case B. Prices cause money (*U*1 and *U*2)	1.23
Case C. Money causes prices (*U*3 and *U*4)	2.54
Case D. Prices cause money (*U*3 and *U*4)	1.66
The *F*-statistic for cases A and C is significant at the 1 percent level.	

a. Analysis of quarterly data, 1956–76; for Sims test, 8 past and 8 future lags were used; for Granger test, 8 lags for each variable (money and prices) were used.

Sims-type regression is indicative of a contemporaneous relationship. Formally, the Sims test is

$$y_t = a_0 + \sum_{i=0}^{m} b_i x_{t-i} + \sum_{i=1}^{m} c_i x_{t+i}.$$

If an *F*-test indicates that the future values, x_{t+i}, are jointly significant in explaining *y*, then *y* causes *x*.

Table 5-15 reports the results for the three tests. Regarding the series *M′ and P′*, the *S**-statistic indicates that the two series are *not* independent. Further, both the Sims and Granger tests indicate that changes in the money supply cause price changes and that there is no reverse causation. The tests then confirm in a striking and unanimous manner the exogenous nature of money in a money-price relationship.

The tests pertaining to *M** and *P** are mixed. The Pierce-Haugh test indicates that the hypothesis that money and prices are independent of each other cannot be rejected at even the 10 percent level of confidence. This finding is a direct contradiction of almost all theories of inflation.[18] The Sims test indicates a one-way relationship between money and prices at the 10 percent level of confidence. The Granger test yields a stronger causal relationship. According to it, money causes prices at the 1 percent significance level. No test yields a relationship that runs from prices to money.

Overall, the results are not as robust as one might have liked. Conflicting results given by the three tests are indicative of the newness of the Box-Jenkins approach to time-series analysis. Since ARIMA modeling is an inexact science, the ARIMA values may not have been correctly identified. The Q-statistic tests would indicate a white-noise structure for the residuals. That the results are sensitive to the type of filter chosen is indicated by the diverse results yielded for two filters, M' and P', and M^* and P^*.

The causality tests indicate that there is at least a weak causal relationship between money and prices, and that it is proper to assume that money supply growth is exogenous in equations like the simple monetarist model of inflation in chapter 3. Not even weak support is obtained for a systematic influence of price changes on money supply.

18. A similar finding for the United States using data for the third quarter of 1953 to the second quarter of 1971 was reached by Edgar L. Feige and Douglas K. Pearce, "Economically Rational Expectations: Are Innovations in the Rate of Inflation Independent of Innovations in Measures of Monetary and Fiscal Policy," *Journal of Political Economy,* vol. 84 (June 1976), pp. 499–522. However, Brillembourg and Khan find with annual data, 1870–1975, and the same test that money and prices are not independent; Arturo Brillembourg and Mohsin S. Khan, "The Relationship between Money, Income, and Prices: Has Money Mattered Historically?" *Journal of Money, Credit, and Banking,* vol. 11 (August 1979), pp. 358–65.

CHAPTER SIX

Central American Accommodation to External Disruptions

GABRIEL SIRI *and* LUIS RAÚL DOMÍNGUEZ

GUATEMALA and El Salvador are small, developing countries with very open economies, fixed exchange rates, and a tradition of conservative monetary and fiscal policy. Their economic structure and policies are representative of the Central American economies.[1] The countries of this region, lying along a narrow isthmus with easy access to the sea, have been heavily oriented toward external trade, and economic policies have reinforced the natural tendency. Tariff barriers have remained relatively low and exchange-rate manipulation has simply been nonexistent. Parity rates with respect to the U.S. dollar have been constant for Guatemala and El Salvador since the early 1920s. Moreover, in Guatemala the purchase of foreign currency has been practically unrestricted. In both economies, expansions in the money supply can be readily diverted to imports with little effect on domestic prices or production.[2]

During the international economic disruptions of the early 1970s, inflation surged from rates traditionally near zero to rates on the order of 13 percent to 19 percent in Guatemala and El Salvador. There is little

WE ACKNOWLEDGE the competent assistance of Ana Rosa Batres de Osorio in the preparation of this paper and the helpful comments of Armando Gonzales Campo, Manuel A. Chavarria, Federico Sanz y Sanz, and Juan Rafael Vargas.

1. Except for Costa Rica, whose more ambitious full-employment policies and resulting balance-of-payments difficulties make it atypical of the region. Nicaragua and Honduras are not included in this analysis because the repercussions of the December 1972 earthquake in Nicaragua and the October 1974 hurricane in Honduras distort the economic profiles of these two countries in the 1970s.

2. This marginal definition of openness, which is sometimes at odds with the more familiar one that relates the size of the external sector to the total product of the economy, is based on Robert Triffin's scheme for the integration of monetary and income analysis in *The World Money Maze: National Currencies in International Payments* (Yale University Press, 1966), app. 1.

room for doubt that the inflation was, to a large extent, imported. In these economies, domestic prices tend to adjust rather rapidly to changes in prices of imports. Undoubtedly the lagged wave of domestic inflation can be altered by internal conditions (particularly in the food production sector) or by governmental policy, but there is no way of avoiding the pull of external prices. This chapter examines both internal and external inflationary factors in the two countries in 1972–76 and the variations in governmental policy for dealing with them.

External Influences on the Economies

During the 1950s and 1960s and, in fact, until the beginning of the world inflation of 1973, the pattern of monetary financing and monetary absorption in Guatemala and El Salvador seemed to be typical of very open economies. Balance-of-trade deficits tended to coincide with the ups and downs of monetary financing (often internal and external financing peaked in unison). Inasmuch as the governments wished and were able to control money supply, they affected global demand, and thus imports and the balance of trade. The pattern bypassed the usual channels of adjustment found in more closed economies, where monetary financing is absorbed largely either through price rises or through real production increases.

As is generally the case in developing countries, the ratio of money to income tended to increase consistently and peak in years when monetary financing sharply increased. This accommodation of the monetary ratio—depicted by Triffin as a reduction of liquidity financing[3]—tends to undo in part the effects of credit creation by the monetary authorities, of external flows of capital, and of surpluses in the balance of trade. In 1972, for example, increases in domestic credit complemented by external financing brought into the two economies through surpluses in the balance of trade were to a certain degree undone by the sharp increase in the monetary ratio (table 6-1). The pattern was much the same in the following years, but price inflation increased the size of the variables, and the oscillations of the money stock and of imports and exports became much less manageable. In particular, balance-of-trade deficits, supported to a large extent by domestic monetary expansion, rose to unprecedented levels. Imports of consumer goods of Guatemala and El Salvador practically

3. Ibid.

Table 6-1. *Sources of Monetary Financing and Absorption in Guatemala and El Salvador, 1967–77*

Millions of U.S. dollars

Source	*1967*	*1968*	*1969*	*1970*	*1971*	*1972*	*1973*	*1974*	*1975*	*1976*	*1977*
Guatemala											
Internal financing (private and government credit)	25.7	23.8	24.7	7.4	24.0	47.3	30.5	108.3	76.0	87.3	104.2
Changes in liquidity (reduction in the monetary ratio)	−7.3	6.4	−13.4	−0.8	−28.0	−69.5	−2.8	42.2	−41.9	−87.7	49.1
External financing (capital flows)	41.1	25.2	2.4	14.0	47.1	41.8	65.4	82.6	145.1	448.2	240.4
Total monetary financing (equal to total absorption)	59.5	55.4	13.4	20.6	43.1	19.6	93.1	233.1	179.2	447.8	393.7
Production increases (real increases of GDP, in monetary terms)	10.7	15.3	21.2	20.9	22.0	33.6	33.7	36.0	14.4	67.4	89.8
Price increases (price increases of GDP, in monetary terms)	0.8	13.0	−1.4	14.8	−2.6	−6.1	76.8	94.1	98.8	118.0	212.9
Domestic prices (sum of the price increases of consumption and investment, in monetary terms)	2.9	12.5	0.0	7.4	5.1	2.2	74.4	112.1	105.3	n.a.	152.7
Import prices (price increases of imports, in monetary terms)	0.1	0.3	1.6	3.0	2.2	9.2	21.5	47.9	20.4	n.a.	30.7
Export prices (price increases of exports, in monetary terms)	−2.0	0.8	0.2	10.4	−5.5	0.9	23.9	29.9	13.9	n.a.	91.3
Deficits (imports minus exports, in current dollars)	48.0	27.1	−6.4	−15.1	23.7	−7.9	−17.4	103.0	66.0	262.4	91.0

El Salvador											
Internal financing (private and government credit)	5.7	14.8	35.6	1.4	29.2	34.7	74.5	125.0	52.2	93.6	127.2
Changes in liquidity (reduction in the monetary ratio)	7.1	−8.6	−12.5	2.5	−11.2	−31.4	−5.2	6.3	−12.7	−47.3	11.9
External financing (capital flows)	26.6	18.3	12.2	21.7	19.7	9.0	29.9	81.1	137.0	112.7	51.5
Total monetary financing (equal to total absorption)	39.4	24.5	35.3	25.6	37.7	12.3	99.2	212.4	176.5	159.0	190.6
Production increases (real increases of GDP, in monetary terms)	12.2	7.9	9.4	8.2	14.7	20.3	19.4	28.1	22.2	28.5	38.6
Price increases (price increases of GDP, in monetary terms)	−0.8	0.6	1.1	12.5	1.5	3.2	39.5	51.6	61.3	102.3	116.1
Domestic prices (sum of the price increases of consumption and investment, in monetary terms)	−0.8	0.6	2.5	2.4	11.5	6.4	32.6	85.7	82.6	9.8	11.5
Import prices (price increases of imports, in monetary terms)	−0.2	0.2	−0.1	1.5	12.9	4.6	18.9	62.2	24.4	11.2	16.7
Export prices (price increases of exports, in monetary terms)	−0.2	0.2	−1.5	11.6	−2.9	1.4	25.8	28.1	3.1	103.7	121.3
Deficits (imports minus exports, in current dollars)	28.0	16.0	24.8	4.9	21.5	−11.2	40.3	132.7	93.0	28.2	35.9

Sources: *International Financial Statistics*, vol. 31 (May 1978); data bank of the Permanent Secretariat of the General Treaty on the Economic Integration of Central America (SIECA), Guatemala.
n.a. Not available.

Figure 6-1. *Growth Pattern of Trade Prices and Real GDP of Guatemala and El Salvador Compared with OECD Pattern, 1971–76*

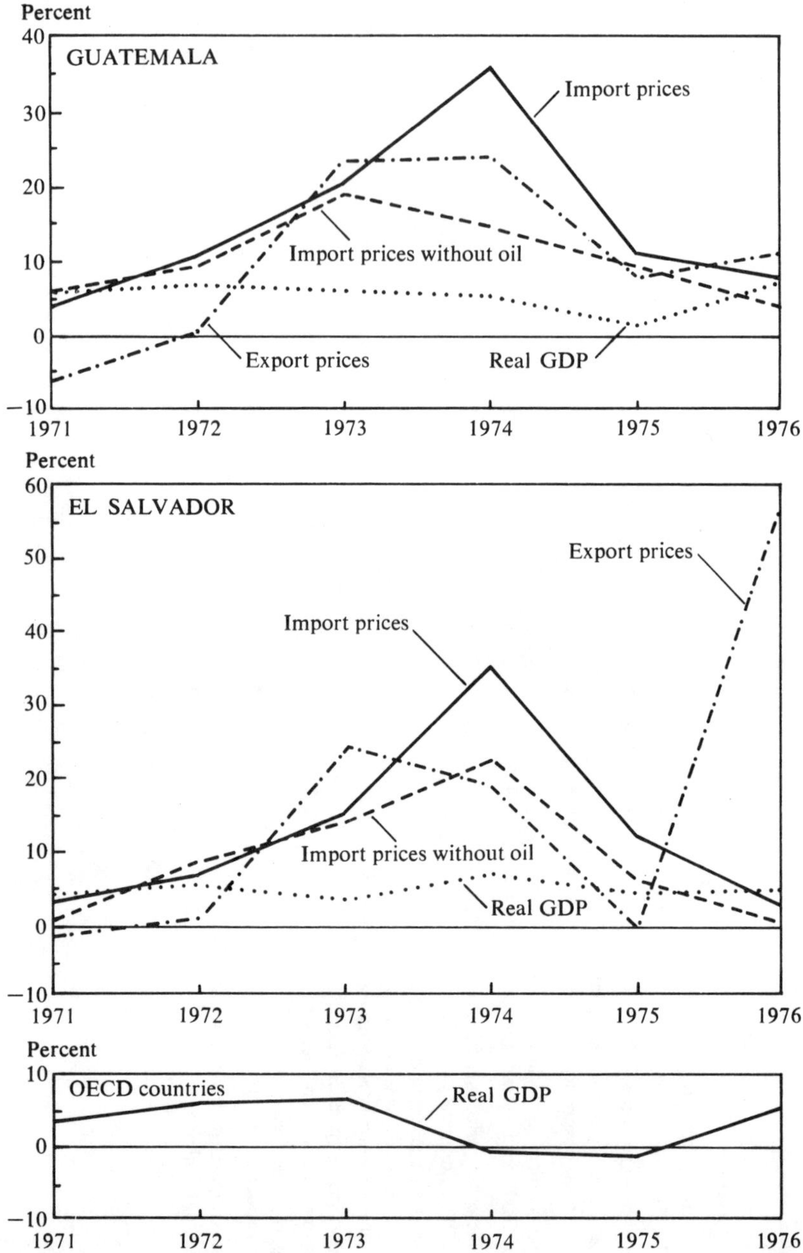

Sources: Central Banks of Guatemala and El Salvador; Organization for Economic Cooperation and Development.

doubled between 1972 and 1974, and again between 1975 and 1977. Basically this was the result of a combination of low price elasticity and high income elasticity with respect to imports, heightened perhaps by the failure of consumers who profited from the export booms to perceive that their profits were being eroded through inflation. The expansion may also have been the result of rapidly acquired habits of higher consumption.

In the years of high liquidity the private sector in both countries rapidly moved to international capital markets to finance imports. Flows of external capital tended to make up for, and at times (as in 1975) to counteract, domestic monetary restrictions. Moreover, the changes in the velocity of money (the rate at which it circulates through the economy, and the inverse of the monetary ratio) were also greater, and at times the historical tendency for velocity to decrease was reversed. In 1974, for example, external prices and inventory accumulation rose so sharply that the usually accommodating monetary financing seemed to be insufficient to finance the outward flow of money. This may explain why the velocity of money increased substantially. (The phenomenon recurred in 1977 in Guatemala, but probably as a direct result of high expected inflation decreasing the time money is held in the public's hands.) As demand for real money balances went down, consumer spending on durable goods and on real stocks rose.

During the period of intense international inflation there were no surpluses in the balance of trade of Guatemala or El Salvador; thus the demand pressure that surpluses sometimes cause was not one of the means through which inflation was imported into these countries. Significantly, there were record deficits in 1974, the year of the great worldwide inflation.

Changing world prices did have a substantial impact on the terms of trade of both countries. With the commodity price boom of 1973 their terms of trade improved, but they deteriorated again in 1974 with the oil price increase. Price movements had a far greater impact than volume movements on the countries' trade balances.

Import prices of Guatemala and El Salvador are primarily a reflection of export prices of the developed countries; they tend to lag somewhat behind the expansion cycles of the developed world and are frequently in turn followed by a peak in export prices. In the mid-1970s, however, the peak in the import price changes was much higher than that in export prices, a direct result of the enormous increase in the price of oil imports (figure 6-1). Normally export prices are more volatile and therefore their

Table 6-2. *Increase in Trade Deficits of Guatemala and El Salvador Attributable to Changes in World Prices of Commodities, 1973–76*
Millions of Central American pesos[a]

Trade item	Change in value over 1972[b]			
	1973	*1974*	*1975*	*1976*
Guatemala				
Imports	68.6	212.9	273.8	322.1
Exports	78.5	178.0	220.3	282.6
Trade deficit	−9.8	34.9	53.5	39.5
El Salvador				
Imports	44.2	164.0	194.1	n.a.
Exports	72.4	144.2	131.5	n.a.
Trade deficit	−28.2	19.2	62.6	n.a.

Sources: Central Banks of Guatemala and El Salvador.
n.a. Not available.
a. One peso is equal to one U.S. dollar.
b. Equals percentage rise in import or export price index over 1972, applied to 1972 value of imports or exports.

growth profile is more jagged than that of import prices. They often vary independently of the business cycle of the developed world, for they comprise mainly prices of agricultural exports whose supply is subject to the vagaries of weather.

The world inflation of 1973 brought sharp rises in both export and import prices but, on balance, the terms of trade changed favorably for Guatemala and El Salvador. Their trade deficits attributable to international inflation decreased during that year (table 6-2). Both export and import prices reached unprecedented levels in 1974 and then dropped sharply in 1975. However, the net effect in each of these two years of world recession was negative for both countries' terms of trade. Balance-of-trade deficits increased, particularly for Guatemala, as the volume of exports dropped below historical growth trends (see table 6-3). (Generally, however, changes in the values of imports and exports resulting from price variations were much larger than those resulting from variations in volume, as is apparent in the magnitudes of values in tables 6-2 and 6-3.)

In each country, manufactured goods account for the bulk of the import price index. After the 1974 oil price increase, the weight of oil in import prices rose sharply (figure 6-2). Oil accounted for approximately half of the increase in import prices in 1974. If oil imports are excluded,

Table 6-3. *Deviation of Export and Import Volumes from 1955–71 Trend, Guatemala and El Salvador, 1972–76*
Percent

Item	Deviation from trend[a]				
	1972	*1973*	*1974*	*1975*	*1976*
Guatemala					
Imports	−20.7	8.3	34.1	−33.7	n.a.
Exports	19.9	−2.2	−3.8	−19.3	−0.8
El Salvador					
Imports	−0.2	9.5	4.8	−5.5	n.a.
Exports	27.5	−26.9	1.9	16.5	n.a.

Sources: Central Banks of Guatemala and El Salvador.
n.a. Not available.
a. For Guatemala the 1955–71 growth trend is 7.6 percent for exports and 5.7 percent for imports, and for El Salvador 7.4 percent for exports and 5.3 percent for imports.

the import price index after 1973 is reduced considerably for both countries, and for Guatemala the terms of trade actually become more favorable.

The export price indexes of the two countries are to a large extent determined by the prices of a few agricultural export commodities. The high degree of specialization of these economies is apparent in Guatemala's dependence on coffee, bananas, cotton, and sugar for about 55 percent of its total exports in 1971–75 and El Salvador's even more dramatic reliance on three products—coffee, cotton, and sugar—which represented about 64 percent of its total exports and about 90 percent of its exports outside the Central American Common Market in 1971–75. Notwithstanding the dominance of a few commodities in the overall export price index, trade in manufactured products within the Common Market is growing. About 5 percent of the total trade of El Salvador and Guatemala was within the region in the early 1960s, when the integration treaties were signed, and by the early 1970s about 25 percent. Even so, trade within the Common Market has limited effects in moderating export cycles because traditional goods dominate all five partners' economies (and therefore their demand for regionally produced manufactured goods).[4]

Both imports from the Central American partners and imports from

4. L. R. Caceres, "Export Instability in a Common Market: The Case of Central America," University of Utah, June 1978.

Figure 6-2. *Indexes of Import and Export Prices and Their Main Components, Guatemala and El Salvador, 1971–75*

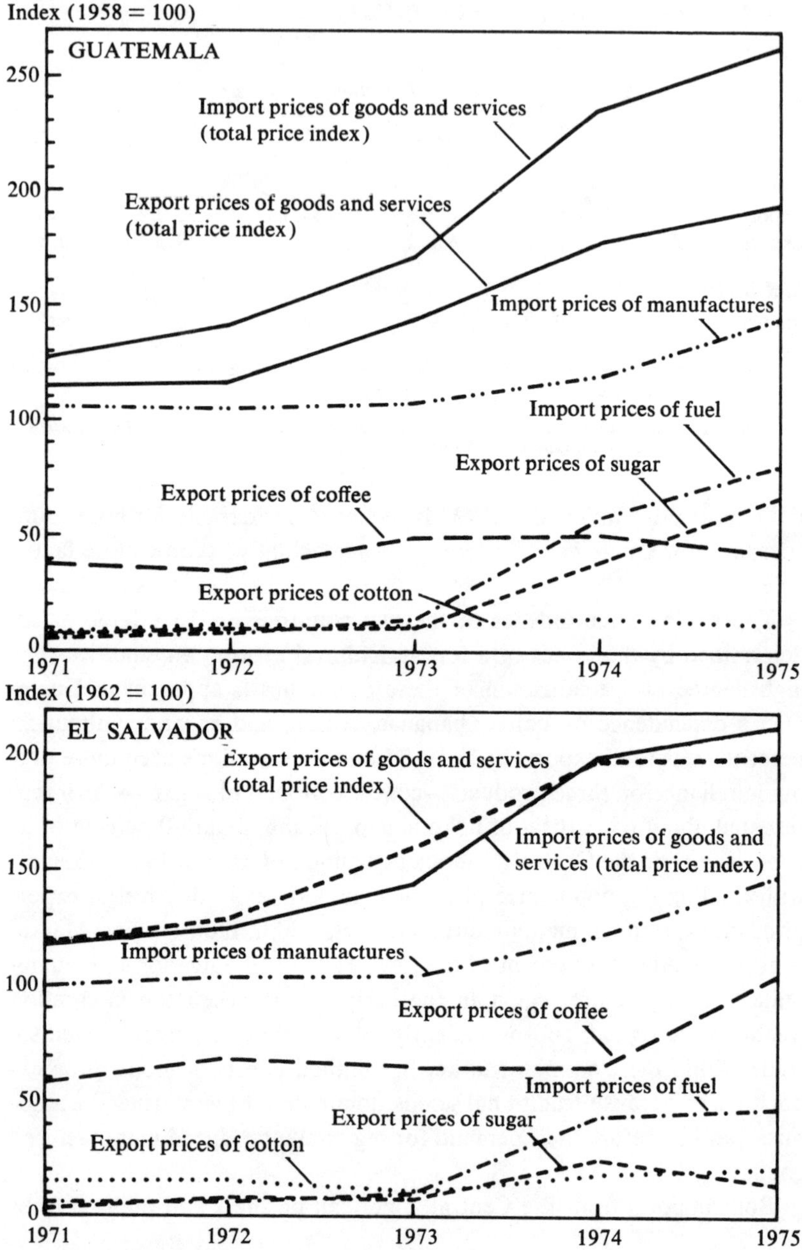

Sources: Central Banks of Guatemala and El Salvador.

the rest of the world are influenced more by consumption and investment, availability of foreign exchange, and excess monetary supplies than by prices. It is significant that 1974, the year that registered the largest increase in volume of imports for Guatemala during the decade, was the year that had the highest increase in import prices on record.[5]

The total imports and exports of the Central American countries represent a very small portion of world trade. Thus their domestic demand for or supply of goods does not affect prices in world markets. The economies are almost perfect price takers, import and export prices being totally outside their control. They can purchase as much as they can afford and can sell nearly everything they can produce at the going prices.[6] Therefore increased demand from developed countries is only relevant for its influence on international prices.

Government Response to Instability

Inflation is such a recent phenomenon in the Central American countries that until 1973 it appeared to be a matter of secondary importance. The concept of full employment seems to be unfamiliar to government planners; in a world where underemployment is permanently high, figures are not even systematically compiled for open unemployment. In recent years, planners have become interested in the concept of economic growth and the growth of industrial production.

The monetary authorities' approach to policy is primarily passive. Liquidity needs are estimated from expected growth of current income (translated into money terms) plus the external deficit. This total minus the anticipated flows of imported capital is a rough measure of the domestic credit expansion that is required.

First and foremost, governments have looked at balance-of-payments signals and have tended to contract their economies in the face of external deficits and let them expand freely when surpluses appear. It has been considered normal to expect fat years and lean, and to accept that the only remedy for the latter is belt tightening. Control of the money supply—the principal anticyclical policy tool—has been used only sparingly and timidly, and fiscal policy has been virtually nonexistent. However, in the

5. Similarly, for El Salvador the increases in volume of imports for 1973 and 1974 coincided with record inflation of import prices.

6. With the exception of bananas and to some extent coffee.

Figure 6-3. *Imports and Exports of Goods and Services and Corresponding Trade Balance, Guatemala and El Salvador, 1950–75*

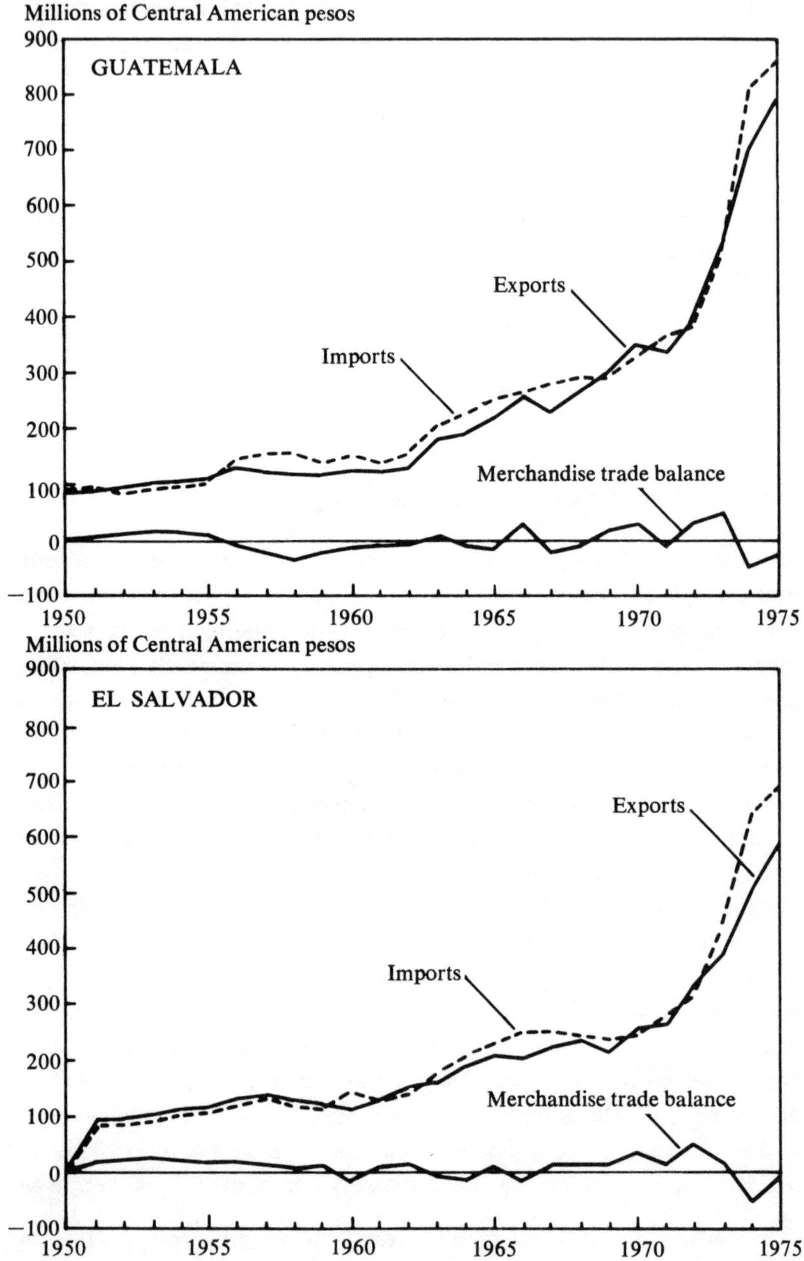

Source: *International Financial Statistics*, vol. 33 (May 1980), pp. 202–03 152–53.

face of growing social pressure in the 1970s, Central American governments have shown some reluctance to continue their traditional policy stance.

The signals that should activate policy adjustments for these open economies tend to be ambiguous. An external boom stimulates domestic inflation, but it usually implies conditions favorable to larger export earnings, and thus balance-of-payment surpluses. On the other hand, a world recession with declining inflation tends to slow down domestic price rises, but at the same time creates external deficits. Policymakers facing the dilemma of signals that call simultaneously for contraction and expansion have given priority to balance-of-payments problems. Thus in 1975 when growth was below normal, inflation high but receding, and the balance of payments deteriorating, the tendency was to contract. But when economic growth and inflation were high and the balance of payments in surplus in 1977, the response was also deflationary. The general policy seems to have been one of keeping the economy at a controlled pace in order to insure internal stability.

Perhaps the most striking economic event that befell the Central American economies—and for that matter, the world economy—in the 1970s was the Great Inflation of 1973–74. These were years of high growth of the value of external trade (see table 6-2 and figure 6-3). In particular, the value of imports increased to unprecedented levels, primarily because of rises in the price of manufactured goods, fuels, and certain raw materials. Faced with this alarming situation, Guatemala and El Salvador sought foreign credit to finance the high growth of imports (the Venezuelan petroleum finance scheme is the best example) and promoted the accumulation of stocks of raw materials and basic grains. Money supply rose because of capital inflows and, in El Salvador, also because of increases in domestic credit. The increase in liquidity supported the growth of imports. Although the balance of payments remained in a rather favorable position during the entire period, the ratio of imports to reserves steadily increased in El Salvador. Guatemala's balance of payments was much more buoyant; however, reserves did drop in 1974.

The governments, concerned about the possibility of excess liquidity and that it might have been reinforcing the imported inflation and, most of all, disturbed by growing balance-of-trade deficits, reacted with unusual resolve to reduce money supply. In 1975 Guatemala's central bank increased the reserve requirements for short-term deposits and reduced to negative values the lines of credit to the government. The central bank of

El Salvador raised the reserve requirements for long-term deposits and cut rediscount credit to domestic banks. The measures certainly restrained imports, but in retrospect they appear to have been ill timed with respect to internal balance. In 1975 domestic prices were already beginning to turn, in line with the reduction of inflation in the developed world. The induced domestic contraction may have accentuated the recession that the countries, particularly Guatemala, suffered during that year.

In their efforts to maintain external equilibrium the monetary authorities have paid close attention to the trade balance, the autonomous external capital flows, and the foreign reserve position of the country. To gauge what the reserve balance, the principal overall indicator, represents in terms of purchasing power in the international markets, the central bankers calculate the number of months that existing reserves can cover the total commitment in imports of goods and services (table 6-4).

With respect to the internal economy, the principal signal has traditionally been the growth of output or of the income of the country (table 6-4 depicts the deviations from the trend of GDP in real terms). Only very recently has the price level become a matter of concern to the Central American countries.

The principal instruments of monetary policy are reserve requirements (which have changed only a few times in each country since 1960), rediscount operations (especially in El Salvador; in Guatemala central bank credit to commercial banks has not been used extensively and in the liquidity glut of the 1970s it became almost irrelevant), control of government finance (before the 1970s fiscal deficits were small), central bank regulation of capital requirements (the chief restrictions to credit expansion of the commercial banks in Guatemala and to a certain extent of the banks in El Salvador) that effectively limits credit growth to the capacity—or willingness—of commercial banks to increase their net worth, and domestic supply stimuli and controls on the prices of goods and of public services.

Some standard monetary instruments have not been used by these countries: parity exchange rates with the U.S. dollar (the exchange rates have been stable for decades), interest rate ceilings on commercial bank loans and deposits (they have been modified only rarely), rediscount rates (they have been practically stable), and open market operations (the thin security market would not support them). Similarly, there is little evidence that governments have applied anticyclical fiscal policies regarding public expenditure and none at all with respect to taxation. On the contrary, public investment has been reduced in periods of economic slowdown and low tax revenue. For example, in years of less than average growth of real GDP in El Salvador (1970, 1973, and 1975), public investment increments were also less than average. During 1975, the only recession year for Guatemala in the decade, the increase in public expenditures was modest and central bank credit to the government was negative (−$21 million).

The possibility of revaluing the dollar exchange rate as a means of avoiding world inflation has never gathered support among the policymakers of Guatemala and El Salvador. The reluctance to do so may well be founded on economic considerations. A large foreign sector concentrated on a few agricultural export products makes the domestic currency particularly vulnerable to international fluctuations. Revaluations might prove tenable as long as the prices of export crops remained high or stable, but these governments have no assurance that world export prices will stay high.

Even though Guatemala and El Salvador were troubled by world inflation under a regime of fixed exchange rates with the U.S. dollar, there are strong arguments to suggest that floating exchange rates would not insulate these economies from external inflation and might even aggravate the degree of imported inflation. Their level of imports is highly inelastic with respect to price changes, more so as the composition of imports has changed in favor of intermediate inputs and raw materials. A rise in import prices—with no change in export prices—would cause a trade deficit, together with a higher demand for foreign exchange. Under flexible exchange rates, the domestic currency would be automatically devalued and the price of foreign goods raised as a consequence. Export proceeds in terms of foreign exchange would not be altered significantly, given that one-half to two-thirds of export earnings are accounted for by four agricultural commodities whose price is determined in the world market. With inelastic import demand and nearly fixed export income the initial devaluation would not suffice for adjusting the trade balance. Further depreciations would be necessary until ultimately import demand became elastic and the trade deficit was eliminated. By then the series of devaluations would have increased import prices by more than the external inflation. Under fixed exchange rates, on the other hand, a rise in import prices would dampen imports since the current account deficit would show up in a reduction of the monetary base and the trade imbalance would result in a multiplied decrease in money income.

Table 6-4. *Pattern of Government's Reaction to External and Internal Imbalance Signals, Guatemala and El Salvador, 1970–76*

Signal	*1970*	*1971*	*1972*	*1973*	*1974*	*1975*	*1976*
Guatemala							
External balance							
Change in balance of trade (millions of current dollars)	5.5	−27.2	27.7	−0.6	−132.1	26.5	−93.0
Net private capital inflow (millions of current dollars)	26.6	63.1	62.3	66.1	88.4	178.0	n.a.
Net foreign reserve coverage (months)	3.6	4.0	5.9	8.8	5.8	7.4	9.1
Internal balance							
Change in cost-of-living index (percent)	1.0	1.0	13.8	16.5	13.1	10.7	n.a.
Deviation in growth of real GDP (percent)	0.7	0.6	2.3	1.8	1.4	3.0	2.6
Monetary policy							
Change in rediscounted loans (millions of current dollars)	0.1	−9.9	0.0	−1.7	2.2	33.4	−24.5
Change in reserve requirement rate							
Short-term deposits (percentage points)	0.0	0.0	0.0	−5.0	0.0	10.0	0.0
Long-term deposits (percentage points)	0.0	0.0	0.0	5.0	0.0	0.0	0.0
Central bank credit to government (millions of current dollars)	−0.8	12.8	6.4	−14.5	69.8	−22.6	100.3
Fiscal policy							
Deviation of real government consumption from trend (percent)[a]	6.9	−11.9	6.1	−4.1	0.2	5.7	1.6
Deviation of real government investment from trend (percent)[a]	−6.9	20.1	12.1	19.8	−24.0	10.0	69.4

El Salvador							
External balance							
Change in balance of trade (millions of current dollars)	29.7	−26.8	27.9	−39.0	−85.8	15.0	102.6
Net private capital inflow (millions of current dollars)	2.5	25.5	0.8	24.1	85.8	127.5	64.7
Net foreign reserve coverage (months)	3.3	2.9	3.0	2.4	1.5	2.0	2.7
Internal balance							
Change in cost-of-living index (percent)	2.8	0.4	1.6	6.4	16.9	19.1	n.a.
Deviation in growth of real GDP (percent)	−1.9	−0.3	0.8	−0.6	1.1	−0.6	1.2
Monetary policy							
Change in rediscounted loans (millions of current dollars)	1.6	5.8	1.4	29.4	25.8	−17.3	16.9
Change in reserve requirement rate							
Short-term deposits (percentage points)	0.0	0.0	0.0	0.0	0.0	0.0	0.0
Long-term deposits (percentage points)	0.0	−30.0	0.0	0.0	0.0	30.0	0.0
Central bank credit to government (millions of current dollars)	20.1	27.7	30.6	18.8	11.4	24.8	n.a.
Fiscal policy							
Deviation of real government consumption from trend (percent)[b]	4.9	−6.6	6.0	−1.2	−10.4	−3.7	3.9
Deviation of real government investment from trend (percent)[b]	−1.2	12.6	30.6	−3.9	36.1	−3.3	−3.2

Sources: Central Banks of Guatemala and El Salvador.
n.a. Not available.
a. The trend is 4.5 percent.
b. The trend is 5.1 percent.

In both economies a large portion of domestic income is spent on foreign goods. Variations in the exchange rate might cause nationals to move out of domestic currency to protect their level of purchasing power. In a small economy, money would be less attractive as a store of value under flexible exchange rates, and nationals would tend to accumulate their cash balances for future transactions in foreign currency. Since the exchange market would be limited, a few speculators might be able to manipulate the market, increasing the swings of the parity changes.

A floating exchange rate subject to monetary manipulation could have disastrous repercussions in the free trade that the Central American countries enjoy in products manufactured within the region. "A currency depreciation," as McKinnon and Oates have pointed out, "is equivalent to an import tariff coupled with an export subsidy. Thus, the desirability of increasing economic integration does point towards a fixed exchange rate."[7]

Empirical Analysis of Inflationary Sources

For over two decades both Guatemala and El Salvador enjoyed stable price levels, with annual increases of less than 3 percent. In 1973 this pattern was abruptly changed and prices began to rise at double-digit rates, in tandem with the global inflation boom. The synchronous behavior of the price levels suggests that inflation in the two small and open economies was largely foreign induced, a hypothesis favored by international monetarists, who claim that under fixed exchange rates domestic prices are closely linked to world prices.

The liquidity of the two economies also underwent a rapid expansion. The money stock of Guatemala had grown at an average rate of 11 percent from 1966 to 1972, and that of El Salvador at 7 percent. With the advent of inflation, the average rate of change reached 20 percent in both countries (table 6-5). An important issue is whether the expansion of the money supply, M_2, stimulated inflation or merely played an accommodating role. The sudden increase in liquidity could have been activated by internal factors—fiscal deficits, wage payments, food prices—or external impulses—import prices, foreign reserve flows—or excess aggregate demand.

7. Ronald I. McKinnon and Wallace E. Oates, *The Implications of International Economic Integration for Monetary, Fiscal, and Exchange-Rate Policy,* Princeton Studies in International Finance, no. 16 (Princeton University, 1966), p. 29.

Table 6-5. *Change in Indicators of Potential Inflation, Guatemala and El Salvador, 1966–76*

Percent

Year	*Cost-of-living index*	*Money supply, M_2*	*Import price deflator*	*Food price index*	*Output gap*[a]
Guatemala					
1966	0.7	12.0	0.2	−0.1	−2.4
1967	0.5	12.1	0.2	0.0	−3.5
1968	1.9	8.9	0.6	3.6	−0.4
1969	2.1	11.0	3.0	1.1	−1.0
1970	2.4	11.3	4.9	4.1	−0.6
1971	−0.5	10.6	3.0	−1.9	−0.3
1972	0.5	24.1	11.1	0.1	1.6
1973	14.4	22.0	21.2	19.3	3.0
1974	15.9	15.4	36.7	15.9	4.0
1975	13.1	21.3	11.3	14.6	0.7
1976	10.7	30.9	8.1	9.6	2.8
El Salvador					
1966	−1.2	7.8	7.8	−1.8	4.7
1967	1.5	2.1	−7.8	4.4	4.9
1968	2.5	5.2	0.4	4.3	3.0
1969	−0.2	10.0	2.8	−4.9	1.3
1970	2.8	6.7	2.5	9.6	−0.8
1971	0.4	11.5	3.0	0.6	−1.1
1972	1.6	20.5	7.0	0.8	−0.9
1973	6.4	19.2	15.9	7.5	−1.0
1974	16.9	17.2	37.2	17.3	0.2
1975	19.1	22.4	11.9	20.5	−0.8
1976	7.0	30.9	n.a.	7.0	−1.6

Sources: Central Banks of Guatemala and El Salvador.
n.a. Not available.
a. Deviation of real GDP from its logarithmic trend.

During the worldwide commodity boom of 1972–73, both countries experienced food price inflation, galloping import prices, and rapid liquidity growth, and Guatemala also faced overheating of aggregate demand (see table 6-5). In 1974 the increase in import prices was enormous, and it was accompanied by the highest trade deficits ever recorded, losses in foreign reserves, and a slower rate of money expansion. This was followed by the 1975 recession and the slowdown of import prices, but continuing food shortages and resurgence of money growth. With the renewal of world economic activity in 1976–77 and the quadrupling of coffee prices, these countries experienced the biggest bonanza ever. International reserves grew to unthinkable magnitudes—three to four times the 1972

Table 6-6. *Deficit in the Central Government Account, Guatemala and El Salvador, 1967–77*

Millions of U.S. dollars and, in parentheses, percent of nominal GDP

Account item	*1967*	*1968*	*1969*	*1970*	*1971*	*1972*	*1973*	*1974*	*1975*	*1976*	*1977*
Guatemala											
Current income[a]	124.3	136.6	149.7	165.2	175.1	185.7	213.8	281.4	358.6	428.0	603.1
Expenditures[b]	151.4	154.0	164.3	189.0	191.7	239.5	260.5	322.9	367.8	574.9	631.9
Deficit	−27.1	−17.4	−14.6	−23.8	−16.6	−53.8	−46.7	−41.5	−9.2	−146.9	−28.8
	(1.9)	(1.1)	(1.4)	(1.3)	(0.8)	(2.6)	(1.8)	(1.3)	(0.3)	(3.4)	(0.5)
El Salvador											
Current income[a]	90.9	92.4	101.6	120.0	120.0	136.0	162.0	194.0	231.5	324.0	473.6
Expenditures[b]	93.5	92.5	115.3	119.7	140.2	148.9	174.7	231.3	275.8	401.8	485.0
Deficit	−2.6	−0.1	−13.7	0.3	−20.2	−12.9	−12.7	−37.3	−44.3	−77.8	−11.4
	(0.3)	(0.0)	(1.4)	(0.0)	(1.9)	(1.1)	(1.0)	(2.4)	(2.4)	(1.4)	(0.2)

Sources: Central Banks of Guatemala and El Salvador.

a. Includes tax and nontax revenues but excludes internal and external financing.

b. Current and capital expenditures excluding amortization. For El Salvador, expenditures include payments for prior year expenditures.

level—and the stock of money rose by 31 percent. Notwithstanding, domestic inflation was alleviated during 1976, falling below the double-digit level for El Salvador, although the abatement was not as great in Guatemala, where an earthquake in 1976 affected the economy.

Fiscal Deficits

A common cause of money growth in less developed countries is the fiscal incapacity to raise enough taxes to pay for government expenditures. This situation is sometimes aggravated by policymakers' commitment to increase effective demand for goods and services in order to foster economic growth. Latin American monetarists have long proclaimed that it is precisely the excess demand generated by government monetary and fiscal policies that provokes inflation.[8]

Guatemala and El Salvador do not appear to belong to this class of overspending countries. Their budget deficits (table 6-6) are more a reflection of conservative and traditional governments than aggressive ones. Fiscal deficits as a percentage of gross domestic product do not show noticeable increases for Guatemala except in 1972, when there was a big leap in money expansion but not in price inflation (and in 1976 when the February earthquake demanded emergency expenditures). For El Salvador the 1974–75 period stands out as different from the rest, but money growth actually decelerated in 1974. Furthermore, it is quite likely that the larger deficits of these two years were brought about by the higher cost of imported goods.

By 1977 the two countries' fiscal deficit had returned to the pre-1972 absolute levels. In both cases the boom in coffee prices brought abnormal increases in income: El Salvador's revenue rose by 40 percent in 1976 and by 46 percent the following year; although Guatemala's government income did not change sharply in 1976, it increased by 40 percent in 1977.[9] The export tax on coffee not only produced significant income that

8. In contrast, Latin American structuralists see inflation as the inevitable outcome of rapid growth coupled with structural bottlenecks, with money being a permissive factor. Monetarists believe that the alleged constraints are the result of government intervention. See C. H. Kirkpatrick and F. I. Nixson, "The Origins of inflation in less developed countries: a selective review," in Michael Parkin and George Zis, eds., *Inflation in Open Economies* (Manchester University Press, 1976), pp. 126–74.

9. Because El Salvador has a progressive export tax, which relates the tax to the sale price, its revenue windfall was 25–30 percent of coffee export earnings whereas Guatemala's was 18–23 percent.

allowed the governments to expand their level of spending but also absorbed some of the excess liquidity created by the quadrupling of coffee prices.[10]

The almost balanced budgets of both countries reflect the governments' slight involvement in the process of economic change rather than their implementation of efficient fiscal reforms. As in many developing countries, tax revenues are inelastic with respect to income and heavily dependent on import duties.

A more fundamental restraining influence on government expenditures is the higher priority given to exchange-rate stability than to social needs. Because of the high import content of public spending, any abnormally high budget not accompanied by a foreign-exchange surplus presents a balance-of-payments problem. Furthermore, the balance of payments may deteriorate still further as the increase in government spending induces multiplier effects on income. In sum, there is no reason to believe that fiscal deficits have stimulated internal monetary growth in Guatemala or El Salvador.

Agricultural Prices

The disruption of household purchasing activities caused by soaring food prices in the 1970s (table 6-5) was an important development both economically and politically, for foodstuffs account for about 50 percent of the average family budget.[11] The only earlier concern about food prices had been in El Salvador immediately after the 1969 armed conflict with Honduras, its main grain supplier. The 1973–75 increases in prices were caused by a combination of bad weather, worldwide scarcity, and internal bottlenecks.

Maize, beans, and rice are the principal staples in Central America. There was a remarkable drop in grain production in both countries in 1972, unmatched by any other period, and a less severe drop in 1974.

Food shortages do not necessarily result in price increases, since they can be alleviated by additional imports. It appears that the Salvadoran government between 1960 and 1976 relied on external suppliers for the procurement of amounts equal to about 22 percent of domestic produc-

10. The Guatemalan government also implemented a forced bond sale to finance reconstruction after the earthquake, which extracted around $50 million from the public.

11. Food items have a weight of 57 percent in the Guatemalan cost-of-living index and 54 percent in the Salvadoran.

tion.[12] But imports of foodstuffs did not keep domestic prices from rising in 1973 because the domestic grain shortage coincided with a worldwide slowdown of food production which almost doubled the prices of most staples. The import prices of basic grains, although more favorable than the internal prices, were very high in comparison with those paid earlier.

The grain marketing agencies were not able to import as much as was needed because of insufficient storage capacity. Guatemala, which had not been dependent on imports in the past (see table 6–7), could store only 3 percent of the production of a year's harvest. El Salvador, as a net importer, had storage capacity for about 9 percent of production volume, but even this was not enough to counterbalance the largest production drop in history. The official marketing agencies also had no appreciable influence on the market price because of the low volume of their operation (because of that experience, both governments by 1976 had increased their capacity to at least 11 percent of the production volume).

To lighten the burden of the food price inflation on the poorer stratum of the population, the governments subsidized the price of the three staples. The Guatemalan marketing agency maintained a price of 5 cents per pound of maize from late 1973 until mid-1975, while the market price fluctuated between 7 cents and 10 cents. The price subsidy unfortunately did not reach households because of the lack of control over the selected distributors. El Salvador's policy was more effective, as the grain agency utilized a rationing system based on family coupons. Rising food prices thus were the outcome of supply deficiencies and internal constraints, exacerbated by the escalation of world grain prices. But demand factors may also have played a role—in particular, increased money incomes derived from the liquidity growth.

Wages

A frequent consequence of rising food prices is the upward adjustment of wages and salaries, which adds fuel to the inflationary process. In Guatemala and El Salvador, wages respond slowly to inflation because of the excess supply of labor. The large number of underemployed per-

12. The production index of El Salvador tends to be systematically correlated with the import ratio of the next period, positive deviation from its trend being followed by a lower import ratio, and so on. The production cycle ends by September, thus determining availabilities primarily for the next year.

Table 6-7. *Production and Imports of Basic Grains, Guatemala and El Salvador, 1960–76*

	Guatemala			*El Salvador*		
Year[a]	*Volume index of grain production (1968 = 100)*[b]	*Deviation of index from trend (percent)*[c]	*Imports of grain as percent of production*[d]	*Volume index of grain production (1968 = 100)*[b]	*Deviation of index from trend (percent)*[c]	*Imports of grain as percent of production*[d]
1960	70.5	0.3	0.1	68.8	8.0	21.0
1961	71.9	−1.6	0.1	60.0	−10.7	19.7
1962	77.3	1.8	4.0	77.9	9.8	27.1
1963	83.0	5.2	2.4	72.0	−3.7	20.0
1964	92.4	12.6	2.2	68.3	−13.5	25.6
1965	90.8	6.5	2.7	75.0	−9.9	35.0
1966	83.4	−5.8	1.1	94.1	7.2	31.0
1967	86.6	−6.0	2.1	84.3	−9.0	15.0
1968	100.0	4.5	3.5	100.0	2.3	24.3
1969	99.9	0.4	1.4	100.0	−3.0	10.1
1970	110.4	6.8	2.5	126.9	16.7	3.5
1971	112.3	4.5	2.6	135.5	18.1	1.0
1972	79.6	−28.7	1.9	88.8	−26.6	0.3
1973	131.4	13.1	4.2	144.2	12.9	14.8
1974	98.6	−18.3	8.3	121.5	−9.8	4.0
1975	142.7	13.8	6.6	156.5	10.1	8.0
1976	144.6	11.0	0.8	163.2	8.8	2.2

Sources: Central Banks of Guatemala and El Salvador.
a. Refers to production cycle, beginning with 1960–61.
b. Index based on 1968 volume weighted for corn, beans, and rice, respectively, by 0.783, 0.174, and 0.043 for Guatemala, and 0.715, 0.149, and 0.136 for El Salvador.
c. Logarithmic trend shows a 3.9 percent growth rate for Guatemala, and 5.4 percent for El Salvador.
d. Domestic production is the average of the current year's volume plus the two prior years. Import ratios based on value weights in note b.

sons provides a check on wage increases and labor unionism.[13] Furthermore, over 50 percent of the labor force is engaged in agricultural occupations, where employment follows the seasonal pattern of the production cycle and the erratic fluctuations of external demand.

Minimum daily wages for agricultural workers in El Salvador's coffee, cotton, and sugar industries were raised by an average of 10 percent in 1973, 8 percent in 1974, and 20–29 percent in 1975. These increases, although at par with the overall inflation rate, were not significant in absolute terms. The important rises occurred in 1976 as a result of the huge surge in coffee prices—minimum daily wages of coffee pickers shot up by 53 percent and those of cotton workers by 33 percent. In manufacturing, wage increases lagged behind the inflation boom of 1973–75. The wage index for industrial workers in San Salvador (the nation's capital) rose 6.4 percent in 1973, 12.3 percent in 1974, and 8.1 percent in 1975.

For Guatemala, minimum wages in industry were increased by an average of 20 percent in December 1973. No source of reliable data is available for studying the evolution of wages vis-à-vis inflation. Between January 1971 and March 1976, the average real salary for the nation as a whole showed a real loss of only 1.9 percent, despite the high levels of inflation (table 6-8). Agricultural workers, who represent more than half of the sample (57 percent), held the country's average salary up. All other economic sectors suffered a loss in real income.[14]

But wages do not appear to have been an important ingredient of the 1970s inflation in either country. The large increases in farm wages came in 1976, when world coffee prices quadrupled. Construction workers in Guatemala also saw their income rise considerably, mainly as an aftermath of the earthquake. Even those rises were not directly inflationary since it is supply and demand that determine agricultural prices.

Import Prices

Higher import prices occupy a prominent place in the 1970s inflation of the two Central American countries. The average of exports and imports as a share of gross domestic product—which is a conservative measure of the size of the foreign trade sector in these economies—rose

13. It is estimated that only 1.9 percent of the economically active population in Guatemala was organized in unions by 1973, and 5 percent in El Salvador.

14. The gain in farm wages may be due partly to the fact that the sample was taken just one month after the February 1976 earthquake; however, the coffee boom was also partly responsible.

Table 6-8. *Monthly Average Salaries in Guatemala, by Economic Activity, 1971 and 1976*

Income group	January 1971 (quetzales)	March 1976: 1976 quetzales	March 1976: 1971 quetzales[a]	Change in real income (percent)[b]
Country average, all activities	50.5	78.0	49.6	−1.9
Agriculture	22.1	37.6	23.9	+8.3
Mining	102.6	153.0	97.3	−5.1
Manufacturing	88.8	127.2	80.9	−8.9
Construction	67.7	94.1	59.8	−11.6
Electricity, gas, and water	130.8	129.4	82.3	−37.0
Commerce	130.5	167.8	106.7	−18.2
Transport, warehousing, and communications	99.2	128.7	81.9	−17.5
Services	93.5	126.1	80.2	−14.2
Average for Guatemala City, all activities	106.5	141.7	90.1	−15.4

Source: Guatemala, Institute of Social Security, "Análisis de salarios enero de 1971 y marzo de 1976." The figures do not include government employees.

a. Adjusted by change in the cost-of-living index since 1971.

b. Difference between 1971 average and 1971 value of 1976 average.

from 18.3 percent in 1970–72 for Guatemala to 22.4 percent in 1973–75, and from 26.3 percent for El Salvador to 34.3 percent.[15]

Of the recorded rises in the overall price of imported products, that of 1974 is the most extreme—over 35 percent (table 6-5). Half of this increase is attributable to the unparalleled rise in oil prices. The effect on these economies was substantial because of their high dependency on imported petroleum. About 98 percent of Guatemala's commercial energy consumption and 93 percent of El Salvador's was based on petroleum products.[16] Neither country produces oil (though oil has been found in Guatemala) and both lack gas deposits and coal mines. With the quadrupling of petroleum prices, both started construction of dams for hydroelectric power, and El Salvador turned to its geothermal resources in hopes of decreasing dependency on oil—by 1976 it was generating 24 percent of its electricity through geothermal energy, the world's highest percentage. In response to the energy crisis the governments also adopted price policies that benefited users of diesel and fuel oil (mostly industry, commercial transport, and electric utilities) over gasoline users (mostly

15. Sizes of the foreign trade sector for OECD countries range from 5 percent to 50 percent. Countries like Austria, Finland, and Sweden have shares comparable to Guatemala and El Salvador.

16. Julio E. Obiols, "La situación energética en Centroamérica y perspectivas para el futuro," SIECA/78/INF/14, Guatemala, August 1978.

Table 6-9. *Exchange Rate Indexes of Guatemala and El Salvador, 1969–76*[a]

Index, 1968 = 100

	Guatemalan quetzales		*Salvadoran colónes*	
Year	*Index*	*Percent change*	*Index*	*Percent change*
1969	100.9	0.9	100.6	0.6
1970	100.9	0.0	100.7	0.1
1971	104.5	3.5	103.8	3.0
1972	104.5	0.0	103.6	−0.1
1973	108.6	3.9	107.1	3.3
1974	110.5	1.7	108.4	1.3
1975	108.6	−1.6	106.6	−1.7
1976	112.1	3.2	109.2	2.4

Sources: Central Banks of Guatemala and El Salvador.
a. Based on the dollar value of major trading partners' currencies, weighted by their share of 1968 imports.

private automobiles). Both countries sought to reduce the drain on their foreign reserves by negotiating long-term loans with Venezuela to cover the increase in the cost of their oil imports—for the full increase over 1973 prices in 1974, and diminishing each year thereafter by 16.7 percent.

Higher import prices reflected not only the rise in the price of oil and manufactured goods but also the parity changes that occurred after the abandonment of the Bretton Woods system. Guatemala and El Salvador of course maintained a fixed parity with the United States, their most important trading partner. Nevertheless, they experienced small changes in their exchange rates since nearly a third of their imports come from countries with floating rates (21 percent from Europe and 9 percent from Japan, on the average).

The international values of the Guatemalan quetzal and the Salvadoran colón declined in 1971 and 1973 by 3–4 percent, then appreciated in 1975 by approximately 1.6 percent, and fell again in 1976 by 2–3 percent (table 6-9). Depreciation accounts for only a small portion of the rise in import prices, even when it is assumed that foreign prices rose by the full amount of the devaluation.

Foreign Monetary Impulses

A major development in the Central American economies in the 1970s was the staggering increase in international reserves. From a stock of

$45 million in 1970, Guatemala's foreign exchange swelled to $280 million in 1975 and to $647 million in 1977. El Salvador's foreign reserves expanded from $52 million in 1970 to $205 million in 1977. Among the most important factors contributing to the accumulation of international reserves was the increase in coffee prices—the value of Guatemala's exports of coffee changed from $164 million in 1975 to $542 million in 1977 and El Salvador's income from coffee sales behaved similarly. Moreover, private net capital flows to Guatemala reached uncommon levels during 1975–77, magnifying the increase in foreign exchange.

Although this was a welcome change, the huge net inflows of foreign reserves, especially during 1976–77, were perceived by monetary authorities as a threat to price stability. Furthermore, the room for action was limited as the instruments of control at the disposal of the central banks are more effective for stopping a contraction than an expansion of the money stock. Required reserves, the principal adjustment tool, would have had to increase so much in order to have a significant effect on money growth that the change would not have been acceptable because of its impact on banks' profits. Other monetary instruments, such as open market operations, are of little use because of the relatively low development of capital markets.

In order to test the effect of foreign reserves on money expansion in Guatemala, the behavior of the two factors over a base period, 1965–72, was compared to that over the longer period, 1965–77, including the years of monetary expansion. The estimated coefficients in a series of regression equations show that the correlation between changes in the two factors increased from 0.5 in the base period to 0.76 in the longer period.[17]

17. Using quarterly data for 1965 through 1972 the regression results were (*t*-values in parentheses):

$$\Delta MS = \underset{(3.27)}{0.50}\,\Delta RES - \underset{(-2.39)}{10.66}\,Q1 \underset{(-2.42)}{-7.51}\,Q2 \underset{(-2.80)}{-9.71}\,Q3 + \underset{(6.26)}{13.60},$$

$\bar{R}^2 = 0.60$; Durbin-Watson $= 1.83$; standard error of estimate $= 5.74$

and for 1965 through 1977 the results were:

$$\Delta MS = \underset{(8.26)}{0.76}\,\Delta RES - \underset{(-3.61)}{29.25}\,Q1 \underset{(-3.41)}{-24.47}\,Q2 \underset{(-3.31)}{-24.73}\,Q3 + \underset{(6.11)}{31.37},$$

$\bar{R}^2 = 0.69$; Durbin-Watson $= 1.60$; standard error of estimate $= 18.28$

where ΔMS is the absolute change in the money stock of Guatemala (defined to include time deposits), ΔRES the absolute change in net foreign reserves, and $Q1$, $Q2$, and $Q3$

The sharp rise in the coefficient on foreign reserves indicates that the influence of reserves on money supply rose in that there was less sterilization of reserve flows than before. The fact that the estimated coefficient was less than one means that Guatemala's monetary authorities may have tried to sterilize foreign reserve inflows. The money supply can be changed by changing either the money multiplier or the monetary base (domestic assets of the central bank, net foreign assets, and other assets). By changing its domestic assets (mainly credit to commercial banks and credit to the government) the central bank may neutralize the changes in foreign assets, as long as the latter change is not extremely large. Assuming that domestic assets of the central bank vary with the level of foreign assets and economic activity, central banks can keep the amount of money in the economy adequate to maintain the expected nominal rate of growth of production by increasing or decreasing domestic credit. If nominal growth is expected to be high, then monetary authorities pump increasing amounts of credit to the economy, and vice versa.[18]

In order to test the sterilization policies of Guatemala and El Salvador before and after 1972, absolute changes in domestic assets of the central banks were compared against changes in nominal gross domestic product and net foreign reserves or the current account balance. The results of the regressions are shown in table 6-10. Before 1972 there appears to have been no systematic relation between changes in domestic assets and changes in foreign assets. But once the sample period is enlarged to include the years of foreign-exchange expansion, there is some evidence of sterilization. For Guatemala the coefficient on changes in foreign reserves is around −0.5, which would mean that about half of the change is being neutralized (a coefficient of −1 would imply complete sterilization). For El Salvador the coefficient has the right sign but is not significant, although there appears to be some sterilization with regard to the current account balance. Moreover, the coefficients of nominal gross domestic product are significant and have the right sign. These simple

seasonal dummies for the first, second, and third quarters of each year. The heterogeneity of the regression slopes was confirmed by the *F*-test and is shown by the different magnitudes of the standard error of the estimate.

18. Their goal may be to have the money stock increase at an equal or lower rate than nominal GDP. See V. Argy and Pentti J. K. Kouri, "Sterilization Policies and the Volatility in International Reserves," in Robert Z. Aliber, ed., *National Monetary Policies and the International Financial System* (University of Chicago Press, 1974), pp. 209–30.

Table 6-10. *Regression Analysis of Changes in Domestic Assets of the Central Banks of Guatemala and El Salvador, before and after 1972*[a]

		Variable			*Regression statistic*	
Country and period	*Constant*	*Nominal gross domestic product*	*Net foreign reserves*	*Current account balance*	*Coefficient of determination,* $\bar{R}^2$	*Durbin-Watson*
Guatemala						
1951–72	3.96 (1.68)	0.01 (0.25)	−0.04 (−0.45)	...	−0.09	2.29
1951–75	−0.48 (−0.17)	0.10 (5.66)	−0.52 (−5.50)	...	0.62	2.73
1951–72	4.90 (1.91)	0.00 (0.16)	...	0.04 (0.61)	−0.08	2.27
1951–75	−4.70 (−1.03)	0.02 (1.13)	...	−0.31 (−2.41)	0.28	2.66
El Salvador						
1953–72	12.18 (1.20)	0.06 (0.61)	−0.23 (−0.86)	...	−0.07	1.98
1953–77	3.13 (0.33)	0.18 (5.62)	−0.23 (−1.29)	...	0.59	2.61
1953–72	12.87 (1.39)	0.00 (0.02)	...	−0.23 (−1.60)	0.03	1.75
1953–77	0.83 (0.10)	0.12 (4.61)	...	−0.26 (−2.88)	0.68	2.41

a. Based on quarterly data. Figures in parentheses are *t*-statistics.

tests do show that both countries were reacting to inflows of foreign exchange, though perhaps less vigorously than the results imply.[19]

Changes in domestic assets of the central bank are not determined solely by monetary authorities but also by commercial banks, to the extent that these banks are given credit on rediscount operations. Their demand for rediscount loans can be partially managed through the rediscount rate, but neither central bank has used this rate as a policy tool. The low demand observed in Guatemala during the 1970s was a conse-

19. The change in net foreign reserves is the sum of the current account balance and capital flows; it may be argued that capital flows change in response to tight or easy money policies, and thus to changes in domestic assets. If so, the change in net foreign reserves would not be independent of the disturbance term and the offset coefficient would be biased.

Table 6-11. *Excess Liquidity of Commercial Banks in Guatemala, 1969–77*

Millions of U.S. dollars at December 31 value

	Assets in excess of minimum required		
Year	*Total*	*Reserves*	*Investment in government securities*
1969	11.4	4.0	7.4
1970	14.6	6.0	8.6
1971	29.0	9.5	19.5
1972	74.4	26.8	47.6
1973	92.0	20.8	71.2
1974	67.5	18.8	48.7
1975	103.0	10.0	93.0
1976	148.7	62.2	86.5
1977	131.8	33.9	97.9

Source: Central Bank of Guatemala.

quence of the substantial excess liquidity of commercial banks since 1972 (table 6-11).[20]

Excess liquidity of commercial banks is measured by the sum of banks' investment in government securities and reserves held in excess of legal requirements. Total excess liquidity has grown rapidly, thus explaining the drop in advances and rediscounts to commercial banks. This phenomenon also accounts for the low impact of the 10 percent increase in reserve requirements imposed in 1974. Commercial banks' excess liquidity was reduced during that year, but partly because the loss in foreign reserves slowed the growth of the money supply.

Guatemala's central bank engaged in open market operations for the first time in 1973 in order to reduce some of the excess liquidity of the banking system. These open market operations consisted of the sale to commercial banks of government securities, which were very attractive because of such features as tax-free interest income and guaranteed repurchase on demand. Commercial banks' excess liquidity was partly invested in these assets, especially in 1973 and 1975; in 1974, when banks needed additional resources, they were able to resell securities.

The high level of surplus liquidity in the banking system was a central

20. Guatemala's excess liquidity was also fostered by a long-established requirement that banks increase their capital as their investments expanded; it proved to be an obstacle to credit operations, especially for banks that had no excess capital.

element in neutralizing the effect of foreign reserve inflows on the money stock. In fact, during the years of heaviest inflow, 1976–77, the money multiplier decreased in both countries:[21]

	1972	*1973*	*1974*	*1975*	*1976*	*1977*
Guatemala	2.20	2.26	2.25	2.29	1.95	1.99
El Salvador	2.01	2.06	2.04	2.08	1.94	1.93

If the money multiplier of 1975 is applied to the monetary base of 1976 in Guatemala, the value of the money stock is raised by $189 million and the rate of change reaches 54 percent instead of the actual 31 percent. For El Salvador the difference between actual and potential is not as great, the growth rate of money increasing from 31 percent to 40 percent. Despite the various factors dampening the impact of foreign reserve flows, they had an important effect on money supply, accelerating its expansion to almost 31 percent during 1976.

Aggregate Demand

In developed economies the pressure emanating from rises in the level of real activity is often regarded as a central factor in inflation. An inverse relation is hypothesized between the inflation rate and the level of slackness or degree of unemployment of resources; the relation has been extended to include expectations about the path of inflation.[22] Regressions of this augmented Phillips-curve relationship for Guatemala and El Salvador in 1950–69 behaved poorly, as could have been expected in view of the low variability of the inflation rate during this period.[23]

The results of empirical tests of an excess demand model that encompasses the swings in domestic inflation in recent years are shown in table 6-12. The dependent variable representing price inflation is the percentage change in the cost-of-living index, which is a weighted average of all important prices in the economy. The change in the index was regressed against independent variables representing excess demand (the percentage deviation of real gross domestic product from its trend), price expectations (the previous inflation rate), and cost-push factors (the percentage change in import prices and the percentage deviation of the grain

21. Central Banks of Guatemala and El Salvador.

22. See, for example, Rodney Cross and David Laidler, "Inflation, excess demand and expectations in fixed exchange rate open economies: some preliminary empirical results," in Michael Parkin and George Zis, eds., *Inflation in the World Economy* (Manchester University Press, 1976), pp. 221–58.

23. See W. A. Bomberger and G. E. Makinen, "Inflation, Unemployment and Expectations in Latin America: Some Simple Tests," *Southern Economic Journal*, vol. 43 (October 1976), pp. 1112–23.

volume index, lagged one year, from its trend or the change in the relative price of food). The model is designed to reflect the importance of external demand in the excess demand of the two Central American economies. Exports are the engines of these economies, determining private investment expenditures as well as government spending. Thus, excess aggregate demand reflects changes in foreign demand more than domestically originated real activity.

The equations fitted with 1957–75 data show no evidence of a relationship between excess demand and inflation in El Salvador. For Guatemala, excess demand is significant only when the cost-push factors are not included in the equation. For El Salvador, neither grain volume nor relative food price is significant whereas for Guatemala both variables have robust parameters.

Thus the pure excess demand model (equations 1 and 2) does not stand by itself, whether judged in terms of explanatory power or significance of coefficients. The results are not conclusive, however, as the measure of excess demand may not be the most appropriate. It is also puzzling that price expectations turned out to be very significant in both countries, but that may be due to the particular measure used.

A robust coefficient on lagged inflation rate can also be interpreted as evidence that any one of the other variables is undergoing adjustment. That possibility was tested by introducing into the equations a variable for lagged import prices (table 6-13). The equations in this cost-push model of inflation examine cost elements alone. However, equations 4–6 of table 6-13 combine cost-push variables with the rate of growth of nominal money supply (defined to include time deposits).

The cost-push specification performs better than the excess-demand model, as measured by the coefficient of determination, $\bar{R}^2$. Lagged import prices turn out to be strongly significant, thus confirming the suspicion that another variable was responsible for the robustness of the price-expectations variable. Again, food prices or food production do not appear as influencing Salvadoran inflation. The growth rate of the money stock adds nothing to the explanatory power of the equations, and its corresponding coefficient is not statistically different from zero.

The results of tests measuring the effect of money growth are reported in table 6-14.[24] This monetary model establishes a positive relation be-

24. The model had been applied to the two Central American economies for 1950–69 without success. See Robert C. Vogel, "The Dynamics of Inflation in Latin America, 1950–1969," *American Economic Review*, vol. 64 (March 1974), pp. 102–14.

Table 6-12. *Regression Results of an Excess Demand Model of Inflation in Guatemala and El Salvador, 1957–75*[a]

		Excess demand						*Regression statistic*		
Equation	*Constant*	*Current*	*Lagged*	*Lagged inflation rate*	*Import prices*	*Lagged grain volume index*	*Relative food prices*[b]	*Coefficient of determination,* $\bar{R}^2$	*Durbin-Watson*	*Auto-correlation*
Guatemala										
1	1.92 (1.76)	0.77 (1.78)	...	0.61 (3.06)	...	...	...	0.61	1.99	0.16
2	2.33 (1.75)	0.65 (1.27)	0.33 (0.63)	0.48 (2.07)	...	...	...	0.59	1.90	0.28
3	−0.03 (−0.04)	0.12 (0.45)	...	0.44 (2.91)	0.34 (4.19)	...	...	0.77	2.19	−0.36
4	−0.38 (−0.98)	−0.18 (−1.06)	...	0.43 (4.89)	0.35 (7.50)	−0.23 (−5.60)	...	0.92	2.39	−0.33
5	0.37 (0.61)	0.05 (0.20)	...	0.53 (4.20)	0.20 (2.75)	...	0.52 (3.60)	0.86	2.13	−0.07

El Salvador										
1	0.68	0.01	...	1.11	...	...	...	0.40	2.04	−0.26
	(0.73)	(0.04)		(4.76)						
2	0.69	−0.01	0.03	1.10	...	...	...	0.36	2.04	−0.25
	(0.72)	(−0.03)	(0.06)	(4.57)						
3	−0.21	0.01	...	0.73	0.31	...	...	0.61	2.06	−0.46
	(−0.31)	(0.07)		(3.07)	(3.20)					
4	−0.22	0.01	...	0.71	0.31	−0.02	...	0.58	2.09	−0.47
	(−0.32)	(0.07)		(2.89)	(3.13)	(−0.36)				
5	−0.43	−0.02	...	0.76	0.30	...	0.24	0.64	1.98	−0.49
	(−0.65)	(−0.09)		(3.32)	(3.23)		(1.51)			

a. The dependent variable is the percentage change in the cost-of-living index. Numbers in parentheses are *t*-statistics. Equations corrected for first-order serial correlation.
b. Food component of the cost-of-living index divided by the other components.

Table 6-13. *Regression Results of a Cost-Push Model of Inflation in Guatemala and El Salvador, 1956–75*[a]

Equation	Constant	Import prices		Lagged grain volume index	Relative food prices[b]	Money supply		Regression statistic	
		Current	Lagged			Current	Lagged	Coefficient of determination, $\bar{R}^2$	Durbin-Watson
Guatemala									
1	0.03	0.44	...	−0.23	...	...	...	0.83	1.84
	(0.05)	(8.56)		(−4.43)					
2	−0.27	0.34	0.19	−0.17	...	...	...	0.91	2.02
	(−0.65)	(7.60)	(4.06)	(−4.52)					
3	−0.10	0.26	0.24	...	0.33	...	...	0.85	1.70
	(−0.20)	(4.31)	(4.27)		(2.48)				
4	0.57	0.28	0.25	...	0.36	−0.07	...	0.85	1.90
	(0.64)	(4.40)	(4.36)		(2.63)	(−0.95)			
5	0.10	0.35	0.19	−0.18	...	−0.04	...	0.91	2.08
	(0.14)	(7.26)	(4.05)	(−4.47		(−0.68)			
6	0.66	0.39	0.20	−0.19	...	−0.02	−0.08	0.91	2.06
	(0.80)	(6.96)	(4.13)	(−4.69)		(−0.39)	(−1.19)		

El Salvador									
1	0.72	0.41	...	0.02	...	...	...	0.36	1.73
	(0.54)	(3.29)		(0.16)					
2	−0.20	0.23	0.41	−0.01	...	...	...	0.72	2.54
	(−0.23)	(2.58)	(4.83)	(−0.24)					
3	−0.17	0.23	0.40	...	0.10	...	...	0.73	2.49
	(−0.21)	(2.72)	(4.73)		(0.77)				
4	−0.85	0.20	0.38	...	0.10	0.09	...	0.73	2.49
	(−0.71)	(2.07)	(4.39)		(0.80)	(0.17)			
5	−0.98	0.20	0.40	−0.02	...	0.09	...	0.72	2.57
	(−0.72)	(2.03)	(4.53)	(−0.38)		(0.77)			
6	−0.40	0.23	0.43	−0.03	...	0.11	−0.12	0.71	2.61
	(−0.26)	(2.16)	(4.46)	(−0.52)		(0.87)	(−0.81)		

a. The dependent variable is the percentage change in the cost-of-living index. Numbers in parentheses are *t*-statistics.
b. Food component of the cost-of-living index divided by the other components.

Table 6-14. *Regression Results of a Monetary Model of Inflation in Guatemala, 1956–75, and El Salvador, 1957–75*[a]

Equation	Constant	Real gross domestic product	Money supply		Acceleration in inflation rate[b]	Import prices		Lagged grain volume index	Relative food prices[c]	Regression statistic	
			Current	Lagged		Current	Lagged			Coefficient of determination, $\bar{R}^2$	Durbin-Watson
Guatemala											
1	0.73	−0.28	0.12	...	0.69	0.25	...	−0.25	...	0.94	2.50
	(1.01)	(−2.23)	(2.28)		(5.54)	(5.11)		(−7.65)			
2	0.72	−0.28	0.12	0.00	0.69	0.25	...	−0.25	...	0.93	2.51
	(0.87)	(−2.12)	(2.18)	(0.02)	(5.22)	(4.11)		(−7.20)			
3	−0.02	−0.04	0.03	...	0.49	0.25	0.13	−0.22	...	0.96	2.73
	(−0.02)	(−0.26)	(0.57)		(3.74)	(6.05)	(2.58)	(−7.48)			
4	0.15	0.00	0.03	−0.04	0.45	0.27	0.14	−0.23	...	0.95	2.71
	(0.20)	(0.01)	(0.47)	(−0.77)	(3.18)	(5.35)	(2.66)	(−7.40)			
5	−0.15	−0.62	0.25	0.23	0.91	...	...	....	...	0.64	2.47
	(−0.08)	(−2.10)	(2.12)	(1.94)	(4.17)						

El Salvador											
1	0.84	−0.31	0.16	. . .	0.24	0.32	. . .	. . .	0.17	0.41	2.40
	(0.36)	(−0.89)	(0.76)		(0.80)	(2.34)			(1.01)		
2	0.24	−0.44	0.10	0.23	0.29	0.24	. . .	. . .	0.16	0.42	2.33
	(0.10)	(−1.21)	(0.46)	(1.09)	(0.98)	(1.56)					
3	0.12	−0.14	0.04	. . .	0.14	0.20	0.38	. . .	0.11	0.71	2.29
	(0.07)	(−0.57)	(0.26)		(0.64)	(2.04)	(3.82)		(0.88)		
4	0.19	−0.12	0.04	−0.03	0.13	0.21	0.39	. . .	0.11	0.69	2.29
	(0.11)	(−0.42)	(0.27)	(−0.19)	(0.56)	(1.87)	(3.35)		(0.85)		
5	−0.42	−0.53	0.18	0.41	0.34	. . .	. . .	. . .	. . .	0.37	2.01
	(−0.18)	(−1.41)	(0.86)	(2.05)	(1.09)						

a. The dependent variable is the percentage change in the cost-of-living index. Numbers in parentheses are *t*-statistics.
b. Inflation rate in prior year minus inflation rate two years previously.
c. Food component of the cost-of-living index divided by the other components.

tween the rate of inflation and monetary growth, a negative relation with respect to proportionate changes in real product, and a positive relation with respect to acceleration of the inflation rate (reflecting the cost of holding liquid money balances). The pure monetary model (with no cost-push variables) is shown in equation 5 of table 6-14. The coefficients have the right signs in the two countries' regressions, although only in Guatemala are these coefficients significant. When the two cost variables (import prices and the grain volume index) are added, the magnitude of the money growth parameter for Guatemala decreases and the model for El Salvador is completely thrown off course. Furthermore, when lagged import prices are introduced, the monetary model collapses in the case of Guatemala.

The statistical tests indicate that changes in import prices of the current and previous year had a definite influence on domestic inflation in both countries. Structural elements such as food shortages played an important role in Guatemala's inflation. In El Salvador the food variable shows no significant contribution, perhaps because its effect is included in the import-price variable, which includes imported foodstuffs. At any rate, El Salvador had a smaller drop in production than Guatemala and it was able to import considerable amounts of grain. This probably explains why El Salvador did not go through double-digit inflation during 1973. The regressions indicate that excess demand was not a source of inflationary pressure. Nor does monetary growth appear to have been a leading stimulus to inflation in either economy.

Conclusions

El Salvador and Guatemala are representative of economic experience in Central America in the 1970s. They have archetypal small, open economies dependent on exports of raw materials. Their economic management typically has been conservative, and their currencies strong and tied in fixed parity to the dollar. Their inflation rates historically have been extremely low, averaging on the order of 1 percent annually. Yet in 1973 and 1974 their inflation rates rose to an average level of approximately 13 percent, and inflation remained at a high average rate of 12 percent in 1975 and 1976.

The statistical results here leave little room for doubt that the recent inflation in Guatemala and El Salvador was largely imported.[25] In these open economies, domestic prices adjust rapidly to import prices. World inflationary impulses set off the unprecedented Central American inflation of 1973 and 1974, and enormous coffee price increases kept inflation at high levels in 1976. In general the region's governments took classic restrictive monetary measures to deal with the inflationary surge, and they refrained from adopting any stimulative measures when the economies entered a significant downturn in 1975.

Import and export prices rose sharply in 1973, leading to improved terms of trade on balance, but with higher oil prices terms of trade declined in 1974. In that year import prices rose by 35 percent, of which half was attributable to higher oil prices. The oil price shock came just as the quantity of imports rose sharply in 1974, partly in response to the governments' promotion of the stockpiling of raw materials and grains. In response to the deteriorating trade balance, monetary authorities restricted monetary growth in 1975. By 1976 the sharp rise in the world coffee price brought a bonanza to the region, causing enormous growth in reserves and in money supply and lessening the progress in reducing inflation.

Throughout 1971–76, external price developments appear to have dominated internal price behavior. Domestic wage policies in the period provided no apparent stimulus to inflation. Economic policymaking in the region adhered to a pattern of passive adjustment to balance-of-payments conditions, allowing the economies to expand in the fat years and contracting them in the lean years; authorities did not apply significant fiscal stimulus to counter the 1975 downturn. In the area of exchange-rate policy, the governments pursued their traditional course of fixed exchange rates tied to the dollar.

From 1970 to 1977, external reserves multiplied fourteenfold in Guatemala and fourfold in El Salvador, as the result of increased coffee prices in 1976–77 as well as large capital inflows. Even though sterilization was not complete, the impact of increased reserves and monetary base was limited, because the private banks typically had excess liquidity. At

25. Some Central American economists adhere to a closed-economy view of inflation, and others who attribute the inflation to monetary phenomena ignore the importance of the price arbitrage mechanism. L. A. Sjaastad, "Additional Observations on the Balance of Payments" (Planning Ministry of El Salvador, March 1976), acknowledges the influence of external factors but concludes that the 1973–75 inflation was made at the Central Bank.

least before 1976, expansion of the monetary base (because of reserve accumulation) did little to expand the money supply; instead, it reduced the money multiplier.

The excess demand and monetarist statistical models of inflation indicate that import price inflation played a large role in explaining inflation; food shortages played a significant role in Guatemala but not in El Salvador (perhaps because food import prices are incorporated in El Salvador's import price index, given its reliance on food imports); excess demand was not a source of inflation; and monetary growth was not a major cause of inflation. Inflation was perhaps the principal disrupting force in the internal and external equilibrium of Guatemala and El Salvador in the 1970s, exacerbating the enormous social and economic welfare problems latent in the economies. Governments were forced to depart from their extremely timid and conservative monetary policies, which, in the name of stability, often sacrificed opportunities for a more rapid development of the economies. In the coming years the monetary authorities are likely to be faced with continuing world inflation and a downturn in the relative prices of the countries' principal export commodities. Given the large share of foreign trade in these economies, their concern should be more how to adapt to external inflation than how to avoid it. This does not mean that government policy should be passive. Governments can make sure that the afterwave of domestic inflation—driven by external prices—is not amplified by internal influences. Governments can create the conditions or take the measures required to dampen domestically generated surges in prices, particularly those originating in the food sector. In responding to abrupt increases in external prices, such as the quadrupling of petroleum prices in 1973, the governments may be justified in arranging and financing a transition scheme designed to soften the disruptive effect of inflation in the allocation of resources within the economies.

To ensure that the burdens of inflation are not simply transferred to those social classes with the least economic and political power, governments must make distributional decisions that will be particularly difficult to implement. In both the public and private sectors there is little experience in managing accelerated inflation, and the goals of the upper classes who control the economies are often shortsighted. The rather high growth of real income[26] during the inflationary surge of the mid-1970s, for example, was largely channeled toward enlarging the income share of capi-

26. Which averaged about 5.5 percent for Guatemala and 5 percent for El Salvador during 1972–77.

tal in the economies. Wages did not keep pace with price rises, except among agricultural workers, many of whom have a subsistence level of income.[27] There is evidence that personal income distribution has become even more skewed than before.[28] Food prices have risen in both countries at a faster rate than prices in any other sector—with the exception of fuel.

In addition to direct responses to inflation, there are measures that the governments can take that will have an effect in the middle and long term. They can diversify exports in order to become less vulnerable to world price conditions. Diversification of import suppliers could also produce some beneficial results.[29] Regional economic integration has already demonstrated the increased bargaining power that a broader market brings in international negotiations. The Central American Common Market also offers the possibility of a larger internal market, somewhat more closed to the world, with some capacity to cushion the impact of external price fluctuations. Greater economic integration would demand closer coordination of fiscal and monetary policies by the member countries, but it would enhance the governments' capacity to manage their economies' response to outside forces.

The governments can also introduce more flexibility into their commercial policy. The import substitution process followed by Guatemala and El Salvador locks a large share of total imports to goods indispensable for industrial development (raw materials, intermediate and capital goods). With the change in composition of imports—from consumer goods to inputs for industry—total imports have become less elastic to price changes; thus, the economy must now bear the full burden of rises in import prices. A possible policy response to this new reality would be to make more flexible and agile some of the instruments used for import control—such as tariffs and commodity consumption taxes. Another obvious line of action would be to join in international cooperative efforts to stabilize world prices of raw materials.

27. Construction workers in Guatemala also kept pace with inflation after the earthquake of February 1976.

28. For a good analysis of labor income, wage profiles, functional and size distribution of income, before and after the establishment of the Common Market, see Clark W. Reynolds and Gustavo A. Leiva, "Employment Problems of Export Economies in a Common Market: The Case of Central America," in William R. Cline and Enrique Delgado, eds., *Economic Integration in Central America* (Brookings Institution, 1978), pp. 181–263.

29. Though it is a highly improbable alternative, it would be profitable to increase the share of imports from the socialist bloc, which in recent years has shown much steadier price behavior, than capitalist countries.

CHAPTER SEVEN

Malaysian Growth and Price Stabilization

R. CHANDER, C. L. ROBLESS, *and* K. P. TEH

AFTER more than a decade of price stability in the domestic economy, Malaysia was shaken by the 1972–75 world cycle of inflation and recession. Malaysia has a very open economy, with exports and imports each ranging between 40 percent and 50 percent of its gross national product (in current prices).[1] Changes in import and export prices and volumes therefore have a significant effect on the domestic price level. Despite this, Malaysia's inflation rates from 1960 to 1971 were low compared to those of other countries. Domestic prices as measured by the consumer price index increased by 12 percent over the period, or about 1 percent a year (table 7-1). In the same period, consumer price levels of the industrial countries rose by 45 percent—the U.S. increase was 37 percent and the U.K. increase 61 percent.[2]

While the slow growth of import prices had a direct effect on domestic prices, the slow growth of export earnings caused by declining export prices affected domestic prices indirectly through changes in money supply. The value of rubber exports—which constituted over 40 percent of Malaysia's export earnings during this period—was 27 percent lower in 1971 than in 1960, despite an increase of 63 percent in the volume exported. Total export value increased only by 2.9 percent a year. Reflecting the sluggish growth of the export sector, money supply M_1 (currency in circulation plus demand deposits of the private sector) increased at a very moderate annual rate of 5.6 percent, the same rate at which GNP was growing (in current prices).

THE VIEWS expressed here are ours alone and should not be attributed to either the government of Malaysia or the World Bank.

1. Malaysia, Treasury, *Economic Report, 1976–77*, table 1.1.

2. *International Financial Statistics Yearbook*, vol. 32 (1979), pp. 60–61, 394–95, 398–99.

Table 7-1. *Consumer, Export, and Import Price Indexes, Malaysia, 1960–71*[a]

Index, 1967 = 100

Year	*Consumer price index*	*Export price index*	*Import price index*
1960	92	n.a.	n.a.
1961	92	n.a.	n.a.
1962	92	108	100
1963	95	106	100
1964	95	108	101
1965	95	114	100
1966	96	109	102
1967	100	100	100
1968	100	95	104
1969	99	108	105
1970	101	105	105
1971	103	97	114

Source: Malaysia, Treasury, *Economic Report, 1973–74* (Kuala Lumpur: [available from] Director General of Printing, 1973), pp. 144, 150, 152.

n.a. Not available.

a. Does not include Sabah and Sarawak, which joined the federation in 1963.

The government's conservative fiscal and monetary policies also contributed to the price stability. Federal budget deficits averaged about 5 percent of GNP from 1961 to 1970 (table 7-2). Moreover, for most of this period the deficits were financed mainly through domestic borrowings from the social security system (by sale of treasury bills and government securities) which substitute public for private aggregate demand. The interest rates offered by the government were also attractive, in relation to the low inflation rates. For example, during much of this period, three-month treasury bills in Malaysia, at 4–5.5 percent, had higher yields than in the United States. Finally, up to 1971, money supply M_1 was backed by more than 115 percent net official foreign reserves; in fact, from 1960 to 1965, reserves were always more than 150 percent of money supply.

Malaysia's foreign reserves were large enough to cover at least seven months of imports. The country's relatively free trade policy allows for effective import competition; excess domestic demand can therefore spill over into imports. Furthermore, in the 1960s Malaysia was able to shift its imports from higher-cost countries like the United Kingdom and the United States to other countries such as Japan, Taiwan, West Germany, and Australia. In 1961, for example, 21 percent of Malaysia's imports came from the United Kingdom and 7.5 percent from Japan; in 1971 the United Kingdom's share had declined to 14 percent and Japan's share had

Table 7-2. *Federal Government Revenue, Expenditure, and Deficits, Malaysia, 1961–76*[a]

Millions of Malaysian dollars

Year	Current revenue	Expenditure: Current	Expenditure: Direct development	Net government lending[b]	Overall deficit	Deficit as a percent of GNP
1961	1,081	847	208	57	31	1
1962	1,097	903	332	83	221	4
1963	1,150	1,032	360	95	337	5
1964	1,458	1,387	413	82	424	5
1965	1,580	1,540	509	68	537	6
1966	1,669	1,619	547	98	595	7
1967	1,842	1,801	519	99	577	6
1968	1,893	1,796	496	115	514	5
1969	2,093	1,930	504	97	438	4
1970	2,400	2,161	565	150	476	4
1971	2,418	2,398	754	316	1,050	8
1972	2,920	3,068	801	422	1,371	10
1973	3,398	3,341	759	347	1,049	6
1974	4,788	4,315	1,107	745	1,379	6
1975	5,117	4,900	1,266	847	1,896	9
1976	5,655	5,600	1,680	680	2,305	9

Source: Treasury, *Economic Report*, various years.
a. For 1960–63 excludes Sabah and Sarawak.
b. Lending to states and public authorities.

increased to 20 percent. Thus Malaysia's import price index increased at only 1.5 percent a year (table 7-1) despite the higher inflation rates of the OECD countries who are Malaysia's major trading partners.

Inflation in the 1970s

The price surge began in Malaysia in the last quarter of 1972. Domestic prices steadily accelerated from an annual rate of 4.3 percent in December 1972 to a high of 21.4 percent in March 1974. During the rest of 1974 prices rose by a more moderate 16.1 percent but the index stabilized only in the second quarter of 1975 as recessionary conditions emerged.

The trends in the overall consumer price index were dominated by food prices, which accounted for 70 percent of the aggregate rise. The index of food prices increased by 3.2 percent in 1972, 15.9 percent in 1973, and 26.1 percent in 1974 (table 7-3), while the nonfood index grew signifi-

Table 7-3. *Consumer Price Index, Malaysia, 1970–75*[a]
Index, 1967 = 100

Component and percent of total index	*1970*	*1971*	*1972*	*1973*	*1974*	*1975*
Food (46.8)	99.1	100.6	103.8	120.3	151.7	157.4
Beverages and tobacco (8.9)	103.0	103.0	107.0	109.0	111.0	121.0
Clothing and footwear (4.8)	102.0	103.0	106.0	129.0	144.0	143.0
Rent, fuel, and power (9.4)	101.0	102.0	103.0	104.0	111.0	119.0
Household equipment and operation (6.6)	106.0	108.0	114.0	129.0	151.0	158.0
Transport and communication (10.4)	103.0	104.0	107.0	109.0	120.0	127.0
Medical care, etc. (2.0)	102.0	103.0	103.0	108.0	116.0	122.0
Recreation and entertainment (5.6)	106.0	111.0	115.0	120.0	127.0	130.0
Miscellaneous goods and services (5.5)	103.0	106.0	113.0	122.0	140.0	148.0
Consumer price index (100.0)	101.3	102.9	106.2	117.4	137.8	144.0

Source: Malaysia, Ministry of Finance, *Economic Report, 1976–77* (Kuala Lumpur: Ministry of Finance, 1976), app. table 7.3.
a. Includes all states except Sabah and Sarawak.

cantly less rapidly: 3.2 percent in 1972, 6.0 percent in 1973, and 9.4 percent in 1974. Not reflected in the CPI was the dramatic rise in the prices of land, residential homes, commercial buildings, and industrial structures. Property values increased substantially, especially in the urban areas where increases of 50–100 percent within a single year were not uncommon.[3]

As prices rose and expectations of further price increases grew, upward wage adjustments became inevitable, especially with the highly regressive incidence of food price increases. Some of the resulting increases were automatically given—in the rubber planting industry, for example, through the gearing, by collective agreement, of the wage of tappers to the rubber price. Others were the result of growing pressure from organized labor on employers to compensate for the rising cost of living. In response, special relief allowances ranging from $15 to $30 a month were provided by the government whose lead was readily followed in the private sector. Although comprehensive wage data are not available, studies covering selected manufacturing industries indicate an overall increase in the average monthly wage of all groups of workers in the manufacturing

3. Bank Negara, Malaysia, *Annual Report and Statement of Accounts, 1973*, p. 95.

sector of about 10 percent in 1973 and 15 percent in 1974, with higher than average rates received by workers in the lower income groups.[4] The special allowances and other wage increases provided a secondary cash-push element in the inflationary process but it is probably not significant.

Domestic factors were partly responsible for the sharp increase in the inflation rate from 1972 to 1974, but the major causes were external. The openness of the economy made imported inflation the primary consideration.

Import Prices

The impact of increased import costs on the consumer price index and other domestic prices was significant. Taking account only of first-round effects, it is estimated that import price increases accounted for 30 percent of the growth in the CPI during 1973 and 1974. As shown in table 7-4, import food price increases were significant, given their weight in both the import index and the consumption basket. Accounting for 80 percent of the rise in the food price index and 32 percent of the overall consumer price index, these increases constituted an important factor in cost and wage pressures during the period.

The most dramatic price increases were in mineral fuels, which increased 13 percent in 1973 and jumped 164 percent in 1974 as a result of the oil crisis. Although these were reflected in domestic prices, and prices of domestically produced oil were adjusted upward, the impact on the CPI was far less severe. Exemptions from import and excise duties and surtaxes were provided for kerosene, diesel, and fuel oil,[5] and price ceilings were imposed, in agreement with industry, on petroleum products and power sales. Thus the transport and communication index grew by 1.9 percent in 1973 and 10.1 percent in 1974, and the rent, fuel, and power index by 1.0 percent and 6.7 percent in those years.

Sharp increases in the import prices of capital goods also directly affected domestic prices in a significant way, since imported capital goods account for 33 percent of total investment. The index of investment goods prices rose progressively from 2.9 percent in 1971 and 8.5 percent in 1972 to 16.4 percent in 1973 before tapering off at 15.7 percent in 1974 and then significantly slowing down to 7.5 percent in 1975.[6]

4. Ibid., *1973,* pp. 96–97, and *1974,* pp. 109–10.
5. Ibid., *1974,* p. 41.
6. Malaysia, *Third Malaysia Plan, 1976–1980* (Kuala Lumpur: Government Press, 1976), pp. 16–17.

Table 7-4. *Import Price Index, Malaysia, 1971–75*[a]
Index, 1967 = 100

Component and percent of total index	*1971*	*1972*	*1973*	*1974*	*1975*
Food (19.4)	103	112	141	194	191
Beverages and tobacco (2.0)	101	97	109	107	130
Crude materials, inedible (9.2)	96	101	114	159	153
Mineral fuels, lubricants, etc. (6.6)	118	119	134	354	425
Animal and vegetable oils and fats (0.6)	149	139	170	258	252
Chemicals (8.4)	108	110	126	213	211
Manufactured goods (20.2)	120	125	147	205	201
Machinery and transport equipment (28.6)	123	132	147	166	195
Miscellaneous manufactured articles (5.0)	122	122	128	153	161
Import price index (100.0)	113	118	137	193	205

Source: Malaysia, *Third Malaysia Plan, 1976–1980* (Kuala Lumpur: Government Press, 1976), p. 128.
a. Includes all states except Sabah and Sarawak.

Apart from their direct effects, higher import prices also pulled up prices of import-competing substitutes, enabling profit margins to be enlarged. They provided an opportunity for manipulation of production as well as distribution margins in the guise of adjustments for the effects of imported inflation. As excess aggregate demand led to growing shortages, imperfections in the distribution system gave rise, as the annual reports of the Central Bank note, to speculative activity, the cornering of markets, and general profiteering.[7]

Export Surplus

Directly reflecting the course of the trade cycle in the industrial countries, export earnings, after increasing by a mere 2.2 percent from 1969 to 1970 and falling continuously after that, increased 51.9 percent in 1973 and 38.3 percent in 1974 before slumping again by 9.6 percent in 1975. The surge in 1973 and 1974 was due primarily to a sharp rise in export prices with export volume playing a much smaller, even negative, role, as is apparent in the changes of rubber, tin, saw logs, petroleum, and palm oil (table 7-5) which together account for about 70 percent of Malaysian exports. Thus, the overall export price index increased by 28.4 percent in 1973 and 34.5 percent in 1974. However, the increase in import prices and expenditures, particularly in 1974, helped to alleviate the expansionary impulse of exports by lowering aggregate demand for domestic production.

7. Bank Negara, *Annual Report, 1973,* pp. 93–95, and *1974,* p. 40.

Table 7-5. *Unit Value and Volume of Malaysia's Major Exports of Primary Commodities, 1971–75*

Commodity and measure[a]	*1971*	*1972*	*1973*	*1974*	*1975*
Rubber					
Price (dollars per pound)	0.48	0.43	0.69	0.83	0.64
Volume (thousands of metric tons)	1,390	1,365	1,639	1,570	1,460
Tin					
Price (dollars per ton)	10,576	10,477	11,178	17,958	15,867
Volume (thousands of metric tons)	87	90	82	86	78
Saw logs					
Price (dollars per ton)	104	92	138	153	109
Volume (thousands of cubic meters)	8,751	9,110	10,116	9,550	8,466
Petroleum[b]					
Price (dollars per ton)	49	52	70	214	227
Volume (thousands of tons)	7,932	4,255	3,827	3,168	3,796
Palm oil					
Price (dollars per ton)	674	529	594	1,224	1,236
Volume (thousands of metric tons)	573	697	798	902	1,163

Sources: *Third Malaysia Plan*, p. 127; Ministry of Finance, *Economic Report, 1976–77*, app. table 3.3.
a. Prices in U.S. dollars.
b. Crude and partly refined.

Capital Inflows

On top of this expansion in export earnings, flows of private capital into the economy jumped 32 percent in 1973 and 114 percent in 1974. Among a number of important monetary decisions in May 1973 were the introduction of a nondiscriminatory and more liberal system of exchange control regulations and the termination of the currency interchangeability arrangements between Malaysia and Singapore. With the breakup of the sterling area in 1972, the new exchange control regulations essentially provided for similar treatment to be accorded to all of Malaysia's trading partners. This meant that the foreign-exchange proceeds from all exports, irrespective of destination, would have to be remitted to domestic commercial banks. The termination of the interchangeability arrangements that had begun with the political separation of Malaysia and Singapore in 1965 was aimed at gradual development of currency and central banking arrangements independent from those of Singapore. One important effect of their termination was significant increases in new deposits and deposit balances by nonresident individuals and businesses with close trading and financial ties with Malaysia.[8] The effect of the increased export earnings

8. Ibid., *1973*, pp. 34–36.

and capital inflow was to increase Malaysia's net external reserves by 12 percent in 1973 and 14 percent in 1974. As in the past, such changes in external reserves provided the impetus for money supply (M_1) growth. This time, increase in net external reserves contributed 70 percent to the growth in money supply between the last quarter of 1972 and mid-1974, before dropping, quarter by quarter, until about mid-1975. Even though credit to the private sector was the largest determinant of money supply, and one which showed the largest increases (table 7-6), a substantial part of this increase was still directly related to the financing of foreign trade.[9]

Thus, money supply, M_1, increased 28 percent in 1972 and 38 percent in 1973 before easing off to 9 percent in 1974, while quasi money, M_2, increased at 11 percent in 1972 and 19 percent in 1973. The spurt in M_1 took place in the third quarter of 1972 and continued until the fourth quarter of 1973.

Exhaustion of Low-Cost Imports

By the early 1970s the scope for shifting Malaysia's import pattern to low-cost exporting countries was virtually exhausted, especially with exchange-rate realignments that appreciated the currencies of countries such as Japan and Germany. Malaysia thus faced similar competing import prices and similar changes of these prices. Moreover, the large foreign reserves that had provided the safety valve for excess domestic demand to spill over into imports was also now of limited effectiveness since these imports could be bought only at high prices.

Public Sector Deficits

Federal government expenditure, investment in particular, increased strongly, relative to revenue, in the early 1970s after sluggish growth in the second half of the 1960s. This expenditure increase reflects both an anticyclical attempt to offset depressed export earnings in 1971 and 1972 and an enlarged public sector effort under the government's New Economic Policy. The ratio of the government deficit to GNP increased greatly to 8 percent in 1971 and 10 percent in 1972 before declining to

9. Ministry of Finance, *Economic Report, 1976–77,* table 9.2. Loans and advances by commercial banks for import, export, and wholesale trade accounted for about 30 percent of the total and grew by 17 percent in 1972, 45 percent in 1973, and 25 percent in 1974 compared with 19 percent, 54 percent, and 16 percent, respectively, for all loans and advances.

Table 7-6. *Money Supply and Its Determinants, Malaysia, 1970–75*

Millions of Malaysian dollars

Item	*1970*	*1971*	*1972*	*1973*	*1974*	*1975*
Determinants						
Net external reserves	2,036	2,177	2,574	2,892	3,292	3,506
Credit to private sector	2,245	2,572	3,015	4,586	5,278	6,077
Lending to government	957	1,174	1,357	1,652	1,999	2,600
Other	180	218	254	471	799	949
Private sector liquidity						
Money supply M_1 (currency in circulation plus demand deposits of private sector)	1,033	2,120	2,716	3,735	4,055	4,349
Quasi money, M_2 (currency in circulation plus deposits with banking system by private sector)	3,025	3,578	3,976	4,925	5,715	6,940

Source: Ministry of Finance, *Economic Report, 1976–77*, table 9.1.

6 percent in 1973 (see table 7-2). The stimulative effect of the 1971 and 1972 deficits continued to be felt in 1973 and 1974, especially since funds earmarked for public development would only be spent after a lag of one to two years. Although foreign market borrowing increased sharply in 1971 and 1972, the bulk of the deficit, or over four-fifths of the total, continued to be financed by nonbank domestic borrowing and foreign project borrowing.[10]

The expansion of aggregate demand stimulated by these external and domestic forces caused Malaysia's real GNP (at 1970 prices) to increase from 6–7 percent in 1971 and 1972 to 11.9 percent in 1973 and 8.4 percent in 1974, before plummeting to 2.5 percent in 1975 when the full impact of the world recession was felt. (The increases in GNP at current prices were: 2.8 percent in 1971, 9.1 percent in 1972, 27.9 percent in 1973, 21.7 percent in 1974, and 2.4 percent in 1975.) The boom period was characterized by domestic supply bottlenecks. Surveys by the Central Bank indicated that as 1973 progressed, most key industries, particularly in the manufacturing and construction sectors, operated under increasing strain. They were increasingly pushed against the effective limits of their productive capacity, while the labor markets in which they operated lightened. More generally, there was mounting evidence of growing scarcity, longer delivery delays, and rising order backlogs for a variety of consumer and capital goods.[11]

The converse situation prevailed from late 1974, when the world recession began, through 1975. Export industries were the first hit and they registered marked output declines. After a short lag, the more domestic-oriented manufacturing, building, and construction industries followed. Excess capacity was prevalent, with cutbacks in the work force reported by a number of industries in the manufacturing, construction, and building sectors.[12]

Policy Issues and Responses

The policy issues facing the government as it sought to deal with cyclical fluctuations in the 1970s were unusually complex. Not only were the fluctuations severe from a purely economic point of view, they had serious

10. Malaysia, Treasury, *Economic Report, 1976–77,* tables 5.1, 5.6.
11. Bank Negara, *Annual Report, 1973,* p. 2.
12. Ibid., *1974,* p. 2, and *1975,* pp. 3–4.

political ramifications as well, arising from the multiracial character of the population and the identification of race with economic function.

There is no question that a key objective of the government during the period was to moderate the pace of inflation and alleviate its impact.[13] Yet containment of inflation had to be achieved without significantly affecting the momentum of socioeconomic development which had been introduced in the twenty-year programs of the New Economic Policy initiated in the government's Second Malaysia Plan, for 1971–75. The country had barely emerged from the 1969 outburst of major racial conflict which threatened the fabric of society and to which the New Economic Policy was the government's overriding response.[14] The two-pronged strategy, designed to eradicate poverty among all Malaysians and to restructure Malaysian society so that the identification of race with economic function would be reduced and eventually eliminated, required a rapid enough pace of economic growth to prevent any group from experiencing any loss or sense of deprivation in the process.[15]

The process of inflation itself affected the racial distribution of income. On one hand, the greatest beneficiaries tended to be the large private rubber, timber, palm oil, manufacturing, and construction concerns, whose ownership was largely in the hands of foreign interests and non-Malay Malaysians. In the first half of 1973, for example, rubber companies showed 50–100 percent increases in profit. On the other hand, among the poor who benefited were rubber smallholders and paddy planters (the largest groups in poverty in the country and largely Malay) and unionized estate workers (about 32 percent Malay and 67 percent other Malaysians). On the average, the income of rubber smallholders in 1973 was nearly double that in 1972. For families in the government's Federal

13. In his 1974 budget message to the House of Representatives in December 1973, for example, the minister of finance called inflation the nation's "No. 1 economic problem. We shall leave no stone unturned to control it as our financial and economic stability depends on our ability to contain it within manageable limits. Either we do this or we may well find the fruits of 16 years of impressive economic growth wiped away." *The 1974 Budget,* p. 43.

14. Malaysia's per capita income is relatively high (about 710 U.S. dollars in 1975) but some 44 percent of all households are estimated to be in poverty. About 36 percent of all household income is earned by the Malays and other indigenous people who are concentrated in agriculture and account for about 55 percent of the Malaysian population compared with 60 percent earned by the Chinese and Indians who are to be found mainly in the secondary and tertiary sectors of the economy and who account for about 43 percent of the population. *Third Malaysia Plan,* chaps. 1, 9.

15. Ibid., chap. 1.

Land Development Authority schemes, the annual income for an average settler in a rubber scheme doubled to about 4,000 Malaysian dollars in 1973 while earnings of settlers in palm oil schemes increased by about 30 percent. Outside agriculture, the real income of construction workers (mainly Chinese) also rose markedly.[16] It was the salaried workers and wage earners (40 percent Malay and 60 percent other Malaysians)[17] who lost significantly. Particularly badly hit were nonunion rural labor and the lower-income groups in the urban areas.

The government's dilemma was to control inflation without upsetting its program to help the poor. Effective control of excess demand required that the windfall gains from export price increases be substantially immobilized (by increasing export taxes, for example). Such action, however, would have deprived many among the rural poor of the gains in the terms of trade which they were enjoying for the first time in many years. Effective action against inflation also required the strictest control of all expenditures that were not directly and immediately productive. Such action again was not possible, given the need for measures that had clearly become necessary to alleviate the plight of those among the poor who were most directly hit by inflation. On the question of income adjustments, the private sector looked to the government for leadership and those adjustments that took place clearly exacerbated cost-push inflation.

The policies and measures adopted by the government followed a middle course. Further, they came to be designed more as a series of measured responses to the situation as it evolved, rather than a set of preemptive strikes, so as to avoid overreaction. They were aimed at moderating the impact on aggregate demand of export earning fluctuations through monetary and fiscal action; expanding the availability, and reducing the cost, of key supplies of domestically produced and imported goods; controlling the prices of basic consumption and investment goods; and alleviating the impact of inflation on the poor.[18]

Monetary Measures

With accumulating evidence that a strong export boom was developing, the Central Bank raised the statutory reserve requirements of the commercial banks in October 1972. In April 1973 the bank increased its

16. Bank Negara, *Annual Report, 1973,* p. 4.
17. *Third Malaysia Plan,* chap. 4, table 4-15, pp. 80–81.
18. Ibid., pp. 129–30.

Table 7-7. *Monetary Measures Affecting Malaysian Commercial Banks, 1972–75*

Percent

Regulated instrument	*1972*	*1973*	*1974*	*1975*
		Interest rate		
Fixed deposits				
One month	3.00	3.50–4.00	4.5	3.5–4.0
Three months	5.00	5.50–6.00	6.5	5.5–6.0
Six months	5.25	5.75–6.25	7.0	6.0–6.5
Nine months	5.50	6.00–7.00	8.0	6.5–7.5
Twelve months	5.75	6.25–8.00	9.0	7.5–8.5
Twenty-four months	6.00	a	a	a
Thirty-six months	6.50	a	a	a
Savings deposits	3.50	4.50–5.50	6.5	5.5–6.5
Minimum advances				
Prime	7.50	8.00–9.00	10.0	9.5
Preferential	7.00	7.50–8.50	9.5	9.0
		Ratio		
Statutory reserve	8.5	8.5	10.0	7.0–8.5
Minimum advances	20.0	25.0	25.0	25.0

Source: Bank Negara, Malaysia, *Quarterly Economic Bulletin*, vol. 9 (March–June 1976), tables 1.18, 4.1.
a. Rates are negotiable.

maximum borrowing and minimum lending rates and raised interest rates on fixed and savings deposits (see table 7-7). These measures, however, were designed only to introduce a modicum of restraint on credit expansion and to encourage higher savings. "The revival of the economy was still in its early stages and any strong measures taken to restrain the expansion of credit would involve the risk of choking off the expected boom prematurely. . . . The national objective of promoting economic growth and reducing unemployment within the framework of monetary and price stability continued to be paramount."[19] In the event, money supply increased from an annual rate of 28.0 percent in the last quarter of 1972 to 33.5 percent in the first quarter of 1973, 41.3 percent in the second—the result of both increasing export earnings and enlarged capital inflows associated with monetary measures adopted in May—and 38.1 percent in the third quarter.[20] Consequently a second series of anticyclical monetary actions was implemented in August 1973 comprising further

19. Bank Negara, *Annual Report, 1973*, p. 37.

20. Bank Negara, Malaysia, *Quarterly Economic Bulletin*, vol. 6 (December 1973), p. P-5.

upward adjustments in the interest rate on fixed deposits and an increase in commercial banks' minimum liquidity ratios. The intent, however, was still that only moderate restraint should be exercised.

> The economic boom was only a few months old. Although strong restrictive measures were called for, the objective of promoting a rapid rate of economic growth and the creation of employment opportunities continued to be overriding. As the policy of expansion had just begun to work through into new investment and capacity build-up, any drastic restrictive monetary measures at [this] stage would [risk] impairing the incentive to invest with the result that the momentum of economic growth which had been so carefully nurtured would be lost.[21]

Only as concrete evidence emerged that the boom had been firmly established and had worked through into new investment and full utilization of productive capacity was the tightest credit squeeze ever experienced in the history of Malaysia imposed. In December 1973, interest rates on deposits and loans were raised across the board, with larger increases for longer term deposits, while the statutory reserve ratios of the commercial banks and the borrowing companies were raised for a second time in just over a year (table 7-7). These measures were followed in April 1974 by another across-the-board increase in interest rates on deposits and loans. In addition, the Central Bank imposed ceilings of 20 percent and 25 percent on the growth of commercial bank and borrowing company credit, respectively.

As a result, the growth of credit to the private sector began to fall. With export receipts also falling from about the third quarter of 1974 as recessionary conditions in world trade appeared, growth of the money supply fell from an annual 37.6 percent in the last quarter of 1973 to 8.6 percent in the last quarter of 1974. The government's task thus turned to ensuring that the economy was protected from recession to the maximum extent feasible without, however, rekindling inflationary forces. The credit growth ceilings that had been imposed on the commercial banks and the borrowing companies were lifted early in 1975, their statutory reserve ratios were reduced, and interest rates were gradually lowered.

In the effort to ensure that monetary action contributed toward curbing inflation without negating the objectives of the New Economic Policy, the exercise of Central Bank influence over the composition of commercial bank credit was a particularly important feature of policy. With every set of monetary measures introduced, the commercial banks were urged

21. Bank Negara, *Annual Report, 1973*, p. 37.

to give priority, within the restraints imposed, to the expansion of productive capacity, residential housing, and the business needs of small borrowers, particularly among the Malays and other indigenous people. As recessionary conditions appeared, the Central Bank went one step further. It exempted loans to small borrowers and the Malay community from the credit growth ceilings it imposed on the commercial banks and stipulated that, within the ceilings, at least 25 percent of the increase would have to be for productive investment in the manufacturing sector. Just under 25 percent of the growth in loans and advances from the commercial banks in 1974 did go to the manufacturing sector, and the Central Bank in its 1974 report commended the banks for their "special efforts in the exercise of restraint generally and in ensuring an equitable distribution of resources in particular."[22]

Fiscal Measures

The principal contribution of fiscal policy on the expenditure front was the stabilization of development spending in 1973 after two years of rapid buildup. Strict expenditure control continued to be maintained in the early months of 1974, although disbursements accelerated toward the end of the year, as policy turned to deal with recession. While low-priority projects, especially those involving the importation of large amounts of capital equipment, were deferred, several quick-disbursing, short-gestation, labor-intensive projects were added to the development program and implemented.[23] Development expenditure increased by 60.7 percent in 1974 and went on to expand further by another 18.5 percent in 1975.

On the revenue front the principal contribution to anticyclical action was made in 1974. The export duty structure for rubber, palm oil, and tin was revised to increase its progressivity, and a land speculation tax was imposed; both measures were specifically designed to siphon off inflationary earnings. With the stabilization of development spending in 1973 and expansion of revenue in 1974, reflecting increased oil revenue in addition to the discretionary tax changes effected, the ratio of the deficit to GNP fell from 10 percent in 1972 to 6 percent in 1973 and 1974, before rising to 9 percent in 1975 during the recession. Furthermore, the share of the deficit financed by foreign borrowing fell to 10 percent in 1973 and 17 percent in 1974.

Apart from its purely anticyclical role, fiscal policy was also aimed at

22. Ibid., *1974,* p. 52.
23. *Third Malaysia Plan,* p. 131.

alleviating the impact of price increases on the poor. Government subsidies were provided for rice, fertilizer, flour, milk, and school textbooks. In addition, the special relief allowances granted to lower salaried public employees and pensioners and similar allowances in the private sector were designed to cushion the impact of inflation on low- and fixed-income groups. These payments accounted for a substantial part of the increase in current expenditure during 1973 and 1974.[24]

Trade and Exchange Policy

The floating of the Malaysian dollar in June 1973 was among the more important measures taken to dampen imported inflation. The trade-weighted average effective rate of exchange of the Malaysian dollar appreciated, reaching a peak of about 15 percent in August and then settling to about 10 percent by the end of the year. In 1974 it appreciated by a further 10 percent.

Trade policy was also liberalized to help expand the availability of imports and, in conjunction with the floating of the dollar, reduce the cost of key supplies of import-competing and imported goods. Thus, import controls were lifted and import duties reduced or eliminated on a large number of basic food and other essential consumer goods and intermediate materials. For exportable goods in these same categories, quantitative controls or special export taxes were imposed. Excise duties were also removed on a wide variety of items. Alongside the liberalization of imports, government investments and promotional action emphasized short-gestation, production-oriented projects in agriculture and manufacturing. To catalyze public commitment, a "grow more food" campaign was launched.

To stimulate competition in the distributive trades—particularly in those sectors where market imperfections exacerbated inflationary forces—a nationwide antihoarding campaign was mounted to focus public attention on trade malpractices; fair price shops were sponsored; and action to extend the network of state trading organizations under the New Economic Policy was accelerated.

Price Control

Comprehensive price and incomes policies were advocated in some quarters but were not adopted. Because of the openness of the economy,

24. Ibid., p. 130.

price controls cannot be effectively implemented for most key tradable goods. Incomes policies aimed at protecting labor would benefit wage and salary earners in urban areas, but would not help the bulk of the poor—agricultural smallholders and unorganized rural labor—who were the government's principal concern. In any case, the statistical, organizational, and manpower requirements of a comprehensive program precluded action of any kind in the near term.

Only rice, the staple of the Malaysian diet, was subjected to extensive price control. In 1974, maximum retail prices were fixed for sixteen grades so that only "reasonable" trading margins would be earned after allowing all production and processing costs. As these prices were significantly below world market prices, private imports ceased. Rice had to be imported by the government and heavily subsidized for sale on the domestic market at the controlled prices.[25]

For the most part, price control was indirect. Domestic price increases were ameliorated in a number of cases by the abolition or reduction of import or excise taxes. Under the Control of Supplies Act of 1961, the designation of individual commodities as controlled items enabled the government to exercise close supervision, if it so chose, of the accounts of producers, wholesalers, and retailers in the endeavor to encourage fair pricing and discourage hoarding and speculation.[26]

An Evaluation

Inflation in Malaysia in 1973 and 1974 appears to have been more pronounced than that in the industrial countries as a whole. It was more in line with inflation in industrial countries from which the major portion of its imports come, and it was less serious than the average for the non-oil-exporting Asian countries (table 7-8).

The degree of openness of the Malaysian economy, the magnitudes of the individual factors underlying inflationary pressure during the period, and the almost simultaneous occurrence of many of the problems clearly made their containment a difficult undertaking. As a relatively small economy, Malaysia is a price taker for imports. Given that imports account for as much as 50 percent of domestic expenditure, the cost-push impact on

25. Bank Negara, *Annual Report, 1974,* p. 40.

26. Malaysia, *Mid-Term Review of the Second Malaysia Plan, 1971–1975* (Kuala Lumpur: Government Press, 1973), p. 118.

Table 7-8. *Increases in Consumer Prices of Malaysia and Selected Industrial and Asian Countries, 1970–75*
Percent

Countries	*1970*	*1971*	*1972*	*1973*	*1974*	*1975*
Industrial countries[a]	5.6	5.1	4.5	7.5	13.1	10.8
Japan	7.6	6.2	4.4	11.8	24.3	11.9
United Kingdom	6.3	9.4	7.3	9.1	16.0	24.2
Australia	3.9	6.0	6.0	9.4	15.1	15.1
United States	5.9	4.3	3.3	6.3	10.9	9.2
Non-oil-exporting Asian countries[b]	5.4	4.9	7.2	16.7	29.0	9.6
Singapore	0.3	1.8	2.1	26.5	22.3	2.6
Malaysia	1.9	1.7	3.2	10.4	17.4	4.5

Sources: *International Financial Statistics*, vol. 31 (May 1978), p. 43.
a. Includes Austria, Belgium, Canada, Denmark, France, Germany, Italy, Japan, Netherlands, Norway, Sweden, Switzerland, United Kingdom, and United States.
b. Includes India, Korea, Malaysia, Pakistan, Philippines, Singapore, Sri Lanka, Taiwan, and Thailand.

the general price level was direct and instantaneous. While changes in export prices had only little direct impact on the general price level, the domestic demand-pull that was exerted as the effects of increased export earnings spread through the economy was clearly substantial.

On top of the externally generated causes there were domestic factors that exacerbated the inflationary pressure. The export boom as it gathered momentum in late 1972 came on top of the expansionary effects that were already beginning to be felt as a result of earlier actions to counter slack and to boost the initiation of the New Economic Policy and the Second Five-Year Plan. The foreign capital inflows associated with the monetary measures of May 1973 further accelerated the expansion in the monetary base. And poor weather in Malaysia in 1972 and 1973 adversely affected food output, particularly rice, and thus compounded excess demand pressure. Any action to contain excess demand, of course, had also to take account of the need to ensure that the momentum of development was not significantly impeded.

In the circumstances, the government's anti-inflation and anticyclical policies can be considered to have attained a creditable measure of success, when compared with other countries'. During the high inflation years of 1973 and 1974, Malaysia was able to keep its inflation rates lower than those of the non-oil-exporting Asian countries as a whole, despite its higher degree of openness. During the worldwide recession year 1975, Malaysia reduced its inflation rate to 4.5 percent, which is much lower than the rates achieved by both the industrial countries and the non-oil-exporting Asian countries.

Malaysia also avoided the potentially serious repercussions of the recession. Although GDP growth fell drastically, unemployment was held down, with cutbacks of only about 16,000 workers in the private sector out of a total labor force of 4.2 million.[27]

Malaysia could of course have done better. The floating of the exchange rate ameliorated cyclical disturbances from the external sector and monetary policy was operated flexibly and in fairly quick response to the changing economic situation. However, the potential countercyclical role of the public budget was less than fully utilized, even allowing for the policy constraints that revenue action was not to affect the poor adversely, and domestic investment cutbacks were to be avoided.

Greater elasticity could have been built into the tax system. For example, earlier introduction of the changes in the export duty structure for rubber, palm oil, tin, and timber—the country's major export commodities—and changing the system of direct tax assessment from a preceding-year basis to a current-year basis would have been helpful. Greater recourse by the public sector to domestic borrowing during the inflation years for financing employment-intensive activity in the recession years would also have helped improve the performance of fiscal and monetary policy during the period.

The experience gained, however, will be invaluable as Malaysia seeks to "ensure that its fiscal and monetary policies are so designed and implemented that the impact of changes in external conditions is cushioned to the maximum extent possible and that national productive capacity is progressively increased so that domestic price increases are kept within reasonable bounds."[28] The prognosis is for continuing fluctuations in export earnings and 6–7 percent increases in international prices each year. It will be difficult to keep domestic prices well below this rate, if substantial contraction of economic growth is to be avoided. The principal task for economic management clearly must continue to be that of moderating the impact of externally induced fluctuations in order that orderly growth may be promoted.

The proposed establishment of buffer stock arrangements for natural rubber, added to those already in operation for tin, should help in moderating price fluctuations in two of Malaysia's key exports and thus facili-

27. *Third Malaysia Plan,* p. 132.
28. Ibid., p. 124.

tate the task of short-run economic management. But above all, adroitness in the management and the combined use of monetary, fiscal, exchange, and trade policies will be of paramount importance. While flexibility in exchange-rate adjustments through the floating of the Malaysian dollar should dampen external cyclical disturbances automatically, it will also affect the allocation of domestic resources. If serious disincentives for the export sector, particularly the nascent trade in manufactured goods, are not to be created, there will have to be clear limits on the extent to which the exchange rate is allowed to appreciate. Monetary authorities should use both interest-rate changes and open market operations to moderate the need for exchange-rate adjustments. Given the openness of the economy, it is exceedingly important that monetary measures be closely coordinated with fiscal policy on both the revenue and expenditure fronts. A useful innovation in the latter connection has been the building up of a reserve list of quick-disbursing, short-gestation, labor-intensive projects that could be injected into or withheld from the economy as and when the situation required expansionary or contractionary fiscal action. Such an instrument is especially germane to Malaysia's overriding aim of moderating cyclical fluctuations without impeding the overall growth process itself.

CHAPTER EIGHT

Policy Response to External Fluctuations

WILLIAM R. CLINE

IN THE GREAT INFLATION of 1973–74 and worldwide recession of 1974–75, developing countries fared relatively well, although the external shocks complicated their economic planning. Their growth rates were high during the worldwide boom of 1973 and did not fall far in the subsequent recession; they obtained substantial windfall gains from the inflationary erosion of their external debt; capital flows to these countries, including concessional assistance (especially from OPEC countries and Europe), more than kept pace with externally provoked changes in their needs; and despite large changes in relative prices, the world distribution of income stayed practically unchanged (or became slightly more equitable).

The developing countries that do not export oil did experience a decline in terms of trade from 1971–72 to 1975. However, when oil is excluded from the calculation of trade values, the great majority of developing countries experienced an improvement in their terms of trade in this period. The source of the overall decline was not inflation in industrial countries but the actions of the Organization of Petroleum Exporting Countries. Terms of trade also became more unstable in the 1970s as commodity prices gyrated more wildly, making planning more difficult.

Inflation was almost universally transmitted into the domestic economies of developing countries; those with traditional price stability faced socially disruptive inflation for the first time, while those with their own inflation found it aggravated by external shocks. Higher prices for imported commodities and expanded reserves and money supply were the principal transmission channels of world inflation. The first of three distinct phases in the international cyclical shocks was the flood of foreign capital into many developing countries in 1971–73, in some cases coupled with rising trade balances, which caused foreign-exchange reserves to rise rapidly. The capital flows appear to have been associated with the flow of dollars out of the United States during the final throes of the Bretton Woods international monetary system. Because the capital inflows were not fully sterilized, money supply grew at exceptionally high rates in developing countries beginning in 1972. This external impulse to monetary growth was stronger in countries more fully integrated into the world financial system because of their relatively strong creditworthiness. Among the cases studied in this volume, the monetary channel for world inflation was especially important for Brazil and to a lesser degree the Central American economies and Malaysia. For India, which is to some extent severed from the world private financial system by its low creditworthiness, the monetary channel for external inflation was not important.

The second major phase of world cyclical disturbance was the rampant commodity price inflation that began in 1973 with sharp increases for food and a number of other commodities and culminated dramatically in 1974 with the fourfold rise in the price of oil. The commodity price boom reflected not only the coordinated economic boom of industrial countries in 1973 but also a wave of speculative stockpiling against still further price increases, both in industrial countries (Japan in particular) and developing countries (as in the explosion of Brazilian imports in 1974). The oil price increase ended any hope of limiting the commodity price inflation. It also was the factor that turned the terms of trade of most developing countries from a positive to a negative trend.

It was in this phase of inflation in the prices of imported commodities (including manufactured goods) that world inflation was thrust most seriously into the internal systems of most developing countries. The statistical tests of thirty countries' price changes and of the experience in Brazil, Guatemala and El Salvador, and India as well as the Malaysian record show the strong influence of the 1973–74 boom in import prices on domestic inflation. In the countries with a tradition of price stability (India, Malaysia, Guatemala and El Salvador) this direct mechanism of import price inflation caused domestic inflation to reach unprecedented heights; in Brazil, where inflation was endemic, import price inflation accelerated the pace of domestic inflation. For the non-oil-exporting developing nations as a group, domestic inflation doubled from 1972 to 1974 (rising from 14 percent to 28 percent). Imported inflation accounted for at least half, and more probably nearly the entire amount, of this increase.[1] Moreover, import price inflation was systematically the more significant factor when set against wage inflation or excess demand. It even provides a better explanation than does monetary growth of domestic inflation in 1973 and 1974 (in the tests on thirty countries and on the Central American economies and Brazil) and of the deceleration of inflation in 1975 (in India especially).

The third phase of world cyclical disturbance, the global recession of 1974–75, caused a reduction in developing countries' exports, aggravating their trade deficits and causing many, especially those unprepared to slow down domestic growth, to accumulate large external debts.

The numerous statistical analyses in this study indicate that a considerable part of the inflationary surge in developing countries may be explained by external inflationary impulses, transmitted primarily through the monetary and import price channels. It would be absurd to interpret the nearly universal pattern of heightened inflation in 1973 and 1974 as the result of a sudden, simultaneous binge by those countries' policymakers embarked on irresponsible fiscal and monetary policies.

Policy Responses in the 1970s

In the face of the common external inflationary and recessionary shocks, developing countries responded in different ways. For the vast

1. From the regression results for individual countries, the contribution of imported inflation amounted to an unweighted average of 47 percent of actual inflation in 1974 (table 3-17, chap. 3, excluding oil-exporting countries, and *International Financial Statistics,* vol. 31 [May 1978], p. 43). Considering that inflation doubled from 1972 to 1974, and that import price inflation was minor in 1972, the implication is that practically the entire increase in domestic inflation came from the surge in imported inflation. The regression results for all developing countries considered as a group suggest a lower contribution of external inflation; of the 10.52 percentage-point acceleration in predicted inflation from 1972 to 1974, 5.17 percentage points are attributed to import price rises (table 3-19, chap. 3), indicating that imported inflation accounted for half of the total rise. Regression analysis for Brazil showed that the import price variable accounted for 10 percentage points out of a total 13.7 percentage-point rise in inflation in 1974 (chap. 4). For Guatemala and El Salvador, the coefficient on import inflation (approximately 0.25, table 6-14) when applied to import price increases in 1974 (40 percent) yields a 10 percent rise in domestic inflation, accounting for approximately two-thirds of inflationary acceleration from 1972 to 1974. *International Financial Statistics,* vol. 31 (May 1978), pp. 43, 51. These various estimates do not include the influence of imported inflation working through the monetary channel, but capture only the impact of price increases for imported goods.

majority of developing countries, external inflation accelerated domestic inflation in 1973–74, but thereafter country experience divided relatively evenly between success and failure in bringing inflation back down. Inflation rates for thirty developing countries (excluding members of OPEC and countries with chronically high inflation) show that about half managed to reduce inflation in 1975–77 below the high rates of 1973–74, and half did not (table 8-1). Even among the group of countries that reduced inflation, however, it remained at levels considerably higher than before the Great Inflation, averaging 9.0 percent in 1975–77 compared with 3.6 percent in the 1960s. The rise was more dramatic for the countries failing to reduce inflation, from 6.6 percent in the 1960s to 25.0 percent in 1975–77.

The figures in table 8-1 confirm the regional data presented in chapter 1 showing much greater anti-inflationary success in Asia than elsewhere. All eight of the Asian countries examined in the table are in the "successful" category. By contrast, Latin American countries are split, with the fiscally conservative Central American countries in the successful group but Mexico, Colombia, and Peru in the unsuccessful group. Similarly, the African countries are split between the two categories. Asian success is underscored when considering the dramatic size of the inflationary reversal in countries such as India, Sri Lanka, Malaysia, and Taiwan.

There is no systematic pattern apparent in table 8-1 to explain why some countries reversed inflation while others did not. The strong Asian bias toward stability is clear but unexplained. If Israel is excluded, there is virtually no difference between the average per capita income of the two country groupings. Nor is country size a determining factor: the stabilizing group includes India at one extreme and El Salvador at the other. Institutional factors such as the British civil servant tradition are equally ineffective in explaining the differences (Egypt, Kenya, and Ghana are found in the nonstabilizing group, for example, while India, Pakistan, and Tanzania are in the stabilizing group).

Nor is there any pattern relating success in reducing inflation to changes in growth rate. The Phillips-curve approach as well as the popular notion that economic stabilization measures (especially of the International Monetary Fund variety) come at the expense of at least short-run growth suggest that growth performance would have been poorer in the group of countries that reduced inflation in the late 1970s. But regression analysis shows no statistical relationship between reduction of

Table 8-1. *Inflationary Experience of Thirty Developing Countries, 1975–77*

Percent inflation

Group	*1960–70, annual average*	*1973*	*1974*	*1975*	*1976*	*1977*
Countries reducing inflation						
Dominican Republic	2.1	15.2	13.1	14.5	7.7	12.9
El Salvador	0.3	6.4	16.9	19.2	7.0	11.9
Guatemala	0.1	13.6	16.6	13.1	10.7	12.6
India	6.9	17.8	27.8	5.6	−7.8	8.5
Korea, Republic of	16.7	3.1	23.8	26.3	15.4	10.3
Malagasy Republic (Madagascar)	3.2	6.2	22.1	8.2	5.0	3.0
Malaysia	−0.3	10.4	17.4	4.5	2.6	4.8
Morocco	2.2	2.7	17.5	7.9	8.6	12.5
Pakistan	3.3	23.0	26.6	20.9	7.2	10.1
Philippines	5.8	14.0	33.5	8.2	6.1	7.9
Sri Lanka	1.8	9.7	12.4	6.7	1.2	1.3
Sudan	3.7	15.3	26.1	23.9	1.7	16.7
Taiwan	4.1	8.2	47.5	5.2	2.5	6.3
Tanzania	1.8	10.3	19.6	26.1	6.9	11.5
Thailand	1.9	11.6	23.4	4.1	5.0	8.4
Tunisia	3.7	4.7	4.2	9.5	5.4	6.6
Average	3.6	10.8	21.8	12.7	5.3	9.1
Countries failing to reduce inflation						
Cameroon	3.7	6.6	16.8	15.1	9.4	14.6
Colombia	11.9	22.8	24.2	25.8	17.4	30.0
Egypt	3.5	4.3	10.8	9.8	10.3	12.7
Ethiopia	2.1	8.8	8.7	6.5	28.6	16.6
Ghana	7.6	10.3	24.2	41.2	52.7	80.4
Israel	6.0	20.1	39.5	39.5	31.4	34.6
Ivory Coast	2.8	11.2	17.3	11.5	12.0	27.5
Jordan	1.1	10.4	20.0	12.0	15.0	31.1
Kenya	1.5	9.4	17.8	19.2	12.4	15.6
Mexico	3.5	11.3	22.5	16.8	16.1	26.4
Peru	9.9	9.5	16.9	23.6	33.5	38.1
Syrian Arab Republic	1.8	21.0	14.7	16.3	15.0	11.3
Zaire	29.9	15.6	27.5	30.7	85.1	63.1
Zambia	7.6	6.3	8.5	10.0	18.7	19.6
Average	6.6	11.9	19.2	19.9	25.6	30.1

Sources: World Bank, *World Development Report 1979*, pp. 126–27; *International Financial Statistics*, vol. 31 (May 1978), p. 43.

inflation and the change in growth rate from earlier trends.[2] This finding is consistent with the results in chapter 3, where the Phillips-curve or output-gap model of inflation was found to perform poorly in explaining inflation. The lack of a statistical pattern relating anti-inflation success to slower growth is encouraging, because it suggests that there are available to developing countries anti-inflationary policies that need not sacrifice growth. Moreover, considering that many of the countries most successful at reducing inflation were Asian countries following essentially policies of monetary restraint, these results suggest that fears of severe loss of economic growth from orthodox stabilization policies may be overstated.

The case studies in chapters 4–7 throw additional light on the pattern of policy response to external shocks in the 1970s. One striking feature of the import pattern in 1974 (especially in Brazil and Central America) is the increase in real imports at a time when extensive import price increases might have been expected to reduce import volume. The same phenomenon shows up at the global level; in 1974 and 1975 the trade deficits of developing countries rose by amounts far in excess of what could be explained by price movements alone. Speculative stockpiling as a hedge against still further commodity price increases probably was at work in 1974. Also it seems likely that in 1974, in a lagged response to the heady days of 1973 when commodity trade prices were highly favorable (at least for countries not heavily importing food), the oil price had not risen, and reserves were mounting, policymakers loosened the reins on imports and allowed them to surge in real terms. This was a clear failure to see through to the end of the commodity cycle, to recognize that the boom was temporary and that reserves should be husbanded against harder times to come. But the real import expansion and trade deficits of 1974 also reflect a determination by policymakers in many developing countries to maintain domestic growth rates despite external imbalance. Clearly that was true of Brazil, as it seems to have been for Korea, another country whose continued high growth targets led to a serious trade deficit in 1974.[3]

2. For the thirty countries in table 8-1, the results of regression analysis were:

$$\Delta g = -0.15 \; -0.024\, \Delta \dot{p},$$
$$(0.4) \quad (0.8)$$
$$\bar{R}^2 = 0.02$$

where Δg is the change in average growth rate from 1960–70 to 1970–77 and $\Delta \dot{p}$ the change in inflation rate from 1973–74 to 1975–77 (t-statistics are in parentheses).

3. See Lawrence B. Krause and Sueo Sekiguchi, eds., *Economic Interaction in the Pacific Basin* (Brookings Institution, 1980).

A broader policy question is the appropriate growth response to a heightened trade deficit caused by international inflation or recession. Should developing countries react to external shock by cutting back growth? This response was clearly chosen by the Central American countries, and the result was discouraging. Economic growth declined, and although the trade deficit declined, the rate of inflation remained high by the region's past standards. The reaction would seem to have been an overly rigid adherence to the traditional policy of allowing the balance of payments to dictate contraction or expansion (even to the point of taking procyclical steps that exacerbate the domestic impact of trade-balance shifts). The opposite response in Brazil was, on balance, healthier. In the face of deterioration in the external account, Brazil pursued high growth combined with aggressive sectoral development designed to replace imports. Brazil's was by far a riskier strategy, and it left a legacy of high foreign debt. But it meant the avoidance of severe real income loss and worsening unemployment. Malaysia stood somewhere in between, allowing a moderate (though acceptable) growth rate in 1975 to follow exceptionally high growth in 1973 and 1974. As one benefit, Malaysia brought down inflation sharply in 1975, while in Brazil inflation persisted at a new high plateau (in part no doubt because the indexing of wages and prices pushed costs higher).

Another theme of fundamental importance is the impact of world inflation and recession on the poor classes within developing countries. The effect of inflation on world income distribution in 1973–74 appears to have been trivial in size although equitable in direction. Not even radical changes in prices of traded goods could be expected to change that result since many of the benefits of higher prices would accrue to rich countries, while much of the gain within developing countries would fall into the hands of the rich minority. The impact of commodity price changes on total income would be slight under any circumstance because external trade is such a small portion of gross national product. Changes in prices of traded goods probably have a much greater effect on internal than international distribution of income. The striking contrast in the responses of Malaysia and India on the one hand and Guatemala and El Salvador on the other to external shock illustrates how the influence of imported inflation on poverty groups can be tempered. Malaysia managed to keep food prices moderate by controlling the price of rice and selling government-imported rice at a subsidy. India also had considerable success in insulating domestic food prices from external food price inflation. Guatemala and El Salvador failed to buffer domestic food prices from meteoric world price increases in 1973. It is tempting to conclude that despite technical (storage) difficulties in Central America, the real difference in the three cases stemmed from the differing political commitment to the impoverished groups.

Malaysia in fact pursued a whole battery of measures designed to help insulate the poor from external shocks. The government subsidized basic consumption items and granted special wage adjustments to low-income civil servants. When higher export taxes became imperative for stabilization, the government raised them by increasing their progressivity, allowing the benefits of higher rubber prices to pass through to at least smallholders. The Central American and Brazilian governments made no such direct efforts. Recession policies in Guatemala and El Salvador must have decreased employment among the poor. Brazil kept its economic activity as high as possible, but the external crisis appears to have led to the shelving or deceleration of earlier efforts at redistribution (primarily through special programs for the impoverished Northeast, for basic education, and for housing).

These patterns suggest the tantalizing conclusion that where the political will is sufficiently strong, adjustment to external shock can be carried out in a way that minimizes adverse impacts on the poor. Because of past racial violence and the fact that the government in Malaysia tends to represent the interests of the poor majority (Malays), the policy response of Malaysia is most informative about the scope for equitably oriented adjustment to external shock.

Exchange-rate policy is another area in which the four case studies offer provocative contrasts. Brazil and Malaysia had flexible exchange rates while the Central American economies tied rigidly to the dollar and India pegged to the pound sterling until 1975. Only Malaysia took advantage of exchange-rate flexibility to appreciate substantially as a means of insulating the domestic economy from external inflation. India did so to a minor degree by remaining pegged to the pound sterling in 1973 (when the dollar declined) and by decoupling from the pound when it began to sink in 1975. However, Malaysia was able to use appreciation as an anti-inflationary device because it enjoyed a rise in terms of trade through 1975, thanks to its self-sufficiency in oil combined with high prices for its exports of rubber, tin, timber, and palm oil. The contrast between Malaysia and the other countries confirms the notion that appreciation is a correct policy for offsetting world inflation only when that inflation has a positive or neutral effect on the country's terms of trade. Appreciation is a luxury no country can afford when it needs to correct its external imbalance.

The rigid exchange-rate policy of the Central American countries meant that in 1971–73 there was a considerable surge in reserves (which appreciation might have discouraged). The fixed peg meant that when the trade balance deteriorated seriously in 1974, the only means of response (barring protection) was repression of the domestic economy. Korea is an excellent illustration of the alternative solution to external imbalance; it undertook a sharp devaluation while maintaining a high growth rate.[4]

Neither the large size of its economy nor the fact that it is closed can guarantee a developing country insulation from external inflationary and recessionary shocks. The regressions in chapter 3 of data on thirty countries show no correlation between openness and the size of the coefficient of domestic inflation on import prices. Large, closed developing economies as well as small, open economies need to take full account of probable international economic trends in their internal economic planning. The more closely the large, closed economy is integrated into the world financial system, the more sensitive it seems to be to world economic fluctuations. Thus, Brazil's intimate integration into world capital markets appears to have undermined the detachment from external shocks that might have been expected for so large and closed economy. India, by contrast, appears to have been well insulated (in view, particularly, of its immunity to capital inflows and reserve growth in the early stages of the 1972–75 cycle).

Future Strategies

Though experience in the Great Inflation will not necessarily be an accurate guide to future policy, it suggests how developing countries might respond to international shocks. If external inflation is accelerating and if the country's terms of trade are either holding constant or improving, a two-step policy sequence appears to be desirable. First the level of protection should be reduced as a means of providing direct relief from higher import prices (it also may provide indirect relief by leading to a more efficient allocation of resources). Malaysia followed this approach and achieved stabilization, in conjunction with other policies. Brazil fol-

4. Ibid.

lowed just the opposite approach—heightened protection—and paid the price of a second round of inflation (1976–77) beyond that induced by higher import prices. A second policy step, for the country with no loss in terms of trade, is to appreciate the exchange rate. In principle, if world prices are inflating and authorities wish to keep domestic inflation below the world level, the exchange rate should appreciate at a rate equal to the difference between external and internal inflation. In an era when the natural tendency of industrial economies was to have price stability or at least much lower inflation than developing countries, this prescription would have been no more than a curiosity. Since the mid-1970s, however, many industrial countries have shown an inability to return to their historically low rates of inflation, and developing countries should search for ways to hold internal inflation below the rates prevalent in industrial countries.

When their terms of trade are falling, it will probably be impossible for developing countries to attempt to offset external inflation by appreciating the currency (or even reducing protection, despite possible efficiency benefits). Instead, devaluation may be necessary. Increased protection should be avoided, however, because it is likely to aggravate rather than soften external inflation, and to do so by a greater degree than would devaluation. Special sectoral policies that encourage domestic substitutes for vital imports (or supply of exports), like the various energy-saving measures adopted in Brazil, India, Central America, and Malaysia, and the Brazilian program of development in raw materials and capital equipment, will also be attractive.

Monetary policies in developing countries need to be much more effectively devised to serve as instruments for sterilizing reserve increases, and sterilization measures need to be more aggressively applied. Otherwise renewed bouts of world inflation and associated increases in reserves seem likely to provoke excessive monetary expansion again, as they did in many developing countries in 1972.

Somewhat unorthodox fiscal measures may be necessary if the poor are to be protected from external economic shocks. For example, domestic food prices should be insulated from international fluctuations, a practice that will require food subsidies at times of external scarcity. To be sure, an international grains agreement with buffer stocks for smoothing price fluctuations would relieve much of this potential fiscal burden. Another flexible fiscal policy, which Malaysia has used, is changes in indirect taxes (and duties) to offset sharp increases in world prices. Again, progressive export taxes that provide needed fiscal stabilization can permit small producers to benefit from higher export prices while taxing the windfall gains of large producers.

The 1970s experience suggests that developing countries should not passively accept external shocks and reduce their domestic growth, but should pursue steady-growth policies, dealing with resulting trade-balance difficulties through devaluation and other stimuli to exports as well as development programs focused on import substitution. This unwillingness to accept recession from abroad should be balanced by a corresponding degree of prudence in the disposition of abundant foreign exchange earned at the favorable peak of the commodity cycle.

The industrial countries must recognize that their macroeconomic policy choices have major implications for the growth prospects of developing countries (see the appendix to this study). In general this fact might not alter their choices, because in seeking to maximize their own medium- and long-term growth, industrial country policymakers would also maximize that of the developing countries. The global externality of macroeconomic policy choices in advanced countries does mean, however, that alternative policy goals may present conflicting national and international preferences, particularly as between price stability on the one hand and higher growth with more nearly full employment on the other. Ideally this might be resolved by some form of global policy coordination that included developing countries. Policy consultation is already accepted practice among industrial countries in the OECD and economic summit meetings, and extension of such consultations to include representatives of developing countries would be desirable.

Another area that should attract industrial countries' concern is commodity price fluctuation. The extraordinary fluctuations in the real values of major raw material exports of the developing countries in the 1970s indicate that establishment of commodity agreements should be given a high priority. There is ample evidence that the prices of imported commodities contributed to high domestic inflation in the industrial countries in 1973 and 1974. Industrial and developing countries need to come to mutually advantageous agreements for ironing out commodity price fluctuations, and squabbles over issues such as the structure of a common fund for commodities should not deter them. Stabilization of grain prices is among the most important arrangements for reducing inflation in developing countries (as the statistical results in chapter 3 and on India and the Central American economies indicate).

Finally, industrial countries must take inflation into account in drawing up their budgets for development assistance. The foreign aid programs of the United States in particular have been savagely eroded by inflation. Increased aid by OPEC and European countries has offset this erosion, but it is unlikely that these sources can be counted on to continue to make good the declining real aid effort of the United States or other advanced-country donors. Furthermore, it appears appropriate for the industrial countries to take into account the heightened degree of externally imposed economic fluctuation when considering measures that affect credit availability to developing countries. Recent increases in the quotas of the International Monetary Fund, new allocations of special drawing rights, and the special Witteveen facility for balance-of-payments lending all work in the direction of increasing the capacity of the official financial mechanisms for dealing with international economic shocks. However, these and other instruments must be continually reviewed to assure they are sufficient to enable developing countries to adjust (with minimum loss of real growth) in a period of global shocks that seems more likely to repeat the turbulence of the early 1970s than return to the steadier, more buoyant environment of the two previous decades.

APPENDIX

Cyclical Growth Links between Industrial and Developing Countries

WILLIAM R. CLINE

THE GLOBAL INFLATION and recession of 1973–75 had a direct impact on the terms of trade and capital requirements of developing countries as well as on their domestic prices. More generally, economic growth in developing countries is affected indirectly by the cyclical phases of the world economy. This appendix analyzes macroeconomic policy choices in industrial countries whose repercussions are likely to be felt in developing countries. It also briefly considers the effects that economic growth in developing countries may have on the maintenance of full employment in the rich countries.

Cyclical Links

The traditional notion that the developed centers of the world determined the demand for exports of raw materials from the peripheral colonial economies carries over to the experience of the developing world in the 1970s. The predominant role of exports in the commercial portion of colonial economies meant that they were very sensitive to the rate of growth in the industrialized nations.[1] During the Great Depression and World War II, developing countries were forced to begin industrializing. The policy of import substitution that they intentionally pursued in the late 1950s and 1960s was supposed to change the dependency of their growth rates on those in industrial countries. Import substitution brought

1. See Thomas B. Birnberg and Stephen A. Resnick, *Colonial Development: An Econometric Study* (Yale University Press, 1975).

Table A-1. *Real Rates of Growth of Gross Domestic Product, OECD and Non-Oil-Exporting Developing Countries, 1960–77*
Percent

Year	*OECD countries*	*Non-oil-exporting developing countries*[a]
1960–65 average	5.0	4.4
1966	5.6	4.7
1967	3.6	5.5
1968	5.5	5.9
1969	4.7	7.0
1970	3.1	6.4
1971	3.7	5.4
1972	5.4	5.5
1973	5.9	7.3
1974	0.2	5.3
1975	−0.9	4.1
1976	5.2	4.8
1977	3.5	4.9

Sources: Organization for Economic Cooperation and Development, *OECD Economic Outlook*, no. 22 (December 1977), pp. 15, 124; International Monetary Fund, *Annual Report, 1978*, p. 11, *1976*, p. 5, and *1973*, p. 9; OECD, *Development Assistance: Efforts and Policies of the Members of the Development Assistance Committee, 1968 Review* (Paris: OECD, 1968), p. 117; United Nations, *World Economic Survey 1967, pt. 1: The Problems and Policies of Economic Development: An Appraisal of Recent Experience*, UN Doc. E/4488/Rev. 1, ST/ECA/104, p. 17.

a. Rates for 1960–72 include oil-exporting countries.

its own new dependency on exports, however, as superfluous imports were eliminated and export earnings became essential to provide the imported raw materials necessary to keep the developing economy operating at full capacity and to supply imported capital equipment necessary for growth.

The Great Inflation of 1973–74, including the sharp and coordinated international boom in 1973, followed by the severe recession of 1974–75, caused a sharp swing in the business cycle for industrial countries which experience dictated would be echoed in the developing countries. The pronounced global cycle did cause a corresponding cycle of boom and recession in the developing countries, but it was less severe than that in industrial countries. The economies of the Organization for Economic Cooperation and Development as a whole reached their highest growth rate for the period in 1973—with aggregate real growth at 5.9 percent (table A-1). In the same year the developing countries that are not oil exporters also reached their highest aggregate growth rate for the entire period, 7.3 percent. In 1974 and 1975, when the OECD growth rate fell precipitously, the developing countries' decline in growth was much less severe, the rate dropping only to 4.1 percent.

During an earlier and milder global cycle in 1968–70, growth rates in industrial countries fell from 5.5 percent to 3.1 percent and developing countries' rates declined also, with a lag of one year (table A-1). But when the growth rate in the industrial countries dipped for a single year, in 1967, there was no visible impact on developing countries, perhaps because of the short slowdown at the center.

In the 1968–70 cycle the growth rate in developing countries declined (with a one-year lag) by two-thirds the amount of the decline in the OECD. During the more severe cyclical downturn of 1973–75, their decline was only about one-half of the decline in the growth rate of OECD countries (a 3.2 percentage-point decline in the former and 6.8 percentage-point decline in the latter).

For the period as a whole, developing country growth is somewhat less sensitive to industrial country growth. A regression relationship between the two growth rates for 1960–77 yields the following results:

$$g_t^{LDC} = 4.67 + \underset{(1.98)}{0.230}\, g_{t-1}^{DC},$$

$$\bar{R}^2 = 0.21$$

where g_t^{LDC} is the growth rate of developing countries in year t, and g_{t-1}^{DC} is the growth rate of industrial countries in the previous year (the t-statistic is in parentheses). The equation shows a relatively high basic growth rate of 4.67 percent in the developing area, affected only moderately by the growth rate in the industrial area in the previous year. The coefficient 0.230 relating the two is statistically significant but its size indicates that for the period as a whole, growth in the developing area was less affected by growth cycles in the industrial area than appears to have occurred in the slumps of 1969–71 and 1973–75.

Some analysts, surprised that the developing countries' decline was not more severe, attribute their supposedly strong performance to massive infusions of foreign capital.[2] They emphasize that the developing countries served as a balancing wheel during the global recession, providing a source of needed demand for the faltering industrial economies. But the developing countries' experience as the result of downturn at the center in 1974–75 was relatively severe in terms of the relationship between

2. See John A. Holsen and Jean L. Waelbroeck, "The Less Developed Countries and the International Monetary Mechanism," *American Economic Review,* vol. 66 (May 1976, *Papers and Proceedings, 1975*), pp. 171–76.

growth in the center and the periphery over the whole period 1960–77. For each percentage-point decline in industrial countries' growth over the longer period the induced reduction of growth in developing countries was approximately one-quarter percentage point, compared with a reduction of one-half percentage point in the 1974–75 recession. Growth in the developing countries appears to have been abnormally responsive to cyclical changes in the industrial countries in the slumps of 1969–71 and 1973–75.

Effects of Macroeconomic Policies in Industrial Countries

One of the most serious negative effects of world inflation on the developing countries may arise from the policies that industrial countries adopt to control their own inflation. Typically those policies lead to domestic recession and a stagnation of demand for developing countries' exports, which stunts economic growth in those countries. The stagnation in demand for developing countries' exports will be reflected in reduction of their capacity to import as their foreign-exchange earnings fall. In the framework of the two-gap model of development, reduction of foreign-exchange earnings can lower the feasible growth rate.[3] Moreover, export decline causes a normal Keynesian demand contraction. When this component of autonomous expenditure in the economy falls, national income declines by a multiple of the export reduction.

In order to judge how macroeconomic policy choices in industrial countries affect growth in developing countries, it is necessary first to determine whether the export earnings and growth of developing countries are in fact smaller during periods of cyclical fluctuation in industrial countries than in periods of moderate but steady growth. That is done by comparing simulation analyses of three different policy approaches to inflation: steady growth at moderate rates of inflation; slower growth with the goal of bringing down inflation; and rapid growth with inflation increasing until it reaches a level so high that low growth is chosen to reduce it. The policies are tested using a model that relates growth in industrial countries to export earnings of developing countries and the relationship in developing countries between GNP and the import requirements that must be financed by export earnings.[4]

3. Hollis B. Chenery and Alan M. Strout, "Foreign Assistance and Development," *American Economic Review*, vol. 56 (September 1966), pp. 680–733.

4. Norman L. Hicks, "A Model of Trade and Growth for the Developing World," *European Economic Review*, vol. 7 (April 1976), pp. 239–55.

It is likely that steady-growth policies in industrial countries will produce a level of demand that is higher than the simple average between the boom and recession levels, since a fluctuation between boom and recession represents an alternation between the two "inefficient" legs of the Phillips curve. Total output over two years of moderate inflation and moderate unemployment would be expected to be higher than the sum of output during one year of high inflation and low unemployment and another of low inflation and high unemployment.[5] With demand under steady growth sufficiently higher than the average of demand between periods of boom and recession, the export earnings of developing countries in the cyclical case would be expected to fall below their export earnings in the case of steady industrial-country growth.[6]

In addition, developing-country planners might find it difficult to anticipate accurately the size and timing of a cycle. As a result, they might spend excessively out of foreign exchange earned during the industrial-country boom, and be unprepared to finance imports out of reserves during the recession. Furthermore, with fluctuating demand and prices the corresponding increase in uncertainty is likely to reduce the rate of investment in export activity.

For all these reasons one would expect developing countries to achieve higher average levels of export earnings if industrial countries followed sustainable, steady-growth paths than if they instead followed stop-go cyclical policies.

High raw materials prices might also prove unfavorable if they feed back into inflation in industrial countries. It is fairly widely accepted that raw materials prices, especially of metals such as copper, are sensitive to the business cycle.[7] Recent attention has also focused on the detrimental

5. As Edward M. Gramlich puts it: "The underlying nonlinearity in the inflation-unemployment tradeoff, which makes high unemployment rates relatively less effective in fighting inflation, encourages policymakers to spread unemployment evenly across the . . . years." "The Optimal Timing of Unemployment in a Recession," *Brookings Papers on Economic Activity, 1:1975*, p. 169. (Hereafter *BPEA*.)

6. This conclusion is based on considerations of export volume. It is conceivable that for some countries, terms-of-trade effects could cause the opposite result (higher earnings with cyclical fluctuation at the center), although asymmetrical assumptions would be required about price behavior in the upswing and in the downswing to reach that result.

7. Hicks, "Model of Trade and Growth"; Rudolf R. Rhomberg, "Transmission of Business Fluctuations from Developed to Developing Countries," in Martin Bronfenbrenner, ed., *Is the Business Cycle Obsolete?* (Wiley-Interscience, 1969), pp. 253–78.

impact of rising commodity prices on inflation and, hence, on the inflation-unemployment trade-off within industrial countries.[8]

This feedback effect suggests that, other things equal, the world economy will function somewhat better with steady industrial-country growth than with very rapid growth initially, followed by stagnation in an ensuing fight against inflation. That is, rapid growth in industrial countries that causes domestic inflation and a run-up in developing countries' raw materials export prices that then feed into still further industrial-country inflation is likely to provoke a subsequent period of recession and stagnation. The extra export earnings gained by developing countries through high prices in the first phase of such a sequence may be less than the export earnings they sacrifice during the later phase. And here there are two considerations—the original one of average level of their exports over a cycle as opposed to that during a period of steady but moderate growth in industrial countries; and a new consideration, the fact that inflation and eventual slowdown in industrial countries are aggravated by the increase in raw materials prices.

The simulation estimates below examine only the effect of industrial-country growth on the exports, and therefore growth, of developing countries. The effects of induced Keynesian demand and of the feedback from changes in export prices are not examined in the simulations.

Each of the policies tested is specified in terms of the relation between unemployment and inflation in developed countries. Though some analysts have concluded that the Phillips-curve relationship collapsed in 1972–75, it remains valid if unemployment is redefined to account for compositional shifts in the labor force and if the influence of lagged inflation, or momentum from the previous period, is taken into account.[9]

8. See Richard N. Cooper and Robert Z. Lawrence, "The 1972–75 Commodity Boom," *BPEA, 3:1975,* pp. 671–715; Joel Popkin, "Commodity Prices and the U.S. Price Level," *BPEA, 1:1974,* pp. 249–59. At the theoretical level, recent attention has focused on the inflationary impact of price run-ups in the "flexprice" (Hicks) or "auction" (Okun) market on the more "sticky" pricing based on "normal cost" (Nordhaus) in the "fixprice" (Hicks) or "customer pricing" (Okun) market. In these approaches, ironically, competitive markets with sensitive price changes are the causes of inflation, and instruments such as buffer stocks to iron out fluctuation in raw materials prices are considered to be important anti-inflationary measures. See John Hicks, *The Crisis in Keynesian Economics* (Basic Books, 1974); Arthur M. Okun, "Inflation: Its Mechanics and Welfare Costs," *BPEA, 2:1975,* pp. 351–90; William D. Nordhaus, "Inflation Theory and Policy," *American Economic Review,* vol. 66 (May 1976, *Papers and Proceedings, 1975*), pp. 59–64.

9. Michael L. Wachter, "The Changing Cyclical Responsiveness of Wage Inflation," *BPEA, 1:1976,* pp. 115–59.

Because of the unusual shocks from international monetary expansion and external commodity inflation in 1972–75, the earlier Phillips-curve relationship is a better guide to policy alternatives for future periods.

The alternative policies call for rapid initial growth and reduction of unemployment, which results in a rapid rate of inflation that then necessitates higher unemployment (a go-stop policy); steady growth at a rate of unemployment that does not accelerate the rate of inflation; and high unemployment maintained in the pursuit of reducing inflation. To specify alternative cyclical patterns a particular point on the Phillips-curve is selected for the initial year reflecting the expansionary, moderate, or anti-inflationary policy approach. For each subsequent year the choice must include the impact of the previous year's inflation on the current year's inflation (using the accelerationist form of the Phillips-curve). This relationship implies the existence of some unemployment rate at which inflation remains unchanged (is not accelerating). Policies seeking still lower levels of unemployment than the nonaccelerating rate (approximately 5 percent unemployment in the United States, based on consensus of the models of the 1970s) must deal not only with high initial inflation but accelerating inflation. Policies that encompass expansion at the non-accelerating unemployment rate permit a steady rate of inflation.

Estimates for the United States

For the United States, Phillips-curve estimates by Modigliani and Papademos are used to examine the alternative policies.[10] In their equation,

$$(1)\quad \dot{p} = -0.42 + 8.2(1/UA) + 0.68\dot{p}_{t-1} - 0.24\dot{\pi} + 0.081\dot{pmx} + 0.059\dot{pf}_{t-1},$$

$\dot{p}$ is the percent increase in the consumer price index excluding food, UA the unemployment rate adjusted downward to reflect shifts in the composition of the labor force since 1956, $\dot{\pi}$ the rate of productivity growth in the private nonfarm business sectors, $\dot{pmx}$ the percent increase in import prices excluding food, $\dot{pf}$ the percent increase in the price index for farm products, and t and $t-1$ the current year and lagged year, respectively. In order to focus on inflation and unemployment, productivity is assigned a constant growth rate of 1.5 percent (which is slightly below the 1960–

10. Franco Modigliani and Lucas Papademos, "Targets for Monetary Policy in the Coming Year," *BPEA, 1:1975*, pp. 141–65. When applied to the years 1975–78, their model predicted inflation rates of 8.2, 7.0, 5.9, and 8.0 percent, respectively (based on nonfood consumer prices). Actual inflation was 9.3, 6.6, 6.5, and 7.2 percent, respectively. The average error of estimates was 10 percent (absolute value).

77 average[11]) and import-price and farm-price inflation are assigned constant rates of 6 percent annually. Although these rates are reasonable, they clearly represent some compromise between avoiding the abnormality of the 1970s and achieving relevance to future conditions. The omission of induced changes in the rates to fit each policy does not introduce a clear bias because of offsetting factors; more rapid recovery, for example, helps reduce inflation by raising productivity growth but also helps raise inflation by boosting international commodity prices and causing a lagged inflationary impact from import prices.

With these assumptions the model becomes:

$$\dot{p}_t = 0.06 + (8.2/UA) + 0.68\dot{p}_{t-1}, \tag{2}$$

which provides the basis for estimating either the adjusted unemployment rate or the rate of consumer price inflation (excluding food). In order to calculate the actual unemployment rate, the constant 0.8 percent is added onto the adjusted rate (to account for extra unemployment that exists because of compositional changes in the labor force).[12]

Assuming that with an unchanged unemployment rate, real GNP grows at 3.5 percent per annum,[13] and that a change of 1 percentage point in the unemployment rate causes output to change by 3.1 percentage points,[14] the growth rate, g, in year t is:

$$g_t = 3.5 + 3.1(U_{t-1} - U_t), \tag{3}$$

where U_t is the unemployment rate in year t. In a five-year period following a year with values for inflation and unemployment equal to those in 1976, the adjusted unemployment rate under the moderate policy designed to keep inflation constant at its rate of the previous year would be 4.0 percent and the actual unemployment rate 4.8 percent. With the unemployment, inflation, and growth rates all held constant over the five years, the inflation rate is 6.6 percent (the lagged or 1976 rate for consumer prices excluding food).

The expansionary policy, which involves initial rapid growth, followed by retrenchment once inflation gets out of hand, begins with reduction of

11. An average of 1.7 percent, based on Edward F. Denison, *Accounting for Slower Economic Growth: The United States in the 1970s* (Brookings Institution, 1979), p. 146.

12. Modigliani and Papademos, "Targets for Monetary Policy," p. 151.

13. *Economic Report of the President Transmitted to the Congress January 1977*, p. 53.

14. George L. Perry, "Potential Output and Productivity," *BPEA, 1:1977*, p. 41.

Table A-2. *Rates of Inflation, Unemployment, and Growth under Various Macroeconomic Policies for the United States*

Percent

	Go-stop policy				Moderate policy				Anti-inflationary policy			
		Unemployment				Unemployment				Unemployment		
Year	*Inflation*	*Ad-justed*	*Un-adjusted*	*Growth rate*	*Inflation*	*Ad-justed*	*Un-adjusted*	*Growth rate*	*Inflation*	*Ad-justed*	*Un-adjusted*	*Growth rate*
Base	6.60	...	7.7	...	6.6	...	7.7	...	6.60	...	7.7	...
1	8.28	2.2	3.0	18.1	6.6	4.0	4.8	12.5	5.55	8.2	9.0	−0.5
2	9.40	2.2	3.0	3.5	6.6	4.0	4.8	3.5	4.83	8.2	9.0	3.5
3	10.19	2.2	3.0	3.5	6.6	4.0	4.8	3.5	4.35	8.2	9.0	3.5
4	7.99	8.2	9.0	−15.1	6.6	4.0	4.8	3.5	4.02	8.2	9.0	3.5
5	7.00	5.4	6.2	12.2	6.6	4.0	4.8	3.5	3.79	8.2	9.0	3.5

unemployment to an ambitious 3 percent; once inflation pierces a 10 percent ceiling, the unemployment rate is raised to the politically acceptable maximum (based on 1970s experience) of 9 percent; when inflation is brought back down to 7 percent, the unemployment rate is reduced enough to keep inflation at 7 percent.

The anti-inflationary policy follows the rule that unemployment remains at the politically acceptable maximum of 9 percent for so long as it takes to reduce inflation to a target rate of 3 percent. As it turns out, even by the end of the fifth year this target cannot be achieved, despite continuously high unemployment.

Table A-2 reports the inflation, unemployment, and growth rates under each of these policies. The policy of bringing inflation down represents paying an extremely high price in terms of continued unemployment (and, to a lesser extent, sacrificing potential growth) for pursuit of the objective of slower inflation. Even after five years of high unemployment the inflation rate is almost 4 percent (a high level by historical standards). Thus if the characteristics of this model estimated from 1953–71 data, which predicted well for 1975–78, continue to apply, it will be very difficult indeed to achieve substantial reduction in the rate of inflation.

The moderate policy approach looks more promising. It provides a target of unemployment generally considered reasonable and steady growth after initial recovery. Its one outstanding flaw is the persistence of inflation at 6.6 percent annually. This rate is dangerous not only because of institutional factors such as the absence of indexing but because businesses are not likely to expect a steady rate of inflation when the basic rate is so high.[15] The negative effect on investment caused by uncertainty about future prices may therefore make steady growth an unrealistically optimistic assumption.

The go-stop policy is inferior to the steady-growth policy on the criterion of inflation as well as steadiness of output growth. It does achieve lower unemployment initially but only at the expense of higher unemployment in the last two years.

Total real GNP at the end of the five-year period is highest under the steady-growth policy—from a beginning index of 100, it grows to 120 under the go-stop policy, 129 under steady growth, and 110 under the anti-inflationary policy. The steady-growth policy achieves higher output than the anti-inflationary (which demands a high price in real output to purchase lower inflation). Steady growth also achieves higher output than

15. Okun, "Inflation: Its Mechanics and Welfare Costs."

the go-stop policy, reflecting the fact that it is inefficient to cycle back and forth between the two inefficient legs of the Phillips curve instead of remaining at a central point where the trade-off between unemployment and inflation is more favorable for the pursuit of both objectives jointly.[16] Because these two policies contain exceptionally high growth rates for the initial year and one very large GNP reduction, which are related to changes in the unemployment rate, additional simulations were run using smoothed versions of the growth rates;[17] they yield the same eventual index of real GNP. The results of the smoothed versions closely resembled those of the unadjusted versions described below.

Estimates for Europe and Japan

For other industrial countries, estimates for 1975 and 1976 based on Phillips-curve models[18] yield predicted rates of inflation that vary widely from rates actually observed. Therefore the policy tests for other industrial countries differ from those for the United States. For the go-stop policy, real growth is assumed during the first two years to be at its average rate for the quartile of high-growth years in 1961–75, for the next two years at its average level for the quartile of low-growth years, and for the fifth year at the average for the lowest 50 percent of annual growth rate. For the moderate policy the average real growth rate for 1961–75 is assumed to hold for all five years. And for the anti-inflationary policy it is assumed to hold steady at its average over the lowest 50 percent of an-

16. Gramlich, "The Optimal Timing of Unemployment in a Recession."

17. For the go-stop policy the first- and second-year growth rates were smoothed to 11.5 percent and 10.0 percent, respectively, and the fourth- and fifth-year rates to −3.0 percent and −2.4 percent, respectively. For the steady-growth policy the first- and second-year rates were smoothed to 8.0 percent and 7.9 percent, respectively.

18. R. J. Ball, "The Prediction of Wage-Rate Changes in the United Kingdom Economy 1957–60," *Economic Journal,* vol. 72 (March 1962), pp. 27–44; S. F. Kaliski, "The Relation Between Unemployment and the Rate of Change of Money Wages in Canada," *International Economic Review,* vol. 5 (January 1964), pp. 1–33; Rajindar K. Koshal and Lowell E. Gallaway, "The Phillips Curve for West Germany," *Kyklos,* vol. 24, no. 2 (1971), pp. 346–49; Geoffrey Maynard and W. van Ryckeghem, *A World of Inflation* (Barnes and Noble, 1975; London: Batsford, 1976), chap. 7; Franco Modigliani and Ezio Tarantelli, "A Generalization of the Phillips Curve for a Developing Country," *Review of Economic Studies,* vol. 40 (April 1973), pp. 203–23; Organization for Economic Cooperation and Development, *Inflation: The Present Problem* (Paris: OECD, 1970), annex A; David J. Smyth, "Unemployment and Inflation: A Cross-Country Analysis of the Phillips Curve," *American Economic Review,* vol. 61 (June 1971), pt. 1, pp. 426–29.

Table A-3. *Rates of Real Growth of Gross National Product under Various Macroeconomic Policies for Europe and Japan*
Percent

Region and year	Rate of growth: Go-stop policy	Moderate policy	Anti-inflationary policy
Europe			
1	6.4	3.7	2.0
2	6.4	3.7	2.0
3	0.4	3.7	2.0
4	0.4	3.7	2.0
5	3.7	3.7	2.0
Japan			
1	13.5	8.5	6.1
2	13.5	8.5	6.1
3	3.2	8.5	6.1
4	3.2	8.5	6.1
5	8.5	8.5	6.1

Sources: Based on frequencies of past growth rates presented in Federal Reserve Bank of St. Louis, *Rates of Change in Economic Data for Ten Industrial Countries: Annual Data 1956–1975* (October 1976). Weights for aggregate growth rates as in *OECD Economic Outlook*, no. 19 (July 1976), p. 11.

nual growth rate in 1961–75.[19] The real growth rates for Europe and Japan are reported in table A-3 (there is no basis for determining unemployment and inflation rates corresponding to growth rates).

Tables A-2 and A-3 indicate that at the end of the five-year period GNP for the industrial countries would have risen from an index of 100 to only 114 under the anti-inflationary policy, to 124 under the go-stop policy, and to 130 under the steady-as-you-go policy (growth for each region is weighted by GNP in the base year). The intermediate policy shows a clear dominance over either the strongly anti-inflationary strategy or the unrealistically ambitious go-stop strategy.

Effects on Developing Countries' Growth

The projected growth rates under the three policies are applied to the World Bank's SIMLINK model to estimate the impact on growth in de-

19. Growth rates are from Federal Reserve Bank of St. Louis, *Rates of Change in Economic Data for Ten Industrial Countries: Annual Data 1956–1975* (October 1976), weighted as in Organization for Economic Cooperation and Development, *OECD Economic Outlook*, no. 19 (July 1976), p. 11.

Table A-4. *Growth Rates and Level of Gross Domestic Product for Developing Countries after Institution of Various Macroeconomic Policies in Industrial Countries*

	Go-stop policy			*Moderate policy*			*Anti-inflationary policy*	
		GDP level, year 5[b]			*GDP level, year 5*[b]			
Developing countries	*Growth rate (percent)*[a]	*Billions of 1975 dollars*	*Percent of anti-inflationary level*	*Growth rate (percent)*[a]	*Billions of 1975 dollars*	*Percent of anti-inflationary level*	*Growth rate (percent)*[a]	*GDP level, year 5 (billions of 1975 dollars)*[b]
Low income	4.2	152.1	108	4.8	155.9	111	2.6	140.7
India	4.1	104.4	106	4.5	106.1	108	2.9	98.3
Other South Asian	4.4	33.7	116	5.5	35.4	122	1.3	29.0
African	4.8	14.0	104	5.1	14.1	105	4.0	13.4
Middle income	5.1	644.0	115	7.5	721.4	128	2.3	561.7
Lower	5.2	100.0	115	7.6	112.3	129	2.3	87.0
Upper	5.1	432.0	114	7.9	491.4	130	2.4	379.1
High	5.1	111.9	117	6.1	117.7	123	1.8	95.6
Total	4.9	796.1	113	7.0	877.3	125	2.4	702.3

a. Five-year average.
b. For purposes of the simulation, the fifth year is 1982.

veloping countries.[20] Increased growth in industrial countries is used to calculate the increase in developing countries' exports of commodities (based on changes in price and to a lesser extent export volumes of various commodities)[21] and of manufactured goods (based on elasticities derived from past experience), the increase in developing countries' imports (derived from equations relating imports to investment), and finally the feasible increase in their gross national product (based on the amount of import requirements that can be financed by export earnings and foreign capital flows). The model's underlying premise that availability of foreign exchange is the key restraint to growth probably tends to overstate the role of exports (for example, the model does not encompass the possibility of increased borrowing abroad when growth in industrial countries is low). Its parameters were estimated for years before 1971 (although commodity prices are adjusted to reflect later levels). The model's strengths include its substantial detail at the regional and, in some cases, country level.[22]

Table A-4, which reports the effects of the three macroeconomic policies in industrial countries, indicates that the intermediate policy results in the highest level of gross domestic product in the developing countries by the fifth year. It yields 25 percent more income for the developing countries than the stern anti-inflationary policy. The go-stop policy is also better than the anti-inflationary but the improvement is only about half as great as that attainable under steady growth (13 percent versus 25 percent).[23]

The impact of industrial countries' growth on the middle-income developing countries is much greater than on the low-income countries. The middle-income countries (primarily East Asian and Latin American) achieve about 30 percent higher real income by the fifth year under the moderate policy than under the strong anti-inflationary policy, while for India and low-income African countries the difference is only 8 percent

20. Hicks, "Model of Trade and Growth."

21. Each product's real price is related to demand and therefore reflects general inflation in the industrial countries.

22. The model is flexible and may be used to examine a variety of policy issues. Holsen and Waelbroeck, "The Less Developed Countries and the International Monetary Mechanism," use it to estimate the effect on developing countries' growth of increased borrowing during the 1975 recession.

23. The results for the smoothed version were almost identical to those shown in the table. The discrepancy between the go-stop and moderate policies is slightly smaller (at 116 percent and 125 percent of the income yielded under the anti-inflationary policy) because the oscillation of the go-stop strategy is damped.

and 5 percent, respectively. Similarly, the difference between the moderate and go-stop policies is greatest for the middle-income countries. These patterns reflect their greater economic responsiveness to business conditions in developed countries and thus a higher degree of integration, or interdependence, with the industrial countries.

All of the regions and income groups, however, show a considerable responsiveness to growth rates in developed countries. The macroeconomic policies that developed countries adopt are consequently of major concern to them. Those that seek to reduce inflation at whatever expense in terms of unemployment are likely to limit seriously the growth prospects of developing countries as well as those of the developed countries themselves. Such anti-inflationary goals lead to an average growth rate among developing countries that is less than one-half that under moderate macroeconomic policies. But when industrial countries pursue overly buoyant growth, moving abruptly to very low levels of unemployment which they are compelled to abandon when inflation accelerates to intolerable levels, the growth prospects of developing countries will be considerably poorer than under the steadier policy of expansion at somewhat higher unemployment rates that do not accelerate inflation.

For the industrial countries as a whole, the rise of GNP from 100 to an index of 114 after five years under the anti-inflationary policy, to 124 under the go-stop policy, and to 130 under the moderate policy would raise the level of GNP under the moderate policy 14 percent higher and under the go-stop policy 9 percent higher than under the anti-inflationary policy. For developing countries the correspondingly higher levels are 25 percent and 13 percent. For each percentage-point difference in total growth for industrial countries the difference for developing countries ranges from 1.79 to 1.44 percentage points. Industrial-country growth therefore appears to have an amplified influence on developing-country growth rather than the diluted effect suggested by the cyclical relationship from 1960 to 1977 (and for 1969–71 and 1973–75 in particular). To some extent this divergence may reflect a tendency of the SIMLINK model to overstate the sensitivity of growth. It is also likely, however, that the divergence reflects a less sensitive response to short-term fluctuations than to the longer-term growth reflected in the five years encompassed in the macroeconomic policy measurements. The analysis indicates that the choice of policy in the industrial countries has major repercussions on growth in the developing countries. The conclusion would hold even if the sensitivity of long-run growth rates in developing countries to growth in industrial countries were somewhat more limited than the SIMLINK model implies.

Effects of Developing-Country Growth

Tradition indicates also that economic growth in the developing world may contribute to growth in industrial countries. In the colonial era the peripheral colony provided raw materials to the center and in turn was a ready market for its manufactured exports; faster growth of income and thus demand in the colonial periphery could stimulate growth at the center.

During the 1974–75 global recession the developing countries maintained relatively high growth rates (through external borrowing), providing sufficient demand for the exports of industrial countries to raise economic growth an estimated 0.5 percentage point in the industrial countries.[24] One econometric analysis of international economic fluctuations in the 1970s concludes that an increase of 3.1 percentage points in the growth rate of developing countries that do not export oil causes growth rates in industrial countries to rise by 1 percentage point.[25] These estimates hinge on the assumption that industrial countries cannot mobilize their underemployed resources but somehow are dependent instead on the emergence of external demand. It is not a compelling economic argument; the successive tax cuts in the United States during the 1975–78 recovery attest that domestic measures are available for addressing Keynesian unemployment in the industrial countries. Furthermore, a 3 percent growth among developing countries (excluding China) that do not export oil and whose per capita incomes are below $2,000 would have amounted to $22 billion in 1975, while a growth of 1 percent among nonsocialist, non-OPEC countries with incomes above $2,000 per capita would have amounted to $39 billion.[26] Assuming that developing countries had a very high marginal propensity to import of, say, 20 percent, the

24. Holsen and Waelbroeck, "The Less Developed Countries and the International Monetary Mechanism," p. 175.

25. United Nations Conference on Trade and Development, *Trade Prospects and Capital Needs of Developing Countries, 1967–1980,* UN Doc. TD/B/C.3/134, April 15, 1976, p. 39.

26. Based on total GNP of $725 billion for the former and $3,909 billion for the latter. *World Bank Atlas: Population, Per Capita Product, and Growth Rates, 1977,* pp. 4, 27–30.

developing group could expect to increase their import demand on the order of $4.4 billion. If this extra demand were expected to raise GNP in industrial countries by $39 billion, the Keynesian multiplier in the industrial countries would have to be an incredibly high 8.9. A Keynesian multiplier of approximately 2 combined with the 3 percent rise in the developing countries' GNP might cause an increase on the order of 0.23 percent in the GNP of industrial countries—which provides a ratio of 13 to 1 (instead of 3 to 1) for the increased growth rate of developing countries relative to the induced increase in industrial countries' growth rate. Although growth in developing countries appears to have had some role in sustaining the growth rates of industrial countries during the trough of global recession in 1975, in general that link is extremely modest. Whereas an extra percentage point of growth in the industrial countries traditionally may induce a short-run increase of 0.5 percent in growth rate to a longer-run increase of more than 1 percent in developing countries, the reverse effect of a 1 percent increase in the developing group is likely to produce as little as a 0.08 percent increase in the growth rate of the industrial nations. And even this minor stimulus arises from the highly unlikely assumption that the developed economies maintain idle plant and labor that cannot be employed except as the result of increased export demand.

Index

Abbott, Philip C., 11n
Accelerationist model of inflation, 111–14
Africa, 231, 253
Aggregate demand, 79n, 114–15, 116, 117. *See also* Excess demand model of inflation
Agricultural prices: econometric models, 80, 81, 82–83; El Salvador and Guatemala, 186–87. *See also* Food price inflation
Ahluwalia, Isher J., 136n
Ahluwalia, Montek S., 38n
Aliber, Robert Z., 193n
Anti-inflation policy, 45–47, 231. *See also* Exchange-rate policy; Fiscal policy; Growth policy; Monetary policy
Argentina, 3, 89n; causes of inflation, 82, 108n; hyperinflation, 55; trade deficit, 23; wage inflation, 67
Argy, V., 193n
ARIMA methods, 161, 162, 165
Atkinson, Anthony B., 43n
Atkinson measure, 42, 43n

Bacha, Edmar, 102n, 103n, 111n, 115n, 122n, 124n, 125n, 128n, 129n, 132n
Baer, Werner, 46n, 103n
Balance of payments: Central America, 234; lending, 239; problems, in Brazil, 107, 114, 115, 117, 122, 124, 126; problems, in El Salvador and Guatemala, 175–77, 186, 205; theory, 54n
Balance of trade, 23–25, 27–28, 229; Brazil, 116, 117, 124, 132, 133, 134; changes in reserves, 72–74, 75; El Salvador and Guatemala, 167, 171, 172, 178, 183, 205
Balassa, Bela, 102n, 113n, 118n
Ball, R. J., 250n
Bangladesh War, 149, 151, 152, 160
Bank for International Settlements, 75n
Bank Negara, 211n, 213n, 217n, 220, 224n
Bank of Brazil, 104
Barros, José Roberto Mendonça de, 120n, 121n, 128n, 129n
Bauxite exports, 16, 39n
Behrman, Jere R., 16n, 39n
Bery, Suman K., 136n
Bhagwati, Jagdish N., 136n
Birnberg, Thomas B., 240n
Black, Stanley W., 5
Bomberger, W. A., 196n
Bond issues, 30n, 34n
Bonelli, Regis, 103n, 107n, 113n, 123n, 129n, 131n
Borrowing, external, 116, 122, 125, 126, 130, 131–32, 133, 134. *See also* Capital, foreign; Capital markets, international
Box, George E. P., 161n
Box-Jenkins method, 161, 165
Brazil, 3, 8, 9, 102–35, 229, 237; aggregate demand, 114–15, 116, 117; balance-of-payments problems, 107, 114, 115, 117, 122, 124, 126; balance of trade, 116, 117, 124, 132, 133, 134; capacity utilization in manufacturing, 113, 123; capital flows, 104; causes of domestic inflation, 106–13; coffee prices, 82n, 116, 117, 121, 124, 126; Council of Industrial Development, 115; creditworthiness, 105, 106n, 131; current account deficit, 116; debt service, 116, 126, 132, 133; devaluations, 102, 103, 108, 117, 119, 120, 127–30, 133; dollar value of exports, 117; dollar value of imports, 108–09, 113, 114, 115, 127; domestic credit, 106, 107, 115; exchange-rate policy, 102, 103, 107–08, 117, 119, 120n, 121, 127–30, 132, 133–35, 235; export earnings, 117, 121, 131, 133, 135; ex-

port incentives policy, 130–35; export prices, 117–21, 135; exports and growth, 1, 103, 117–22, 130–33; exports and world industrial activity, 119–22; exports, models for world demand for, 119–22; export subsidies, 130–31, 133; export volume, 115, 116, 117–19, 133, 233; external borrowing, 105–06, 116, 125, 129, 131–32, 134; external debt, 116, 122, 125, 126, 130, 131–32, 133, 134; food prices, 82; foreign reserves, growth of, 69n, 70, 103–06, 114, 116; foreign reserves, sterilization of, 104, 105, 106; gross domestic product, 115; gross national product, 102n; growth policy, 102–03, 116, 117, 122–27, 131–33, 134, 233, 234; hyperinflation, 55; import prices, 103, 104n, 106–15, 122, 132, 134, 229, 230, 233; imports, reserves relative to, 132; import substitution, 115, 122, 124, 126, 133, 134; import volume, 107, 115–16; inflation models, 109–15; monetary/fiscal policy fluctuations, 122–24, 129, 130, 131, 132, 133; money supply, growth of, 104–06, 107, 109, 110n, 111–13, 115, 123, 125; National Bank of Economic Development, 115; oil price increases, 107, 122, 123, 124, 127, 132, 133, 134; price indexing, 103, 108–09, 112; protectionist trade policy, 45, 103, 110–17, 122, 124, 130, 132, 133, 134; regression analysis, 230n; tariff liberalization, 103; terms of trade, 13, 14, 126, 128, 133, 134–35; trade deficit, 116, 122, 125, 133; wage indexing, 112n; windfall debt erosion, 36; world capital markets, 236; world recession, 103, 117–22, 133–35, 235
Bretton Woods monetary system, 1, 8, 35n, 104, 147, 191, 229
Brillembourg, Arturo, 78n, 165n
Bronfenbrenner, Martin, 244n
Brunner, Karl, 79n
Bruno, Michael, 86n, 92n
Budget deficits: El Salvador and Guatemala, 185–86; and full employment, 65n; and industrial countries, 64; and liquidity problems, 95; Malaysia, 209, 215, 217, 222; and money supply, 64–67

Caceres, L. R., 173n
Campo, Armando Gonzales, 166n
Capacity utilization, 113, 123
Capital flows, 228–29; Brazil, 104; and changes in reserves, 72, 74–76; Malaysia, 214–15, 220, 225; and world inflation, 7
Capital, foreign, 72n, 75, 94, 95, 228
Capital markets, international, 75, 170; Brazil, 236; El Salvador, 170; Guatemala, 170; Malaysia, 217, 222
Capital requirements, 9, 21–28, 47, 240
Carneiro, Dionísio Dias, 104n, 115n
Central America, 8, 166, 176, 178, 229, 237, 238; balance of payments, 234; exchange-rate policy, 182, 236; export volume, 175; food price inflation, 235; foreign reserves, 191; grain production, 186; growth policy, 234; import prices, 233; import volume, 175, 233. *See also* El Salvador; Guatemala
Central American Common Market, 173, 175, 207
Central banks, and monetary policy: El Salvador and Guatemala, 177, 178, 179, 192, 194–95, 205; Malaysia, 213, 217, 219–22
Chavarria, Manuel A., 166n
Chenery, Hollis B., 22n, 243n
Chile: copper prices, 14; domestic inflation, 3, 108n; Harberger's model of inflation for, 78; hyperinflation, 55, 89n; terms of trade, 14; wage inflation, 68
Christ, Carl F., 68n, 152n
Clark, Peter B., 83n
Cline, William R., 11n, 42n, 44n, 52n, 102n, 105n, 107n, 116n, 132n, 207n
Cocoa, 13, 17, 18, 39n, 40, 42, 43, 44, 117
Coffee exports, 17n, 18, 39n, 185–86
Coffee prices, 13, 17, 18, 116, 117; Brazil, 82n, 116, 117, 121, 124, 126; El Salvador and Guatemala, 183, 185, 189, 192, 205
Colón, depreciation of, 191
Commercial banks: El Salvador and Guatemala, 178, 194, 195; Malaysia, 215n, 219–21
Commodity price increases, 1, 3, 12, 17, 18, 141, 228, 229–30, 233, 234, 238, 245; and distribution of world income, 9, 11, 37–43; and domestic inflation, 52, 63; Guatemala and El Salvador, 171, 183; and industrial countries, 229, 238; Japan, 229; and real income, 42, 44; and terms of trade, 5, 6n, 10, 12–17, 18
Commodity terms of trade, 17, 18

Concessional development assistance. *See* Development assistance; Foreign aid
Conjuntura econômica, 107
Consumer price increases, 34n, 55, 62–63
Consumer price index: India, 136, 153n; Malaysia, 208, 210, 212; and models of inflation, 82n, 83
Contador, Claudio, 102n
Cooper, Richard N., 140n, 245n
Copper, 14, 17, 18, 39n, 244
Cost-push variables and inflation, 153, 159. *See also* Structural factors in inflation
Cotton, 17, 18, 39n, 140
Credit. *See* Domestic credit, Foreign credit
Credit ceilings, 221–22
Creditworthiness, 229; Brazil, 105, 106n, 131; India, 229
Crop failures, 63–64, 94–95
Cross, Rodney, 196n
Cruzeiro, devaluations of, 102, 103, 108, 117, 119, 120, 127–30, 133
Currency, purchasing power and exchange rates, 37–38. *See also* Devaluation; Dollar, U.S.; Exchange-rate policy
Current account deficits, 27–28, 116
Current income, 92n

Davis, Jeffrey M., 85n
Debt erosion, windfall, 7, 9, 10, 28–37; equations for determining, 48–50
Debt service, 30–31, 116, 126, 132, 133
Delgado, Enrique, 207n
Demand, 152. *See also* Aggregate demand; Excess demand model of inflation; Export demand; External demand; Inflation models, demand-related
Denison, Edward F., 247n
Deutsche marks, 35n
Devaluation, 46, 237, 238; as anti-inflationary policy, 45–47; of colón, 191; of cruzeiro, 102, 103, 108, 117, 119, 120, 127–30, 133; exports and, 46n; of quetzal, 191; of rupee, 136, 142, 147–49; of U.S. dollar, 46, 128
Developing countries, non-oil-exporting: anti-inflationary policies, 45–47; average traded-goods index, 81n–82n; balance of trade, 23, 28, 229; budget deficits, 64–67; capital flows, 228–29; capital requirements, 9, 21–28, 47, 240; commodity price inflation, 229–30, 233, 234; creditworthiness, 229; current account deficits, 27–28; debt service, 30; devaluation, 46, 237, 238; development assistance, 19, 21, 26, 27, 228; domestic inflation, 2, 3, 52, 108n; economic instability, 4–5; exchange-rate policies, 37–38, 237; export growth, 26; export prices, 30–31; export values, 7, 10, 23, 31; export volume, 26; external debt, erosion of, 7, 11, 28–37, 47, 228; fiscal policies, 237; foreign bond issues, 30n, 34n; foreign capital, 72n, 75, 94, 95, 228; foreign reserve erosion, 34–37, 47; foreign reserves, 69–76, 94, 228, 229; global inflation, 1, 4, 6–7, 10, 52; growth links between industrial countries and, 240–43, 255–56; growth rates, 1, 4, 60–62, 228, 231, 233–34, 238; import policies, 27–28; import prices, 30, 228–30; import substitution, 240–41; import values, 7, 10, 23, 30; interest rates, 84; and macroeconomic strategies of industrial countries, 7, 238, 240, 243–55; monetary policies, 237; money supply, 69–76, 94, 228, 229; oil price increases, 1, 6, 228; real activity, 60n; terms of trade, 5–7, 9, 10, 11–16, 23, 33n, 47, 228, 229, 237, 240; trade deficits, 47, 233–34; UN development strategy for, 22; wage inflation, 230; world distribution of income, 37–45, 47, 228, 234; and world recession, 1, 2, 4, 95, 230. *See also* Brazil; El Salvador; Guatemala; India; Malaysia
Development assistance, 19–21, 26–27, 228; from communist countries, 19, 27n; from industrial countries, 239; from OPEC countries, 10, 17, 19, 27n, 228, 239; total world flow, 27. *See also* Foreign aid
Development Assistance Committee, OECD, 30
Diaz-Alejandro, Carlos F., 68n
Diesel oil, Malaysian surtax on, 212
Distribution of income, 38, 39, 40n, 207, 218. *See also* Real income; World income distribution
Dollar, Malaysian, 223, 226, 227
Dollar, U.S.: and Brazilian exchange rate, 128; depreciation, 46, 128; El Salvador, Guatemala parity rates with, 166, 178, 179, 191, 204; and foreign reserves, 34–36; suspension of con-

vertibility into gold, 1. *See also* Bretton Woods monetary system; Eurodollar market
Domestic borrowing, 209, 226
Domestic credit: Brazil, 106, 107, 115; El Salvador and Guatemala, 167, 177
Domestic prices, 177, 178, 182, 204, 205, 206. *See also* Consumer price increases; Food price inflation
Dornbusch, Rudiger, 86n
Drought, 136, 137, 138, 149, 151

Econometric tests of price inflation, 76–101
Economist, 12
Edgren, Gösta, 81n
El Salvador, 8, 9, 108n, 166–207, 231; agricultural prices, 186–87; balance-of-payments problems, 175–77, 186, 205; balance of trade, 167, 171, 172, 178, 183, 205; budget deficits, 185–86; capital flows, 167, 178, 192, 194, 196, 205; central bank, 177, 178, 192, 194–95, 205n; coffee export tax, 185–86; coffee price increases, 183, 185, 189, 192, 205; commercial banks, 194, 195; commodity price boom, 171, 183; domestic credit, 167, 177; domestic prices, 177, 178, 182, 204, 205, 206; excess demand model of inflation, 196, 204, 206; excess liquidity, 177, 179, 183, 186, 195–96; exchange-rate policy, 166, 178, 179, 182, 186, 191, 205; export prices, 171, 172–73, 179, 183, 205; export volume, 172, 173, 175; fiscal policy, 166, 175, 178; food price inflation, 183, 186–87, 207, 235; foreign credit, 177; foreign reserves, 178, 183, 191–96, 205; import prices, 171, 172–73, 175, 179, 183, 187, 189–91, 204, 205, 229, 230; import values, 177; import volume, 167, 169, 175, 177; international capital markets, 171; labor unionism, 189; monetary financing, 167, 171, 177, 192; monetary model of inflation, 204, 206; monetary policy, 166, 175, 177, 178, 206; monetary ratio, 167; money supply, 166, 167, 175, 177, 182, 192, 196, 206; oil price increases, 171, 172–73, 190, 205, 206; open market operations, 195; parity rates with U.S. dollar, 166, 178, 179, 191, 204; personal income distribution, 207; production index, 187n; public investment, 179; recession policy, 235; rediscount operations, 178, 194, 195; reserve requirements, 178; reserves, sterilization of, 193; taxation, 178, 185, 186; velocity of money, 171; Venezuelan petroleum finance scheme, 177, 191; wages, 187–89, 205, 206
Emmanuel, Arghiri, 44n
Eurodollar market, 1, 75, 94
Europe: concessional aid to developing countries, 228, 239; real income, 41–42; simulation estimates for, 250–51
Excess aggregate demand, 79n
Excess demand model of inflation, 79, 84; El Salvador and Guatemala, 196, 204, 206
Exchange-rate policy, 37–38, 45, 236–37; Brazil, 102, 103, 107–08, 117, 119, 120n, 121, 127–30, 132, 133–35, 235; Central America, 182, 236; El Salvador and Guatemala, 166, 178, 179, 182, 186, 191, 205; India, 147–49, 235; Malaysia, 223, 226, 227
Exchange rates, 81, 83; flexible, 8; purchasing power and, 37–38; realignment of, 1. *See also* Bretton woods monetary system
Export demand, 13, 72, 119–22
Export earnings: Brazil, 117, 121, 131, 133, 135; Malaysia, 213–14, 215, 220
Export growth, 26, 75n
Export incentives, 130–35
Export prices, 17, 18, 63n; and balance of trade, 25; Brazil, 17–21, 135; and debt service, 30–31; and domestic inflation, 81n–82n; and foreign-exchange reserves, 34, 35; Guatemala and El Salvador, 171, 172–73, 179, 183, 205; India, 142–43; for major commodities, 17–18; Malaysia, 208, 213, 219, 225, 226; and world distribution of income, 38–39. *See also* Terms of trade
Exports: 46n; and domestic growth, 222, 223, 226, 240, 241, 243–55
Export subsidies, 130–31, 133
Export taxes, 185–86, 222, 223, 226
Export value, 7, 10; Brazil, 117; India, 142, 143
Export volume, 25–26; Brazil, 115, 116, 117–19, 133, 233; Central America, 175; Guatemala and El Salvador, 172, 173, 175; Korea, 26n; Malaysia, 208, 213
External borrowing, 105–06, 116, 125, 129, 131–32, 134. *See also* Capital markets, international; Creditworthi-

ness; Debt erosion, windfall; Debt service
External debt: Brazil, 116, 122, 125, 126, 130, 131–32, 133, 134; erosion of, 7, 11, 28–37, 47, 228
External demand, 53, 55, 56

Faxen, Karl-Olof, 81n
Federal Reserve Bank of St. Louis, 251n
Feige, Edgar L., 78n, 165n
Fiscal policy, 237; El Salvador and Guatemala, 166, 175, 178; India, 149–52, 160; Malaysia, 209, 222–23, 227
Fishlow, Albert, 112n, 125n, 132
Food price inflation, 1, 7, 11, 52, 64, 82, 85, 229; Brazil, 82; Central America, 235; and consumer price index, 89; El Salvador and Guatemala, 183, 186–87, 207, 235; India, 136, 138–41, 142, 152, 158, 234; Malaysia, 210, 212
Food shortages and inflation, 63–64, 95; and econometric models, 76, 77, 80–81; India, 136, 138–41, 152, 153, 160
Food subsidies, 223, 237
Foreign aid, 19, 20–21, 27n. *See also* Development assistance
Foreign bond issues, 30n, 34n
Foreign credit, 72n, 75, 94, 95, 177, 228. *See also* Capital markets, international
Foreign exchange. *See also* Exchange-rate policy
Foreign reserves. *See* Reserves, foreign
France, 20–21, 128
Frank, Charles R., Jr., 105n
Full-employment budget deficits, 65n. *See also* Unemployment-inflation trade-off
Furuguem, Alberto S., 115n

Gallaway, Lowell E., 250n
Germany, 20–21, 76n, 128
Gini coefficient, 42–43
Global equity, 11
Global inflation. *See* Inflation, global
Global price index, 39. *See also* Export prices; Import prices; Oil price increases
Gold reserves, 11, 34, 35
Gold standard, 35n. *See also* Bretton Woods monetary system
Goldstein, Henry N., 76n
Goldstein, Morris, 83n
Gordon, Robert J., 79n, 81, 83n
Grain agreements, 237, 238
Grain prices, 11, 94
Grain production, 186
Gramlich, Edward M., 244n, 250n
Granger, C. W. J., 161
Granger test, 161, 163, 164
Great Depression, 240
Great Inflation. *See* Inflation, global
Gross domestic product (GDP), 83, 115
Gross national product (GNP), 2, 4, 102n, 215, 217, 222
Growth policy: Brazil, 102–03, 116, 117, 122–27, 131–33, 134, 233, 234; Central America, 234
Growth rates: of developing countries, 1, 4, 60–62, 228, 231, 233–34, 238; exports and, 1, 103, 117–22, 130–33, 222, 223, 226, 240, 241, 243–55; of industrial countries, 4, 60–62; link between developing and industrial countries, 60–61, 240–56
Guatemala, 8, 9, 108n, 166–207, 231; aggregate demand, 183; agricultural prices, 186–87; balance-of-payments problems, 175–77, 186, 205; balance of trade, 167, 171, 172, 178, 183, 205; budget deficits, 185–86; capital flows, 167, 178, 192, 194, 196, 205; central bank, 177, 178, 179, 192, 194–95; coffee export tax, 185–86; coffee price increases, 183, 185, 189, 192, 205; commercial banks, 194, 195; commodity price boom, 171, 183; domestic credit, 167; domestic prices, 177, 178, 182, 204, 205, 206; earthquake (*1976*), 185, 189; excess demand model of inflation, 196, 204, 206; excess liquidity, 177, 179, 183, 186, 195–96; exchange-rate policy, 166, 178, 179, 182, 186, 191, 205; export prices, 171, 172–73, 179, 183, 205; export volume, 172, 173, 175; fiscal policy, 166, 175, 178; food price inflation, 183, 186–87, 207, 235; foreign credit, 177; foreign reserves, 178, 183, 191–96, 205; import prices, 171, 172–73, 175, 179, 183, 187, 189–91, 204, 205, 229, 230; import values, 177; import volume, 167, 169, 175, 177; international capital markets, 171; labor unionism, 189; monetary financing, 167, 171, 192; monetary model of inflation, 204, 206; monetary policy, 166, 175, 177, 178, 206; monetary ratio, 167; money supply, 166, 167, 175, 177, 178, 182, 183, 192–96, 205–06; oil price increases, 171, 172–73, 190, 205, 206; open market operations, 195; parity roles with U.S. dollar, 166,

178, 179, 191, 204; personal income distribution, 207; public investment, 179; recession policy, 235; rediscount operations, 178, 194, 195; reserve requirements, 178; reserves, sterilization of, 193; taxation, 178, 185, 186; velocity of money, 171; Venezuelan petroleum finance scheme, 177, 191; wages, 187–89, 205, 206

Gupta, Babi, 52n

Harberger, Arnold C., 46, 68n, 152n

Harberger model, 78, 152

Harvey, Stephen, 10n

Hathaway, Dale F., 140n

Haugh, Larry D., 161

Heller, H. Robert, 69n

Heston, Alan W., 37, 38

Hicks, John, 245n

Hicks, Norman L., 243n, 244n, 253n

Holsen, John A., 242n, 253n, 255n

Honduras, 108n, 166n, 186

Hyperinflation, 53, 55, 89n

Import prices, 6–7, 9, 63n, 228–30; Brazil, 103, 104n, 106–15, 122, 132, 134, 229, 230, 233; Central America, 233; as deflators of debt service, 30–31; as deflators of foreign-exchange reserves, 34, 35; and domestic inflation, 81n–82n; and econometric models, 76, 77, 80–83, 85, 89, 94, 95; Guatemala and El Salvador, 171, 172–73, 175, 179, 183, 187, 189–91, 204, 205, 229, 230; India, 142–43, 145, 147, 152, 153, 158, 159, 160, 229, 230; Malaysia, 208–10, 212–13, 224–25; and world distribution of income, 7, 38–39. *See also* Terms of trade

Imports: protectionist policies, 46n–47n, 224; ratio of reserves to, 69, 132

Import share, 86

Import substitution, 240–41; Brazil, 115, 122, 124, 126, 133, 134

Import values, 7, 10; Brazil, 108–09, 113, 114, 115, 127; India, 143

Import volume, 25–26, 27–28; Brazil, 107, 115–16; Central America, 175, 233; and current account deficits, 27–28; Guatemala and El Salvador, 167, 169, 175, 177; India, 141–42; Malaysia, 208

Income distribution. *See* Distribution of income: Real income; World income distribution

Income policy, 224

India, 8, 9, 136–65, 229, 231, 236, 238, 253; Bangladesh War, 149, 151, 152, 160; concessional aid, 25; consumer price index, 89, 136, 153n; cost-push variables, 153, 159; creditworthiness, 229; demand and cost factors, 152; devaluation, 136, 142, 147–49; export prices, 142–43; export volume, 141–42; fiscal policies, 149–52, 160; food prices, 140, 142, 152, 158, 234; food supplies, 136, 138–41, 152, 153, 160; foreign reserves, 149; import prices, 142–43, 145, 147, 152, 153, 158, 159, 160, 229, 230; industrial production, 136, 153n; inflation models, 151–65; monetary policy, 149–52, 160; money supply, 78n, 149, 151; real aggregate activity, 137; terms of trade, 13, 14; windfall debt erosion, 36

Indonesia, 95; commodity price increases and real income, 42, 44; hyperinflation, 53, 55; windfall debt erosion, 36

Industrial activity, world, and exports, 119–22

Industrial countries: budget deficits, 64; commodity price increases, 229, 238; consumer price increases, 34n; development assistance, 239; distribution of world income, 37; domestic inflation rates, 3; export demand, 13, 72; foreign aid, 19, 20–21; gross national product, 2, 4; growth links with developing countries, 240–43, 255–56; growth rates, 4, 60–62; industrial production, 60; inflation models, 80; macroeconomic strategies and developing countries, 7, 238, 240, 243–55; money supply, 54n; reserve expansion, 69; windfall debt erosion, 7, 29, 31, 33; world recession, 4, 95

Industrial exports, 12

Industrial imports, 13–16

Industrial price inflation, 6n

Industrial production, 60, 136, 153n

Inflation, domestic, 2, 3, 52, 108n; Brazil, 106–13; and export prices, 81n–82n; and industrial countries, 3; and lagged prices, 89, 95; and protectionist trade policy, 45–47. *See also* El Salvador; Guatemala; India; Malaysia

Inflation, global, 1–4, 9, 10, 19, 47, 52, 228, 231, 236, 240, 241; and balances of trade, 23–25, 27–28; and capital flow, 7; capital requirements, 21–28; and concessional development assistance, 19, 21; and domestic inflation,

52; effect on Central America, 177; excess liquidity and, 53, 54; external demand and, 53; future strategies for, 236–39; and savings/trade gap, 22; and terms of trade, 5–6; transmission of, to domestic economies, 6–7, 52–101; universal and synchronous nature of, 53; and windfall debt erosion, 7, 11, 28–37; and world distribution of income, 7, 37–45. *See also* Brazil; El Salvador; Guatemala; India; Malaysia
Inflation models, 109–15; accelerationist, 111–14; closed-economy, 81n; demand-related, 80–82; Harberger's monetarist, 78, 152; for India, 151–65; and industrial countries, 80; monetarist, 77–79, 80, 82, 84–86; nondemand structural, 80–81; output-gap, 233; real activity, 76, 77, 79–80; reduced-form, 82, 84–85
Inflation-output trade-off, 83n
Inflation, price, econometric tests for, 76–101
Inflation-unemployment trade-off, 83n, 244–45
Interest rates, 34, 84, 220–21
International Monetary Fund, 5, 27n, 54n, 134, 231; current account deficits, 28n; export price index, 26n; Interim Committee, 35n; net reserve position, 34, 35; quota increases, 239; special drawing rights, 34
Iron ore, 17, 39n, 117

Jain, Shail, 38n
Japan, 128; commodity price increases, 229; exports to Malaysia, 209, 215; foreign aid, 20–21; foreign-exchange reserves, 35n; real income, 41–42; simulation estimates for, 250–51
Jenkins, Gwilym M., 161n
Johnson, Harry G., 54n
Jute, 17, 39n

Kadota, Décio, 120n, 121n, 128n, 129n
Kaliski, S. F., 250n
Kapur, Ishan, 75n
Kerstenetzky, Isaac, 46n, 103n
Keynesian multiplier, 256
Khan, Mohsin S., 78n, 165n
Kirkpatrick, C. H., 185n
Korea: concessional aid, 25; export volume, 26n; growth rate, 1, 233, 236; and monetarist model of inflation, 84; terms of trade, 13, 14
Koshal, Rajindar, 250n
Kouri, Pentti J. K., 193n
Krause, Lawrence B., 2n, 53n, 103n, 233n
Kravis, Irving B., 37, 38
Krugman, Paul, 86n
Kubitschek regime, 102
Kuwait, 41, 44
Kwack, Sung Y., 83n, 86n

Labor unionism, 189
Laffer, Arthur B., 53n
Laidler, David, 79n, 196n
Latin America, 231, 253
Lawrence, Robert Z., 52n, 136n, 140n, 245n
Layton, Marion, 10n
Leiva, Gustavo A., 207n
Lemgruber, Antonio, 102n, 103n, 105n, 108, 110n, 112n
Likar, Linda, 52n
Liquidity, excess: El Salvador and Guatemala, 177, 179, 183, 186, 195–96; and inflation, 53, 54, 89, 94, 95
Logue, Dennis E., 83n
London interbank overnight rate (LIBOR), 30
Lopes, Francisco Lafaiete, 104n

McKinnon, Ronald I., 182n
Macroeconomic strategies, 7, 238, 240, 243–55
Makinen, G. E., 196n
Malan, Pedro, 102n, 103n, 107n, 113n, 123n, 129n, 131n
Malaysia, 208–27, 231, 236, 237; budget deficits, 209, 215, 217, 222; capital flows, 214–15, 220, 225, 229; Central Bank, 213, 217, 219–22; commercial banks, 215n, 219–21; consumer price index, 208, 210, 212; Control of Supplies Act, 224; credit ceilings, 221–22; currency interchangeability, 214; development expenditures, 222; distribution of income, 218; domestic borrowing, 209, 226; domestic prices, 208, 210, 212; exchange control regulations, 214; exchange-rate policy, 45, 223, 226, 227, 235; excise duties, 212; export duties, 222, 223, 226, 235, 238; export earnings, 213–14, 215, 220; export prices, 208, 213, 219, 225, 226, 235; export volume, 208, 213; Federal Land Development Authority, 218–19; fiscal policy, 209, 222–23, 227, 237;

floating of dollar, 223, 226, 227; food price inflation, 210, 212, 234; food subsidies, 223, 234, 235; foreign market borrowing, 217, 222; foreign reserves, 209, 215; government securities, 209; gross national product, 215, 217, 222; import duties, 212, 224, 237; import prices, 208–10, 212–13, 224–25, 229; import volume, 208; income policy, 224; interest rates, 220–21; monetary policy, 209, 219–22, 225, 226, 227; money supply, 208, 209, 215, 220, 221; New Economic Policy, 215, 218, 221, 223, 225; oil price increases, 212; oil revenues, 222; openness of economy, 208, 223, 224, 225, 227; per capita income, 218n; price ceilings, 212, 223–24; property values, 211, 222; quasi money supply, 215; racial conflict, 218; relief allowances, 211–12, 223; rubber exports, 208; Second Malaysia Plan, 218, 225; statutory reserve requirements, 219–21; surtaxes, 212; terms of trade, 235; trade deficit, 23; trade policy, 209, 223; treasury bills, 209; wage adjustments, 211–12, 235; wages, 218, 219, 224

Malloy, Mike, 29n

Manufactured goods, 5–6, 12, 39, 44, 117–18

Marcos, Ferdinand, 29

Maynard, Geoffrey, 250n

Meiselman, David I., 53n

Meltzer, Allan K., 79n

Mexico, 23, 36, 82, 108n, 231

Models of inflation. *See* Inflation models

Models of world export demand. *See* Export demand

Modigliani, Franco, 83n, 86n, 246n, 247n, 250n

Monetarist model of inflation, 77–79, 80, 82, 84–86; for El Salvador and Guatemala, 204, 206; for India, 152, 153, 158, 160, 161, 165; for Korea, 84

Monetary financing, 167, 171

Monetary policy, 237; Brazil, 122–24, 129, 130, 131, 132, 133; El Salvador and Guatemala, 166, 175, 177, 178, 206; India, 149–52, 160; Malaysia, 209, 219–22, 225, 226, 227

Money supply, 54–55, 62, 69–76, 85, 94, 95, 228, 229; Brazil, 104–06, 107, 109, 110n, 111–13, 115, 123, 125; budget deficits and, 64–67; and consumer price increases, 55, 62–63; domestic causes for growth in, 63–68; econometric models, 76, 83; exchange-rate depreciation, 83; exogeneity of changes in, 78n; foreign reserves and, 69–76; Guatemala and El Salvador, 166, 167, 175, 177, 182, 192, 196, 206; India, 149, 151; in industrial countries, 54n; Malaysia, 208, 209, 215, 220, 221; wage inflation and, 67–68

Munhoz, D., 111n

National Bank of Economic Development, 115

Nelson, Charles R., 162n

Netto, Delfim, 133n

New Economic Policy, 215, 218, 221, 223, 225

Nixson, F. I., 185n

Non-oil-exporting countries. *See* Developing countries, non-oil-exporting

Nordhaus, William D., 83n, 245n

Oates, Wallace E., 182n

Obiols, Julio E., 190n

Odhner, Clas-Erik, 81n

OECD. *See* Organization for Economic Cooperation and Development

Oil-exporting countries, 31n, 70

Oil price increases, 1, 2, 6, 8, 54, 82n, 93, 95, 141, 228, 229; Brazil, 107, 122, 123, 124, 127, 132, 133, 134; and distribution of world income, 37, 39, 40, 41, 43–44; effect on terms of trade, 6, 10, 11, 13, 14, 17, 18, 47; Guatemala and El Salvador, 171, 172–73, 190, 205, 206; India, 145–47, 152, 160; Malaysia, 212, 222

Okun, Arthur M., 245n, 249n

OPEC. *See* Organization of Petroleum Exporting Countries

Openness, 86, 93, 166n. *See also* Malaysia, openness of economy

Organization for Economic Cooperation and Development (OECD), 11n, 12n, 17, 19, 27n, 31n, 33n, 53n, 76, 79n, 83, 92, 122, 190n, 238, 241, 242, 250n, 251n

Organization of Petroleum Exporting Countries (OPEC), 6, 13–14, 37, 41, 74, 125n, 231; balance of trade, 23; development assistance, 10, 17, 19, 27n, 228, 239. *See also* Oil price increases

Osario, Ana Rosa Batres de, 166n

Otani, K., 79n

Output-gap model of inflation, 233
Output-inflation trade-off, 83n

Pakistan, 13, 14, 36, 42, 231
Palm oil, 222, 226, 235
Papademos, Lucas, 83n, 86n
Parkin, Michael, 53n, 54n, 81n, 82n, 185n, 196n
Pastore, Affonso Celso, 102n, 106n, 120n, 121n, 128n, 129n
Pearce, Douglas K., 78n, 165n
Per capita income, 38, 39, 218n
Permanent income, 92n
Perry, George L., 247n
Petrobras, 127
Philippines, 13, 14, 36, 79n
Phillips, A. W., 83n
Phillips curve, 77, 79–80, 231, 233, 245, 246, 250
Pierce, David A., 161
Pierce-Haugh test, 161, 163, 164
Popkin, Joel, 245n
Pounds sterling, and devaluation of rupee, 35n, 147, 149
Prebisch, Raúl, 11
Price ceilings, 212, 223–24
Price inflation, econometric tests for, 76–101
Prices. *See* Agricultural prices; Coffee prices; Export prices; Food price inflation; Global price index; Grain prices; Import prices; Oil price increases; Raw materials prices
Protectionist trade policy: Brazil, 45, 103, 110–17, 122, 124, 130, 132, 133, 134; and domestic inflation, 45–47
Public Law 480, 140, 160

Quasi money supply, 215
Quetzal, depreciation of, 191

Raw materials prices, 244
Real activity: econometric tests, 76, 79, 80, 85; and global inflation, 54, 61, 63; India, 137; industrial production as index of, 60
Real activity model, 79, 85, 92, 95, 152, 153; alternative, 84, 95
Real income, 42, 44, 78n
Recession, world, 1, 2, 4, 95, 103, 117–22, 133–35, 225, 228, 230, 235, 240, 243, 255; and capital flow, 7; capital requirements of developing countries, 21–25, 27–28; and development assistance, 19, 21; effect on industrial countries, 4, 95; money supply changes, 78n; and savings/trade gap, 22. *See also* Brazil; El Salvador; Guatemala; India; Malaysia
Rediscount operations, 178, 194, 195
Reduced-form models of inflation, hybrid, 82, 84–85, 92, 95
Regression analysis, 230n
Regression models of inflation, 152, 159
Relief allowances, 211–12, 223
Reserves, foreign, 9, 11, 52, 69–76, 94, 95, 228, 229; Brazil, 69n, 70, 103–06, 114, 116; Central America, 191; El Salvador and Guatemala, 166, 167, 175, 177, 178, 182, 183, 192–96, 205–06; erosion of, 29, 34–37, 47; and excess liquidity, 53; fluctuation, 69; India, 149; Malaysia, 209, 215; and money supply, 69–76; requirements, 177, 178, 192, 219–21; sterilization of, 75, 76, 94, 104, 105, 106, 193, 237
Resnick, Stephen A., 240n
Reynolds, Clark W., 207n
Rhomberg, Rudolf R., 244n
Rice, 64, 85n, 140
Roett, Riordan, 102n, 124n
Rubber, 17, 18, 39n, 44, 208, 222, 226, 235
Rupee, devaluation of, 136, 142, 147–49

Sa, Angelo Calmon de, 127n
Saito, Katrine, 145n
Salant, Walter S., 2n, 53n, 103n
Sanz, Federico Sanz y, 166n
Sarris, Alexander H., 11n
Saudi Arabia, 41, 44
Savings gap, 22
Sawyer, Malcolm, 38n
SDR. *See* Special drawing rights
Sekiguchi, Sueo, 233n
Shaw, Edward S., 105n, 106n, 127
SIMLINK model, 251–55
Sims, Christopher A., 161
Sims test, 161, 162, 163, 164, 165
Sjaastad, L. A., 205n
Skidmore, Thomas E., 124n
Smith, Gordon W., 31n, 33n
Smyth, David J., 250n
Souza, Angelo Jorge de, 112n
Souza, Janes Angelo de, 112n
Soybeans, 117
Special drawing rights (SDRs), 34, 35–36
Srinavasan, T. N., 136n
Stagflation, 80

Sterilization of reserves, 75, 76, 94, 104, 105, 106, 193, 237
Strout, Alan M., 22n, 243n
Structural factors in inflation, 80–81, 85–86, 92–93, 95, 185n. *See also* Cost-push variables and inflation
Structural inflation model, nondemand, 80–81
Structuralist-monetarist debate, 134
Sugar, 17, 18, 39n, 40, 43, 44, 117, 140, 142
Summers, Robert, 37, 38
Surtaxes, 212
Sweden, 190n
Sweeney, Richard J., 53n, 83n

Tarantelli, Ezio, 250n
Tariff liberalization, 103
Taxation, 178, 185, 186
Taylor, Lance, 11n
Tea, 13, 39n
Terms of trade, 10, 11, 13–17, 18, 45; aggregate index, 12–13; Brazil, 13, 14, 126, 128, 133, 134–35; and commodity price fluctuations, 5, 6n, 10, 12–17, 18; of developing countries, 5–7, 9, 10, 11–17, 23, 33n, 47, 228, 229, 237, 240; global inflation and, 5–6, 9, 11–17; losses vs. debt erosion gains, 33n–34n; Malaysia, 235; oil prices and, 13–17
Timber, 235
Tin, 17, 18, 222, 235
Trade balance. *See* Balance of trade
Trade deficits: Brazil, 116, 122, 125, 133; global inflation and, 23–25, 27–28; and protectionism or devaluation, 46–47
Traded goods. *See* Exports; Imports; Manufactured goods; various commodities
Trade gap, 7, 10, 22, 23, 25
Treasury bills, 209
Triffin, Robert, 166n, 167

UN Conference on Trade and Development (UNCTAD), 5, 6, 7, 12, 22, 23, 25, 28, 33n–34n, 45, 126n, 255n
UN Development Program, 5, 25
UN Economic Commission for Latin America, 107–08
Unemployment-inflation trade-off, 83n, 244–45. *See also* Full-employment budget deficits
United Kingdom, 82n, 128, 147, 149, 208, 209
United Nations, 11, 22, 26, 27n, 82n
United States, 13, 30n, 83; and Brazilian tariffs, 130–31; capital outflows, 6, 8, 94, 104–05, 229; consumer price increases, 208; foreign aid, 20–21, 239; as import source for Malaysia, 209; oil price increases, 42n; simulation estimates for, 246–50; tax cuts, 255
U.S. dollar. *See* Dollar, U.S.

Van Ryckeghem, W., 250n
Vargas, Juan Rafael, 166n
Velloso, João Paulo dos Reis, 116n, 124, 125, 126n
Velocity of money, 171
Venezuela, 44, 89, 108n, 177, 191
Vogel, Robert C., 78n, 84n, 158n

Wachter, Michael L., 245n
Wachter, Susan M., 78n, 82n, 84n, 158n
Waelbroeck, Jean L., 242n, 253n, 255n
Wage adjustments, 211–12
Wage indexing, 112n
Wage inflation, 67–68, 95, 230
Wages, 82n; El Salvador and Guatemala, 187–89, 205, 206; Malaysia, 218, 219, 224
Wellons, P. A., 75n
West Germany, 209, 215
Wharton econometric forecasting model, 132
Wheat prices, 40, 43–44, 64, 85n, 140, 152; and world distribution of income, 39
Willett, Thomas D., 53n
Windfall debt erosion, 7, 9, 10, 28–37; equations for determining, 49–50; and industrial countries, 7, 29, 31, 33
Witteveen facility, 239
World Bank, 31, 34, 42n, 145n, 208n; capital needs estimates, 22, 23; SIMLINK model, 251–55
World income distribution, 7, 50–51, 228, 234; commodity price inflation and, 9, 11, 37–43; export prices and, 39; and global inflation, 7, 37–45; and industrial countries, 37; and manufactured goods, 39, 44; and national income distribution, 38, 39, 40n; and oil price increases, 37, 39, 40, 41, 43–44; and wheat prices, 39
World industrial activity, exports and, 119–22
World recession. *See* Recession, world

Zis, George, 53n, 185n, 196n